Science and Homosexualities

Science and Homosexualities

Edited by
Vernon A. Rosario

Routledge
New York London

Published in 1997 by

Routledge
29 West 35th Street
New York, NY 10001

Published in Great Britain by

Routledge
11 New Fetter Lane
London EC4P 4EE

Printed in the United States of America on acid-free paper.

Library of Congress Cataloging-in-Publication Data

Science and Homosexualities / edited by Vernon A. Rosario II.
p. cm.
Includes bibliographical references and index.
ISBN 0-415-91501-5 (hard cover). — ISBN 0-415-91502-3 (pbk.)
1. Homosexuality—Genetic aspects. 2. Homosexuality—Research.
3. Homosexuality—Philosophy. I. Rosario, Vernon A.
HQ76.25.S48 1996
306.76'6—dc20 96-9673
CIP

To our parents of the mind:
teachers, activists, and mentors.
Thanks for the intellectual and political legacy!

Contents

Acknowledgments

This volume grew out of a pair of panels entitled "Science and (Homo)Sexualities" which were held at the 1994 History of Science Society (HSS) Annual Meeting. These were the first panels at the HSS meeting to deal with the history of homosexuality. In addition to thanking Garland Allen, Alice Domurat Dreger, Anne Fausto-Sterling, and Jennifer Terry (whose essays in this anthology were originally delivered at the conference), I would like to thank the others who participated in and helped organize these panels, including Evelynn Hammonds, Bert Hansen, Gregg Mitman, Robert Nye, Maggie Osler, Londa Schiebinger, and, especially, Joan Cadden for doing most of the networking. I am grateful to Bill Germano and Eric Zinner of Routledge for their enthusiastic support of this project. Finally, I thank all the contributors for tolerating my gentle, regular, electronic prodding and my repeated demands for revisions.

Homosexual Bio-Histories
Genetic Nostalgias and the Quest for Paternity

Vernon A. Rosario

> I have some reason for believing that some of my relatives (on the paternal side) were not normal in their sexual life. . . . [L]ong before puberty—which was early with me—I remember being greatly attracted to certain boys, and wishing to have an opportunity of sleeping with them. . . . As a medical student, the first reference bearing definitely on the subject of sexual inversion was made in the class of Medical Jurisprudence, where certain sexual crimes were alluded to . . . as manifestations of the criminal depravity of ordinary or insane people. . . . I felt that this teaching must be based on some radical error or prejudice or misapprehension, for I knew from my own very clear remembrance of my own development that my peculiarity was not acquired, but inborn; my great misfortune undoubtedly, but not my fault.
>
> —Dr. E. S. (1897)

> Two hot pussies bumping in the night.
> There's not even a single guy in sight.
> That's 'cause they're dykes. It's what they like.
> For them, it's natural! It's natural! Hello! Hello!
> They're not sick, they don't need to heal.
> It's about as natural as oatmeal.
> It's natural! It's natural! Right? Hello!
> When I was a boy, I had a little toy.
> It wasn't really much at all.
> It was a doll. You see, I was gay.
> My daddy said, "Why you gotta be that way?"
> I said, "Why? Because, because, because, because, because, because!
> Because it's natural! It's natural!
> You see, for me, it's natural!"
>
> —Tabboo! (1995)

An ocean of cultural differences and a century separate Dr. E. S.'s poignant self-analysis from drag queen Tabboo!'s defiant pæan to queerness sung to the crowds at *Wigstock* (New York's annual drag extravaganza). Yet the two men seem like homosexual relatives. The fifty-year-old Victorian physician's confession to pioneering British sexologist Havelock Ellis (1897, 100–105) evokes a variety of issues that are as relevant to the present scientific and cultural analysis of homosexuality as they were to the late nineteenth-century Euro-American exploration of "sexual inversion." Then, as now, two points are especially important. First, numerous avowed homosexuals declared that their same-sex erotic attraction was *innate*. As another of Ellis's correspondents expressed it: "I cannot regard my sexual feelings as unnatural or abnormal, since they have disclosed themselves so perfectly naturally and spontaneously with me" (Ellis, 108). Second, since these subjects and their doctors perceived homosexual attraction to be congenital, they believed it to be "natural"—in other words, bodily and biologically ingrained. This, in turn, justified the ethical conclusion expressed by one of Ellis's homosexual colleagues: "As a medical man, I fail to see morally any unhealthiness, or anything that nature should be ashamed of, in connection with, and sympathy for, men" (Ellis, 162). In other words, it's as natural and wholesome as oatmeal!

In the past five years, enormous media attention has been devoted to research on the biological basis of homosexuality. The U.S. popular press has represented this neurobiological and genetic research as thoroughly innovative and groundbreaking (see for instance, Burr 1993b, 47–48). The impression of novelty has been perpetuated by the scientific researchers themselves.[1] For example, Dean Hamer, a biologist particularly identified with the "search for the gay gene," summarizes what is most likely the popular understanding of the medical history of homosexuality:

> Beginning in the late 1800s, psychiatrists and psychologists turned their attention to homosexuality and concluded that it was a mental disorder caused by a misguided upbringing. This disease model remained the primary way of thinking about homosexuality during most of the twentieth century. More recently, however, some scientists have begun to view both heterosexuality and homosexuality as natural variations of the human condition that are at least as deeply rooted in nature as in nurture. (Hamer & Copeland 1994, 20)[2]

This is a serious misrepresentation that tries to dismiss earlier research as psychologizing and pathologizing while glorifying current "scientific" work (including Hamer's) that vindicates homosexuals by naturalizing them. This volume will show that since the mid-nineteenth century, when medical scientists began grappling with what they perceived as a *new* behavioral and psychological disorder, a continuous line of researchers has assumed that homosexuality is a biological phenomenon. As the title of this anthology suggests, numerous diagnostic names were employed: contrary sexual feeling, psychosexual hermaphroditism, sexual inversion, unisexualism, sexual perversion; in the case of men, sodomy, pederasty, and effeminacy; and in the case of women, lesbianism, tribadism, feminism, and eviration (to name just a few). Multiple explanations were also proposed, yet most of these relied on strict biologically determinist mechanisms. The essays in this volume will examine these hereditarian, hormonal, anthropometric, neurobiological, and genetic theories that have circulated in a variety of incarnations for over a century. Even the psychoanalytic theories to which Hamer alludes, although hugely influential in the twentieth century, never completely eclipsed organic approaches to research on homosexuality, nor were the psychoanalytic models free of biological foundations.[3]

If this anthology largely sets aside clinical psychoanalytic explanations of the origins of homosexuality, it is not because I discount them as wrong or ideologically tainted, but because they have been examined elsewhere,[4] and because the pendulum of popular and scientific opinion (particularly in the United States) has swung back to favoring biological hypotheses. This is not to say that biological theories are more objective or apolitical in their scientificity than psychoanalytic ones—as defenders of sexology proclaim.[5] It is historically and sociologically naïve to imagine that Science is a pure, descriptive pursuit of nature's Truth, independent of the political interests, social concerns, or the cultural and religious values surrounding the practice of science.[6] Ever since the mid-nineteenth century, same-sex love has been studied biologically as a "natural" phenomenon in order to legitimize opposing political aims: the normalization and defense of homosexuality, or its pathologization and condemnation. The natural and the unnatural, nature and nurture, essentialism and constructionism, and other binarisms have all been invoked in these medico-political battles.

The Binarisms That Divide Us

> DR. BORDEU.—Anything that exists cannot be either against nature or unnatural. I do not even make an exception for voluntary chastity or continence, which would be amongst the greatest crimes against nature—if it were possible to sin against nature—and one of the greatest crimes against the social laws of a country where actions were weighed on a balance other than that of fanaticism and prejudice.
>
> —Diderot (1769, 939)

Through the authoritative voice of Dr. Théophile de Bordeu, Diderot cleverly unmasked the folly of condemning any sexual act as "against nature" since all that exists in the world is necessarily part of nature. Nevertheless, the social and religious fanaticism and prejudice he ridiculed have persisted, and so has the notion of the "unnatural." Arguments for the "naturalness" of homosexuality commonly associate the "natural" with the biologically determined, in opposition to the freely "chosen" and thereby, potentially, "sinful" and "against nature." This "natural" versus "chosen" distinction has great cultural and political weight in the U.S., where a *New York Times* poll (March 5, 1993) found more tolerant attitudes towards homosexuals among respondents who believe homosexuality is immutable than among those who feel it is chosen. Not surprisingly then, well-intentioned defenders of gay civil rights also appeal to the notion that "principled [social] policies" can be established only once it is proven that homosexuality is a "*natural* sexual orientation" (Burr 1993a; emphasis added).[7] The simplest proof of this is often sought in animal sexual behavior (Ford & Beach 1951), but this tells us nothing about how animals *conceptualize* their erotic attractions or identities. As Kirsch and Weinrich (1991) point out, numerous observations of homosexual *behavior* between wild animals in "nature" do not support the claim that human homosexual *orientation* is "natural," nor does such evidence mollify homophobes (for instance, Cameron 1992). Human homosexuality is no more nor less "natural" than human heterosexuality. In any case, civil rights protection need not be founded on a claim of innateness, naturalness, or immutability: for instance, religious *choice* can be declared an inalienable right without being theorized as biological. The labeling of any sexual activity or identity as immoral or criminal is a matter of religious, cultural, and legal convention and tradition, not transcendental "naturalness."

While the natural/unnatural binarism can be set aside as specious (albeit culturally persistent), the *nature/nurture* dichotomy is a rather more complex and confusing distinction that is still evoked in the scientific disciplines but with varying meanings.[8] For example, a geneticist considers all non-genetic effects (even intrauterine ones) as "environmental," and recognizes that environmental factors may be necessary for triggering genetically determined predispositions (Hamer & Copeland 1994, 81–82). For a neurobiologist, however, the nature/nurture divide is quite different. Simon LeVay (1991) provided some suggestive evidence for a neuroanatomical dissimilarity (in a region called the INAH 3) between presumed heterosexual men and men labeled as homosexual in their medical charts.[9] In LeVay's book on the neurobiology of sexuality, *The Sexual Brain* (1993), he makes it clear that, for a neurobiologist, even intrauterine hormonal effects on the developing embryo and its nervous system are classified as "natural" forces. Given the greater plasticity of neurons and nerve synapses compared to that of genes, a variety of "environmental" effects and *learned* behaviors have been shown to produce microanatomical and neurochemical effects. For LeVay, therefore, the range of nurture effects (that is, non-neuroanatomical effects) is limited to phenomena that exist only as transient, dynamic states of the nervous system.[10] LeVay goes further, however, in broadening the realm of the Natural (understood by him as the biological rather than the psychological): he notes that "even the most nebulous and *socially determined* states of mind are a matter of genes and brain chemistry" (1993, xii; my emphasis). For the monist neurobiologist (who denies the mind-matter duality) there is no immaterial "mind," or, as neurophilosopher Patricia Churchland puts it, no "spooky stuff" beyond the body and its neurochemical states. In other words, for the monist, the nature/nurture dichotomy proves to be as fictitious as the natural/unnatural divide: all learned behaviors should be reducible to biological, that is, natural, phenomena.

Readers philosophically aligned with materialist monism may, nevertheless, be uncomfortable with such *biological reductionism*.[11] Why would philosophical materialists—who logically should agree that mental phenomena have a biological, material substrate—sometimes appear to be anti-science, genetic Luddites in their objection to genetic and neurological theories of homosexuality?[12] One reason is the confusion of biological reductionism with *biological determinism*, where the latter implies the absence of human agency. However, as the conclusion to LeVay's study makes clear, the possibility that there may be an anatomical difference between homosexual and heterosexual men's brains tells us nothing about the causation of sexual orientation; in other words, a larger INAH 3 might be either one of the *causes* of male heterosexuality, or the by-product of a heterosexual lifestyle *choice*. Even in the sphere of genetics, no researcher has suggested that genes *fully* determine sexual orientation. Indeed, the boldest prediction from a study of individuals who share *identical genes* (monozygotic or "identical" twins) is that, if one of the pair is homosexual, the chances that the co-twin is also homosexual are slightly more than 1:2 (52 percent)—not much better predictive value than flipping a coin (Bailey & Pillard 1991). Although data at present do not permit researchers to claim that biology *fully* determines behavioral traits, this presumption seems to guide their work. LeVay, for example, betrays his biological-determinist as well as reductionist inclinations in the conclusion to his popular book: "In *reality*," he confides, "our range of individual development is *defined and limited* by what we are born with" (1993, 138; emphasis added).

For the (crypto)biological determinist, free choice (more specifically, sexual choice) is an illusion. Reality is immutably inscribed in the genes at conception and in the nervous system at birth (or at least by the time of puberty). All the vicissitudes of individual and social histories are merely the elaborate and as yet ill-understood manifestations of the "realities" of genes and the nervous system. In some brave new world of total biological knowledge—once the Human Genome Project and, presumably, a Human Neurone Project have been successfully completed—we will be able to understand every political decision made by Ronald Reagan during his presidency in terms of his genetic and neurological construction and dynamics.[13] This brings me to another binarism: the *normal* versus the *pathological*.

One regular objection to biological research on homosexuality is that such work is necessarily pathologizing and stigmatizing. While few people, not even LeVay or Hamer, would deny that the majority of research into the causes of homosexuality has explicitly approached it as a pathology, that does not necessarily mean that all biomedical research pathologizes every subject it touches. Particularly in the current context of governmental retreat from basic research funding, biomedical scientists must compete for dwindling grants by promising that their work has proximate applications in medical therapeutics. Nevertheless, under the cover of entrepreneurial pragmatism, basic research is conducted into all forms of biological phenomena. That is certainly not to say that basic research on fruit flies is devoid of social and political implications—the best example being the recent description of "gay" Drosophila (Zhang & Odenwald 1995; see also Horton 1995; Thompson 1995). If, as Zhang and Odenwald (1995, 5526) believe, they have genetically and environmentally *produced* "homosexual activity" (daisy chains of foreleg-touching, genital-rubbing, fellating male flies), is it possible to call such behavior "pathological" or "abnormal"? By analogy, we would also have to describe most varieties of hybridized plants and breeds of domestic and farm animals as "pathological." As Canguilhem (1966) argued, "normal" and "pathological" are concepts that arose in the nineteenth century out of developments in instrumentation, statistics, anatomy, and physiology. The "pathological" does not exist as an isolated and objective phenomenon, but in contradistinction to what is arbitrarily designated the "physiological." Similarly, the "normal" applies to an arbitrarily delimited range of possibilities around the statistical "norm" (average) (Canguilhem 1966, 228–229). Unlike the category of the "unnatural," which they displaced from the scientific lexicon, the "normal" and the "pathological"—in their very quantitative arbitrariness—disguise the cultural and moral values they perpetuate.[14] However, to search for the biological substrate of an ab-normal (that is, non-average) trait or behavior does not necessarily stigmatize it as pathological and socially evil. Recall that the founder of eugenics, Sir Francis Galton, first studied *genius* (1869), which is, by definition, abnormal: intelligence beyond the norm. Similarly, the classification of homosexuality as abnormal or pathological does not exist in an essential way within its examination by scientists, but is constructed from a complex interaction of social values and individual researchers' and subjects' approaches, methods, and presuppositions.

This brings me to my final binarism: *essentialism* versus *constructionism*.[15] The quarrel between "essentialists" and "constructionists" has preoccupied gay and lesbian studies since the 1980s (and feminism since the 1970s). Those already familiar with the dispute probably cannot imagine anything new or productive coming of it. *Forms of Desire: Sexual Orientation and the Social Constructivist Controversy* (Stein 1992) provides a valuable survey, and Stein's concluding essay reviews the philosophical stakes and mistakes involved in the debate. Stein points out that there are many types of essentialism and contructionism—there can be essentialist theories of homosexuality that emphasize nature or nurture (as we saw above), and there can be constructionist theories that are socially or culturally determinist. Since there is such variety, let me explain my use of the terms in the context of this anthology.[16] Essentialist theories propose that homosexuality is a biologically determined, objectively detectable, erotic orientation that can be identified in all cultures and throughout history, albeit under diverse behavioral appearances and at different prevalence rates. Constructionist theories propose instead that "homosexuality" is a concept and a phenomenon that arose relatively recently in Euro-American cultures to describe a specific type of person and that person's erotic interest in others of the same sex.[17] Homosexuality is thereby theorized as historically and socially contingent. The precise dating for the emergence of the first "true" homosexuals is a matter of debate. Foucault (1976, 59) identifies the earliest homosexuals in the pages of Karl Westphal's article on "contrary sexual sensation" of 1869. Halperin (1990, 15) claims that homosexuality was invented in 1892 with Charles Chaddock's introduction of the word into the English language. Kimmel (1990) and Trumbach (1989) take the genesis further back to the early eighteenth century. Whatever the exact date of birth, most constructivists would agree that homosexuality *per se* could not be located much earlier than the eighteenth century, and certainly not in the Classical period, Middle Ages, or Renaissance, as Boswell (1980, 1994), Rowse (1977), and the *Encyclopedia of Homosexuality* assume. It should be noted that both essentialists and constructivists generally agree that there has been male-male and female-female erotic and sexual activity documented throughout the historical record as well as in most cultures (Weinrich & Williams 1991). But neither camp is interested merely in any same-sex sexual activity (for example, the "situational" homosexuality of prisoners or sailors restricted to a single-sex environment). It is the more elusive issue of same-sex *desire* or sexual *orientation* ("true" homosexuality or "gayness") that is the matter of concern.

This important point of overlap between essentialist and constructivist theories is not as simple or unproblematic as it might initially appear. Constructivists, taking their cue from Foucault (1976, 59), insist that there is a major conceptual leap between thinking of *sex* in terms of sexual (particularly genital) acts, and theorizing *sexuality* as a deeply ingrained feature of a subject's feelings, self-definition, and social functioning. As an analogy, the American Revolution created the new possibility for people to identify themselves and *feel* like "American citizens." This ontological revolution is reenacted today through the performative ritual of "naturalization," officiated by the United States Immigration and Naturalization Service.[18] Those people who were born and raised in the United States and are "natural" American citizens tend to sense this national identity as congenital and integral to their personal identity, and not as a lifestyle choice. This is quite different from the foreigner who, in order to be "naturalized," usually has to undergo numerous, often trying, changes in lifestyle and, ultimately, must make a citizenship choice. Who, then, would you include in a history of "Americans" or a medical study of some aspect of "American" lifestyle: "Native" Americans, descendents of the Pilgrims, descendents of those forcibly brought over on slave ships, yesterday's "naturalized" citizens, second generation "illegal aliens," all the inhabitants of the "Americas," expatriate U.S. citizens? Both the historical and synchronic identifications of a population involve difficult and arbitrary criteria based on subjects' self-perceptions, and historians' or scientists' "objective" distinctions.

Constructivist studies explicitly define homosexuality as a modern phenomenon of subjective self-definition. Unwittingly, many biological essentialists are also examining a historically and culturally contingent phenomenon since they are interested in gayness as a *mode of being* and not simply as the performance of homosexual acts. Three recent studies widely publicized for demonstrating partial genetic determination of homosexuality are about "sexual orientation" and not just homosexual activity (Bailey & Pillard 1991; Bailey et al. 1993; and Hamer et al. 1993). For example, Hamer and coworkers claim from the start that "human sexual orientation is variable. Although most people exhibit a heterosexual *preference* for members of the opposite sex, a significant minority display a homosexual orientation." Heterosexuality itself is presented as a "preference" for the opposite sex, and the article notes that "the subjects studied were *self-acknowledged* homosexual men" (Hamer et al. 1993, 321; my emphasis). In particular, a modified Kinsey scale was used to allow subjects to *self-rate* their "identity," from a "0" for exclusively heterosexual, to a "6" for an exclusively "gay" identity (Hamer & Copeland 1994, 329), rather than *researchers* rating subjects' "overt experience" and "psychic reactions," as did Kinsey et al. (1948, 639). Therefore, to the degree that Hamer and his colleagues' findings of a genetic basis for homosexuality prove robust and replicable, they are evidence of a genetic linkage for being an "out" "gay" man (that is, a self-acknowledged and publicly known gay man whatever his actual genital activities), not just an objectively defined, homosexually active individual. The study protocol specifically excluded "closeted" gays from genetic analysis (they were designated "false negatives") (Hamer et al. 1993, 323).

The population of interest to the contemporary biologists of homosexuality is that group of men who have chosen to declare themselves members of the "gay" citizenry (or, we might say, have chosen to be naturalized as Gay Americans). Although it may very well be the case, as Burr suggests, that "homosexuals have long maintained that sexual orientation, far from being a personal choice or lifestyle . . . is something neither chosen nor changeable" (1993b, 48), being an "out" "gay" man is a historical and social novelty in the same sense that being "American" is; furthermore, to many non-Americans, being "gay" or "queer" is specifically an Anglo-American phenomenon.[19] Therefore, the search for a "gay gene" is the quest for the genetic basis of a sociohistorical construct. In arriving at this conclusion, I do not mean to suggest that this research is therefore self-deluded, futile, or hopelessly flawed. On the contrary, it is perfectly consonant with much other research that investigates the genetic basis of other social constructions. For example, *Huntington's chorea* is a term not much older than *homosexuality*. The wild, dancelike movements associated with it were also described in people suffering from demonic possession in the Middle Ages, from *chorea lascivia* in the Renaissance, and from pediatric rheumatic fever, but it was not until an American doctor, George S. Huntington, described in 1872 a "medical curiosity"—a *hereditary*, incurable form of chorea affecting adults, leading to insanity and suicide—that *Huntington's disease* (HD) was born. Since then, its "definitive" diagnosis has relied on a changing variety of clinical symptoms, neuropathological findings, genetic linkages, and, most recently, a specific gene on chromosome 4 (Gusella et al. 1993). With HD, as with AIDS and anorexia nervosa, the selection of people diagnosed under a medicohistorically constructed label varies over the years as theories of disease causation and pathophysiology evolve. The discovery of an HD gene establishes, for now at least, a specific historical incarnation of this disease as the "correct" and biologically true one. This is not to say that HD is a fiction—a figment of an oppressive medical profession's imagination—or that the current genetic explanation of HD is wrong, but that biomedical science, particularly genetics, has become the major authority entrusted with officiating the naturalization of human behaviors and ailments. Therefore, even if confronted with replicable evidence of a "gay gene," it would be premature to abandon social constructivism, as Halperin promises to when he concedes that "if it turns out that there actually is a gene, say, for homosexuality, my notions about the cultural determination of sexual object-choice will—obviously enough—prove to have been wrong" (1990, 49).[20] Not only is the cultural phenomenon of "gayness" a construct, but genes themselves and the "molecular vision of life" are an elaborate sociohistorical construct (Kay 1993).

I have spun this argument that both the subject and methodologies of the science of homosexuality are sociohistorical constructs, not to reduce science to constructionism, but to point out that biologically essentialist conceptions of "contrary sexual sensation," "inversion," "homosexuality," or "gayness" coexist with and are codependent on constructionist models. Like wave and particle theories of light, both essentialism and constructionism may be useful explanatory models in different contexts and for various aims. The century and a half of diverse biomedical theories of same-sex love and behavior that will be examined in the following essays can be understood and applied only to the different national, historical, and cultural contexts that identified and conceptualized those behaviors. While many of these scientific theories and identity labels may seem bizarre and antiquated to contemporary readers, it is likely that our current sexual identities and our scientific or sociological explanations of them will seem equally ludicrous to people a century hence, or indeed, to our contemporaries who do not share the cultural and scientific inheritance that bred present day Western gays and medicine. If cultural and biomedical analyses of contemporary "gay" men and "lesbians" are not mutually contradictory, how might we begin to understand the specific historical and cultural meanings of the "search for the gay gene," or as journalist Natalie Angier (1991a) phrased it, the quest for the "biology of what it *means* to be gay"? Let me turn now to one possible explanation of the current vogue among American scientists as well as gay men and lesbians for genetic explanations of gayness.

The Legitimacy of Origins and the Teleology of Homosexuality

> We do not even in the least know the final cause of sexuality. The whole subject is hidden in darkness.
>
> ——Charles Darwin

Darwin's words appear as the epigraph to Hamer's book on the *Science of Desire* (1994, 11). Darwin's second appearance in the volume is even more portentous. In reconstructing the "turning point" in his career, Hamer identifies Darwin's *Descent of Man, and Selection in Relation to Sex* as one of the decisive books that converted him from research on the metalothionein (MT) gene to the "search for the gay gene." Reading the "father of modern biology" for the first time, Hamer discovers that Darwin had devoted three quarters of the book to sexual selection, and had particularly suggested that behavioral differences between species and individuals might be inherited. This was the "Aha!" moment when, inspired by the father's seed of genius, Hamer realized that sexuality, specifically homosexuality, "most likely has a significant genetic component" (26). Suddenly, the quest for the genetics of sexual orientation struck Hamer as a fulfilling, exciting alternative to the "boredom" of MT research.

Equally important, it was an area where he felt he could do "some real science," free of politics (27).

Hamer most likely had thought of these issues before this seminal moment during a flight from Oxford to Washington, D.C. (metaphorical capitals of intellectual and political power). He admits that in addition to disinterested, scientific curiosity, he was also motivated by personal reasons (25). I dwell on this dramatization of scientific inspiration because I believe it stages many of the latent motivations fueling the current U.S. fascination with genetic explanations of sexual orientation. Most significantly, the Darwinian epigraph identifies the central aim of this research as a teleological one—a search for final causes. Furthermore, by invoking the Darwinian legacy, Hamer draws upon the notions of natural selection, evolution, genetic fitness, and sexual selection.

More than any other scientific figure, Darwin is associated in the popular imagination with the idea that the great diversity of animal forms and behaviors is the product of "natural" forces (except where breeders intervene), and that all these variations contribute to the fitness and survival of the individual species. For some trait to have "evolved" and persisted must mean that not only is it "natural," but it is also useful to the individual and the species in some immediate or ancient way. In the *Origin of Species* (1859), Darwin proposed that "natural selection will never produce in a being anything injurious to itself, for natural selection acts solely by and for the good of each." Beyond simply avoiding noxious traits, "natural selection tends to make each organic being as perfect as, or slightly more perfect than, the other inhabitants of the same country with which it has to struggle for existence" (201). Darwin's one caveat to this "utilitarian doctrine" was that past useful traits might persist or recur, so long as they were harmless, since "by far the most important consideration is that the chief part of the organization of every being is simply due to inheritance: and consequently, though each being assuredly is well fitted for its place in nature, many structures now have no direct relation to the habits of life of each species" (199).

In *The Descent of Man, and Selection in Relation to Sex* (1871), Darwin extended these conclusions to humans, and further elaborated his theory of sexual selection: male characteristics (for example, strength, intelligence, virility) are evolutionarily favored in the competition for females, who will be selected for beauty, health, and fecundity (1:296). Darwin also suggested that the two motors of evolution—natural selection and sexual selection—had produced the social instincts that were the foundations of human morality and virtue (1:104). While Darwin preferred to view the "moral qualities" as products of habit, reason, instruction, and religion rather than natural selection (2:404), E. O. Wilson, the leading proponent of sociobiology, goes further when he proposes that even morality is an *evolved instinct.* "If that perception is correct," Wilson concludes, "science may soon be in a position to investigate the very origin and meaning of human values, from which all ethical pronouncements and much of political practice flow" (1978, 5). Applying this scientifico-political speculation to the matter of homosexuality, Wilson hypothesizes that homosexuality exists in all cultures and throughout time because it is "normal in a biological sense":

"homosexuals may be the genetic carriers of some of mankind's altruistic impulses" (143). The sociobiologist's functionalist logic is that even if homosexuals reproduce less, genes for homosexuality might have been maintained in a prehistoric, "primitive society" if homosexuals' altruistic works favored the natality and survival of their kin (144–145). No matter how little contemporary homosexuals might *actually* contribute to the child-rearing of their kin—or, indeed, how homophobes might panic at the thought of armies of gay child-care workers—a genetic theory of homosexuality evokes a prehistoric, imaginary narrative and invokes a Darwinian, evolutionist teleology to prove that gays are natural and good.

The geneticization of homosexuality founds vertical and horizontal lines of imagined, gay kinship.[21] Extending vertically into the past, the "gay gene" legitimizes a homosexual metahistory that transcends conventional genealogies. Genes are the primordial "stuff of life," and to the degree that a "homosexual gene" is presumed to even exist in animals (for example, "fruit" flies), gayness becomes eternal, enduring, and universal. Akin to owning a commemorative swatch of the 1994 International Pride mile-long rainbow flag, posessing "our" gay gene—a snippet of the thread of life that bears "our" name and identity—is a promise of a Positive bio-history: an ideological and fantasmatic global link to the past and the future.[22] A "gay gene" figuratively establishes a confraternity with other famous "homosexuals in history": Plato, Alcibiades, Erasmus, Richard the Lion-Hearted, Sir Francis Bacon, Michelangelo, King Henri III, Byron, Proust, Gide, and all the other luminaries in the *Encyclopedia of Homosexuality* (also Rowse 1977 and Spencer 1996). They would all share that genetic seed of homosexual genius, and a gay man today could claim an illustrious paternity far more congenial to his "sexual identity" than his actual father who, quite likely, was hostile toward the boy's homosexuality and who failed to initiate the child into gay culture and identity (the way African-American, Jewish, WASP, or other culture might be transmitted through generations).

Analogous to the case of deaf children struggling to consolidate an identity in a hearing family (Lane 1992, 227), most gays and lesbians lack familial role models for developing a "homosexual identity" if they grow up in a heterosexual household. The search for an alternative filiation, a reaffirming culture, and a historical tradition in the creation of a gay identity is most easily found in essentialist approaches to homosexuality (whether biological or historical) (Fuss 1989). A "gay gene" establishes a paternal link to collateral gay offspring who otherwise would have been brought into the family only by gay acculturation (or as homophobes would claim, queer recruitment). This is the horizontal imagined kinship enabled by the "gay gene": the objective, biological confirmation of "gaydar," which assures one that the cute guy (hanging on to his girlfriend's arm in Greenwich Village or in a gay bar) really is "family," but just hasn't figured out (his genes) yet. Beyond national boundaries, an essentialist model also legitimizes the gay cultural imperialism epitomized by the bible of gay tourism, the *Spartacus International Gay Guide*, which cheerfully identifies where to find exotic "gay" sexual partners from Abu Dhabi to Zimbabwe even if "they don't believe that there is anything homosexual about their actions" (797)![23]

A genetic theory adds a new level of scientific realism to these vertical and horizontal homosexual bio-histories, as well as a good dose of hereditarian chauvinism. Converting gay identity into genetic currency (coining "our" own gene) boosts the trait's value in the genetic economy of the United States, where vast funds go to molecular biology research, and where genes are valuable commodities (Hubbard & Wald 1993). A gay gene would also necessarily be a particularly crafty and subversive gene—one that has endured since human prehistory while evading the traditional heterosexual reproductive imperative, and outdoing the Darwinian tenet that those who reproduce most are the victors in the evolutionary struggle. This peculiar genetic internarrative arises through the anthropomorphizing of genes inspired by Richard Dawkins's *The Selfish Gene* (1976). In striking contrast to Wilson's altruistic gay gene, both LeVay and Hamer invoke the image of selfish genes operating through time and individuals for the genes' own good. Nostalgically evoking an image of 1970s gay male hedonism, LeVay claims that "genes do not care about these long-term prospects [of the species] any more than they care about the general welfare of the planet. Genes demand instant gratification" (1993, 6). Specifically rejecting the quest for teleologies of homosexuality (with which he nevertheless opened his book), Hamer announces that "genes don't care about us. . . . The point is that evolution works at the level of genes and individuals, not at the level of populations or societies. This may seem selfish—but then, genes always are" (1994, 186). This tale of our genetic Id, managing to survive the evolutionary wars by whatever means necessary, uncannily mirrors (while historically trivializing) those fearless and ingenious gays and lesbians who have struggled to gain social visibility and political clout in the twentieth century. As a biohistorical operon, the "gay gene" secretly reassures us that, no matter what social and cultural oppression gays may suffer today, or whatever political activism or inaction we personally espouse, *gayness* will survive!

Despite Hamer and LeVay's protests that scientific research on homosexuality should and can be "objective" and apolitical, it should be clear that even if it adheres to the methods and standards of scientific correctness, such research is inevitably interlaced with deeper narratives and hidden motivations that reflect the political climate of the moment as well as the personal aspirations of individual researchers. After all, it must be remembered that much of the current work and perhaps much of the nineteenth-century biological research on homosexuality has been conducted by homosexually inclined scientists. LeVay has been most candid in linking his research on homosexuality to his gayness and, more specifically, his mourning over his lover's death from AIDS (Kevles 1995, 86; Gelman 1992, 49). Richard Pillard, the co-author of several gay twin studies, was the sole "out" psychiatrist in the early 1970s struggling to have the diagnosis of homosexuality expunged from the *Diagnostic and Statistical Manual of Psychiatric Disorders* (Bayer 1981). It therefore seems misguided to accuse these scientists of internalized homophobia or a will to pathologize homosexuality (unless it is through false consciousness). Such indictments seem equally inapplicable to the lesbians and gay men who have warmly embraced the geneticization of homosexuality. I have suggested here that gays' support for such work is rooted not in homophobia, but in a homo-chauvinism that seeks cultural approbation in biological "reality" and extracts from genetic metanarratives a mythical history of gay paternity, endurance, wiliness, and social utility.

The genetic hypothesis of homosexuality would undoubtedly have equally thrilled the Victorian doctor quoted at the beginning of this essay who was convinced his sexual orientation was innate. Likewise, it would have pleased the many proud and unrepentant homosexuals who wrote to early sexologists and participated in biomedical research in an attempt to bolster the evidence for the biological basis of homosexuality. While we should debate the legal and political expediency of such arguments, we must recognize that biological explanations have enormous "natural" appeal to lesbians and gay men (Wishman 1996). Another of Ellis's correspondents probably echoes the sentiments of many contemporary gays who share his personal and class experience:

> My parentage is very sound and healthy. Both my parents (who belong to the professional middle class) have good general health. . . . I cannot regard my sexual feelings as unnatural or abnormal, since they have disclosed themselves so perfectly naturally and spontaneously within me. All that I have read in books or heard spoken about the ordinary sexual love, its intensity and passion, lifelong devotion, love at first sight, etc., seems to me to be easily matched by my own experiences in the homosexual form. . . . I am sure that this kind of love is . . . as deeply stirring and ennobling as the other kind, if not more so. (Ellis 1897, 107–108)

Bio-Histories / Culturing Science, Gender, and Sexuality

If I have used only male examples in the argument above, it is specifically because I suspect that gay men have a greater investment than lesbians in genetic theories of homosexuality.[24] The *New York Times* also implies this by illustrating two articles on gays and biology with photographs of gay male couples (Angier 1991a, 1993a; see also Angier 1993b). In part, this is due to the fact that most of this research—predominantly by white, male scientists—has been devoted to gay men. Lesser interest on the part of lesbians (particularly lesbian feminists) in the biologization of homosexuality is undoubtedly due to a tradition of feminist scholarship devoted to "denaturalizing" gender and demonstrating the male bias of science. In the past two decades, feminist historians and philosophers have shown how science (particularly biomedicine) has systematically marginalized women from scientific institutions, has pathologized female bodies and sexualities, and projected its masculinist fantasies and values upon the landscape of "Mother Nature."[25] If it has been politically expedient to demonstrate that the "mind has no sex" (to borrow Poulain de la Barre's felicitous phrase), it seems equally wise to show that genes have no sexuality.

Sarah Schulman (1995) argues that women have historically been ill-served by a patriarchal, heterosexist science, whereas men have put greater trust in biological over social or political explanations. Given that Euro-American societies are still largely patriarchal (in the anthropological sense), it seems likely that gay men, who might otherwise worry that their family name terminates with them, would find some comfort in an imagined transcultural, transhistorical "patrinomy" of the gay gene.[26] One can further understand the particular attractiveness of bourgeois-supportive science to gay men if gay identity itself is a by-product of capitalism (as suggested by D'Emilio [1993]).[27] If there was a major conceptual shift in the nineteenth century from an aristocratic social symbolism of *sanguinity* to a bourgeois analytics of *sexuality* (Foucault 1976, 194–195), then in contemporary North America the "gay gene" seeds a bio-history that *equates* consanguinity and (gay) sexuality. Particularly for bourgeois, gay, white men, the "gay gene" is the blazon of a distinguished, imaginary homosexual lineage. For those men who by birthright had a greater investment in the hegemonic culture but were disowned by the heteropatriarchy when they "came out" socially, a scientific "coming out" stakes a claim for the restitution of that patrimony. But can such a claim, and scientific research agenda, expand the list of beneficiaries of that patrimony?

White, heterosexual, male, bourgeois-dominated science has historically not been a friend to women, people of color, homosexuals, "sexual perverts," working-class people, and other groups it has pathologized, denigrated, and abjectified.[28] However, as Harding (1986) and Haraway (1991, 184–201) point out, this does not necessarily mean that science is inevitably and eternally hostile to all these groups, nor that science cannot be transformed to serve the broader weal of humanity and the natural world. This would involve not an abandonment of science, but an intensive, self-analytical engagement with and criticism of all layers of scientific knowledge production and application.

As the essays in this anthology demonstrate, the subjects of science (those curious and troubling perverts, inverts, viragints, and homosexuals), far from being passive guinea pigs, have in multiple ways, for divergent political purposes, and with variable results wrestled with biomedical science. Science's goal of turning homosexuals into objects of knowledge has always been met with their countervailing efforts to turn science into a vehicle of self-knowledge—an objective consonant with the conventional aims of all natural scientific discourse (Eagleton 1983, 210). The exploitation of homosexual "pathology" as a means to advance the sciences of genetics, embryology, anatomy, endocrinology, psychology, and neurosciences has been regularly reappropriated by the use of these sciences to publicize, explore, and normalize homosexualities. To return to my earlier question: How can we make sense of the quest for the "biology of what it means to be gay"? The science of homosexuality is not a disembodied pursuit simply of what homosexuality *is* but of what it *means*—in other words, it is an integral part of the scientific interrogation of what it means to be human in a particular time and environment. As such, the questions and answers of science are profoundly historical ones, and in analyzing them, we not only grapple with the past culturing of science, but can seed the sciences of the future.

The essays in this volume take as a premise that science is not an isolated laboratory activity, but a cultural practice deeply intertwined in the shaping of the very phenomena it examines. While the contributing authors bring different methodological and political commitments to their analyses, three major themes run through this anthology. First, the volume examines the major trends and figures in a century and a half of scientific research on same-sex sexuality, and sets this research in its broader social and cultural context.[29] Second, it explores the role experimental and clinical subjects themselves played in the scientific enterprise, and suggests a variety of reasons for their participation. Third, this anthology studies the ways in which this interaction between the doctor and the patient or experimental subject shaped not only scientific theories of homosexuality, but also cultural perceptions and self-perceptions of sexuality generally.

Beginning in the mid-nineteenth century, a variety of European doctors (neurologists, alienists, public hygienists, medical forensics experts, and even general practitioners) began encountering a growing number of people "afflicted" with erotic desires for others of the same sex. Many of these cases arose in the context of legal proceedings over sodomy or "crimes against public morals" (public sex), particularly in countries that still criminalized "crimes against Nature." Central Europe particularly witnessed an efflorescence of such cases alongside claims for the naturalness of same-sex love. Karl Heinrich Ulrichs, a Hannoverian lawyer, vocally and insistently argued for the decriminalization of sodomy. Hubert Kennedy's essay examines how Ulrichs relied on existing research in embryology and animal magnetism to develop scientific theories of sexuality useful to his defense of the "Urning" (a female caught in a male body) and the "Urningin" (a male caught in a female body). Initially relying on a personal sense of the innateness of his sexuality, Ulrichs elaborated increasingly complex models to try to encompass the diversity of sexualities he later encountered. His poignant, confessional tracts and his model of sexual inversion were hugely influential on subsequent sex researchers.

One of the most important of these was the Viennese psychiatrist, Richard von Krafft-Ebing, whose *Psychopathia Sexualis* (1886) became the grand encyclopedia of sexual perversities. Harry Oosterhuis focuses on the special place of homosexuals' correspondence with Krafft-Ebing in transforming the psychiatrist's representation of homosexuality. Although Krafft-Ebing, like most of his colleagues, had originally described "contrary sexual feeling" as a product of hereditary degeneration, he subsequently presented it as a harmless variation in human sexual behavior, and he became a strong advocate for homosexual civil rights in Germany.

The biomedical study of the "third sex" and the vindication of homosexual rights in Germany continued under the influence of the German-Jewish, homosexual psychiatrist Magnus Hirschfeld and his Institute for Sexual Science until Hitler's political victory in 1933. Hirschfeld published prolifically on the full spectrum of human sexual "intermediacy," which he held to comprise hermaphroditism, androgyny, homosexuality, and transvestism. Although his defense of homosexuals seems quite modern, his outlook remained deeply rooted in the scientific paradigms and political programs of the late nineteenth century, and was informed by monistic naturopathy (an alternative to allopathic medicine), by debates over Darwinism and degeneracy, and by socialist optimism.

While the model of sexual inversion, psychosexual hermaphroditism, or "third sex" (between male and female) seemed natural and politically expedient to Ulrichs and Hirschfeld, it has proven problematic to researchers and a variety of people with "unorthodox" sex/sexualities (Herdt 1994). Not least among these were anatomical hermaphrodites or intersexed people. Alice Dreger illustrates the huge challenges such individuals posed to French and British categorizations of sex, gender role, and sexuality. Having gonads of one sex and genitalia of the other, such *pseudohermaphrodites* were always, simultaneously, homo- and heterosexual with any partner of either sex. Dreger points out how such sexually "ambiguous" people were—sometimes unwittingly, at other times self-assertively—powerful disrupters of cultural gender conventions.

Anne Fausto-Sterling's essay brings the analysis of intersexes up to the present time. In focusing on four decades of influential work by psychologist John Money and his colleagues at the Psychohormonal Research Unit at the Johns Hopkins University, Fausto-Sterling demonstrates how scientific theories of hormonal and genetic sex development incorporate popular stereotypes of gender roles. The heterosexist, male bias of these stereotypes not only shapes sexological formulations of homosexuality and "normal" sexuality, but also surgically reshapes bodies that do not conform to genital "normality."

While the penis has been seen as the genital norm by a male-dominated medical profession, the clitoris was a site of intense scrutiny and concern at the turn of the century. American doctors particularly relied on anthropometry (the comparative measurement of bodily parts) as a means of detecting deviance. Margaret Gibson uncovers a wealth of late nineteenth-century medical literature on the clitoris. She argues that in linking lesbianism with clitoral pathology, doctors associated female inverts with a variety of "sociopathic" women (masturbators, prostitutes, women of color, and poor women), and thereby also attempted to discredit the feminist political projects spearheaded by independent, "masculine" women.

Masculinity and femininity were also of huge concern to French doctors, particularly after France's humiliating defeat in the Franco-Prussian War. French physicians, therefore, made major contributions to the study of "sexual inversion" and other "sexual perversions" (both terms coined by the French). In my essay, I discuss the prominent role played by inverts themselves in shaping scientific conceptions of inversion and in criticizing physicians' hypocrisy. Relying on the nationalistic contributions of fiction writers to the medical literature on inversion, I argue that the fin-de-siècle "homosexual" was a fictional character (albeit culturally and politically real) spun from the pre-existing figures of the sodomite, the hysterical male, and the degenerate.

The theory of degeneracy—of evolution in reverse, or atavism—continued to inform even socially liberal sexologists, such as Britain's Havelock Ellis, in the early part of the twentieth century. Julian Carter shows how evolutionary narratives allowed Ellis and his Anglo-American colleagues to map their norms of racial and class progress upon sexological models of "normal," white, bourgeois sexuality. According to this logic, homosexuality was understood as a "primitive" or developmentally stunted behavior. Paralleling these precarious routes of sexual, racial, and class progress, the mastery of both literary and scientific language was traced as the sole path to "normal," "civilized" sexuality.

By the 1920s, American sexological research on lesbianism was putting aside the work of Ellis and earlier German physicians who had dominated the field. Erin Carlston documents a proliferation and diversification of medical theories of lesbianism in the 1930s that distinguished themselves from or incorporated Freud's increasingly popular psychological theories of the origins of homosexuality. In the process of constructing models of healthy heterosexuality, doctors paid growing attention to homosexuality as a challenge to psychiatry and society. Nevertheless, throughout these debates, several tolerant voices emerged from both the somatic and the psychoanalytic camps, and lesbians themselves were loudly, insistently proclaiming their normality.

Mounting evidence of homosexuals' external anatomical normality increasingly challenged the old hermaphroditic models. Researchers in the early twentieth century, therefore, turned to new biomedical fields such as neurophysiology and endocrinology to explain the presumed psychosexual inversion of homosexuals. Stephanie Kenen examines these early hormonal theories of homosexuality and the strong challenge posed to them by Alfred Kinsey's sociological model of sexuality. Kinsey's widely publicized demographic research on "normal" Americans shocked the world with its evidence that nonheterosexual behavior was surprisingly common, and his work problematized all the neat categories of gender and sexuality that preceded it.

The increasingly dominant fields of genetics and molecular biology have provided a constant stream of provocative, albeit tenuous, suggestions that homosexuality and other traits are inherited. Garland Allen traces the history of this work, beginning with the eugenics movement in the early part of this century, proceeding through to the homosexual twin studies of the 1950s and the 1990s. Allen examines in detail the theoretical and methodological flaws of the most recent and widely publicized of the genetic approaches, Hamer and coworkers' linkage study. The recourse to sociobiological and genetic explanations of human behavior, Allen observes, has been fraught with overhyped results that mask a dangerous political and social conservatism.

The politics of the biomedical search for the "cause" of homosexuality and of gay and lesbian identities themselves is a recurrent theme throughout these essays. Jennifer Terry places these issues at the head of her critique of the science of homosexuality. Surveying the field, Terry devotes special attention to the research of Hamer and LeVay, which was economically, materially, and emotionally fueled by the AIDS epidemic. Terry locates the reason for the current confidence in biologically determinist "explanations" of homosexuality in the high cultural valuation of genes as the "key of life" and in cultural anxieties surrounding sex itself—particularly in the era of AIDS.

Finally, Richard Pillard reviews the evidence for a genetic contribution to the determination of sexual orientation, setting this research agenda in the context of gay political involvement in the psychiatric profession since the 1970s. He associates the current debates with the old controversy in psychology between empiricists and nativists. Most contemporary scientists, however, agree that both perspectives must be synthesized, particularly in the complex study of human traits. Like the other contributors to this anthology, Pillard recognizes the social and ethical dangers of genetic research on sexual orientation (particularly given the growing reality of genetic engineering). However, these dangers demand not an end to science, but keen political awareness and intervention on the part of scientists and public alike—whatever their sexual orientation.

Although the essays in this anthology cover the major areas of biomedical research on the ætiology of homosexuality in the past 150 years, I have to acknowledge gaps in this account: the twentieth-century material primarily focuses on the United States; the volume concentrates on clinical, human studies rather than animal studies; and we overlook numerous researchers who have not attracted popular attention. Nevertheless, the following essays present an extensive introduction to the topic, and also display a diversity of analytic approaches inspired by science studies, queer studies, and feminist studies. This volume does not set out to *resolve* the question: What causes homosexuality? On the contrary, in examining the scientific pursuit of that question, the following essays serve to confound the neat taxonomies of sex, gender, and sexuality, and of homosexuality, heterosexuality, and bisexuality. In demonstrating how these biomedical categories were produced, we gain a better appreciation of the methods and aims of the scientific manufacture of knowledge and of the active role of those very beings science struggles to know. As the objects of the scientific gaze, inverts, gays, lesbians, and queers have not simply been performing homosexually on the stage of the microscope, oblivious to that scientific voyeurism. They have been critically staring back up the barrel, into the inquiring eyes of Science. Sometimes those eyes have been those of other homosexuals who double as objects and subjects of science. But their curiosity is that of all those who would turn science into a magical mirror of inner truths. The political urgency, however, is to recognize science as an instrument of our own creation—a tool for writing alternative, liberatory bio-histories of the future.

Notes

An abridged version of this essay was presented at the UCLA Center for the Study of Women. I thank the audience at that colloquium as well as Christopher Kelty, Andrew London, Henry Rubin, and Drs. Joel Braslow, Maggie Magee, and Diana Miller for their valuable comments.

1 Simon LeVay, for example, is reported as claiming that his novel neurobiological work demonstrates that the study of homosexuality is "not just in the province of the psychologists and psychoanalysts any more" (qtd. in Angier 1991b). See also *Scientific American* (1994).

2 Although the book is co-authored with Peter Copeland, Hamer explicitly states that he is

"solely responsible for its scientific content and interpretation" (6); therefore, I discuss its ideas as Hamer's alone.

3 See Sulloway (1979). As one example of the marriage of psychoanalytic and organic approaches to homosexuality, Freudian psychiatrist Newdigate Owensby advocated the "correction of homosexuality" through metrazol pharmaco-shock therapy, which he proposed "liberates this previous fixation of the libido and the psychosexual energy becomes free once more to flow through physiological channels" (1940, 65).

4 For the history of psychoanalytic theories and therapies of homosexuality, see Aardweg (1986) and Lewes (1988).

5 See for example Bullough (1994, 278).

6 For recent, influential sociological and political analyses of science, see Shapin (1982), Latour (1986), Bloor (1991), and Proctor (1991).

7 For a detailed legal critique of the naturalizing strategy or "argument from immutability," see Halley (1994).

8 By way of example, on the side of hypotheses giving primacy to "nature," one could simplistically place genetic theories: namely, that the genetic combination (*genotype*) established at conception determines an organism's subsequent traits (*phenotype*), including sexual orientation. Among theories giving primacy to "nurture" (or the environment), we could place psychoanalytic models of homosexuality as a product of family dynamics in infancy: for example, a "preoedipal nuclear conflict" involving dread of mother-child unity resulting in fixation to the mother and a narcissistic object choice (Socarides 1968).

9 The INAH 3 is the interstitial nucleus of the anterior hypothalamus 3. For a review of neuroanatomical research on the hypothalamus, see Swaab and Hofman (1995).

10 These are phenomena that would be eliminated if the nervous system were brought to a standstill, for example, by chilling. An analogy to the distinction between neuroanatomical versus neurodynamic phenomena is the difference between data stored on a floppy disk versus a file currently in RAM. If your computer suddenly lost all power, including back-up battery power, the data stored on the diskette would still be there (physically recorded in magnetic form), while your current file (since the last auto-save) would be lost in electronic oblivion.

11 On the history of philosophies of knowledge and perception, see Churchland (1986, 239–276).

12 For example, Sarah Schulman, in an otherwise politically astute essay, opposes all biologically determinist theories of homosexuality with the defeatist conclusion, "How can homosexuality have a cause? Like light and water it just is" (1995, 21). She overlooks the fact that the study of light is one of the most ancient preoccupations of physics. Later, however, she proposes: "Wouldn't society be better served by social and scientific inquiries into the causes of homophobia?" (21). Although I agree with her on the greater social utility of research on homophobia, how would this research agenda be based on any different methodological or epistemological principles than research on homosexuality?

13 See Mendelsohn's (1993) equally satirical suggestion that Republicanism be viewed as a genetic disorder.

14 For example, to be of a "normal" weight, particularly in weight-conscious U.S. society, is not simply to be within a certain range of the average for a highly specific group of people (i.e., of the same age, height, nationality, sex, race, historical period, etc.), but also to be "healthy" and "responsible." Recent claims of the discovery of "obesity" genes may shift the pathologization of being overweight, but probably not alter its cultural stigmatization.

15 My list of binarisms certainly does not exhaust the possibilities that have been evoked

around the matter of homosexuality. Another important one that deserves mention is the realist vs. nominalist divide, which Boswell (1989) maps to the essentialist vs. constructionist opposition. Halperin (1990, 43) however notes that claiming heterosexuality and homosexuality to be culturally constructed does not (or, at least, need not) mean that they are "unreal" in the present historical setting. Fuss (1989) provides a broader analysis of the debate in the contexts of feminist and race/ethnicity theories.

16 While genetic theories of homosexuality may epitomize essentialist models, there can be non-biological essentialisms: e.g., psychoanalysis also provides theories of homosexuality as a transhistorical and transcultural phenomenon of specific parent-child dynamics. Constructionist models are also diverse, and may give primacy to sociological, cultural, or familial *historical* forces in the shaping of sexualities, including "homosexuality."

17 Numerous references could be given to examples and discussions of social constructivist theories of homosexuality; some of the more influential articles include Halperin (1990), Vance (1989), Padgug (1992), Stein (1992), De Cecco and Elia (1993).

18 This is paradigmatic of a performative, illocutionary speech act as formally defined by linguists: speech that does something in the process of its enunciation (Austin 1962).

19 For an analysis of French constructions of homosexuality, and the view that "gay" and "queer" are American imports, see Rosario (1992). On Queer nationalism, see Duggan (1992) and Berlant and Freeman (1993).

20 I should note that Halperin (1995, 187–188 n. 3) has recently shifted away from his earlier position that constructionism is a synonym for cultural determinism.

21 Compare this notion of "imagined kinship" with Anderson's model (1991) of the "nation" as an imagined community, particularly in relation to my earlier example of "American citizenship" as a constructed, "naturalized" identity. The various "Queer Nation" groups in the early 1990s implicitly associated nationality and sexual community. Gay men's and lesbians' fondness for kinship (both traditional and alternative) is poignantly documented in Weston's anthropological analysis of "chosen families" (1991),

22 Foucault used the term *bio-history* to refer, rather vaguely, to "the pressures by which the movements of life and the processes of history interfere with one and other" (1976, 188). I use the term specifically in this context to describe the synchronic and diachronic narratives of historical identity-filiation built upon biological, particularly genetic, frameworks.

23 *Spartacus* editor Bruno Gmünder notes that: "The nationalism typical of the 19th century was never of particular interest to gay men. As long as gay love has been around, we have tried to focus on things that unite, not divide us" (xvi). I am grateful to Lawrence Cohen for alerting me to the gay imperialist subtext of such tourism books.

24 Wishman (1996) found that the "dominant account" of the origins of homosexuality among the seventy-two lesbians and gay men she interviewed is predominantly a determinist one. She also suggests, as I do, that this determinist model better suits men than women. Unfortunately, her sample does not allow her to generalize her conclusions, or extend them to racial or class subgroups.

25 For feminist critiques of biomedical constructions of women's bodies and sexuality, see Bleier (1984), Fausto-Sterling (1985), Hubbard (1990), Russett (1989). For feminist critiques of the sciences, more broadly, see Longino and Doell (1983), Schiebinger (1989), Harding (1986), Haraway (1991). Indeed, these analyses have been so convincing that a band of threatened men have appointed themselves the defenders of Science against what they perceive as a wave of irrationalist, romantic anti-science (Park 1995; Holton 1993; Gross & Levitt 1994).

26 It is nevertheless ironic, and pregnant with oedipal interpretations, that the gay, male her-

itage Hamer described is *matrilineal*—a, perhaps fortuitous, line of gay male resistance to a patriarchy especially hostile to effeminate gays. Hamer's laboratory has failed to show a similar genetic linkage for lesbianism (Hu et al. 1995)

27 Compare with Martin (1987) on middle-class women's acceptance of biomedical models of female reproductive physiology versus working-class women's resistance.

28 On race and class issues in science and medicine see Harding (1993), Larson (1995), Vaughan (1991), Prins (1989), Jones (1993), Gilman (1985), Cameron (1995).

29 De Cecco and Parker's (1995) informative anthology on the "biology of sexual preference" presents a more internalist and biomedically oriented criticism of methodology in the field than this volume. It also offers meta-analyses, and new scientific studies. Also see Byne (1994) for a methodological critique of the recent research.

References

Aardweg, G. J. M. van den. 1986. *On the Origins and Treatment of Homosexuality: A Psychoanalytic Reinterpretation.* New York: Praeger.

Anderson, Benedict. 1991. *Imagined Communities: Reflections on the Origin and Spread of Nationalism.* London: Verso.

Angier, Natalie. 1991a. The biology of what it means to be gay. *New York Times* (September 1) sect. 4: 1, 4.

———. 1991b. Zone of brain linked to men's sexual orientation. *New York Times* (August 30): A1, D18.

———. 1993a. Bias against gay people: hatred of a special kind. *New York Times* (December 26) sect. 4: 4.

———. 1993b. Study of sex orientation doesn't neatly fit mold. *New York Times* (July 18) sect. 1: 24.

Austin, J. L. 1962. *How To Do Things With Words.* Oxford: Clarendon.

Bailey, J. Michael, and Richard Pillard. 1991. A genetic study of male sexual orientation. *Archives of General Psychiatry* 48:1089–1096.

Bailey, J. Michael, Richard C. Pillard, Michael C. Neale, and Yvonne Agyei. 1993. Heritable factors influence sexual orientation in women. *Archives of General Psychiatry* 50:217–223.

Bayer, Ronald. 1981. *Homosexuality and American Psychiatry: The Politics of Diagnosis.* New York: Basic Books.

Berlant, Lauren, and Elizabeth Freeman. 1993. Queer nationality. In *Fear of a Queer Planet,* ed. Michael Warner, 193–229. Minneapolis: University of Minnesota Press.

Bleier, Ruth. 1984. *Science and Gender: A Critique of Biology and Its Theories on Women.* New York: Pergamon.

Bloor, David. 1991. *Knowledge and Social Imagery.* 2nd ed. Chicago: University of Chicago Press.

Boswell, John. 1980. *Christianity, Social Tolerance and Homosexuality: Gay People in Western Europe from the Beginning of the Christian Era to the Fourteenth Century.* Chicago: University of Chicago Press.

———. 1989. Revolutions, universals and sexual categories. In *Hidden from History: Reclaiming the Gay and Lesbian Past,* ed. M. B. Duberman, M. Vicinus, and G. Chauncey, Jr., 17–36. New York: New American Library.

———. 1994. *Same-Sex Unions in Premodern Europe*. New York: Villard.

Bullough, Vern L. 1994. *Science in the Bedroom. A History of Sex Research*. New York: Basic Books.

Burr, Chandler. 1993a. Genes vs. hormones. *New York Times* (August 2): A15.

———. 1993b. Homosexuality and biology. *Atlantic Monthly* 271(3): 47–65.

Byne, William. 1994. The biological evidence challenged. *Scientific American* 270 (May): 50–55.

Cameron, Kenneth N. 1995. *Dialectical Materialism and Modern Science*. New York: International Publishers.

Cameron, Paul. 1992. What causes homosexuality and can it be cured? Lincoln, NE: Family Research Institute.

Canguilhem, Georges. [1966] 1989. *The Normal and the Pathological*. Trans. Carolyn Fawcett. New York: Zone.

Churchland, Patricia. 1986. *Neurophilosophy: Towards a Unified Science of the Mind-Brain*. Cambridge, Mass.: MIT Press.

Darwin, Charles. [1859] 1964. *On the Origin of Species*. Facsimile of the first edition. Cambridge: Harvard University Press.

———. [1871] 1981. *The Descent of Man, and Selection in Relation to Sex*. Photoreproduction of the first edition. Princeton: Princeton University Press.

Dawkins, Richard. 1976. *The Selfish Gene*. Oxford: Oxford University Press.

De Cecco, John, and John Elia. 1993. A critique and synthesis of biological essentialism and social constructionist views of sexuality and gender. *Journal of Homosexuality* 24(3/4): 1–26.

De Cecco, John, and David A. Parker, eds. 1995. *Sex, Cells, and Same-Sex Desire: The Biology of Sexual Preference*. Binghamton: Harrington Park.

D'Emilio, John. 1993. Capitalism and gay identity. In *Gay and Lesbian Studies Reader*, ed. H. Abelove, M. A. Barale, and D. M. Halperin, 467–476. New York: Routledge.

Diderot, Denis. [1769] 1951. *La Suite de l'Entretien* [entre d'Alembert et Diderot]. In *Oeuvres*, 935–942. Paris: Pléiade.

Duggan, Lisa. 1992. Making it perfectly queer. *Socialist Review* 22(1): 11–31.

Eagleton, Terry. 1983. *Literary Theory: An Introduction*. Minneapolis: University of Minnesota Press.

Ellis, Havelock [and John A. Symonds]. [1897] 1936. *Sexual Inversion*. In *Studies in the Psychology of Sex*, Vol. II, Part 2. New York: Random House.

Encyclopedia of Homosexuality. 1990. Ed. Wayne Dynes. New York: Garland.

Fausto-Sterling, Anne. 1985. *Myths of Gender. Biological Theories About Women and Men*. New York: Basic Books.

Ford, Clellan S., and Frank A. Beach. 1951. *Patterns of Sexual Behavior*. New York: Harper.

Foucault, Michel. 1976. *Histoire de la sexualité; Vol. 1: La volonté de savoir*. Paris: Gallimard.

Fuss, Diana. 1989. *Essentially Speaking: Feminism, Nature and Difference*. New York: Routledge.

Galton, Francis. [1869] 1884. *Hereditary Genius*. New York: Appleton.

Gelman, David, with Donna Foote. 1992. [Is homosexuality] Born or bred? *Newsweek* (Feb. 24): 46–53.

Gilman, Sander L. 1985. *Difference and Pathology: Stereotypes of Sexuality, Race, and Madness*. Ithaca: Cornell University Press.

Gross, Paul R., and Norman Levitt. 1994. *Higher Superstition: The Academic Left and Its Quarrels with Science*. Baltimore: Johns Hopkins University Press.

Gusella, James, Marcy MacDonald, Christine Ambrose, and Mabel Duyao. 1993. Molecular genetics of Huntington's disease. *Archives of Neurology* 50:1157–1163.

Halley, Janet E. 1994. Sexual orientation and the politics of biology: A critique of the argument from immutability. *Stanford Law Review* 46:503–568.

Halperin, David. 1990. *One Hundred Years of Homosexuality*. New York: Routledge.

———. 1995. *Saint Foucault: Towards a Gay Hagiography*. New York: Oxford University Press.

Hamer, Dean, and Peter Copeland. 1994. *The Science of Desire: The search for the gay gene and the biology of behavior*. New York: Simon & Schuster.

Hamer, Dean, Stella Hu, Victoria L. Magnuson, Nan Hu, and Angela Pattatucci. 1993. A linkage between DNA markers on the X chromosome and male sexual orientation. *Science* 261:321–7.

Haraway, Donna. 1991. *Simians, Cyborgs, and Women. The Reinvention of Nature*. New York: Routledge.

Harding, Sandra. 1986. *The Science Question in Feminism*. Ithaca: Cornell Univesity Press.

———, ed. 1993. *The "Racial" Economy of Science: Toward a Democratic Future*. Bloomington: Indiana University Press.

Herdt, Gilbert, ed. 1994. *Third Sex, Third Gender: Beyond Sexual Dimorphism in Culture and History*. New York: Zone.

Holton, Gerald J. 1993. *Science and Anti-Science*. Cambridge: Harvard University Press.

Horton, Richard. 1995. Is homosexuality inherited? *New York Review of Books* 42(July 13): 36–41.

Hu, Stella, Angela M. L. Pattatucci, Dean Hamer, et al. 1995. Linkage between sexual orientation and chromosome Xq28 in males but not in females. *Nature Genetics* 11:248–256.

Hubbard, Ruth. 1990. *The Politics of Women's Biology*. New Brunswick, NJ: Rutgers University Press.

Hubbard, Ruth, and Elija Wald. 1993. *Exploding the Gene Myth*. Boston: Beacon.

Huntington, George S. 1872. On chorea. *Medical and Surgical Reporter* (Philadelphia) 26:317–321.

Jones, James H. 1993. *Bad Blood: The Tuskegee Syphilis Experiment*. New York: Free Press.

Kay, Lily E. 1993. *The Molecular Vision of Life: Caltech, the Rockefeller Foundation, and the Rise of the New Biology*. New York: Oxford University Press.

Kevles, Daniel. 1995. The X factor: The battle over the ramifications of a gay gene. *New Yorker* 71(6) (April 3): 85–90.

Kimmel, Michael, ed. 1990. *Love Letters Between a certain late Nobleman and the famous Mr. Wilson*. Binghamton: Harrington Park.

Kinsey, Alfred C., Wardell B. Pomeroy, and Clyde E. Martin. 1948. *Sexual Behavior in the Human Male*. Philadelphia: W. B. Saunders.

Kirsch, John A. W., and James Weinrich. 1991. Homosexuality, nature, and biology: Is homosexuality natural? Does it matter? In *Homosexuality: Research Implications for Public Policy*, ed. John Gonsiorek and James Weinrich, 13–31. Newbury Park, CA: Sage.

Lane, Harlan. 1992. *The Mask of Benevolence. Disabling the Deaf Community*. New York: Knopf.

Larson, Edward J. 1995. *Sex, Race, and Science: Eugenics in the Deep South*. Baltimore: Johns Hopkins University Press.

Latour, Bruno. 1986. *Laboratory Life: The Construction of Scientific Facts*. Princeton: Princeton University Press.

LeVay, Simon. 1991. A difference in hypothalamic structure between heterosexual and homosexual men. *Science* 253: 1034–1037.
———. 1993. *The Sexual Brain*. Cambridge: MIT Press.
LeVay, Simon, and Dean Hamer. 1994. Evidence for a biological influence in male homosexuality. *Scientific American* 270 (May): 44–49.
Lewes, Kenneth. 1988. *The Psychoanalytic Theory of Male Homosexuality*. New York: Simon & Schuster.
Lewontin, Richard C., Steven Rose, and Leon L. Kamin. 1984. *Not in Our Genes: Biology, Ideology, and Human Nature*. New York: Pantheon.
Longino, Helen, and Ruth Doell. 1983. Body, bias, and behavior: A comparative analysis of reasoning in two areas of biological science. *Signs* 9:206–227.
Martin, Emily. 1987. *The Woman in the Body: A Cultural Analysis of Reproduction*. Boston: Beacon.
Mendelsohn, Daniel. 1993. Republicans can be cured! *New York Times* (July 26): A15.
Owensby, Newdigate. 1940. Homosexuality and lesbianism treated with metrazol. *J. Nervous and Mental Diseases* 92: 65–66.
Padgug, Robert. 1992. Sexual matters: on conceptualizing sexuality in history. In *Forms of Desire: Sexual Orientation and the Social Constructivist Controversy*, ed. Edward Stein, 43–67. New York: Routledge.
Park, Robert L. 1995. The dangers of voodoo science. *New York Times* (July 9) sect. 4: 15.
Prins, Gwyn. 1989. But what was the disease? The present state of health and healing in African Studies. *Past and Present* 124:159–179.
Proctor, Robert N. 1991. *Value-Free Science? Purity and Power in Modern Knowledge*. Cambridge: Harvard University Press.
Rosario, Vernon. 1992. Sexual liberalism and compulsory heterosexuality. *Journal of Contemporary French Civilization* 16:262–79.
Rowse, A. L. 1977. *Homosexuals in History*. New York: Macmillan.
Russett, Cynthia E. 1989. *Sexual Science: The Victorian Construction of Womanhood*. Cambridge: Harvard University Press.
Schiebinger, Londa. 1989. *The Mind Has No Sex. Women in the Origins of Modern Science*. Cambridge: Harvard University Press.
Schulman, Sarah. 1995. Uncontrollable instincts. *Rouge* 20:20–21.
Scientific American. 1994. Is homosexuality biologically influenced? 270(May): 43.
Shapin, Steve. 1982. History of science and its sociological reconstruction. *History of Science* 9:157–211.
Socarides, Charles. 1968. A provisional theory of ætiology of male homosexuality. A case of preœdipal origin. *International Journal of Psycho-Analysis* 49:27–37.
Spartacus International Gay Guide. 1990–91. 19th edition. Ed. Bruno Gmünder and John D. Stamford. Berlin: Bruno Gmünder Verlag.
Spencer, Colin. 1996. *Homosexuality in History*. New York: Harcourt Brace.
Stein, Edward. 1992. Conclusion: The essentials of constructionism and the construction of essentialism. In *Forms of Desire: Sexual Orientation and the Social Constructivist Controversy*, ed. Edward Stein, 325–353. New York: Routledge.
Sulloway, Frank J. 1979. *Freud, Biologist of the Mind: Beyond the Psychoanalytic Legend*. New York: Basic Books.
Swaab, D. F., and M. A. Hofman. 1995. Sexual differentiation of the human hypothalamus in relation to gender and sexual orientation. *Trends in Neuroscience* 18:264–270.

Tabboo! and Peter Fish. 1995. It's Natural. Sound recording on *Wigstock: The Movie. Music from the Original Soundtrack.* Performed by Tabboo! New York: Sire Records.

Thompson, Larry. 1995. Search for a gay gene. *TIME.* 145(June 12): 60–61.

Trumbach, Randolph. 1989. The birth of the queen: Sodomy and the emergence of gender equality in modern culture, 1660–1750. In *Hidden From History*, ed. M. B. Duberman, M. Vicinus, and G. Chauncey, Jr., 129–140. New York: New American Library.

Vance, Carole. 1989. Social construction theory: Problems in the history of sexuality. In *Homosexuality, Which Homosexuality?*, ed. Denis Altman, et al., 13–34. London: GMP Publishers.

Vaughan, Megan. 1991. *Curing Their Ills: Colonial Power and African Illness.* Stanford: Stanford University Press.

Weinrich, James, and Walter Williams. 1991. Strange customs, familiar lives: Homosexualities in other cultures. In *Homosexuality: Research Implications for Public Policy*, ed. John Gonsiorek and James Weinrich, 44–59. Newbury Park, CA: Sage.

Weston, Kath. 1991. *Families We Choose: Lesbians, Gays, and Kinship.* New York: Columbia University Press.

Wilson, Edward O. 1978. *On Human Nature.* Cambridge: Harvard University Press.

Wishman, Vera. 1996. *Queer by Choice: Lesbians, Gay Men, and the Politics of Identity.* New York: Routledge.

Zhang, Shang-Ding, and Ward F. Odenwald. 1995. Misexpression of white(w) gene triggers male-male courtship in Drosophila. *Proceedings of the National Academy of Science U.S.A.* 92:5525–5529.

Karl Heinrich Ulrichs
First Theorist of Homosexuality

Hubert Kennedy

Karl Heinrich Ulrichs was the first to formulate a scientific theory of homosexuality.[1] Indeed, his theory implicated, as Klaus Müller has emphasized, "the first scientific theory of sexuality altogether" (1991, 24). It was set forth and elaborated in five writings published in 1864 to 1865. The series of writings was continued—there were twelve in all, the last appearing in 1879—but with only slight revisions in the theory. Ulrichs's intention in his writings was not merely explanatory, but also—and especially—emancipatory. This was based on his view that the condition of being homosexual is inborn. This was a major departure from previous and subsequent theories that saw the practice of homosexuality/"sodomy" as an acquired vice. In this Ulrichs was the first in a long and continuing line of researchers who believe that a proof of the "naturalness" of homosexuality, that is, the discovery of a biological basis for it, will lead to equal legal and social treatment of hetero- and homosexuals. If this attempt seems quixotic, it is nevertheless of historical importance to investigate its origins in the writings of Ulrichs. We shall see that Ulrichs's influence goes beyond any "emancipatory" intent.

The son of an architect in the service of the Kingdom of Hannover, Karl Heinrich Ulrichs was born on August 28, 1825, on his father's estate of Westerfeld near Aurich. Following his father's death in 1835, Ulrichs moved with his mother to Burgdorf, to live with her father, a Lutheran superintendent. Ulrichs studied law in Göttingen (1844 to 1846) and Berlin (1846 to 1847) and, after the official examination in 1848, was in the civil service of Hannover until December 1854, when he resigned in order to avoid being disciplined. His homosexual activity had come to the attention of his superiors, and although homosexual acts were not then illegal in Hannover, as a civil servant he could be dismissed. For the next few years, Ulrichs earned his living as a reporter for the important *Allgemeine Zeitung* (Augsburg) and as secretary to one of the representatives to the German Confederation in Frankfurt am Main. He also received an inheritance from his mother on her death in 1856.

The first five of his writings on the riddle of "man-manly" love (as Ulrichs's translator has rendered Ulrichs's coinage *mannmännlich*) were written in the years 1863 to 1865, and published under the pseudonym Numa Numantius. This series was later continued under his real name; the twelfth and last volume appeared in 1879. Ulrichs's activism for the homosexual cause was hampered in part by a lack of money and was interrupted by his engagement in another political cause. A trained lawyer and administrator, he was hindered from using his abilities to earn a living by the mean-spirited vindictiveness of the authorities in Hannover, who refused him any certification of service, thus barring him from practicing as a lawyer and forestalling his candidacy for mayor of Uslar in 1865. But even this did not stem his patriotic feelings, for when Prussia invaded and annexed Hannover in 1866, Ulrichs protested publicly, and was twice imprisoned for it. As an activist Ulrichs fought not only for the equal rights of homosexuals, but also for the rights of ethnic and religious minorities, as well as the rights of women, including unwed mothers and their children (see *Prometheus*, 9).[2] In 1880, Ulrichs left Germany to spend the last fifteen years of his life in exile in Italy, where he earned his living by tutoring foreign languages and publishing a journal that was written entirely by him in Latin; its goal was to revive Latin as an international language. He died in Aquila, Italy, on July 14, 1895.[3]

In his published writings on homosexuality, Ulrichs posited the existence of a "third sex" whose nature is inborn. The essential point in his theory of homosexuality is the doctrine that the male homosexual has a female psyche, which he summed up in the Latin phrase: *anima muliebris virili corpore inclusa* (a female psyche confined in a male body). In his attempt to understand himself and others he thought were like him, however, he did not immediately arrive at this theory. An autobiographical manuscript of 1861 shows that he had still not arrived at this concept. In it, he mentioned his good health and added: "A physical-mental characteristic of mine is a certain passive magnetism of the animal world," and he attached an outline of this "Animal Magnetism," beginning:

> The mental-physical passive animal magnetism mentioned is passive, not active, for the reason that the person for whom it is a characteristic does not attract, but rather feels himself attracted, just as a passive magnetism dwells in a piece of soft iron, since it does not attract, but is attracted by the steel magnet, whereas active magnetism is in the attracting steel magnet (perhaps a passive magnetism as well, but at least an active is there). (Cited in Kennedy 1988, 44)

The existence of animal magnetism had been postulated in the eighteenth century by Friedrich Anton Mesmer (1734–1815), but interest in it fell off after a commission appointed by the medical faculty of Paris (which included Benjamin Franklin) concluded in 1784 that this magnetic fluid did not exist.[4] But a generation later, Alexandre Bertrand (1795–1831) revived it, and in 1831 a committee of the Academy of Medicine of Paris reported favorably upon "magnetism" as a therapeutic agent. In Germany its acceptance as a scientific theory was strengthened in 1845, when Karl Ludwig Freiherr von Reichenbach (1788–1869), who was already known for his investigation of paraffin (1830) and creosote (1832), announced the discovery of a magnetic force he called Od. Ulrichs was clearly acquainted with Reichenbach's theory of "odylic force," as it was called in English, but gave no indication of other sources of his own theory.[5] At any rate, he soon abandoned this explanation, which appears to have had no connection with his later study of hermaphroditism.

Although Ulrichs continued to use the language of animal magnetism in describing sexual attraction, he believed that he had discovered a scientifically more acceptable theory of the cause of homosexuality. Nevertheless, he published in 1864 a report from a correspondent, who wrote that he saw a spark on his penis when it was touched by his young soldier friend while they were sitting on a park bench and he was also touching his friend's penis. Ulrichs asked: "Was this spark Reichenbach's Od? Was it positive animal electricity?" (*Formatrix*, 64). When Magnus Hirschfeld (1868–1935) published a somewhat truncated edition of Ulrichs's writings in 1898, he left out this passage. By then the theory of animal magnetism was out of favor.

Noteworthy in Ulrichs's 1861 manuscript is his sense of himself as a pioneer in the scientific study of the phenomenon. He also castigates scientists and others for their neglect:

> Until now science has not sought to investigate this passive animal magnetism (by no means an isolated phenomenon), although the doctor, the anthropologist and physiologist, the jurist, the psychologist, and the moralist could cultivate an entirely new field. In fact they have made not the slightest effort to investigate its nature: rather (misled by poorly understood Bible passages and by laws based on such Bible passages—laws whose moral value stands on the same level as those against witchcraft and heresy in the Middle Ages) they have believed they should ignore or disdain it with hatred and scorn, examples of which are in scientific books. (Cited in Kennedy 1988, 44)

Ulrichs's confidence in the logical and liberating possibilities of science was inherited from the eighteenth century, of which Wolfgang Breidert writes: "There appeared to be no limits set to the technical-scientific command of nature; one had indeed in Newton's theory of gravitation a theory that was extended to the whole cosmos, even its farthest parts. The rational penetration of phenomenal fields became the Enlightenment goal of an epistemologically optimistic time" (1994, 3). And Ulrichs saw himself in this tradition of the Enlightenment.

Ulrichs, however, must have felt the inadequacy of the theory of animal magnetism as a scientific explanation.[6] At any rate, when he next wrote about the subject in letters to a circle of close relatives in 1862, he made no mention of magnetism. Instead, through observing others like himself, he wrote, he perceived a "female element" that is part of their nature, and he stated that the principal part of this female element is their erotic attraction to men. A member of this "third sex" he called a *Uranier*, as opposed to the "true" man, the *Dionäer* ("Vier Briefe," 45). (In his published writings, from 1864, these terms became *Urning* and *Dioning*, respectively.) The term "third sex" (*drittes Geschlecht*) had been used earlier, from Plato (*Symposium*) to Théophile Gautier (*Mademoiselle de Maupin*, 1835), with very diverse meanings. What they all have in common is that "sex" is not viewed solely from the aspect of reproduction.[7] The term's blending of sex, sex role, and gender (and the confusions produced) continues today.[8]

Ulrichs arrived at his new theory as a result of his study of the literature on hermaphrodites. He assumed it to be a rule of nature that human beings were born with either male or female sexual organs. At times, however, there were exceptions to this rule of nature that he found described in the scientific literature, namely, physical hermaphrodites. Correspondingly, Ulrichs accepted it as a rule of nature that persons with male sexual organs are sexually attracted to women, and he assumed that there could also be exceptions to this rule, namely that some persons with normal male sexual organs could be attracted not to women, but to men. But what could cause this? It could not be the body with its male sexual organs, for if the body determined the direction of the sex drive, it would obviously be directed toward women. Hence, the direction of sexual attraction must be caused by the person's psyche. But since, according to Ulrichs, sexual attraction to men is always of a female nature, it follows that the psyche of those who are attracted to men must be female.

In reviewing Ulrichs's ideas, Jonathan Ned Katz comments:

> In Ulrichs's eroticized update of the early Victorian true man, the real man possessed a male body and a male sex-love for women. The Urning was a true man with the feelings of a true woman. The Urning possessed a male body and the female's sex-love for men.
>
> As we've seen, the Victorian concept of the "true" mechanically linked biology with psychology. Feelings were thought of as female or male in exactly the same sense as penis or clitoris: anatomy equaled psychology, sex physiology determined the sex of feelings. Sex-love for a female was a male feeling, sex-love for a male was a female feeling. A female sex-love could inhabit a male body, a male sex-love could inhabit a female body.
>
> According to this theory there existed only *one* sexual desire, focused on the other sex. . . . Their desire was therefore "contrary" to the one, normative "sexual instinct." Ulrichs accepted this one-instinct idea. (Katz 1995, 51–52)

But to explain this attraction scientifically, Ulrichs needed to find a substrate for it. We may recall that the chromosomal basis of sexual differentiation was discovered only in the twentieth century. Since the sexual organs are not differentiated in the early stages of the embryo, Ulrichs argued that there was a possibility of developing either way, and saw this view confirmed by the existence of hermaphrodites with both types of sexual organs.[9] He postulated the existence of a germ (*Keim*) of development that would determine whether the sexual organs developed as male or female. To explain the possibility of a sexual drive in apparent disharmony with the individual's sexual organs, he likewise postulated the existence of a germ that determines the direction of the sexual drive. Thus, Ulrichs argued, while the rule of nature was that these two germs in an individual give the same direction of development, male or female, there could be occasional exceptions that would produce people like himself, who were neither fully men nor fully women, but rather, as he called it in his first publication on the subject in 1864, a "third sex." From this also followed the theoretical possibility of a "fourth sex," with a female body and a male psyche, but he was unacquainted with any at that time.[10]

Ulrichs's goal was to free people like himself from the legal, religious, and social condemnation of homosexual acts as unnatural. For this, he invented a new terminology that would refer to the nature of the individual, and not to the acts performed. The forensic medical expert Johann Ludwig Casper (1796–1864), for example, had earlier used the term "pederasty" from the classic Greek for "boy-love."[11] Yet the meaning of this term had been confused with the Latin *paedicatio* (anal intercourse), so that the two had become synonymous.[12] Ulrichs's most important coinage, in an attempt to counteract the previously used pejorative terms, was *Urning* (the subject of man-manly love), in contrast to *Dioning* (the real man). The term "homosexuality" (*Homosexualität*) was first published (anonymously) by Karl Maria Kertbeny (1824–1882) in 1869, but was used by him the year before in correspondence with Ulrichs.[13] Ulrichs never used "homosexual," preferring Urning and the positive connotations it had for him.[14] By the turn of the century both terms—and others besides (contrary sexual, homogenic, invert, sexual intermediate, similisexual)—were used for this phenomenon; by the mid-1900s "homosexual" had become the commonly used term.

Ulrichs later recalled that he had noticed signs of his homosexuality at the age of fifteen, but it was only when he was twenty-one, as a student in Berlin, that he became convinced of the inborn nature of his sexual orientation. Ulrichs wrote to his sister Ulrike in 1862:

> But everything else [that you wrote], dear sister, rests on false assumptions. With great love you admonish me to make the decision now to turn myself around. You admit that this will be very difficult. But God will help.
>
> That sounds very beautiful—and would be quite correctly said, if my inclination were a habituation or an aberration. But, dear sister, to love even the most beautiful woman is *absolutely impossible* for me, and indeed solely because no woman instills even a trace of love feelings in me; no one, however, can instill love toward certain persons or sexes through his own strength of will. This has also always been so with me. ("Vier Briefe," 40–41)

Casper (1852, 62) had already stated that "pederasty" was inborn in some cases, but Ulrichs learned of this only in 1864. Ulrichs also appears to have been unaware of an article of 1849 by Claude François Michéa in which, according to Gert Hekma, Michéa "hypothesized that the feminine habits and preferences of same-sex lovers were perhaps rooted in biology" (Hekma 1994, 215). Most probably it was his own experience and feelings that led Ulrichs to this conviction; in his writings he often used himself as an illustration for his arguments. As a confirmation of his theory, Ulrichs cited the "female characteristics" that he found in himself and other Urnings. (He saw the "female characteristics" as a necessary result of having a "female" psyche.) Thus, whereas Casper and other forensic experts, for example, Ambroise Tardieu (1818–1879) in Paris, identified the "pederast" by telltale signs, such as a funnel-shaped anus in the receptive partner and a pointed penis in the penetrator—signs presumably resulting from their forbidden activity—Ulrichs looked for signs that indicated the female nature of the Urning, which he would possess whether he engaged in any sexual activity or not.[15] He described many of them in his writings, including indications in young children. This particularly confirmed his theory of the inborn nature of homosexuality, since they occurred before the age of puberty when, as he thought, the sex drive first awakens. In one of his first publications, Ulrichs stated:

> This outwardly recognizable female essence I call the female habitus of the Urning. . . . The female habitus is quite particularly in us in our childhood, before we have been reared into an artificial masculinity, and before we have had the depressing experience that every expression of our female essence will be ascribed to us as a disgrace (!) by our playmates as well as adults, before, that is, suffering under this external pressure, we began to carefully hide that female trait.
>
> The Urning shows as a child a quite unmistakable partiality for girlish activities, for interaction with girls, for playing with girls' playthings, namely also with dolls. (*Inclusa*, 13–14)

By the end of 1864, his increasing contacts with other Urnings—both direct contact and through correspondence with readers of his first publications—had convinced Ulrichs that things were not as simple as he had originally thought. Thus, there were men who loved women and men alike, there were men who loved other men "tenderly and sentimentally" but desired women sensually, and so on. To accommodate these possibilities, he expanded his theory and assumed that there was not one germ for the sexual drive (as he had at first assumed), but two: one for "tender-sentimental" love and one for sensual love. The terminology for these new varieties likewise expanded to include the terms "*Uranodioning*," "*konjunktiver Uranodioning*," "*disjunktiver Uranodioning*," and others. Rolf Gindorf has schematized sixteen distinct sexual natures that are implied by Ulrichs's system (1977, 132–133). Eventually, this system became so complicated that it began to resemble the epicycles of the later Ptolemaic system of the universe. Ulrichs was aware of this, writing in 1867:

> I suppose a future researcher will discover an underlying law for this apparent chaos of varieties, a law according to which the seeming arbitrariness of the mixture becomes a necessity of nature. Needed for this is a comprehensive observation of individuals who belong to the particular varieties and, of course, a bit of talent for gaining new insight by taking a synoptic view of the variety. One must find a formula for this law, I might say, just as exact as that formula Kepler once found for the laws of the motions of the planets and comets. (*Memnon* 2, 116; modified translation from Ulrichs 1994b, 419)

The complexities in Ptolemy's system were brought about in part by his unquestioning assumption that all celestial motion must be circular. Just so were the complexities in Ulrichs's theory caused in part by his unquestioning assumption that sexual love for a man must be feminine. Although this assumption has often been questioned (already before the end of the nineteenth century by, for example, James Mills Peirce [1834–1906], mathematics professor and first dean of the Graduate School of Harvard University), it has continued until today to be a leitmotif in the search for physical characteristics of homosexuals, both in the popular mind and in the scientific community. In a letter of 1891 to John Addington Symonds (1840–1893), Peirce pointed out the circularity in Ulrichs's argument:

> There is an error in the view that feminine love is that which is directed to a man, and masculine love that which is directed to a woman. That doctrine involves a begging of the whole question. . . . The two directions are equally natural to unperverted man, and the *abnormal* form of love is that which has lost the power of excitability in either the one or the other of these directions. It is *unisexual* love (a love for one sexuality) which is a perversion. The normal men love both. . . .
>
> I clearly believe . . . that we ought to think and speak of homosexual love, not as "inverted" or "abnormal," as a sort of colour-blindness of the genital sense, as a lamentable mark of inferior development, or as an unhappy fault, a "masculine body with a feminine soul," but as being in itself a natural, pure and sound passion, as worthy of the reverence of all fine natures as the honourable devotion of husband and wife, or the ardour of bride and groom.[16]

The originality of Ulrichs's theory has occasionally been questioned, and sometimes connections have been drawn that do not exist. That Casper stated earlier that homosexuality was inborn in some cases has led some to draw the conclusion that Ulrichs adopted this idea from him, and Warren Johansson has stated, regarding Ulrichs's idea that the Urning has an *anima muliebris virili corpore inclusa*: "He took the notion from *Eros: die Männerliebe der Griechen* . . . by Heinrich Hoessli" (Johansson 1990, 580). Indeed, Ulrichs mentioned both

Casper and Hössli (1784–1864), but expressly stated that he arrived at these notions before reading those authors. I think there is no reason to doubt Ulrichs's honesty in this matter. He cites them only as confirmation of his own views. Ulrichs quite carefully reported his sources of information and, while his intent was obviously to change the opinions of others, this was more in the spirit of the Enlightenment (and here Ulrichs was perhaps somewhat behind his times) and not in the propagandistic way that later became the fashion, such as that practiced by his successor Magnus Hirschfeld, who was a master of the half-truth.[17]

Although Ulrichs's theory was original, it was certainly influenced by the scientific discourses of the time and reflected "the perceptual interest in the new science of the human being" that, around 1800, as Claudia Honegger has pointed out, "was directly concerned with determining more closely the connection between the bodily disposition and psychological capacity" (1991, 56). Ulrichs was influenced above all by nineteenth-century advances in biology, especially in embryology. And on one point he was very much a man of his time. Thomas Laqueur's statement, "Sexuality as a singular and all-important attribute with a specific object—the opposite sex—is the product of the late eighteenth century. There is nothing natural about it" (1990, 13), would have had no meaning for Ulrichs. It is precisely its "naturalness" of which he was most convinced. Laqueur speaks of the "new slogan" (new in 1800) that "opposites attract" (152); for Ulrichs the principle that "opposites attract" was an assumption of his theory that caused him great difficulty, but which he never questioned.

Ulrichs's views were often dismissed by the medical establishment since he was not one of the guild, and especially since, as a self-declared Urning, he was arguing *pro domo*. What medical researchers did not say—as was repeatedly asserted by Ulrichs—was that he was able to make many more observations than they of homosexuals, especially of "ordinary" homosexuals. As Ulrichs pointed out: "My scientific opponents are mostly psychiatrists. They are, for example, Westphal, Krafft-Ebing, Stark. They made their observations on Urnings who were in institutions for the mentally ill. They appear not to have seen mentally healthy Urnings. The rest follow the published views of the psychiatrists" (*Critische Pfeile*, 96; 1994b, 688).

When Ulrichs noted that his "scientific opponents" had not seen healthy Urnings, he omitted, as Günter Dworek has pointed out, "that the doctors were far distant from accepting him as a scientific opponent of equal rank. For them, Ulrichs's arguments were those of a sick man, a potential patient" (1990, 42). Dworek's article reproduces two reviews of Ulrichs's *Inclusa* of 1864, in which he first spelled out the biological basis of his theory. Since these were not taken into consideration in my biography of Ulrichs and have not before appeared in English, they may be quoted at length to illustrate the early reception of Ulrichs's theory. Both were published, in 1864 and 1865 respectively, in *Der Irrenfreund* (Heilbronn), which Dworek describes as "a small, reform-psychiatric oriented journal." The first, signed only "Dr. F," begins with the book's title, "Anthropological Studies of Man-Manly Sexual Love," to which, typically, the author added in parentheses, as if it were part of the title, "Pederasty" (which, we recall, meant anal intercourse), and he continued to use the term in what he presents as quotations from Ulrichs. For him, Ulrichs is another "case," for which, as Dworek pointed out, "to his question, 'Is this sickness curable?' he grotesquely announces for the author of *Inclusa* a reservedly optimistic prognosis" (43).

> N[uma] N[umantius] wants to justify pederasty. He is of the opinion: the law and morality condemn pederasty because it is not recognized that it is inborn in certain men. . . .
>
> He seeks to correct public opinion through all kinds of mostly irrelevant observations, quotations, anecdotes, outpourings of his heart. . . .
>
> He is so full of his feelings that he writes books about it. The actual physical arousal stands in the foreground with him; the whole circle of his imagination is constantly filled with it.
>
> About the personal circumstances, the occupation, the way of life, the biography of N. N., we indeed learn nothing. But we may assume that his efforts are directed to maintaining and promoting physical arousal, which plays such a role in his imagination.
>
> The healthy, vigorous life does not conduct itself thus. . . .
>
> How does such a condition of sick lust develop?
>
> N. N. is at pains to furnish all kinds of things in order to show that "nature has created pederastic lust." What could he be thinking of with the word "nature"? His statements want to be scientific. So we would remind him that the so-called natural sciences constantly have to do with the determination of certain facts and with their conditions. The conditions of his state can be called his disposition.
>
> Without it, without the germ, nothing arises. Because of the lack of information from the earlier life of N. N., nothing may be said about how this disposition came about.
>
> Is this sickness curable?
>
> It depends on how far all the other emotions have suffered and how far the circumstances are in a position to promote healthy efforts.
>
> It is a good sign that he feels uncomfortable in his condition, that he is making an effort to justify it.
>
> To his lack of courage (he believes that what nature has given him he cannot change), may be objected that sick tendencies dissolve if their nourishment is lacking, that even slightly healthy dispositions come to development through teaching; he should remember that his teachers have developed for him so much knowledge and skill, for which he had just a weak disposition, that there is also a training that will teach him to be vigorous and manly, that law and morality are such teachers, which are continually trying to develop the good in the individual. (Cited in Dworek 1990, 44–45)

It is not clear here whether this reviewer accepted the inborn nature of the condition. Even if he did, it still remained a sickness for him, a view that was strengthened by his inability to see it as anything other than "pederasty." The second reviewer, who avoided the term "pederasty," decisively rejected the view that it is inborn.

Dworek notes that the second reviewer, who used his complete name (Dr. D. Lissauer), does not otherwise appear to have published in the field of sexual pathology, and so "all the more remarkable for the process of the medicalization of homosexuality is the way he, several years before the fundamental works of Westphal and Krafft-Ebing, self-evidently classifies male-male sexuality in the sphere of responsibility of the doctors" (43). This may be seen in the first half of the review:

> The present booklet furnishes no proof of the naturalness of that immorality, but rather is a contribution to the literature of partial mental disturbances. According to the natural idea that coupling should take place only for the goal of reproduction of human beings, this other release of the sexual drive, which immorality, refinement, or inverted direction of thought calls forth, is abnormal and for a human being is in the highest degree unworthy or morbid. That the latter is the case more often than one believes, is shown by the kind of description of man-manly sexual love in the brochure mentioned. Therefore, in cases before the courts, the medical experts should investigate the mental condition of the party concerned and decide whether immorality or mental illness is present; then perhaps many who are now put into a prison or penitentiary would through an appropriate treatment in a reformatory or mental institution gain insight into the direction of their love and return to living with views of the satisfaction of the sexual drive in accordance with nature.
>
> Now, to also comment, unnecessarily, on several views of the author, I first stress that his inborn sexual love exists just as little as inborn ideas; the former develops only little by little with the development of sexual conditions. (Cited in Dworek 1990, 46)

There were, however, those who, following Casper, believed that homosexuality was inborn, at least in some cases, and they may have also been influenced to some extent by Ulrichs. Ironically, the man who became the major proponent of the sickness model of homosexuality, Richard von Krafft-Ebing (1840–1902), became interested in studying the subject precisely as a result of reading Ulrichs's writings, as he explicitly stated in a letter to Ulrichs of January 29, 1879 (*Critische Pfeile*, 92). Already in 1877, Krafft-Ebing had written that Ulrichs was "afflicted with this perverse drive" and that Ulrichs "still has not furnished proof that he, as an inborn phenomenon, is *eo ipso* a physiological and not perhaps a pathological one" (Krafft-Ebing 1877, 305–306). With only a slight change in the wording, this statement was included in his *Psychopathia sexualis* (1886, 58) and it remained in all later editions of this perennial bestseller.

Although Krafft-Ebing became interested in the subject because of Ulrichs, his understanding of it was rather along the lines of the degeneration theory of Bénédict Auguste Morel (1809–1873), as presented by Morel in 1857. This is shown already in the title of Krafft-Ebing's 1877 work, which may be translated: "On certain anomalies of the moral drive and the clinical-forensic evaluation of them as a probable functional sign of degeneration of the central nervous system." Nevertheless, Giovanni Dall'Orto sees a positive influence of Ulrichs on Krafft-Ebing, in that Krafft-Ebing "softened, thanks to him, the original premise, which saw in the homosexual a serious degenerate, and a criminal for life" (Dall'Orto 1985, 66).

Ulrichs's impact on sexology was more significant for directing medical researchers' attention to the subject of homosexuality than in changing their view of it. This is evident in a five-page entry on "contrary sexual feeling" in a medical encyclopedia of 1885, where only Ulrichs's name and pseudonym, Numa Numantius, are printed in boldface. After noting that Casper had divided "those peculiar individuals who are sexually inclined to persons of their same sex into two categories: those whose inclination is *acquired* and a consequence of a surfeit of the natural sexual pleasures, and those in whom it is *inborn* and a symptom of a *psychopathic* condition," the author continues:

> If the view of Casper was now challenged, it was by the anonymous author who hid under the name "**Numa Numantius**" and through a series of years in numerous, strange-sounding pamphlets [Blumenstok names the seven published up to then] has been at pains to justify the existence and contest the criminality of a large clan of individuals that one was rather used to characterizing as depraved libertines. But his behavior was all the less suited to shake the belief in the moral depravity of his protégés. Numa Numantius, who later turned out to be the "private scholar and former Hannoverian official" **K. H. Ulrichs**, brought too much system in and deprived the same of a basis, not so much through his repulsive declamation as much more through the fact that he rolled out a whole tableau of sexes, on which, according to his custom, he conferred poetic sounding, but in fact meaningless names (Urnings, Dionings, Uranodionings). Since the time, however, when at the assembly of jurists in Munich (1867) he called forth universal indignation with his proposal for a revision of the German criminal code in favor of sexual satisfaction contrary to nature, his muse became silent and with it the question defended by him appeared to be removed from the order of the day once and for all. (Blumenstok 1885, 515–516)

Blumenstok then notes that only two years later the subject was taken up by Karl Westphal (1833–1890) and others, and he briefly reviews the cases discussed by them. Although he does not accept Ulrichs's explanations, it does appear that he has been impressed enough by him not to accept entirely the reported results of the others. He writes:

> There can be no doubt, for daily experience teaches it, that aberrations of the sexual feeling appear not only in the case of nervous and mental illness, but also in indi-

> viduals for whom neither any kind of disturbance of the psychic functions nor any anomaly in the nerve center may be demonstrated. It is further certain that in the ranks of the latter those aberrations are more often met with than among the former. . . . In the large cities we have to deal with the clan of active and passive pederasts, whose behavior we would like to attribute to every other cause, only not conceive of as a neuropathic or psychopathic phenomenon. . . . Casper, therefore, goes too far when he views the abnormal sexual direction in most individuals as a symptom of a psychopathic condition: for even if it may be assumed that the number of those suffering from contrary sexual feelings is much greater than the small number of cases described up to now lets one suppose, . . . it is still vanishingly small in comparison with the greater number of pederasts. (Blumenstok 1885, 517)

By the time this was written, Ulrichs had published his estimate that one adult man in five hundred in Germany was an Urning. No doubt most readers thought this figure too high, but it probably had an influence, as appears here, especially since Ulrichs seemed to be acquainted with many Urnings. By the end of the nineteenth century, Ulrichs's theories had also reached English readers, primarily through the writings of Symonds, who became personally acquainted with Ulrichs in 1891 on a visit to Aquila.[18]

Just as Ulrichs was forced to modify his first, oversimple biological explanation of the Urning because of contact with an increasing variety of sexual types, so too he had to modify the strict division of male body/female psyche. Allowing that the body influenced the psyche, and vice versa, he was better able to account for the variety he saw. His search for physical characteristics that distinguish Urnings from "real" men was the beginning of a flood of similar investigations that continues unabated today, whether done by those with an emancipatory intent like Ulrichs (for instance, Magnus Hirschfeld in the early twentieth century and Simon LeVay near its end) or by those with less benevolent intentions (for instance, the Nazi doctor Carl Vaernet and, since about 1967, Günter Dörner).[19]

Rainer Herrn has noted that "the most comprehensive constitutional investigation" was carried out at the Prague Institute for Sexual Science around 1960.

> They compared weight, stature, length of trunk, shoulder and hip width, size of the skeleton and the muscular apparatus, the laying on of fat, as well as hairiness on the four regions of the body. The diameter of the areola of nipple was noted and the prostate examined by hand and classified. In addition the length of the flaccid penis and the longitudinal axis of the testicles were measured. Even the voice and the vocal apparatus were evaluated. Those tested were divided into three groups: feminine homosexuals, non-feminine homosexuals, and heterosexuals. This exhaustive investigation concluded that no differences in the bodily measures could be found among the three groups. What was established was merely that homosexuals are somewhat lighter and have a significantly "larger penis" than heterosexuals. If we ignore the possible implication of the longer penis, then it becomes clear that there were obviously

> no constitutional differences. Since then the premise has not been pursued further; the theory of bodily differences between homosexuals and heterosexuals has finally been abandoned. (Herrn 1995, 43–44)

Herrn's concluding statement is a bit too strong, however. Even as I write, an Associated Press report comes to my attention, with the headlines: "Genetic Link to Male Homosexuality—Unusual Pattern of Fingerprints Is Focus of Study" (*San Francisco Chronicle*, 26 Dec. 1994). Pudd'nhead Wilson strikes again![20]

If Ulrichs's ideas were dismissed by the medical establishment as those of a "potential patient" who was far from being their scientific equal, his fellow lawyers found their own way of dealing with him. When Ulrichs spoke at the Congress of German Jurists in Munich on August 29, 1867, to support his proposal to repeal the antisodomy laws of Germany and Austria, he was simply shouted down and not allowed to speak. His treatment in Frankfurt two years earlier was even more bizarre.

When Ulrichs moved to Frankfurt in 1859 he immediately joined the Freies Deutsches Hochstift für Wissenschaften, Künste und allgemeine Bildung (Free German Foundation for Science, Art, and General Culture), which had been founded there earlier that year. (The Hochstift still exists today. Goethe's birth house with its museum belongs to the Hochstift.) When Ulrichs began to discuss his ideas, the Hochstift removed his membership on the rumor that a criminal prosecution was pending against him. Ulrichs showed that this was not the case and, in 1865, sent copies of his first publications for their consideration. The leaders of the Hochstift then read just enough to find another excuse to expel him: since Ulrichs asserted that, in addition to the two previously recognized sexes, there was a third sex which he called Urnings, and he declared that he belonged to it, then Ulrichs could not be a member of the Hochstift, whose statutes made no mention of admitting such a being to membership (see Kennedy 1988, 64–66).

Ulrichs was a pioneer in many ways. For example, he anticipated Freud in his assertion of the importance of dreams for sexology, stating in 1865: "Very unjustly, therefore, the importance for sexual science of those dream phenomena has been entirely overlooked until now, unfortunately: certainly to the great detriment of [sexual science]" (*Formatrix*, 12). But the impulse he gave to the study of homosexuality did not go in the direction he wished. Nor were his efforts to repeal the antisodomy laws successful. Indeed, in his lifetime the harsh Prussian law was extended to all parts of Germany with the foundation of the German empire in 1870, and the law was not relaxed until 1968 (East Germany) and 1969 (West Germany), with a further reform in 1994 (in the united Germany) that set a gender-neutral age of consent of sixteen, thus making no distinction (in theory) between homo- and heterosexual activity.

As an "activist," Ulrichs was ahead of his time. He was the first self-declared homosexual to speak out publicly for the civil and legal rights of homosexuals; he published the first homosexual journal, but it had only one issue (1870); he even wrote by-laws for a proposed homosexual organization in 1865—all ideas that were not revived until the turn of the century, when Hirschfeld and others founded the Wissenschaftlich-humanitäres Komitee (Scientific Humanitarian Committee) in 1897, and the journal *Der Eigene* (The Self-Owner)—which began publishing in Berlin in 1896 as an anarchist journal under the direction of the egoist philosopher Max Stirner (1806–1856)—became openly homosexual in 1898.

Although Ulrichs's "third sex" theory of homosexuality was superficially dismissed by the medical establishment of his day, it nonetheless appears to have had an influence—best seen, perhaps, in the continuing search by biological determinists for a bodily substrate for homosexuality.[21] A century after Ulrichs's death, we may not be entirely comfortable with the development of ideas that followed Ulrichs's introduction of a "third sex," but it was the first scientific theory of homosexuality, and he deserves credit for it. On the other hand, we can unreservedly admire the courage and integrity of the man who fought so hard against impossible odds for the equal rights of all: women, religious and ethnic minorities, and homosexual and other sexual varieties.

In 1869, Karl Westphal had introduced the term "contrary sexual feeling," and defined it as an illness in the title of his article: "The Contrary Sexual Feeling: Symptom of a Neuropathic (Psychopathic) Condition." Since that time, for more than a century, most psychiatrists represented homosexuality as an illness by definition. Nor was the vote in 1973 to remove homosexuality from the American Psychiatric Association's official diagnostic manual of mental disorders overwhelming (58 percent of the membership ratified the recommendation of the APA Board of Trustees). But survey after survey has been done, each trying to be more comprehensive than the other, so that today there is a vast, relatively objective literature on the subject of homosexuality in general. Along with this has come a change in the public perception. In order to gain an insight into the earlier view of homosexuality, let us consider the current "expert" and popular view of pedophilia. The parallels are striking.

There is first of all the term itself: whereas in nineteenth-century Germany the term "pederasty" (from the classic Greek for "boy-love") was equated with anal intercourse, the current term "pedophilia" (a more general Greek term for "boy-love") is equated with child sexual molestation. Like nineteenth-century homosexuality, pedophilia is considered by definition an illness, and little effort has been made to learn about the "ordinary" pedophile. (We recall Ulrichs's complaint that the psychiatrists "appear not to have seen mentally healthy Urnings.") In the United States, the literature continues to be dominated by psychiatry and, more recently, victimology. Indeed, as a result of the popular misidentification of child sexual molestation with intergenerational sex, any scientific survey of ordinary pedophiles has become impossible due to the legal requirement to report any suspected cases. Some research in the Netherlands has been reported (for example, Sandfort 1981; Bernard 1985). And in Germany, sixty pedophile men were interviewed by a team led by Rüdiger Lautmann of the University of Bremen, who described his report as "the first German-language project to empirically research the socio-sexual sides of pedophilia" (Lautmann 1994, 12). Among those adults who had sexual contact with children, Lautmann distinguished three types:

> (1) the true pedophile, who is in general interested in social contacts with children, including the sexual side;
> (2) the substitute-object perpetrator, who satisfies himself sexually on a child because he does not gain access to an adult;
> (3) the aggressive-sadistic perpetrator, who resorts to force from pathological grounds. (Lautmann 1994, 10)

For their report, Lautmann's team interviewed only men of type one, the true pedophile. Their report paints a rather different picture from that usually seen in the United States.

So long as research in the United States is by necessity limited to populations such as patients and those institutionalized or threatened by legal punishment, we will not have a clear picture of true pedophiles—a situation that in some ways parallels an earlier situation in Berlin regarding homosexuality in general. In 1903 Magnus Hirschfeld distributed three thousand questionnaires to university students, asking about their sexual orientation. Five students denounced Hirschfeld for offending them "through the distribution of obscene writings," and in fact Hirschfeld was found guilty and sentenced to pay a fine (Herzer 1992a, 63).

In California, for example, such research is forbidden with regard to those who are interested in "children" below the age of eighteen, since sex is legally forbidden to them and suspected sexual contacts are required to be reported. One wonders what Ulrichs would have thought about this situation. That research could not be done would likely have offended his Enlightenment views. Certainly he thought the age of consent too high. Although he had pretty much abandoned his cause during the last fifteen years of his life in Italy, he nevertheless wrote one last plea to the Austrian Minister of Justice on June 18, 1894, apparently prompted by a monograph of Richard von Krafft-Ebing that year, which he refers to in his letter. In it he says that he will send in a few days two short discussions concerning points in Krafft-Ebing's work, one "about an unjustifiable age limit, i.e., aimed too high; eighteenth year, proposed by Krafft-Ebing."[22] Krafft-Ebing had written: "Regarding [homosexual] sodomy, the completed eighteenth year appears to me to be the correct limit, since from there up, according to experience, the ability to judge and the ability to make moral distinctions is already sufficiently developed to determine for oneself the question of morality and to no longer need the protection of the law" (1894, 33).

I have suggested that we may gain insight into the situation of homosexuality in the nineteenth century by a comparison with the current situation of pedophilia. The comparison may also be telling the other way around. It may be that the current confusion of pedophilia with child sexual molestation will disappear the way nineteenth-century pathologization of masturbation has.[23] When it does, hopefully, we will have a more sane and rational view not only of homosexuality, but of other sexual variations as well.

Notes

1 Homosexuality is, of course, a complex phenomenon, much more complex than Ulrichs—and many others up to the present—imagined. It includes, but is not limited to, erotic attraction to someone of the same sex. But it is precisely this element that Ulrichs's "Urning theory" of homosexuality principally seeks to explain scientifically.

2 Unless otherwise specified, citations of Ulrichs's work refer to titles collected in *Forschungen über das Räthsel der mannmännlichen Liebe* (Ulrichs 1994a). His complete writings are available in English translation in Ulrichs (1994b).

3 For a complete biography, see Kennedy (1988 and 1990).

4 The story is actually more complex. The secret report explained that it actually did work and, therefore, was really dangerous (see Darnton 1968).

5 The term "odylic force" had a vogue in Britain following the translation in 1850 of Reichenbach's *Untersuchungen über Dynamide des Magnetismus, der Elektrizität, der Wärme, des Lichtes, . . . in ihren Beziehungen zur Lebenskraft* (1849), as *Researches on Magnetism . . . in Relation to Vital Force*, by Dr. Gregory, professor of chemistry at the University of Edinburgh. See the entry on "Odylic Force" in *The Encyclopaedia Britannica*, 11th ed. (1911) 20: 10–11.

6 Ulrichs seems to have abandoned his theory of animal magnetism after 1861. His later descriptions in terms of magnetism are probably best seen as a popular, figurative usage that continues today when, for example, we speak of the erotic "attraction" that "radiates" from certain persons.

7 The possibility of an organism that requires more than two sexes in order to reproduce has been investigated by Kennedy and Cull (1970). They showed that, if the sexes are to be reproduced in approximately equal numbers and are determined by a "Mendelian" mechanism (like the human X,Y chromosomes), then an organism with more than two sexes is mathematically impossible.

8 This has been investigated from several viewpoints in Herdt (1994).

9 Ulrichs notes only a few cases of hermaphrodites, citing the *Prager Vierteljahrsschrift für praktische Heilkunde* (Prague Quarterly for Practical Medicine) of 1855, Casper's *Vierteljahrsschrift für gerichtliche Medicin* (Quarterly for Forensic Medicine) of 1856, and Casper's *Wochenschrift* (Weekly) of 1833 (see Ulrichs 1994a, *Inclusa*, 5). He may have obtained further information about hermaphrodites and embryology from personal correspondence; he notes that in 1862 he was already in correspondence with "a German physician well known in medical science" (*Inclusa*, 11).

[10] Ulrichs (*Inclusa*, 50). But later that year he could write: "Of women with male love-drive . . . so numerous and so attested examples are available to me that the factual existence of female as well as male Uranismus thus appears completely warranted" (*Formatrix*, 40).

[11] It is in the title of his 1852 article "Ueber Nothzucht und Päderastie und deren Ermittelung seitens des Gerichtsarztes" (On rape and pederasty and their investigation on the part of the forensic doctor).

[12] For example, in a forensic medicine textbook of 1867: "Unnatural lust is that satisfaction of the sexual drive which deviates from intercourse according to nature. The most decisive form of this is *commasculatio* or pederasty, the insertion of the member through the anus from man to man" (Buchner 1867, 182).

[13] On Kertbeny and his coinages, including "heterosexual," see Herzer (1985) and Herzer and Féray (1993). On Kertbeny's contact with Ulrichs, see Herzer (1987 and 1992b).

[14] There were probably several reasons why Ulrichs never used Kertbeny's term, "homosexual." First, as a classical scholar, he would have objected to the "impure" combination of Greek and Latin elements in "homosexual." In contrast, his own terms, *Urning* and *Dioning*, were "pure" Greek derivatives from a classical passage in Plato's *Symposium* (the speech of Pausanias). Second, "homosexual" pointed directly to the sexual and could be given a negative connotation, whereas Ulrichs's terms were intimately bound up with his theory of the Urning's (and Dioning's) inborn nature and thus had, for Ulrichs, positive connotations. Third, there was probably also a personal factor involved. The brief contact between Ulrichs and Kertbeny apparently ended in 1868 in conflict. In an unpublished manuscript of 1869, Kertbeny mentions "Urnings—which name was invented by one of the most unclear heads from their set" and referred to Ulrichs as "the thoroughly crazy author of *Incubus*" (Herzer 1992b, 73–74).

[15] See Casper (1852), Tardieu ([1857] 1878), Aron and Kempf (1978).

[16] Peirce's letter was published anonymously; see Peirce (1897). Jonathan Ned Katz reprinted the letter (1976, 374–376) and suggested that the author was James Mills Peirce. This was confirmed by Hubert Kennedy (1982). For Peirce as a mathematician, see Kennedy (1979).

[17] For example, in discussing the case of Johann Baptist von Schweitzer (the first Social Democrat to be elected to a European parliament), who was arrested in a park in Mannheim in 1862 and convicted of causing "public offense," Hirschfeld invented an adult occupation for Schweitzer's companion (who had managed to run away), namely that of bricklayer. But the available evidence suggests that he was, rather, a boy of fourteen. Hirschfeld's petition to the German Reichstag, urging a revision of the antisodomy law, suggested setting an age of consent at sixteen. For Schweitzer, see Kennedy (1995).

[18] Symonds published a summary of Ulrichs's theory in 1891 in his privately printed *A Problem in Modern Ethics* (included in Symonds 1964) and expanded the summary for his collaboration with Havelock Ellis (see Ellis and Symonds 1897, 258–272).

[19] See LeVay (1993). Regarding LeVay's research, Gilbert Herdt notes: "The 'gay brain' theory is but the latest form of anatomical reductionism, however well intentioned the

theory" (1994, 498 n.124). For Vaernet, see Plant (1986, 175–178). For Dörner, see Herrn (1995).

20 Mark Twain's fictional character Pudd'nhead Wilson used fingerprints to convict a criminal in a novel of that name published in 1894, several years before fingerprints became part of the official means of identifying criminals by the police.

21 For a critique of biological determinism, see De Cecco and Parker (1995).

22 Ulrichs's letter is reproduced in Sulzenbacher (1994, 26–29); the two discussions mentioned are not in the Austrian file.

23 For a comparison of the child sexual molestation and masturbation hysterias, see Kennedy (1992).

References

Aron, Jean-Paul, and Roger Kempf. 1978. *Le penis et la démoralisation de l'occident.* Paris: Grasset.

Bernard, Frits. 1985. *Pædophilia: A Factual Report.* Rotterdam: Enclave.

Blumenstok, L. 1885. Conträre Sexualempfindung. In *Real-Encyclopädie der gesammten Heilkunde*, 2nd ed., ed. Albert Eulenburg, 4:515–519. Vienna/Leipzig: Urban & Schwarzenberg.

Breidert, Wolfgang, ed. 1994. *Die Erschütterung der vollkommenen Welt: Die Wirkung des Erdbebens von Lissabon im Spiegel europäischer Zeitgenossen.* Darmstadt: Wissenschaftliche Buchgesellschaft.

Buchner, Ernst. 1867. *Lehrbuch der gerichtlichen Medicin für Aerzte und Juristen.* Munich.

Casper, Johann Ludwig. 1852. Ueber Nothzucht und Päderastie und deren Ermittelung seitens des Gerichtsarztes. Nach eigenen Beobachtungen. *Vierteljahrsschrift für gerichtliche und öffentliche Medicin* 1:21–78.

Dall'Orto, Giovanni. 1985. Il concetto di degenerazione nel pensiero borghese dell'Ottocento. *Sodoma: Rivista omosessuale di cultura* 2(2):59–74.

Darnton, Robert. 1968. *Mesmerism and the End of the Enlightenment in France.* Cambridge: Harvard University Press.

De Cecco, John P., and David Allen Parker, eds. 1995. *Sex, Cells, and Same-Sex Desire: The Biology of Sexual Preference.* Binghamton, NY: Harrington Park.

Dworek, Günter. 1990. "Ist diese Krankheit heilbar?" Zwei Irrenärzte kommentieren Karl Heinrich Ulrichs. *Capri: Zeitschrift für schwule Geschichte*, no. 8:42–56.

Ellis, Havelock, and John Addington Symonds. 1897. *Sexual Inversion.* London: Wilson and Macmillan. Facsimile reprint, New York: Arno Press, 1975.

Gindorf, Rolf. 1977. Wissenschaftliche Ideologien im Wandel: Die Angst vor der Homosexualität als intellektuelles Ereignis. In *Der unterdrückte Sexus: Historische Texte und Kommentare zu Homosexualität*, ed. Joachim S. Hohmann, 129–144. Lollar: Achenbach.

Hekma, Gert. 1994. A female soul in a male body: Sexual inversion as gender inversion in nineteenth-century sexology. In *Third Sex, Third Gender: Beyond Sexual Dimorphism in Culture and History*, ed. Gilbert Herdt, 213–239. New York: Zone Books.

Herdt, Gilbert, ed. 1994. *Third Sex, Third Gender: Beyond Sexual Dimorphism in Culture and History*. New York: Zone Books.

Herrn, Rainer. 1995. On the history of biological theories of homosexuality. In *Sex, Cells, and Same-Sex Desire: The Biology of Sexual Preference*, ed. John P. De Cecco and David Allen Parker, 31–56. Binghamton, NY: Harrington Park.

Herzer, Manfred. 1985. Kertbeny and the nameless love. *Journal of Homosexuality* 12(1):1–26.

———. 1987. Ein Brief von Kertbeny in Hannover an Ulrichs in Würzburg. *Capri: Zeitschrift für schwule Geschichte*, no. 1:25–35.

———. 1992a. *Magnus Hirschfeld. Leben und Werk eines jüdischen, schwulen und sozialistischen Sexologen*. Frankfurt/New York: Campus Verlag.

———. 1992b. Zastrow—Ulrichs—Kertbeny: Erfundene Identitäten im 19. Jahrhundert. In *Männerliebe im alten Deutschland: Sozialgeschichtliche Abhandlungen*, ed. Rüdiger Lautmann and Angela Taeger, 61–80. Berlin: Verlag rosa Winkel.

Herzer, Manfred, and Jean Claude Féray. 1993. Karl Maria Kertbeny. In *Homosexualität: Handbuch der Theorie- und Forschungsgeschichte*, ed. Rüdiger Lautmann, 42–47. Frankfurt/New York: Campus Verlag.

Honegger, Claudia. 1991. *Die Ordnung der Geschlechter. Die Wissenschaften vom Menschen und das Weib, 1750–1850*. Frankfurt/New York: Campus Verlag.

Johansson, Warren. 1990. Incarceration Motif. In *Encyclopedia of Homosexuality*, ed. Wayne R. Dynes, 580–582. New York: Garland.

Katz, Jonathan Ned. 1976. *Gay American History: Lesbians and Gay Men in the U.S.A.* New York: Thomas Y. Crowell.

———. 1995. *The Invention of Heterosexuality*. New York: Dutton.

Kennedy, Hubert. 1979. James Mills Peirce and the cult of quaternions. *Historia Mathematica* 6:423–429.

———. 1982. Fierce and quixotic ally. *Harvard Magazine* (November–December): 62–64.

———. 1988. *Ulrichs: The Life and Works of Karl Heinrich Ulrichs, Pioneer of the Modern Gay Movement*. Boston: Alyson.

———. 1990. *Karl Heinrich Ulrichs. Sein Leben und sein Werk*. Trans. Menso Folkerts. Stuttgart: Ferdinand Enke.

———. 1992. Sexual hysteria—then and now. Review of *Male Intergenerational Intimacy: Historical, Socio-Psychological, and Legal Perspectives*. *Empathy: An Interdisciplinary Journal for Persons Working to End Oppression on the Basis of Sexual Identities* 3(1):128–130.

———. 1995. Johann Baptist von Schweitzer, the queer Marx loved to hate. In *Gay Men and the Sexual History of the Political Left*, ed. Gert Hekma, Harry Oosterhuis, and James Steakley, 69–96. Binghamton, NY: Harrington Park.

Kennedy, Hubert, and Paul Cull. 1970. The Mendelian model for polysexual populations. *BioScience* 20:162.

Krafft-Ebing, Richard von. 1877. Ueber gewisse Anomalien des Geschlechtstriebs und die klinisch-forensische Verwertung derselben als eines wahrscheinlich functionellen Degenerationszeichens des centralen Nerven-Systems. *Archiv für Psychiatrie und Nervenkrankheiten* 7:291–312.

———. 1886. *Psychopathia sexualis. Eine klinisch-forensische Studie*. Stuttgart: Ferdinand Enke.

———. 1894. *Der Conträrsexuale vor dem Strafrichter. De Sodomia ratione sexus punienda. De lege lata et de lege ferenda. Eine Denkschrift.* Leipzig/Vienna: Franz Deuticke.

Laqueur, Thomas. 1990. *Making Sex: Body and Gender from the Greeks to Freud.* Cambridge: Harvard University Press.

Lautmann, Rüdiger. 1994. *Die Lust am Kind. Portrait des Pädophilen.* Hamburg: Klein.

LeVay, Simon. 1993. *The Sexual Brain.* Cambridge: MIT Press.

Morel, Bénédict Auguste. 1857. *Traité des dégénérescences physiques, intellectuelles et morales de l'espèce humaine et des causes qui produisent ces variétés maladives.* Paris: J.-B. Baillière.

Müller, Klaus. 1991. *Aber in meinem Herzen sprach eine Stimme so laut. Homosexuelle Autobiographien und medizinische Pathographien im neunzehnten Jahrhundert.* Berlin: Verlag rosa Winkel.

[Peirce, James Mills] Professor X. 1897. [Letter]. In *Sexual Inversion*, by Havelock Ellis and John Addington Symonds, 273–275. London: Wilson and Macmillan. Facsimile reprint, New York: Arno Press, 1975.

Plant, Richard. 1986. *The Pink Triangle: The Nazi War Against Homosexuals.* New York: Henry Holt.

Sandfort, Theo. 1981. *The Sexual Aspect of Paedophile Relations.* Amsterdam: Pan/Spartacus.

Sulzenbacher, Hannes. 1994. "Man bekommt aber den Eindruck, als ob Ulrichs nicht recht normal wäre." Acht Petitionen gegen den österreichischen Unzuchts-Paragraphen. *Capri: Zeitschrift für schwule Geschichte*, no. 17:21–9.

Symonds, John Addington. 1964. *Studies in Sexual Inversion.* New York: Medical Press of New York.

Tardieu, Ambroise Auguste. [1857] 1878. *Etude médico-légale sur les attentats aux moeurs.* 7th ed. Paris: J.-B. Baillière.

Ulrichs, Karl Heinrich. [1864–79] 1994a. *Forschungen über das Räthsel der mannmännlichen Liebe.* Ed. Hubert Kennedy, 4 vols. Berlin: Verlag rosa Winkel.

———. 1994b. *The Riddle of "Man-Manly" Love: The Pioneering Work on Male Homosexuality.* 2 vols. Trans. Michael A. Lombardi-Nash. Buffalo, NY: Prometheus.

Westphal, Karl Friedrich Otto. 1869. Die conträre Sexualempfindung. Symptom eines neuropathischen (psychopathischen) Zustandes. *Archiv für Psychiatrie und Nervenkrankheiten* 2(1):73–108.

Hermaphrodites in Love
The Truth of the Gonads

Alice D. Dreger

In the summer of 1892, one not-so-ladylike individual by the name of Louise-Julia-Anna presented herself to Dr. François Guermonprez of Lille. She had been referred to him by his colleague, Dr. Reumeaux of Dunkirk, with "no other information than this: 'subject interesting from the psychological point of view' " (Guermonprez 1892, 337).[1] Though her face had been shaven clean just before their encounter, and though she came wearing a lady's dress, corset, gloves, and hat (see Figure 1), Louise-Julia-Anna still struck Guermonprez as a rather poor specimen of a woman:

> Her outfit is rather badly adjusted, lacking in grace and lightness . . . her broach is placed poorly to the side; her girdle goes more to one side than the other; the flowers and the ribbons of her hat are disposed without taste and the entire ensemble bespeaks a sort of negligence, which is not the consequence of bad intentions, but which results mainly from absence of good taste. (338–339)

Still, Louise's unrefined taste in *dress* was not what made her so "psychologically interesting" to the doctors. It was, rather, her taste in *lovers*: she desired only men. Indeed, she had had sexual intercourse with more than one man, but never a woman.

What did the doctors find so remarkable about this? Though Louise had been raised as a girl, and though she appeared, and believed herself, to be female, Reumeaux and Guermonprez were convinced she was really a man. The patient had first come to Reumeaux seeking treatment for an inguinal hernia. But during a preliminary examination, the first doctor had discovered, much to his surprise, testicles, as well as what looked very much like a small penis:

> Stupefied, [Reumeaux] interrogated [Louise] with prudence. This person thought herself a woman; she had had relations with men and showed no attraction toward persons of the feminine sex. There was nonetheless no doubt anatomically about the masculine sex of the subject [because she had testicles]; the questions were rephrased

> in vain: it always resulted in receiving responses which revealed the exclusive penchants of the feminine sex. (338)

If Louise was a man, as the doctors were certain, the doctors wondered why she desired other men, and only men. In Guermonprez's and Reumeaux's eyes, the combination of thc subject's "male" anatomical sex (because of her testicles) and her "feminine" desires (because directed towards men) constituted a "bizarre contradiction between the anatomical worth of the subject and the psychic characteristics of her sexual tendencies!" (338) This "man" had "womanly" desires, so, the doctors figured, there must be something wrong *psychologically* with Louise. Guermonprez and Reumeaux concluded that their patient was "truly a teratological being morally as well as physically" (370).[2]

Figure 1. Louise-Julia-Anna, drawn by Fleuret. (Reprinted from Guermonprez [1892]).

Guermonprez did not spare Louise the full brunt of his opinion: he told her she was a man, and instructed her to stop pretending otherwise. As might have been expected, "the revelation of the masculine nature of [her] sex troubled [the patient] profoundly." Guermonprez triumphantly noted, however, that there was "not a tear, not a sigh, not the least vestige of an attack of nerves! There was nothing of that profound distress of a true woman found in the presence of an event which reverses her life all at once" (370). The fact that Louise took the life-altering news with "a firmness thoroughly virile" convinced Guermonprez that his diagnosis was right: she must indeed be a "true male," a subject of "pseudohermaphroditism." Her sexual desires for men were therefore, in his eyes, thoroughly inappropriate.

Long before and throughout the nineteenth century, "hermaphrodite" was the name given to a person who possessed something other than one of the two sets of sexual organs common to most people. That is, a hermaphrodite was a person who appeared to be anatomically something other than a "typical" man or a woman. People like Louise-Julia-Anna were called more precisely by nineteenth-century medical and scientific men "*pseudo*hermaphrodites" because, as far as the men who studied them were concerned, the subjects did not possess all the organs *essential* to both the male and the female. Interestingly, what has counted as "essential" to "true" malehood or "true" femalehood has changed over time (see Dreger 1995), but for Reumeaux, Guermonprez, and their contemporaries, the gonads (that is, the testes or ovaries) were the markers of true sex. Louise would have to possess both ovaries and testicles to be a "true" hermaphrodite. Three feminine names, coiffed hair, a dress, a corset, sexual desires for men—all these supposedly "feminine" traits were not enough to make Louise a woman as far as the doctors were concerned. Her testes defined her as a man, and her doctors thereby demanded "manhood" from her—bravery in the face of terrifying revelations, and "masculine" desire for women even after a life of "mistaken" womanhood.

As is evident in this case, personal and social identity had no role in the medical determination of "true sex" at the end of the nineteenth century, nor did, for that matter, the external genitalia. "Truth" was determined by that which was contained inside the body—the gonads—even if that "truth" were invisible and unsuspected. The label of pseudohermaphroditism, then, could denote one of two general kinds of anatomical situations: (1) when a person had only ovaries or testes, but her/his genitalia displayed elements of both the conventional male and the conventional female anatomy (as when a person had both a "penis" and a "vagina"); or (2) when the genitalia looked female while the gonads were male, and vice versa.

A whole range of anatomical hermaphroditism had been documented for centuries before Louise was born and declared a girl (only to have her sex reversed twenty-three years later), but scientific and medical interest in the phenomenon increased greatly in the late nineteenth century. In part, this was because the medical and scientific communities were undergoing tremendous growth, particularly in the area of anatomicopathological research (see Ackerknecht 1967; Foucault 1975, chap. 8). In the 1860s, the highly publicized sex change and suicide death of the French hermaphrodite Herculine Barbin served to focus medical and lay attention on the bizarre problems of hermaphroditism (see Barbin 1868), and there was no lack of subsequent cases to hold that attention. At the fin de siècle, hermaphrodites attracted the curiosity of many medical and scientific men because it was also then that social tensions surrounding issues of sex and sexuality burgeoned with the growing visibility of people who socially challenged traditional images of two distinct sexes (just as hermaphrodites anatomically challenged them)—people such as feminists, who questioned assumptions about the natures and destinies of men and women, and people such as "inverts," who challenged dominant ideas about sexuality by acting on their passionate attractions to people of their own sex. Like feminists and "inverts," hermaphrodites posed conceptual and practical problems for those (including members of the scientific and medical communities) who adamantly claimed men and women were naturally, fundamentally, and obviously different, and who also claimed that sexuality (specifically heterosexuality) was the natural result of the evolution of the two distinct sexes.

Anne Fausto-Sterling notes in this volume the tradition in the medical profession which holds that "the abnormal requires management." She demonstrates how medical doctors have, in this century, treated intersexed bodies in ways designed to fit them into culturally dominant assumptions about the nature of sex, gender, and sexuality. Guermonprez and his colleagues were also participants in this long tradition; late nineteenth-century medical men strove, conceptually and practically, to "manage" anatomically and psychologically "teratological" beings, to understand their anatomy and behavior in the context of mainstream biomedical paradigms of sex, and, whenever possible, to use "abnormal" cases to strengthen those paradigms. One such critical assumption framing the treatment of hermaphrodites concerned sexual desire: Reumeaux and Guermonprez, like most of their colleagues, expected "true" males like Louise naturally to desire women, not men. As illustrated below, although hermaphrodites ostensibly threatened these paradigms, French and British medical men instead found ways to reconstruct the desires and acts of hermaphrodites such that they would actually support the paradigms.

Today distinctions are typically drawn between *sex* (which is considered an anatomical category), *gender* (which is thought of as a category of self- and/or social identification), and *sexuality* (a term used to refer to sexual desires and/or acts). However, at least until the late nineteenth century, such a division did not exist.[3] The characteristics we conventionally associate with these categories were believed to belong naturally together. The case of Louise illustrates this point. Guermonprez and Reumeaux assumed testicles (a matter of sex to us) meant bravery (a matter of gender to us) and desire for women (a matter of sexuality to us). They could not fathom why this subject's sexual desires did not "match" the anatomical sex as they expected it should. They assumed the sex-sexuality link was so tight that, even if Louise did not know she was a man, her body would know it, and her internal "male" anatomy would drive her to desire women.[4]

Guermonprez's and Reumeaux's French and British colleagues documented a number of cases in which pseudohermaphrodites had (unlike Louise) the sorts of desires predictable for their "true" sex, even though they apparently did not consciously identify with that "true" sex. For instance, Aline C. looked to most people like a woman, but the doctors to whom she confessed that her "tastes carried her toward women" found those desires understandable, because they had decided she was anatomically "truly" a male (Sorel & Cherot 1898, 367). Similarly, it did not surprise a Parisian surgeon to discover that Louise Bavet, apparently a woman, "has a very pronounced taste for women, and men inspire no desire in her," or that "in her dreams, it is always women whom she holds in her arms" (Pozzi 1885a, 312, 313). It was no surprise because "Louise B[avet] has testicles, thus Louise B[avet] is a man" (316).

In France, medical men were especially persistent in their attempts to ferret out information about hermaphroditic subjects' sexual pursuits. Two young Parisian surgeons who performed a postmortem on the body of Marie, a person thought by her companions to be a woman, discovered that she had testicles (and no ovaries). Unable to interrogate their now-dead subject, the surgeons instead sought out Marie's concierge. The concierge reported, to the satisfaction of the surgeons, that Marie manifested desires "inappropriate" to a woman: When the concierge's husband went away, Marie pursued the concierge with "caresses and lewd touching," relations which the concierge found "*ridiculous between women*" (Pozzi & Grattery 1887, 308; original emphasis).

These vignettes illustrate a key point, namely that the status of a behavior or desire depended on the surrounding conceptual framework and the perception of what was "real" and "true." So, for instance, Marie's desire for her concierge seemed inappropriate to one who knew Marie in her lifetime, but to the doctors, who (literally) saw Marie quite differently, the behavior seemed natural. Behavior apparently "perverse" became understandable when the internal "truth" was revealed, and inversely, the gonadal "truth" could uncover unsuspected "perversity," as in Louise-Julia-Anna's case. The result was that hermaphrodites often possessed two different identities, one personally and socially, another medically and scientifically. To scientifically minded French doctors, the "truth" was always internal, even when invisible and seemingly unmanifested. In fact, Guermonprez refused to treat Louise's "hernia" because she refused to live by his truth; she made it fairly clear that she intended to go on living as a woman, and she only wanted her hernia fixed because it made relations with men difficult. As far as Guermonprez was concerned, "the operation requested appeared to me to become, no longer an *operation of complaisance*, but rather an *operation of complicity*; something like a profanity of the art [of surgery]. This is why I have refused!" (1892, 376). He would not participate in enabling a "man" to have sex with other men.

Compared to their French counterparts, British medical men were much less interested in inquiring into hermaphroditic patients' sexual penchants and exploits—or at least, less inclined to report their findings in this realm. Nonetheless, they did share with their French colleagues the assumption that gonads determined sex and sexuality. On both sides of the Channel, medical experts fretted over the possibility that a masked male (a "true" male who appeared to most people to be female) might make his way among girls and women unsuspected, like a wolf in sheep's clothing. Surely, they reasoned, given a masked male among females, the burning desire for sexual connection with females that supposedly necessarily came with manhood would emerge, and rain down "demoralization and scandal" (Laurent 1894, 217). One could hardly expect a "real" man to suppress his desires swimming in a sea of feminine bodies.

Franz Neugebauer, a Polish gynecologist and a leading authority on hermaphroditism at the turn of the century, sent a special report to the British Gynecological Society (of which he was a member) warning them of these dangers. In his communication on "Information upon Hermaphrodism Indispensable to the Practitioner," Neugebauer imagined in lurid detail "the supposed young girl of 16," really a masked man,

> her sexual instincts aroused by reading romances; sharing the dormitory of her fellow pupils, she watches every night and morning these maidens at their toilet, and without any restriction has opportunities of learning to admire the bodily charms of persons of the opposite sex. (1903, 244)

Such circumstances, Neugebauer presumed, would naturally serve to "awaken in him, however innocent hitherto in regard to sexual matters, desires that might easily lead him to abuse the situation, in a way which might be followed by consequences even more serious perhaps for the companions sacrificed to his masculine desire than for himself" (244–245). It is worth noting that Neugebauer so firmly associated naturally strong desires for females with masculinity that he switched the gender of his pronouns midway through his fantasy. The hermaphrodite began as a "she," but became a "he" as powerful desires for "his" girl classmates emerged.[5]

Neugebauer and other medical men concerned with the "dangers" of sexual ambiguity dispensed advice to practicing colleagues about what to do with children whose "sex" (that is, whose internal organs) could not be determined with certainty. The English gynecological surgeon Lawson Tait, for example, suggested that when faced with a child of uncertain sex, if "no genital orifice can be discovered, let the patient be considered as a male, for if brought amongst males but little harm can come to him." "Little harm" meant that no vaginal intercourse could occur, since there was no vaginal opening. Tait's anxiety ran parallel to Neugebauer's: "If, however, an individual were brought up amongst girls who turned out to be a semi-competent male, no end of mischief might accrue" (Tait 1879, 22). Clinical practice sometimes followed these fearful beliefs about the irrepressible desires of the gonads. Upon discovering testicles in nine-year-old "Christina," a Glasgow surgeon decided to excise them immediately, "as it would [have been] a singularly unfortunate thing for a person with all the outward appearance of a female to develop into a man as to internal organs and feelings" (Buchanan 1885, 214).

In France, medical men warned that hermaphrodites who looked like men externally but had ovaries internally were likely to seduce unwitting men.[6] In 1885, one French writer hysterically warned about the two-way perils of mistaken sex:

> Put one or the other of these mal-sexed individuals into religious orders or a teaching position, and morality will be gravely compromised. If a man-woman [that is, a mannish-looking woman] were admitted to the seminary, what would become of the young Levites at her contact . . . ? Still much more dangerous would be a woman-man [that is, a womanish-looking man] like Brade [a male who mistakenly landed in a nunnery]; there too the fire of the convent consumed the nuns! It would be worse still in the schools, in the boarding schools, the grammar schools. What would happen in the barracks if the current preliminary examination of recruitment did not assure against similar mistakes? (Garnier 1885, 289)

A hundred years ago, hermaphrodites in the military posed a frightening risk since their natural sexuality seemed irrepressible and uncontrollable. Not only did they threaten to seduce other soldiers, but sometimes, by doing so, they even "brought a child into the world in open camp!" (Garnier 1885, 289). Faced with a pseudohermaphrodite, one could not be assured of a clear separation of the sexes, and therefore one could not ensure against mixing "true" men and women where they ought not be mixed lest their supposed "natural" sexual drives toward each other forced them to couple.

Yet some medical experts also feared pseudohermaphrodites (and those people who intentionally cross-dressed) because they might, by *appearing* to belong to the other sex, tempt unwitting souls into same-sex coupling. Émile Laurent, a French doctor who readily immersed himself in the exploration of the anatomy and psychology of sexual peculiarities, insisted that "to place a young man with the breasts and grace of a woman in a barracks would be practically to encourage pederasty" (1894, 110). Laurent bemoaned how often "accidental hermaphrodites" were formed when young boys and men, "already feminine in their form and their allure, become more so by education" (that is, through "indoctrination into pederasty") until "their souls become feminine, too" (181). In England, a 1901 editorial in *The Lancet* expressed profound contempt for "the vilest of the vile," namely those "men of effeminate appearance dressed as women" who enticed men seeking female prostitutes into unwitting same-sex intercourse (Wakley & Wakley 1901). The fear that "normal" males might be tempted by feminine-looking men into sexual relations directly contradicted the running assumption that sexual desire would always be determined by one's "true" anatomical sex, no matter how masked that sex! Obviously a blanket fear underlay all these anxious pronouncements, namely a fear of all sexual encounters that did not conform to particular kinds of socially sanctioned heterosexual relations.

Biomedical experts on hermaphroditism expressed profound horror at the very real possibility that two persons might enter into marriage without anyone, even the spouses, realizing that both spouses were "really" (meaning gonadally) the same sex. French hermaphroditism specialists blamed "ignorant matrons," "prudish midwives," and "myopic doctors" for contributing to the spread of mistaken sex (Garnier 1885, 288), but English medical men instead faulted the poor sex education of the nation's children, especially those raised as girls (Tait 1879, 21). The editors of the *British Medical Journal* railed against "this secrecy, this 'conspiracy of silence,' [which] has gone too far" to keep children ignorant of sexual matters, so far as to be "productive of serious evils" (Hart 1885), not the least of which was the discovery by some pseudohermaphrodites on their wedding nights that their parts were not what were expected of a person of their supposed sex.

French doctors, burdened with a national population crisis and a deep concern for productive marriages, were especially troubled by marriages that, though proper in the eyes of the partners and their acquaintances, were, in the view of the doctors, "malformed." An anxious French doctor reminded his colleagues in 1899 that:

> The question [of mistaken sex] which occupies us has only a relative gravity if it concerns only contested heritages, electoral rights, or military service; but it is entirely otherwise when marriage intervenes. One can then be found in the presence of monstrous alliances, and see, for example, two men or two women united together, by a mistake which engenders social disorders, causes scandalous divorce, or creates some wretchedly equivocal situations. (Delore 1899a, 229)

Time and again, doctors' discoveries of an unexpected "true" sex arrived at a point when "the law had already sanctioned a union against nature" (Pozzi 1885a, 308). One French physician warned that these "monstrous marriages" (like the one of the couple shown in Figure 2, in which the "wife" was a male pseudohermaphrodite) would only wind up disastrously unhappy, because "the sexual appetite of the individuals cannot be satiated" (Leblond 1885, 26). Leblond implies that a relationship between two men, because "unnatural," could never be sexually satisfying, *even* if everyone believed one of the two was a woman. Yet there was much evidence to the contrary. Neugebauer's ever-growing collection of "marriages made between persons of the same sex" (1899; 1900) made it absolutely clear that pseudohermaphrodites often married persons of the same gonadal sex, and that in many cases they remained so married until (or even after) a medical expert or an unexpected happenstance of physiology (for instance, the onset of menstruation in a supposed man) revealed a long-standing "error of nomenclature" (Tait 1879, 21).

Figure 2. Photograph of married couple, both gonadally male. Original caption: "A. S., married for sixteen years, male hypospade. Error of sex" due to pseudohermaphroditism. (A. S. is the "wife.") (Reprinted from Neugebauer [1900, Figure 1])

Some hermaphrodites' anatomy allowed for vaginal-like intercourse, so that, as far as the partners were concerned, nothing about their relationship was bothersome. But the genitalia of a hermaphrodite could be such that it was impossible to engage in intercourse without serious pain or difficulty, a condition which often precipitated a medical examination and the declaration (to the patient or privately to colleagues) that one spouse was not the sex that everyone had assumed. In France this occasionally led to divorce or annulment of marriage "by reason of error of sex," and in Britain, to desertion of the anatomically confused spouse.

In France, errors of sex were announced to the patient (and sometimes the public) and legally amended, but in Britain, matters of mistaken sex proceeded along more confidential lines. So, for instance, two adult sisters in Scotland were informed that they were both men, and had their sexual identities quietly changed. They were then dispatched to pursue manly occupations in the colonies where no one would know they had once been women (Croom 1898). By contrast, in France, sex-change proceedings were often quite public.[7] For instance, late in 1885 the tribunal of Château-Gontier called three medical experts to pronounce their opinion on the sex of one Joseph-Marie X., formerly known as Marie X. Joseph-Marie sought to have his legal status formally changed to conform to what he thought was his true sex, that is, male. The panel of experts agreed that the plaintiff was a male, in part because "on various occasions, she claims to have had some erotic dreams pushing her to be drawn to persons of the feminine sex" (Benoist 1886, 85). They assumed this meant that "she" had testicles.

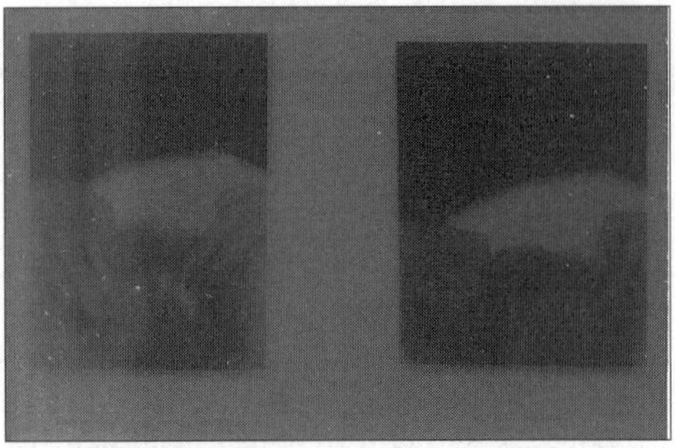

Figure 3. Photograph of the genitals of A. E., held open "Showing Penis, Groove, and Urethral Orifice." Reprinted from Green (1898, Fig. 3). (Courtesy of the History of Medicine Division of the National Library of Medicine, Bethesda)

Meanwhile, British surgeons made a virtual habit of removing apparent female's testicles, as in the case of Christina, the nine-year-old girl from Glasgow mentioned previously. At least one English surgeon actually removed his patient's testicles without ever revealing the truth to her or her entourage, for the patient had "always lived as a woman [and] I did not think it necessary or even fair to inform her of what we had discovered, and when she left the hospital she believed, as far as I am aware, that she had been suffering from an ordinary rupture which had been cured" (Clark 1898, 719). Perhaps the surgeon in this case figured that, since the patient was by then elderly and left widowed by her husband of sixteen years, it would not matter if she went on in a female role. Probably, like his compatriot colleagues, Clark assumed that since he had removed her testicles, he had in fact "unsexed" her, so that she was then, if not a woman, at least not a man and thereby free of any latent "male" desires. In the same year, another English surgeon, G.R. Green of Sheffield, told his patient, a local resident who "had been living in domestic service as a housemaid for some years," that he had discovered male organs in her (see Figure 3). This certainly explained the lack of menstruation which had been her chief complaint. Green noted that "the question now arose as to what should be done, and as the patient in mind and habit is more a woman than a man, and it is illegal for him to remain as he is in female attire, he expressed a desire to have the testicles removed and continue a woman" (1898, 132). Though it is remarkable that castration would be necessary and sufficient for the patient to dress and live as a woman, the surgeon obliged, and reported that the patient "made a good recovery, and having been unsexed, has now returned to domestic service as a housemaid" (132). With a mostly feminine body, a small penis, and no testicles, it was apparently safe to send the patient back into the land of women. No complaints about these "unsexing" procedures were lodged in the British medical literature.

French doctors were given to initiating legal proceedings when a case of mistaken sex was uncovered (see, for example, Barbin 1868). Occasionally though, a French surgeon did allow an apparently same-sex union to continue rather than taking on the "ungrateful role" of destroying a happy marriage (Delore 1899a, 229). Take, for instance, the case of Madame X of Angers. Though she received several proposals of marriage as a young woman, her parents "did not judge it honest to consent to a marriage destined to remain sterile . . . since the young girl never had the menses" (Blondel 1899, 75). When Madame X reached the age of forty-four in 1898, a sixty-year-old widower who already had several children and grandchildren found her sterility a fine selling point, and asked this "woman" to marry him. Try as he might, Monsieur X could not penetrate his new wife to the depth he desired, and his attempts caused her some pain. The two, however, did not find the situation entirely unsatisfying: "she felt voluptuous sensations when ejaculation was produced in her husband, [and] these sensations reached their climax in the form of rhythmic spasms accompanied by a shaking of the whole body and an emission of sticky liquid in the area of the vulva" (76). After Madam X suffered a fall, she discovered two new "tumors" in her labia majora, and this, combined with the painful intercourse and several other complaints (dizziness, giddiness, vague pains), convinced her to confer with a doctor in 1899, although her friends assured her the symptoms merely signaled menopause.

During her consultation with Dr. Raoul Blondel in Paris, Madame X took the opportunity to ask whether the surgeon could not do something to enable "more complete relations with her husband" (Blondel 1899, 76), for she "loved her husband tenderly" (Neugebauer 1899, 198). A rather troubling question really, since Blondel had already decided the "tumors" in the patient's labia signified not menopause, but manhood: they appeared to be testicles. Other signs also pointed toward mistaken sex, including her flat-chestedness, sizable "clitoris," and failure to menstruate. On the other hand, her "voice, pelvis, character, and inclinations" were all rather "feminine" (Neugebauer 1899, 198). True enough, she managed some sexual relations via her short, blind, "pseudo-vagina," but as far as Blondel was concerned, "from the social point of view, it [was] evident that the marriage of this unfortunate [was] null" by virtue of his belief that her "true" sex was male. Two men could not be legally married. Nevertheless, Blondel and a colleague decided that their nagging "doubt should be interpreted in favor of the subject's intentions." Blondel therefore offered Madame X the help she sought: he "decided to section her hymen and elongate her pseudo-vagina by an incision at the base of its cul-de-sac . . . [and] by means of grafts" (Blondel 1899, 77). She agreed to undergo the surgery (apparently unaware of his chief diagnosis) and made an appointment for the procedure, though she did not keep it, for reasons unknown.

Unlike in Britain, in France such aiding and abetting by doctors of accidental same-sex marriages did not go unchallenged. One French physician, Dr. Xavier Delore, sharply reprimanded Blondel and other doctors who would let continue, and even promote, such "essentially immoral" unions of two males or two females, no matter how honorable the intentions of the parties. In Delore's opinion, the similarity of the partners' sexes constituted "a most profound vice in the origin of the marriage and consequently in its validity" (Delore 1899a, 229). The practitioner faced with such a discovery must be "guided by reason and sentiments of high morality" (1899a, 229), and see to it that the marriage be dissolved, not remedied, lest a doctor like Blondel lend himself "to a conjugal onanism of a new genre!" (Delore 1899b,

70). Delore summarized the situation thus: "From the scientific point of view, the *hermaphrodite* is very interesting; but from the practical point of view it has provoked . . . deceptive and equivocal situations" (1899b, 70). Surely "the hermaphrodite is a trouble to society" (1899a, 226). Delore was not alone in this damning conclusion. Given the conceptual, moral, and practical messes created by hermaphrodites, it was no wonder that medical men of every nationality wished such beings were never born. Some turned their heads while traumatized mothers apparently left genitally ambiguous babies to waste and die (Phillips 1886, 167). Perhaps many thought what one American physician dared to say: that the best treatment for this sort of congenital abnormality was prussic acid—a strong poison (Gross 1852).

Remarkably, despite so many well-documented instances in which people of a hidden "true" sex expressed the desires proper to their "apparent" rather than their "true" sex (cases like Louise-Julia-Anna's), French and British physicians continued to labor under the assumption that testicles naturally meant desire for women, and ovaries meant desire for men. In fact, one reason Blondel maintained some doubt as to Madame X's "true sex" was that her "tastes and penchants were clearly feminine, and at every moment the subject indicated no inclination for women" (Blondel 1899, 77). Throughout the century in France and Britain, people of doubtful sex were quizzed by medical men about their sexual predilections in the belief that answers would elucidate the nature of their gonads.[8] Occasionally the biomedical belief in the natural, irrepressible desire for the "true" opposite sex found its affirmation in cases of mistaken sex. In a number of instances the "true" sex of apparently female horses, goats, and people was questioned because of unexpected "masculine" sexual behavior. In 1897, for instance, a Scottish filly fell under suspicion "because this seeming filly was quite vicious with other female equines, teasing and tormenting them like any entire colt or stallion. In fact, as the season came in she got quite unmanageable with other females in the fields" (Macgillivray 1897, 581). A veterinarian was summoned to perform a thorough investigation, and discovered, to his surprise, two testicles and a penis. He castrated the horse, removing the testicles and the "erratic penis" and was "very glad to say that the filly [no longer the "seeming filly"] . . . made a splendid recovery in every way" (582). The pursuit of females ceased. Conversely, in a human case, the sudden descent of testicles in an apparent woman was considered responsible for the abrupt turn of her sexual interests from men toward women (Laurent 1894, 205). In short, these cases were (quite easily) interpreted in such a way as to support the sex/sexuality paradigm.

Still, in a disturbing number of cases of pseudohermaphroditism, as in that of Louise-Julia-Anna, ambiguous people displayed desires unequivocally for beings of the same gonadal sex as themselves. Such apparent anomalies required explanation in ways that true-male/true-female coupling did not. In France, where an elaborate psychology of sex was being developed, experts on hermaphroditism (many of whom also maintained an active interest in sexual "inverts") suggested that "education can . . . push the sexual instinct in an opposite direction to that which it should be, and thus produce a sort of sexual inversion" (Laurent 1894, 205). Still, some French authors preferred the explanation favored by British medical men: Confused sexual desires (desires for the "wrong" sex) were the inevitable result of confused sexual anatomy. They were of one pathology: strange anatomy, strange sexuality. Louis Blanc, for instance, told lay readers of his picture-packed book on monstrosities, "morality itself is often modified by this perversion of the genital apparatus" (1893, 209).[9]

British medicine did not experience the burgeoning interest in "sexual inversion" that French medicine did (Ellis 1908, v). Indeed, as Bert Hansen has noted, British physicians remained "rather reticent on this subject through the 1890s" (1992, 105). This undoubtedly contributed to the British concentration on more strictly anatomical explanations for same-sex coupling in pseudohermaphrodites, as British doctors found ways to fault anatomical limitations for this "peculiar" sexual behavior. Take, for example, the case of Pauline S., thought to be a true woman in spite of her large clitoris. Pauline's "sexual inclinations [which were] entirely towards women" were blamed on the fact that "the [medical] opinion [had] been expressed [to her] that if pregnancy occurred it would be necessary to remove the child by an operation, which might prove fatal" (Targett 1894, 274). So Pauline did not have a female partner because this was "natural" or even a matter of simple choice; she did it because her anatomy (or self-consciousness of her dangerous anatomy) forced her. In theory, as in practice, the British were inclined to deal with anatomy rather than psychology, as when British surgeons "desexed" (removed the testicles from) apparently female patients. Had Louise been a British subject, might she have had her testicles removed and her hernia repaired rather than being labeled "psychologically interesting"?

Although medical approaches in France and Britain toward "women" with testicles may have differed considerably, at their foundation they shared the same basic assumption that has been illustrated repeatedly above: It did not make sense for people with testicles to have the desires "naturally" and exclusively appropriate to women, nor did it make sense for people with ovaries to have the desires that supposedly belonged to men. Indeed, many medical observers wondered aloud whether a person with "sexual inversion" might not also have something *anatomically* amiss. Voice was occasionally given to the floating suspicion that close examination of a sexually inverted person might turn up some anatomically hermaphroditic traits. So, for instance, in a "Note on Hermaphrodites" in his *Archives of Surgery*, Jonathan Hutchinson wondered "whether in . . . instances [of inverted sexuality] organic peculiarities which have been overlooked do yet really exist" (1896, 65–66). Perhaps those oddly "feminine" and "masculine" desires had a physical basis, as they seemed to in the sexually "normal"?

When given the opportunity, those investigating sexual inversion often made thorough examinations of the bodies of subjects. Case studies frequently contained remarks on the "femininity" or "masculinity" of the face, chest, skeleton, and genitalia. Reports abounded, for instance, of the prevalence in inverted men of gynecomastia, a condition in which there was an enlargement and "feminization" of the breasts (usually associated with undescended or atrophied testicles), even to the point that the male subject's nipples secreted milk (Ellis 1908, 170; Laurent 1894, 20). Usually, like pointy penises and infundibuliform anuses (Rosario 1996), gynecomastia was figured to be a stigmata of pederasty, in this case a bodily metamorphosis that signaled prolonged indulgence in supposedly "feminine" forms of sexuality. Still, questionnaires designed to investigate the bodies, desires, and habits of the sexually inverted often contained questions about the condition of those physical traits commonly thought to be congenitally sex-specific, like the build of the body, the weight and shape of the bones, the distribution of body hair, and the type of "sex organs," including the genitalia and breasts.[10] Suspicions hovered that hermaphroditic bodies went with inverted desires.

Those medical writers who gathered large amounts of data on inverts often noted, as did Richard von Krafft-Ebing in Germany and Havelock Ellis in England, that anatomical ambiguity was not always—or even frequently—found in conjunction with sexual inversion. Collected evidence instead suggested that in most cases "the genitals are normally developed, the sexual glands perform their functions properly, and the sexual type is completely differentiated" (Krafft-Ebing 1921, 222). As Robert Nye has noted, outside France, with its national sexual dilemmas, sexologists "could readily conceive of homosexual men who were masculine in every visible way and differed from other men only in their interior psychic constitutions" (1991, 399).

However, this image of the anatomically "normal" invert was not always the picture painted, and many sexologists inside and outside France still retained nagging suspicions that the bodies of at least some inverts leaned toward the hermaphroditic. Ellis, for instance, noted that:

> It seems to me, on a review of all the facts that have come under my observation, that while there is no *necessary* connection between infantilism [the persistence of childish features], feminism ["feminine" features in a man], and masculinism ["masculine" features in a woman], physical and psychic, on the one hand, and sexual inversion on the other, yet that there is a distinct tendency for the signs of the former group of abnormalities to occur with unusual frequency in inverts. (Ellis 1908, 171; emphasis added)

Krafft-Ebing similarly suggested that, while the genitals of "those individuals of contrary sexuality" were virtually always clearly differentiated into the normal male and female types, their "skeletal form, [their] features, voice, etc.," might be such that "the individual approaches the opposite sex anthropologically" (1921, 304).

Moreover, while it is true that the men who wrote about inverted men often found it quite easy to imagine thoroughly "masculine" male inverts (anatomically speaking), by contrast the female subjects and archetypes of inversion were regularly described as "masculine" (see for example, Krafft-Ebing quoted in Laurent 1894, 290). So, for instance, in his *History of Similisexualism*, privately distributed in the early twentieth century, Xavier Mayne (the pseudonym of Edward Irenaeus Prime Stevenson) insisted the "Uranian, or Urning," that is, a man who desired men, "may be defined as a human being that is more or less perfectly, even distinctively, masculine in physique" (Mayne [1908?], 72). He admitted that "Uraniads," that is, women who desired women, did not necessarily display anatomical ambiguity:

> As is the Uranian continually in externals "perfect man," so also is the Uraniad, incessantly a "perfect woman," in her physical appearance, her manner, and all that is not intimately sexual. There is no necessary question of hermaphroditism. . . . Often a perfect Uraniad is a veritable Venus, realizing the fullest feminine loveliness and grace. [But, Mayne continued,] there is to be admitted in the Uraniad class a tendency toward imperfect sexual organization and functions; to divergences from the delicacy of the female anatomy. The Uranian is likely to have nothing saliently feminine as to his general physique and personality, and to possess most perfectly male organs. On the contrary, the Uraniad is often obviously "boyish" when a girl, has unfeminine proportions, bizarre muscular strength, and activity. . . . Also as she matures she frequently coarsens in body. When this occurs . . . we have the heavy-set, "mannish" woman, with a masculine walk and carriage, with a male timbre of voice. . . . The Uraniad's [facial] features can be in due female proportion, but often of hirsute tendency, even to her showing a beard or moustache. Almost all "bearded women" are more or less Uraniad, and of "contrary" sexualism. (Mayne [1908?], 124)

Ellis similarly suggested that inverted women were often quite "feminine" in external appearance, but noted that "truly" inverted women—those who carried a "congenital predisposition" for inversion—were known often to betray "a more or less distinct trace of masculinity" (Faderman 1978, 81).

In a sense, the congenital invert was always a hermaphrodite of a sort, even if not anatomically one, as long as the desire for men was implied to be a "feminine" trait, and the desire for women a "masculine" trait. This lingering mentality revealed itself especially in the term *psychosexual hermaphroditism*. The "psychosexual hermaphrodite" was not a person with any anatomical peculiarity *per se*. Instead the label was used to denote an invert (Allen 1897) or, more commonly, an individual in whom "there exists a sexual attraction to both sexes"—what we would call (with not much different connotation) a "bisexual" (Ellis 1908, 112; see also Krafft-Ebing 1921, 230). The psychosexual hermaphrodite earned her/his title precisely from the idea that she/he had not a unique sort of desire, but a *doubly* natured desire, part "masculine" and part "feminine." Indeed, just as scientific and medical men expressed doubt that there could be more than a smattering of true anatomical hermaphrodites among humans (so inconceivable was the simultaneity of male and female traits), even those sexologists who believed in a "congenital" form of inversion expressed doubts that true psychosexual hermaphrodites could exist in any significant numbers. Ellis, for instance, suggested that in most supposed psychosexual hermaphrodites, either the homosexual or the heterosexual "instinct" was congenital, with the other added through circumstances of life (1908, 112).

Writings on the subject of sexual inversion had always been laced with references to hermaphroditic states partly because many subjects themselves described the feeling of having some important characteristics of the "opposite" sex—characteristics that included (but were by no means limited to) seemingly incongruous "masculine" or "feminine" desires. For instance, in the 1860s and 1870s, the would-be legislative reformer, Karl Ulrichs, in describing the "third sex" in which he placed himself, posited the existence of a "feminine soul confined in a masculine body" (see Kennedy in this volume). Ulrichs viewed this sort of soul/body hermaphroditism as a variation on a theme of nature, just like the gradations in sexual anatomy manifested in the forms of anatomical males, females, and hermaphrodites.

Following Ulrichs's lead in the search for a more tolerant explanation of homosexuality, Mayne made the homosexual/hermaphrodite analogy explicit, arguing that those possessed of a "similisexual instinct" formed "a series of originally intermediary sexes—the so called intersexual theory—rather than mere aberrations, degeneracies, psychic tangents, from the male and female" (Mayne [1908?], x). Like Ulrichs, Mayne did not suggest the variation of the "intersexes" had a corporeal basis to it, that homosexuals were hermaphroditic (though, as shown above, he did imagine rather hermaphroditic lesbians). Instead, he used gradations in Nature, including in sexual anatomy, to construe "intersexuality" as an element of "Nature's Endless Unity":

> Between the whitest of men and the blackest negro stretches out a vast line of intermediary races as to their colours. . . . Between a protozoan and the most perfect development of the mammalia, we trace a succession of dependent intersteps. . . . A trilobite is at one end of Nature's workshop: a Spinoza, a Shakespeare, a Beethoven is at the other: led-to by cunning gradations, Nature can "evolve" an onion into a philosopher, or a mollusk to a prime-minister. The spectrum is a chain. (Mayne [1908?] 14)

By what right then, Mayne asked, have we

> gone on insisting that each specimen of sex in humanity must conform absolutely to [one of] the two theories [the "normal" male or "normal" female], must follow out [one of] two programmes only, or else be thought amiss, imperfect, and degenerate[?] Why have we set up masculinity and femininity as processes that have not perfectly logical and respectable inter-steps? (Mayne [1908?], 16)

Ulrichs and Mayne thus suggested a congenital origin of homosexuality and likened it to the anatomical hermaphroditism that arose occasionally in nature in the hopes that the social status of homosexuality might be recalibrated and made acceptable because of its "naturalness."

Of course, such an analogy to the hermaphrodite and its position in the chain of being left open the possibility for two conclusions that Mayne did not wish to evoke: first, that "intersexuality" was pathological, a "monstrous" state, like anatomical hermaphroditism;[11] second, that the "intersex," because it was a gradation between the two sexes, was at best an inferior form of life. (Few of Mayne's contemporaries would have argued that the mollusk, though perhaps a necessary part of the "Unity of Nature," was the prime minister's equal.) In France, where "sexual inversion, was a terrifying nexus of medical, social, and moral deviations" (Rosario, this volume), the "variation" of the invert ranked among inferior forms that needed explaining and treatment. Throughout the nineteenth century, French teratological theorists often used the notion of arrested development to explain a whole host of variations,[12] so it is not surprising that some biomedical thinkers suggested that both anatomical hermaphroditism and "contrary" sexual desires originated from (or at least indicated) a "weakened procreative capacity," a failure of energy in the ascent up the sexual ladder (Nye 1991, 395, 399; Nye 1989, 36). Dr. Émile Laurent imagined in his 1894 text, *Les Bisexués*, that a human being could slip down the sexual evolutionary scale in several ways: morphologically (in having confused sexual parts, that is, the traditional "hermaphrodite"); physiologically (in emitting the physiological signs of the "opposite" sex, as when a man lactated); or indeed, psychologically (in lacking the desire for the "opposite" sex, and/or in evincing desire for the same sex). All these intertwined conditions represented "a return to inferior forms of hermaphroditism, a return to the monoecious creatures" (Laurent 1894, 138). No mere natural varieties, these were devolutions, signs of "degeneracy" in both the physical and moral sense.

Although Ellis concurred that "strictly speaking, the invert is degenerate," he preferred not to use the term because of the regrettable pejorative connotation it had acquired. According to Ellis, the invert was a "degenerate" only in the most scientific sense, namely that "he [sic] has fallen away from the genus" (1908, 188). He insisted that, "in sexual inversion we have what may fairly be called a 'sport,' or variation, one of those organic aberrations which we see through living nature" (186). Ellis's opinions, like those of Krafft-Ebing, were clearly in the tradition of Ulrichs and Mayne, the tradition that held "that inverted sexual instinct was 'abnormal' but not a disease; it was instead a variation in a range of natural possibilities" (Nye 1991, 391).

Like those scientists today who would find a biological basis for homosexuality, Ulrichs, Mayne, Krafft-Ebing, and Ellis advanced evidence that inversion was "congenital" or a "natural variation" in the hopes that their data would lead to legal and social tolerance. Their strategy, so remarkably similar to that of Simon LeVay and other supporters of gay rights who advance biological theories of homosexuality, was to argue that a judgment on the acceptability of a given person's sexuality ought to be calibrated to that person's physical nature. Yet a fundamental difficulty built into this otherwise seemingly progressive approach was, and is, the potential collapse to the homosexual-hermaphrodite analogy. Simon LeVay's work, for instance, on the "sexual brain" reinscribes the gay brain into a hermaphroditic model: LeVay suggests that a portion of the hypothalamus differs in gay and straight men, and he explicitly likens this feature of the "gay brain" to the same feature in the brains of women (LeVay 1991). Yet this sort of attempt to free the homosexual via scientific evidence of the "congenital" nature of her/his sexuality winds up again associating the homosexual with the hermaphrodite—a being who has never been the object of real social tolerance in Western culture. This unfortunate alliance of the homosexual and the hermaphrodite springs from the persistent division of desire into two sorts, often thought of as "masculine" and "feminine," a division that forever renders the homosexual person conceptually (if not physically) hermaphroditic. With the constant harkening back to issues of two sexualities, the two sexes and their "true" natures and "true" desires, the image of the homosexual risks perpetual entanglement with the image of the hermaphrodite, the being who is part male and part female, and as such, never really "normal," never really fully evolved, never really acceptable.

We seem to return continually to the idea that it is anatomy, however unsuspected, however invisible, that determines all else and constitutes the "truth." With the advent of genetic research into the "roots" of sexuality, will a homosexually active man lacking a supposed "gay gene" become now a "pseudohomosexual"? Will a heterosexually active woman with a "lesbian gene" become a "pseudoheterosexual"?

We are left with the image of that "homosexual" "hermaphrodite," Louise-Julia-Anna, who, for several years after her encounter with Reumeaux and Guermonprez, wandered northern France in search of a doctor who would allow her—help her—to go on loving men, in search of a man of medicine or science who would see her as she saw herself, a person who by nature desired men. Yet the doctors believed the truth was in her body, and not in her desires, not in her acts.

Notes

I would like to thank Vernon A. Rosario, whose assistance with this article has proven unfailing and invaluable. Thanks also to Aron Sousa, M. Jeanne Peterson, Ann Carmichael, Fred Churchill, and the members of OUT! at Indiana University's Bloomington campus for their help with and support for this project. Funding for this research was provided by Indiana University and by a Charlotte Newcombe Doctoral Dissertation Fellowship from the Woodrow Wilson National Fellowship Foundation.

1 Unless otherwise noted, all translations are my own.

2 Teratology is the scientific study of malformations or "monstrosities." The term was coined by the French anatomist Isidore Geoffroy Saint-Hilaire (1805–1861), who published a three-volume work on the subject in 1832–1836, entitled *Histoire générale et particulière des anomalies . . . ou, Traité de tératologie* (see Dreger 1993).

3 Arnold Davidson (1992, 98) relies on the *Oxford English Dictionary* to trace back to 1879 the appearance of the modern usage of "sexuality" (i.e., "possession of sexual powers, or capability of sexual feeling") in the English language. Specifically, Davidson marks the shift in an illustrative passage provided by the *O.E.D.* and drawn from J. M. Duncan's *Diseases of Women* of 1879: "In removing the ovaries, you do not necessarily destroy sexuality in a woman." While I do not disagree with Davidson's general point that the modern idea of sexuality, as distinct from sex, began to emerge only in the late nineteenth century, he has unfortunately assumed Duncan meant what we currently understand by "sexuality" and has therefore misinterpreted Duncan's phraseology. Duncan almost certainly did *not* draw a sex/sexuality distinction, nor did his colleagues; instead, they used the broad term "sexuality" to denote all those characteristics (anatomical features, behaviors, penchants, talents, and abilities) typically associated with one or the other sex.

Even as late as 1899, the *New Sydenham Society's Lexicon of Medicine and the Allied Sciences* defined "sexuality" as broadly and vaguely as Duncan probably would have: "the characteristics of sex; those special characters which go to constitute either a male or a female." So, when Duncan said a woman whose ovaries were removed did not necessarily lose her sexuality, he most likely meant that she did not necessarily lose her "femininity," i.e., her basically "feminine" anatomy, tastes, talents, and so on. Ironically, in his remark, Duncan was actively demonstrating the lack of a distinction between sex and sexuality that Davidson assumes Duncan displayed by the remark. (Davidson's confusion is quite understandable, given the *O.E.D.*'s poor choice of illustration for this meaning of "sexuality.")

4 Articulating this general notion, the renowned British surgeon Jonathan Hutchinson declared in 1896 that "roughly speaking, and in a general way" the "special organs of [a] sex are inseparably connected with [that sex's] moral and emotional characteristics" (1896, 65). Compare with Trélat (1881, 59): "Louise D. had a uterus and an ovary; the genetic sense thus existed in her."

5 Authors of English texts were forced to chose between "he," "she," and "it" when referring to the hermaphrodite, but French writers learned a trick to avoid this difficulty. The French commonly designated the hermaphrodite as **le** *sujet,* which then enabled them to employ masculine pronouns agreeing with *sujet,* rather than specific to the sex of the hermaphrodite him/herself (a sex that might be double or undetermined).

6 By contrast, British medical men did not share this worry about female pseudohermaphrodites invading and corrupting the ranks of men, perhaps because British women were not considered as dangerously and naturally seductive as French women.

7 The difference in publicity levels might explain why the French lamented that hermaphrodites "literally [ran] about on the streets," and warned that any infertile couple might be victims of mistaken sex (Garnier 1885, 287)—suspicions the British did not share.

8 The English Dr. Webster, for instance, took as profound evidence for a patient's "maleness" that C.D., a sexually ambiguous kitchen maid, confessed that her "sexual and sensual indications . . . are for a female and not for a male; . . . a longing for connection with a girl has been experienced, though never indulged" (Webster 1866, 146). Unlike C.D., the French pseudohermaphrodite Eugénie Remy did indulge in relations with women. Although raised a girl, Remy displayed a "sexual appetite directed toward the feminine sex, [with] coitus easy" (Petit 1891, 297). Remy even "affirmed having provided by coitus venereal orgasm in several women" (Petit 1891, 297)—supposedly a sure sign of a man! According to the author of the medical report on Remy, this "ensemble of her psychic genital state plead[ed] in a positive and energetic fashion in favor of [her true] virility" (299). A tiny minority of medical writers suggested sexual desires had "no importance for the determination of sex in doubtful cases" (Pozzi 1885b, 111), but few practitioners heeded their warnings. In fact, when medical men did ignore the claims of a patient with regard to sexual preferences, this was not because they doubted "true" males would desire females and vice versa, but rather because they believed that in general "no attention ought to be paid to the declarations of the individual, or of his or her relations" (Ogston 1876, 191). The veracity of the anatomy was not the issue; the veracity of the patient was.

9 Still, Blanc assured readers that the "true" sex (and sexuality) would usually emerge, and troubles would end: "In more than one case, the individual, whose sex has been the subject of error, presented during a part of his life the tendencies of his supposed sex, then spontaneously recouped *his natural instincts*" (1893, 209; original emphasis). Blanc offered as an example a classic story of the hermaphrodite made good:

> Worbe reported the history of a hermaphrodite born in 1775 in the area of Dreux, and baptized under the name Marie-Jeanne. Raised a girl, this subject for a long time wore the dress of the young village girls; but, toward the age of twenty, the masculine tendencies made themselves known: Marie-Jeanne frequented the cabarets, got drunk often, smoked a pipe, hunted, and was pleased to lead and attend horses. Later she took on the clothes of her true sex, and married. (209–210)

[10] For example, Appendix A, "A Categoric Personal Analysis for the Reader" in Mayne [1908?]; also "Questionnaire on Homosexuality" by Earl Lind, reproduced in Hansen (1992, 112–113).
[11] Interestingly, although the term "intersexuality" originally denoted homosexuality, it later came to be the blanket term used to describe various forms of anatomical sexual ambiguity.
[12] "Arrested development" connoted the failure of an organism to develop to its full potential, leaving it stuck in an "inferior" state (see Gould 1977, 49–52).

References

Ackerknecht, Erwin H. 1967. *Medicine at the Paris Hospital.* Baltimore: Johns Hopkins University Press.

Allen, C. W. 1897. Report of a case of psycho-sexual hermaphroditism. *Medical Record* (New York) 51:653–655.

Barbin, Herculine. [1868] 1980. *Herculine Barbin. Being the recently discovered memoirs of a nineteenth-century French hermaphrodite.* Intro. Michel Foucault. Trans. Richard McDougall. New York: Pantheon.

Benoist, Alcide. 1886. Rapport sur un cas d'hermaphrodisme. *Annales d'hygiène publique et de médecine légale,* 3rd ser., 16:84–87.

Blanc, Louis. 1893. *Les anomalies chez l'homme et les mammifères.* Paris: J.-B. Baillière.

Blondel, Raoul. 1899. Observation de pseudo-hermaphrodisme.—Un homme marié à un homme. *Journal de médecine de Paris,* 2nd ser., 11:75–77.

Buchanan, George. 1885. Hermaphrodite, aged 9, in whom two testicles were excised from the labia majora. *Glasgow Medical Journal* 23:213–217.

Clark, Andrew. 1898. A case of spurious hermaphroditism (hypospadias and undescended testes in a subject who had been brought up as a female and been married for sixteen years). *The Lancet* 1 (12 Mar.): 718–719.

Croom, J. Halliday. 1898. Two cases of mistaken sex in adult life. *Transactions of the Edinburgh Obstetrical Society* 24:102–104.

Davidson, Arnold. 1992. Sex and the emergence of sexuality. In *Forms of Desire: Sexual Orientation and the Social Constructionist Controversy,* ed. Edward Stein, 89–132. New York: Routledge.

Delore, Xavier. 1899a. Des étapes de l'hermaphrodisme. *L'Écho médicale de Lyon* 4 (7): 193–205; 4 (8): 225–232.

———. 1899b. De l'hermaphrodisme dans l'histoire ancienne et dans la chirurgie moderne. *Journal des sciences médicales de Lille* 2:63–70.

Dreger, Alice. 1993. "Nature is One Whole": Isidore Geoffroy Saint-Hilaire's *Traité de tératologie.* Master's thesis, Indiana University.

———. 1995. Doubtful sex, doubtful status: Cases and concepts of hermaphroditism in France and Britain, 1868–1915. Ph.D. diss., Indiana University.

Ellis, Havelock. 1908. *Studies in the Psychology of Sex: Sexual Inversion.* 2nd ed. Philadelphia: F. A. Davis.

Faderman, Lillian. 1978. The morbidification of love between women by 19th-century sexologists. *Journal of Homosexuality* 4 (1): 73–90.

Foucault, Michel. 1975. *The Birth of the Clinic: An Archaeology of Medical Perception.* Trans. A. M. Sheridan Smith. New York: Vintage Books.

Garnier, Pierre. 1885. Du pseudo-hermaphrodisme comme impédiment médico-légale à la déclaration du sexe dans l'acte de naissance. *Annales d'hygiène publique et de médecine légale,* 3rd ser., 14:285–293.

Gould, Stephen Jay. 1977. *Ontogeny and Phylogeny.* Cambridge: Harvard University Press.

Green, G. R. 1898. A case of hypospadias in a patient, aged 24, who had always passed as a woman. *Quarterly Medical Journal* 6:130–132.

Gross, S. D. 1852. Case of hermaphrodism, involving the operation of castration and illustrating a new principle in juridical medicine. *American Journal of the Medical Sciences,* new series, 14:386–390.

Guermonprez, François Jules Octave. 1892. Une erreur de sexe, avec ses consequences. *Journal des sciences médicales de Lille* 2:337–349, 361–376.

Hansen, Bert. 1992. American physicians' "discovery" of homosexuals, 1880–1900: A new diagnosis in a changing society. In *Framing Disease,* ed. Charles E. Rosenberg and Janet Golden, 104–133. New Brunswick, NJ: Rutgers University Press.

Hart, Ernest. 1885. Sexual ignorance. *British Medical Journal* 2:303–304.

Hutchinson, Jonathan. 1896. A note on hermaphrodites. *Archives of Surgery* 7:64–66.

Krafft-Ebing, Richard von. 1921. *Psychopathia Sexualis, With Special Reference to Contrary Sexual Instinct.* Authorized translation of the seventh enlarged and revised German edition. Trans. Charles Gilbert Chaddock. Philadelphia: F. A. Davis.

Laurent, Émile. 1894. *Les Bisexués. Gynécomastes et hermaphrodites.* Paris: Georges Carré.

Leblond, Albert. 1885. Du pseudo-hermaphrodisme comme impédiment médico-légal à la déclaration du sexe dans l'acte de naissance. *Annales de gynécologie* 24:25–35.

LeVay, Simon. 1991. A difference in hypothalamic structure between heterosexual and homosexual men. *Science* 253:1034–1037.

Macgillivray, A. E. 1897. Operation on an hermaphrodite; Castration. *Veterinarian* (London) 70 (838): 580–582.

Mayne, Xavier [pseudonym for Edward I. P. Stevenson]. [n.d.; preface dated 1908] 1975. *The Intersexes. A History of Similisexualism as a Problem in Social Life.* Privately printed. Reprint, New York: Arno Press.

Neugebauer, Franz. 1899. Cinquante cas de mariages conclus entre des personnes du même sexe, avec plusieurs procès de divorce par suite d'erreur de sexe. *Revue de gynécologie et de chirurgie abdominale* 3:195–210.

———. 1900. Une nouvelle série de 29 observations d'erreur de sexe. *Revue de gynécologie et de chirurgie abdominale* 4:133–174.

———. 1903. Hermaphrodism in the daily practice of medicine; being information upon hermaphrodism indispensable to the practitioner. *British Gynaecological Journal* 29:226–263.

Nye, Robert A. 1989. Sex difference and male homosexuality in French medical discourse, 1830–1930. *Bulletin of the History of Medicine* 63:32–51.

———. 1991. The history of sexuality in context: National sexological traditions. *Science in Context* 4 (2): 387–406.

Ogston, Francis. 1876. Select lectures on medical jurisprudence: Doubtful sex. *Medical Times and Gazette* (London) 1:161–162, 189–191.

Petit, Paul. 1891. Pseudo-hermaphrodisme par hypospadias périnéo-scrotal. *Nouvelles archives d'obstetrique et de gynécologie* 6:297–299.

Phillips, John. 1886. Four cases of spurious hermaphroditism in one family. *Transactions of the Obstetrical Society of London* 28:158–168.

Pozzi, Adrien, and P. Grattery. 1887. Pseudo-hermaphrodite (hypospadias périnéal). *Le Progrès médical*, 2nd ser., 5:308–312.

Pozzi, Samuel. 1885a. Homme hypospade (pseudo-hermaphrodite) considéré depuis vingt-huit ans comme femme. *Bulletin de la Société de Médecine Légale de France* 8:307–317.

———. 1885b. Note sur deux nouveaux cas de pseudo-hermaphrodisme. *Gazette médicale de Paris*, 7th ser., 2:109–112.

Rosario, Vernon A. 1996. Pointy penises, fashion crimes, and hysterical mollies: The pederasts' inversions. In *Homosexuality in Modern France*, ed. Jeffrey W. Merrick and Bryant Ragan, 146–176. New York: Oxford University Press.

Sorel, R., and M. Cherot. 1898. Un cas de pseudo-hermaphrodisme. *Archives provinçales de chirurgie* 12:367–369.

Tait, Lawson. 1879. *Diseases of Women*. New York: William Wood.

Targett, J. H. 1894. Two cases of pseudo-hermaphroditism. *Transactions of the Obstetrical Society of London* 36:272–6.

Trélat, Ulysse. 1881. De l'hermaphrodisme féminin (leçon recueillie par M. G. Marchant). *Journal des connaissances médicales pratiques et de pharmacologie*, 3rd ser., 2:41–42; 58–59.

Wakley, Thomas H., and Thomas Wakley, Jr., eds. 1901. Social leprosy [Editorial]. *The Lancet* 1 (2 Feb.): 346.

Webster, John H. 1866. Case of hermaphrodism. *British Medical Journal* 1 (10 Feb.): 145–146.

Richard von Krafft-Ebing's "Step-Children of Nature"
Psychiatry and the Making of Homosexual Identity

Harry Oosterhuis

> Although I fear to pester you, Sir, with my letter—after all, in the preface of your *Psychopathia sexualis*, you mention the "innumerable letters by such step-children of nature"—I still trustingly turn to you, hoping that a layman might report something to the scholar that is not entirely without interest: even the most inconspicuous thing may gain importance in the right place and may be worth the researcher's scrutiny.[1]

In 1900 a young nobleman, Von R., addressed himself in this manner to the renowned German-Austrian psychiatrist Richard von Krafft-Ebing (1840–1902), author of *Psychopathia sexualis* and one of the founders of scientific sexology. For the most part, Von R.'s letter is an elaborate introspection on his problematic sexuality. When he was ten years old, Von R. ascertained retrospectively, his "contrary sexual feeling" and "masochistic" impulses had already revealed themselves in his fantasies, reading habits, and games. The lust he experienced as a boy when he made a ceremony out of decapitating flowers was a clear symptom of his deep-seated proclivities. His urge to be humiliated by his male subordinates especially caused inward conflict. Torn between his irresistible sexual desire and his class prejudice, Von R. was weighed down by shame and guilt. He meticulously explored and evaluated every circumstance that might shed light on his anomaly: his particular way of acting and feeling, his childhood and puberty, his upbringing in an exclusively female environment, the fantasies and the moral conflicts that accompanied his self-abuse, his failure to copulate with a prostitute, his character and intellectual faculties, his state of health (he detected a slight "nervousness" in his behavior), and his family background, especially possible hereditary taints.

The way Von R. framed his autobiographical account is noteworthy. As if to underline its structure and to add an objective comment to his intimate confession, he took notes in the margins of the pages. The composition of his life story and his marginal notes are reminiscent of many handwritten case histories I found in the Krafft-Ebing archives.[2] After Krafft-Ebing's assistants had written down the patient's biography, symptoms, and anamnesis, Krafft-Ebing added the diagnosis and other remarks in the margins. Thus the individual case was likened to others, classified, and fitted into Krafft-Ebing's taxonomy. One of the leading clinically oriented psychiatrists of his time, he had a reputation for extensive case histories. Although he was influenced by the natural-scientific approach in psychiatry that sought to classify mental diseases on the basis of anatomical pathology, Krafft-Ebing focused not so much on the specific characteristics of a particular illness as on the detailed histories of individuals. In his *Lehrbuch der Psychiatrie auf klinischer Grundlage* (Textbook of Clinically Based Psychiatry) (1879–1880), which was widely used by medical students, he laid down a standard for the taking of psychiatric case histories and listed the elements of what was characterized as the individual case approach. Next to the patient's name, age, occupation, dates of admission and consultation, there should be information about his or her ancestry, family medical and mental health history, childhood and puberty history, onset and development of mental disorders, and subjective condition: moods, imaginative powers, dreams, fantasies, perceptiveness, intellectual capacities, decisiveness, and moral awareness.

Much of Krafft-Ebing's work was descriptive and consisted primarily of case histories and sometimes autobiographies written by his patients. The contents and the form of Von R.'s own writing mirror the psychiatric model of the individual case description. Krafft-Ebing's *Psychopathia sexualis*, which contained many case reports and autobiographies, must have inspired Von R. to write his own case history and to diagnose himself. Using the language of psychiatry, his autobiography reflects medical explanations of sexuality. Offering his life story as grist for the interpretative mill, Von R. seems to have placed his fate into the hands of the psychiatrist and his confession appears to be typical of what Michel Foucault (1976) has designated as the medical construction of sexuality. Foucault argues that the modern idea of sexuality was historically constituted by medical science, which delimited deviance. Before medical theories emerged that lumped together behavior, physical characteristics, and the emotional makeup of individuals, there was no entity that could be delineated as sexuality. Thus, by differentiating between the normal and the abnormal, and by stigmatizing sexual variance as sickly deviation, physicians, as exponents of an anonymous "biopower," were controlling free and easy pleasures of the body.

Although Foucault himself stressed that sexuality was shaped rather than repressed by the scientific will to know, several historians have associated the emergence of a science of sexuality with a deplorable medical colonization, replacing religious and judicial authority with a new form of medico-moral tyranny. Therefore, Krafft-Ebing's work has been damned as "an unmitigated disaster," and he has been blamed for "the confusion which continues to surround the subject of sexual variation today" (Brecher 1969, 56). For the prophet of antipsychiatry, Thomas Szasz, it is clear that "Krafft-Ebing was not interested in liberating men and women from the shackles of sexual prejudice or the constraints of antisexual legislation. On the contrary, he was interested in supplanting the waning power of the church with the waxing power of medicine." Adding that "*Psychopathia sexualis* is full of falsehoods pretentiously presented as if they were the fruits of hard-won scientific discoveries," Szasz's opinion (1980, 19–20) is typical of the way historians have viewed Krafft-Ebing's work from a presentist perspective.

Contemporaries like Von R., however, experienced it in a different way. Reading *Psychopathia sexualis* had made him aware of the fact that:

> I am not the only "step-child of nature." . . . I would never have believed that my pride could convince me to make such confessions. Only your work has opened my eyes. It made the world and myself not appear in the gray light of disdain any longer, and, reassuring and rehabilitating, it inspired my confidence. (Freiherr von R. to Krafft-Ebing, July 1900. Krafft-Ebing Estate)

For Von R., Krafft-Ebing's work was a revelation. Von R. was not the only one who made references to the salutary effects of *Psychopathia sexualis.* "A heavily suffering person turns to the benign and great help of your science," another man wrote. "It is incredibly hard for me to expose myself. And I can only do it to you, to you alone in the entire world, because I know from your book *Psychopathia sexualis* that I wouldn't be saying totally strange things" (G.P. to Krafft-Ebing, March 10, 1899. Krafft-Ebing Estate). Especially homosexuals who addressed themselves to Krafft-Ebing and sent him their autobiographies expressed themselves in a similar tone. "I read your essay in the *Zeitschrift für Psychiatrie* [Journal of Psychiatry]," a man reported to Krafft-Ebing in 1882.

> Through it, I and certainly thousands with me are revindicated in the eyes of every thinking and halfway honest man and I thank you warmly for it. You yourself probably know to what degree our subject is being frowned on, despised, and persecuted. (Krafft-Ebing 1884, 2)

Also typical was a man who made clear that recognizing himself in *Psychopathia sexualis* had brought him great relief:

> Your book *Psychopathia sexualis* brought me much comfort. It contains passages that I might have written myself; they seem to be unconsciously taken from my own life.—My heart has been considerably lightened, since I learned from your book of your benevolent interest in our disreputable class. It was the first time that I met someone who showed me that we are not entirely as bad as we are usually portrayed. Anyway, I feel a great burden has been lifted from me. (Krafft-Ebing 1890a, 55)

How should such expressions be qualified? Are these individuals, as the Foucaultian interpretation would have it, trapped in a medical discourse that constitutes not only power relations and social control of deviant sexualities, but also sexual subjects themselves? The radical implication of Foucault's reasoning is that before 1870 there did not exist "perverts" like homosexuals, fetishists, and masochists, nor their counterparts, "normal" heterosexuals. This contention might be defended, but the problem is that the conclusion has been drawn too readily that new sexual categories and identities were merely medical constructions. As far as the individuals who are labeled as "perverts" are concerned, they have mainly been presented as passive victims of a medical juggernaut, having no other choice than to conform to medical stereotypes.

The emphasis on medical labeling in the creation of "deviants," such as homosexuals, presents a social-deterministic model in which individuals are pawns of social forces with no will of their own. To explain how sexual "perversion" in general and homosexuality in particular were constructed,[3] it is necessary to enter the subjective world of individuals who read Krafft-Ebing's work and responded to it, and to take their intentions, purposes, and meanings seriously on their own terms. How was Krafft-Ebing's work read and used by contemporaries? Who were his patients and informants? What were their social and cultural backgrounds? How did they interpret medical theories, and how did they come into contact with psychiatrists? In what way did medical theories and individual experiences interact, and how did these interferences between scientific and autobiographical constructions of meaning develop?

Moral Offenders and Degenerates

Although Richard Freiherr von Krafft-Ebing was one of the most prominent psychiatrists of his time in Central Europe and worked in numerous fields of psychiatry, he is remembered today as the author of *Psychopathia sexualis* and as one of the founding fathers of scientific sexology. The first edition of his much quoted book appeared in 1886, followed soon by several new and expanded editions—seventeen in German between 1886 and 1924—and by translations in several languages. Krafft-Ebing revised it several times, especially by adding new categories and case histories. By naming and classifying virtually all nonprocreative sexuality, he was one of the first to synthesize medical knowledge of what was then labeled "sexual perversion." Although in retrospect *Psychopathia sexualis* can be considered an important milestone in the development of what later became sexology, Krafft-Ebing probably did not intend to establish a new medical discipline. His interest in the broader aspects of sexual deviance emerged from experience in asylum psychiatry, which viewed disorders such as masturbation as symptoms of preexisting mental diseases, and he was even more influenced by the preoccupation of forensic medicine with criminal acts such as sodomy. Before the 1890s, his interest in sexual pathology was intrinsically linked to forensic psychiatry, an area in which he was a pioneer and leading expert (Krafft-Ebing 1879).

Psychopathia sexualis was therefore written for lawyers and doctors discussing sexual crimes in court. Krafft-Ebing's main point was that in many cases perversion was not a sin or a crime, but a disease—a common position of liberal physicians of the period from 1870 to 1900. "Deviant," nonprocreative sexual acts, traditionally considered immoral and criminal, increasingly came under psychiatric evaluation, as they were regarded not simply as sins and crimes, but as symptoms of an illness caused by natural laws. Since mental disease often diminished responsibility, Krafft-Ebing argued that most sex offenders should not be punished, but treated as patients suffering from mental diseases. Although perversion left reason intact, as a form of "moral insanity" it selectively damaged the moral faculties. Unable to control their strong, irresistible, sexual drives and obsessions, "perverts" could not be held personally responsible for their inclinations because their free will was impaired. Only those who possessed insight into their actions were responsible in a legal sense. Krafft-Ebing distinguished between immoral "perversity," on the one hand, and sickly "perversion" on the other, and he stressed that neither lawyers nor common sense, but only professional psychiatrists were qualified in court to distinguish mental illness. Judgment had to be geared toward a medical diagnosis. Although it was debated whether perversion was inborn or acquired, psychiatrists such as Krafft-Ebing shifted the focus from immoral and criminal acts, a temporary deviation of the norm, to a pathological condition.

In the second half of the nineteenth century, neuropathology and theories of degeneration played an important part in psychiatric explanations of mental illness in general and sexual disorders in particular. Krafft-Ebing was influenced by Charles Darwin (1809–1882) and especially by the French alienist Bénédict Auguste Morel (1809–1873). Morel focused on heredity as the underlying cause of mental diseases, and claimed that these got progressively worse over generations. Following in the wake of Morel, Krafft-Ebing believed that the extraordinary demands of modern civilization on the nervous system were responsible for a rise in mental disturbances, and that acquired disorders could be inherited from "tainted" relatives. Although he believed that perversion might be acquired through bad environmental agents, seduction, and corrupt habits such as masturbation, he increasingly stressed that many sexual disorders were inborn.

Krafft-Ebing's first systematic work on sexual pathology was published in 1877 in a leading German psychiatric journal. Following the dominant clinical-anatomical approach in psychiatry that situated mental disorders in the nervous system and particularly the brain, and adopting Morel's preoccupation with "pathological family," Krafft-Ebing supposed that degeneration was the underlying cause of inborn perversion. His initial classification distinguished between classes of sexual abnormalities that were of a quantitative and qualitative nature. The first group comprised absence and pathological increase of the sexual drive, and sexual activity during an abnormal period, that is, childhood or old age. The second covered the perversions proper. As far as the last category was concerned, he discussed three subgroups: lust murder, necrophilia, and contrary sexual feeling (1877). Same-sex attraction, which was associated with an inverted gender identity, figured prominently in the last group, but that group also included various biological and psychological fusions of manliness and femininity that would gradually be reclassified in the twentieth-century as radically separate phenomena, such as hermaphroditism, androgyny, and transvestitism.

Krafft-Ebing and other physicians such as Karl Westphal (1833–1890) (who published the first psychiatric study of contrary sexual feeling in 1869) were influenced by the writings of the Hannoverian lawyer, Karl Heinrich Ulrichs (1825–1895), who introduced the concept of "Uranism" in 1864 (see Kennedy in this volume). In his dozen brochures (published 1864–1879), Ulrichs advocated the decriminalization of the "vice against nature" on the grounds that "Uranism" was a natural phenomenon of "migration of the soul": a woman's soul in a man's body and vice versa. Ulrichs's and Krafft-Ebing's explanations of homosexuality as a form of inversion demonstrates how, in the nineteenth century, sexual attraction was not conceivable without a physical or psychological polarization and matching of male and female elements. Although Ulrichs argued that Urnings' love was natural because it consisted of an attraction between male and female elements, psychiatrists like Krafft-Ebing identified inversion with degeneration and its associated "inverse tendency" toward dedifferentiation.

Krafft-Ebing premised his initial theory of sexual pathology on a comparatively small number of generally severe cases, such as lust murder and necrophilia, often derived from criminal proceedings. New categories of perversion were created and underpinned more or less by systematically collecting and publishing new case histories. In the 1880s, Krafft-Ebing published several articles on contrary sexual feeling, containing extensive case studies and autobiographies. Relabeling already collected cases and assembling new ones, he expanded his taxonomy, and new perversions entered *Psychopathia sexualis* around 1890. Along with "contrary sexual feeling," he introduced "fetishism" (the erotic obsession with certain parts of the body, hair, shoes, nightcaps, handkerchiefs, gloves, ladies' underwear, fur, and silk), and he coined "sadism" and "masochism" as the most fundamental forms of psychosexual perversion. In the last decades of the nineteenth century, especially in France and Germany, several prominent psychiatrists were classifying and explaining the wide range of deviant sexual behaviors they discovered.[4] Several taxonomies were proposed, but the one developed in *Psychopathia sexualis* around 1890 eventually set the tone. Although he also paid attention to voyeurism, exhibitionism, pedophilia, gerontophilia, bestiality, necrophilia, urolagnia, coprolagnia, and other sexual behaviors, Krafft-Ebing distinguished four main perversions: sadism, masochism, fetishism, and contrary sexual feeling (or inversion).

The Psychology of Sexual Desire

Psychopathia sexualis has been characterized as the climax of the medicalization of sexuality and a typical expression of Victorian hypocrisy. True, there are elements that would substantiate such a judgment, but a close reading of this work makes clear that it cannot be regarded only as a medical and moral disqualification of sexual aberration. Krafft-Ebing's views were far from static or coherent, and in several ways his scientific approach to sexuality was ambivalent. The differentiation of pathological and healthy sexuality—reproduction being the touchstone—was the basic assumption in his taxonomy; at the same time, the barriers between the normal and abnormal were subverted in his discussion of the main perversions. Sadism, masochism, and fetishism were not only disease categories, but also terms that described extremes on a graded scale of health and illness, and explained aspects of "normal" sexuality. He construed sadism as a pathological extension of the normal sexual psychology of males, and masochism as an exaggeration of the female sexual nature. Sadism and masochism were inherent in normal male and female sexuality, the first being of an aggressive and the second of a submissive nature. (However, most of Krafft-Ebing's cases were of male masochists, and therefore he assumed that masochism in males was related to inversion.) In his view, the distinction between sadomasochism and "normal" heterosexuality was quantitative rather than qualitative. Fetishism was also defined by Krafft-Ebing as part and parcel of normal sexuality, because the individual character of sexual attraction and monogamous love was grounded in a distinct preference for particular physical and mental characteristics of one's partner. "Normal" sexuality appeared to have features of perverted desire. In addition, the boundary between masculinity and femininity was blurred. Inversion, spanning the gulf between the masculine and the feminine, occupied a major place in Krafft-Ebing's sexual pathology. The extensive discussion of several forms of physical and mental inversion highlighted the idiosyncratic and chance character of sex differentiation, and hinted that exclusive masculinity and femininity might be mere abstractions. Despite the effort to distinguish perversion from normalcy, there was a clear tendency in *Psychopathia sexualis* to undercut distinctions between divergent desires and to make various forms of normal and abnormal sexuality equivalent and interchangeable, thus abolishing a clear boundary between health and perversion.

Krafft-Ebing's psychiatric theorization of sexuality opened up a new continent of knowledge, not only because it treated sexual abnormality as disease instead of sin, crime, or decadence, but, more importantly, because he made it clear that sexuality deserved serious study since it was central to the existence of the individual and society. He pointed to the danger of the sexual instinct threatening civilization, but at the same time he also drew attention to its constructive role in culture and society, religion, social ethics, and esthetics. For him, love as a social bond was inherently sexual. "Ethical surroundings are necessary in order to elevate love to its true and pure form, but nevertheless, sensuality remains its strongest root. Platonic love is an absurdity, a self-deception, a misnomer for kindred spirits" (Krafft-Ebing 1912, 11–12). The longing for physical and psychological union with a partner was valued as a purpose in itself. His discussion of same-sex love indicates that procreation was no longer considered to be an unshakable norm—notably, Krafft-Ebing did not mention contraception in his discussion of abnormality. In fact, he assigned primacy to the satisfaction of desire and psychological matters.

Krafft-Ebing's biological approach to sexuality has often been contrasted with Freud's psychological one (Gay 1988, 120). However, in *Psychopathia sexualis* there is a striking inconsistency between organic explanations and clinical descriptions. Although in his case histories he often mentioned physical examinations of his patient's sexual organs, and sometimes even anatomies of the brain if they died while still under medical supervision, these were not very relevant for his classification and definition of perversion. The introduction of fetishism, sadism, and masochism was not only an important broadening of terminology, but also a significant step from a predominantly forensic focus and a physiological explanation to a psychological approach to human sexuality. Not so much bodily characteristics nor actual behavior were decisive in the diagnosis of perversion, but functional disorders, individual character, personal history and emotional life, dreams and fantasies. Although the underlying causes of perversion remained degeneration and heredity, Krafft-Ebing shifted the medical discussion away from explaining sexuality as a series of interrelated physiological events to a more psychological understanding. In this way, he foreshadowed Freud: like Freud, Krafft-Ebing viewed human sexuality as distinct from animal instincts. His analysis primarily had to rely on what "perverts" were telling him; therefore, (auto)biographical accounts were most important to his work. Especially because his case histories displayed an individualization and psychologization of sexuality, his approach marks a central moment in the constitution of the modern concept of sexuality in general and of homosexuality in particular.

"Plato Was Not a Filthy Swine"

As indicated before, *Psychopathia sexualis* was illustrated with hundreds of case histories and autobiographical accounts. The twelfth edition (1903), the last to be edited by Krafft-Ebing himself, contained almost 250 of these. In his earlier work, many of them were borrowed from colleagues, or were based on cases of "moral offenders" whom he examined in his capacity as an expert witness. Each new edition presented larger numbers of patients hospitalized in the asylums or university clinics where he was a medical superintendent. Also represented were individuals who contacted Krafft-Ebing of their own accord as private patients, or who corresponded with him because they had recognized themselves in published case histories. Some of them sent in their autobiographies hoping to have them published in a subsequent edition of *Psychopathia sexualis*. Although most cases in his early work were rather short and factual, later editions contained more extensive ones. In publishing autobiographies and quoting his patients, many case studies focused especially on the patient's subjective experiences.

The subjects of Krafft-Ebing's case histories were drawn from various social groups. This was closely connected to his endeavor to expand the boundaries of his psychiatric practice by changing its institutional setting and recruiting new types of patients (Hauser 1992, 85–132). When Krafft-Ebing started his career as an Extraordinary Professor of Psychiatry in Graz, his professional élan must have been severely challenged. In the overcrowded Feldhof Asylum, where he was a medical superintendent, he was faced with generally poor, uneducated, chronic, and sometimes violent inmates, who were barely treatable and with whom it was difficult to sympathize. In such an institution, psychiatry consisted mainly of custodial care, and offered few gratifying professional and scientific experiences. For teaching and publishing purposes and for successful treatments, he needed greater variety and a higher turnover of acute cases. His successful struggle for a clinical ward in the university hospital was not only a strategic move to strengthen his position in academia, but was also important for the shaping of psychiatry as a respectable medical specialty. The founding of a private sanatorium for an elite, wealthy clientele suffering from relatively mild disorders like "nervousness" and "neurasthenia" may have been inspired by similar considerations. In asylums and clinical wards, Krafft-Ebing treated mainly lower-class patients, while in the commodious sanatorium and his private practice he catered to men and women from the higher ranks of society, for whom hospitalization was undesirable. Among them were several members of the German, Austrian, and Hungarian aristocracy, and affluent patients from all over Europe. While hospitalized patients and suspected moral offenders had no other choice than to conform to standard medical procedures and have their stories recorded, many of his aristocratic and bourgeois patients, who generally had contacted him of their own accord, were given ample opportunity to speak for themselves. Homosexual men particularly seized this opportunity.

The autobiographies Krafft-Ebing received from Urnings were by members of the upper and educated classes, who often were familiar with his work on sexual pathology and eager to reveal their lives to him. In his early articles on contrary sexual feeling, he had made it clear that he needed more cases to substantiate empirically his taxonomy, and he encouraged Urnings to contact him. They responded with letters and autobiographies. "You ask for biographies of several Urnings," one university graduate wrote in 1885. "In the interest of science I won't make a fuss about giving you an autobiography that is as detailed as possible, and in which I will attempt to give all data as objectively as possible" (Krafft-Ebing 1885, 42–43). The almost exclusively male cases he collected in the 1880s, either by direct contact or through letters, were of merchants, civil servants, aristocrats, scholars, writers, artists, and, remarkably, of medical students and physicians.[5] Generally, they were economically independent and, in most cases, living apart from the traditional family. Krafft-Ebing probably had expected them to be nervous and effeminate "degenerates"; however, they argued convincingly that they enjoyed perfect health and that they were physically indistinguishable from their fellow men. The case of G., Ph.D. published in 1882, is typical of this group. This man, who had been arrested in Graz on immorality charges while traveling from Italy to Vienna, and who ended up in Krafft-Ebing's clinic, made clear that he did not consider himself a sinner or a patient. On the contrary, he was perfectly happy, especially because he often stayed in Italy where homosexuality was not punishable. "He reports," Krafft-Ebing wrote in G.'s case history, "with great contentment and remarkable cynicism that he has an innate contrary sexual sensitivity. . . . G. refers to his poetic works with great confidence and asserts that people of his mold, without exception, are talented at poetry." Referring to famous predecessors, like Plato, who, according to G., "certainly was not a filthy swine," he even stated that same-sex love was elevating (Krafft-Ebing 1882, 215–216). Similar statements were made by others: "Our love also sprouts the most beautiful, precious blooms, develops all the more precious drives and encourages the mind, as much as the love of a young man for his girl" (Krafft-Ebing 1884, 5). Count Z., whose case history also appeared in 1882, was characterized by Krafft-Ebing as "intellectually well-talented . . . , an open, generous character," and

> neither unhappy about the inversion of his sexual sensitivity, nor capable of recognizing it as unhealthy. He is even less capable of doing so, since he feels morally dignified, happy, and relieved because of the contact with men. How could it be unhealthy, that which makes a man happy and inspires in him beautiful and lofty things! His only misfortune is that social barriers and penal codes stand in the way of "naturally" expressing his drive. This would be a great hardship. (Krafft-Ebing 1882, 213–214)

Written by educated and often cosmopolitan men, some of the autobiographies were full of learned and literary references, philosophical and medical speculations, and detailed self-analysis. The letters also vividly demonstrated a considerable degree of subjective suffering, not so much because of the author's sexual orientation as such, but because of social condemnation, legal persecution, the need to disguise their real nature, and fear of blackmail and loss of social status. Several men stressed that their sexual behavior could not be immoral or pathological because they experienced their sexual desire as "natural." "Since I gave way to my Urning nature, I am happier, healthier, and more productive!" a forty-eight-year-old academic wrote to Krafft-Ebing (1885, 46). Another man, who had been convicted for "unnatural vice," was of the opinion that in a moral sense he was not guilty at all: "I did not offend against nature, a thousand times no, therefore a part of the other guilt falls away from me and onto an antiquated law" (Krafft-Ebing 1884, 4). Krafft-Ebing reported that Count Y., first interviewed in 1882, also "does not feel unhappy with his perverse sexual sensitivity, but the fact that the highest sexual pleasure is denied to him because of social reasons often makes him entirely sad, unhappy, embittered, and increases his neurasthenic troubles" (Krafft-Ebing 1884, 7).

These stories must have touched Krafft-Ebing. In 1884 he introduced an article containing six case histories on contrary sexual feeling with the statement that the task of science was to differentiate disease from immorality. "Scientific research would hereby contribute to the vindication and betterment of the social lot of so many unhappy [men]" (Krafft-Ebing 1884, 1–2). In the introduction to the second edition of *Psychopathia sexualis* (1887), which was newly subtitled "With Especial Reference to the Contrary Sexual Feeling,"[6] he stated that some lawsuits in which the accused had been treated unjustly, had given him occasion to draw special attention to these unhappy "step-children of nature" (Krafft-Ebing 1887, vi, 139). In the chapter on the legal aspects of same-sex behavior, he included a long letter of a highly placed man from London, who criticized Krafft-Ebing for sticking to the opinion that it was an illness:

> Your opinion that the ultimate origin of the phenomenon in question must be attributed in most cases to a congenital "unhealthy" disposition, may, perhaps, make it possible very soon to overcome existing prejudices and to arouse compassion rather than abhorrence and contempt for us poor "sick" men.
>
> Much as I believe that your perspective is most advantageous for us, I am notwithstanding, in the interest of science, unable to accept the word "unhealthy" just like that, and I indulge in giving you some more relevant explications. (Krafft-Ebing 1912, 430)[7]

Psychological suffering was indeed widespread among Urnings, the man continued, but experience had taught him that the cause was not so much their inborn disposition as the legal and social obstacles with which they contended:

> Such a forcible repression of a deeply implanted drive primarily causes, in my humble opinion, the unhealthy phenomena that we can observe in many Urnings, but it is not necessarily a consequence of the Urning's disposition. (Krafft-Ebing 1912, 430)

Similar statements could be found in other case histories and autobiographies. For example, a 50-year-old Belgian Urning wrote to Krafft-Ebing:

> Even though I am an Urning, I cannot admit that my nature is an "unhealthy" [one], otherwise you would also have to classify as unhealthy other entire categories of men who are usually considered normal. . . . Unfortunately, we are considered sick for a completely valid reason, namely, that we really became sick and that one then confuses cause and effect. . . . We certainly become sick, as animals are stricken by rabies if they are prevented from engaging in the sexual act which is adequate to their nature. (Krafft-Ebing 1890b, 129–130)

By publishing such arguments without any additional medical comment, but instead remarking that they strikingly typified the feelings and suffering of Urnings, Krafft-Ebing made a powerful statement for those concerned. In new editions of *Psychopathia sexualis*, he included more and more extensive autobiographies in which Urnings made clear that they did not seek a cure, since it was not their disposition that made them unhappy, but the social condemnation. "He does not want to become another person nor to lose the sweet memories," reported Krafft-Ebing on the outlook of the 42-year-old C. v. Z. "If one suggested he give up men, he would be unhappy. He could not and would not want to 'switch,' because his whole ethics, etc. are developed around this peculiar sexuality" (Krafft-Ebing 1890a, 58). In his elaborate autobiography, a 36-year-old cosmopolitan man insisted:

> I cannot imagine that my condition might appear unnatural, because as far back as I can think I have always felt the same way. . . . I morally suffered a lot, quite a lot,

> not because I recognized my drive as unhealthy, but because of the common contempt we encounter all around us. (Krafft-Ebing 1890a, 55)

Another man, who had found many sexual partners while traveling all over Europe, indicated that the positive points of his experiences—"the mysterious and enchanting temptations this matter offers"—amply outweighed the prohibitions (Krafft-Ebing 1890a, 60–61). Emphasizing that many of his sexual partners were in perfect health and with nerves of steel, he hoped that his confession would give others courage. Some correspondents criticized Krafft-Ebing in no uncertain way for surrounding Uranism with the stigma of pathology. The letter of a 33-year-old man, who had contacted Krafft-Ebing in 1889, was very clear in this regard.

> Your essay "Die conträre Sexualempfindung vor dem Forum" [Considering Contrary Sexual Sensitivity], which I just put down, greatly aroused my interest. It is but a poor attempt at making the abnormal phenomenon (which occurs more often than you know) clear to wider circles and at proving that the actions of the natural drive, even if different from the conventional form, are impossible to punish.
>
> One should not consider the Urning an inferior being, that would be erroneous. Under circumstances, he is the most perfect creation of nature. I know some whose disposition of mind is so noble—unlike that of normal men I have observed. (Krafft-Ebing 1890b, 113–114)

Between 1882 and 1900, Krafft-Ebing published a series of articles on the legal aspects of homosexuality (Krafft-Ebing 1882, 1884, 1885, 1892a, 1892b, 1894, 1900). At first he did not attack the German and Austrian laws criminalizing "unnatural vice" (§ 175 and 129), but only stressed the need to distinguish crime from disease. Although in 1882 he declared that one of his patients, G., Ph.D. (who criticized German and Austrian legislation) showed "incredible cynicism" and was mentally deranged (Krafft-Ebing 1882, 216), a few years later—after having published several autobiographies which showed the harmful effects of penalization—he himself would begin to favor judicial reform. In the early 1890s, Krafft-Ebing put his name to petitions for the abolition of § 175, and he added to *Psychopathia sexualis* that the book should contribute towards changing the law, thus ending the errors and hardships of many centuries. When, at the end of the nineteenth century, homosexuals began to organize protest movements, they referred to Krafft-Ebing as a scientific authority who was on their side,[8] and he indeed supported the homosexual rights movement that was founded in 1897 in Berlin by Magnus Hirschfeld (1868–1935). After he had signed Hirschfeld's petition advocating the abolition of § 175, he admitted in his last article on homosexuality, published in Hirschfeld's *Jahrbuch für sexuelle Zwischenstufen* (Yearbook for Sexual Intermediaries), that the scientific conception of Uranism had been one-sided, and that there was truth to the opinion of many of his homosexual correspondents (Krafft-Ebing 1901). Having referred earlier to the decline of Greece and Rome as warning examples from the past, he now believed that Uranism was not incompatible with mental health or even with intellectual superiority. It was not a pathological phenomenon, but a biological and psychological condition that had to be accepted as a more or less deplorable but natural fate. Focusing less on the sexual acts and more on the relational aspects of sexuality, he also attributed an equal ethical value to same-sex and heterosexual loves.

Science and Humanity

The case histories and autobiographies of Urnings make clear that so-called "perverts" did not play a passive role vis-à-vis the psychiatrist. On the contrary, there is no doubt that Krafft-Ebing's views were influenced by his patients and informants. Not only did Krafft-Ebing delight in scrupulous analysis and in the invention of new categories and subcategories, but also some of his patients were eager to confess the truth about their inner self, and they displayed great diagnostic and classificatory zeal. "I tell everything here, because I want to write only the truth and the whole truth," one of the autobiographers assured Krafft-Ebing. "I hand over these lines to you in the interest of future fellow-sufferers. Publish from it whatever you feel suits the interests of science, truth, and justice" (Krafft-Ebing 1890b, 162–164). A 34-year-old merchant also made clear that in his autobiography he strove for absolute truth:

> Permeated by the conviction that the mystery of our existence can only be solved or at least examined by unprejudiced, thinking men of science, I describe my life solely with the intention that I may contribute to elucidating this cruel error of nature and hereby be useful to comrades in fate of later generations . . . I will strive for the most severe objectivity . . . in my communications. And I note concerning my drastic, often even cynical style, that I want to be true above all and, therefore, I do not avoid strong statements because they characterize the matter I am discussing most strikingly. (Krafft-Ebing 1890b, 189)

A man who sent in an elaborate life history and who, with the help of *Psychopathia sexualis*, had come to the painful conclusion that his anomaly was "a mixture of sadism and masochism, complicated by homosexuality, with fetishistic concomitants," underlined that his confession originated from scrupulous and objective self-observation. "I am always capable of fully imagining myself in the situation and feelings of another as well as I myself can judge accurately and mercilessly from an impartial perspective" (Krafft-Ebing 1912, 165–166).

The active role of several subjects of Krafft-Ebing's case studies in the genesis of his theories suggest that psychiatry enabled the individuals concerned to speak out and be recognized. While Krafft-Ebing's work has been regarded as a cultural defense against the corruption of morals and "decadence" in fin-de-siècle society—and he may have intended it as such—it nevertheless failed to conceal its own tendency to make sexual variance imaginable and to enlarge the sphere allotted to idiosyncratic desires. Although a scientific work intended for physicians and lawyers, *Psychopathia sexualis* probably became a best-seller thanks to laymen interested in the case histories and its pornographic qualities (even if the "offensive" passages were in Latin). In addition to scientific expositions, there were extensive descriptions of sexual experiences, fantasies, erotic temptations and amusements in big cities, examples from history and literature, fragments of semipornographic writings, candid advertisements, and journalistic descriptions of events such as "the Woman-haters Ball" for Urnings in Berlin. Some subjects of case histories made perfectly clear that they knew just where to go to satisfy the perverse desires catalogued by Krafft-Ebing. Specialized forms of prostitution and meeting places had developed in response to new desires. Subcultural pursuits entailed certain roles and a sense of community—"the comfort of belonging together and not being alone anymore"—as one of Krafft-Ebing's correspondents wrote (Krafft-Ebing 1884, 4). A 31-year-old homosexual man, who made clear to Krafft-Ebing that he did not want a cure for his leanings, because they had given him so many "unforgettably lovely hours," claimed: "I could write volumes about my acquaintances, which are over 500" (Krafft-Ebing 1912, 279–280). A German physician who had written a novel about the life of Urnings, was, like others, familiar with the homosexual underground in several cities. "Since I am aware of my abnormal drive, I have come in contact with far more than a thousand men of the same kind. Almost every larger city has some meeting place, as well as a so-called cruising area" (Krafft-Ebing 1912, 288).

By publishing letters and autobiographies and by quoting statements of his patients *ad verbatim*, Krafft-Ebing enabled voices to be heard that were usually silenced. Therefore, medical discourse as represented in his work is characterized by multivocality: one can find different, even contradictory, sets of values in *Psychopathia sexualis*, and the book was open to dialogue and divergent meanings. Evidently, contemporary readers interpreted Krafft-Ebing's work in various ways and, to a large extent, "perverts" gave their own meaning to their sexual feelings and experiences. For several of them the book was clearly the impetus to self-awareness and self-expression. Some of the autobiographers took the opportunity to give expression to their criticism of current social norms and even those of the medical profession. For example, a highly placed German civil servant—who sent in not only an autobiography but also a carefully detailed criticism of § 175—concluded that this law was based on prejudice and ignorance. Same-sex love was no sin or crime, but part of nature, and medical scientists had the duty to enlighten the general public (Krafft-Ebing 1892b). Even more self-assured and militant was a 22-year-old medical student whose autobiography appeared in 1890:

> I intentionally and consciously condemn contemporary moral standards, which force sexually abnormal people to offend against arbitrary laws. And I think that sexual contact between two people of the same sex is at their individual discretion, without the legislator having any right to object. . . . I only yearn for a time, when I can pursue the same [sexual contact] in a more comfortable way and with less danger of

being discovered, in order to give myself a pleasure that does not harm anyone. (Krafft-Ebing 1890a, 63, 66)

A 48-year-old doctor's autobiography—thirteen pages of small print regularly republished in *Psychopathia sexualis*—was also outstanding because of its criticism of the medical profession. Through his life story this man explained that he had always felt like a woman. In a letter accompanying his autobiography, he advocated that women should be allowed to study medicine, because they showed more intuition than men:

> Finally, I wanted to present you with the results of my recollections and reflections to prove that one can be a doctor given female feeling and thinking. I think it a great injustice that medicine is closed to women. A woman discovers the traces of many maladies through her intuition, while a man gropes in the dark despite diagnostics, at least for women's and children's diseases. If I could make it happen, every doctor would have to undergo a quarter year of femininity. He would have more understanding and more respect for the side of humanity, from which he descended. He would respect women's greatness of mind, and at the same time also the hardness of their fate. (Krafft-Ebing 1890a, 79)

The impact of Krafft-Ebing's medical work was multifaceted: it served not only as a guide for professionals, but also as a mouthpiece and panel for the individuals concerned. To a certain extent, they used psychiatry for their own purposes; for example, the psychiatric concept of hereditary causes was used by homosexual men to argue that their leanings were part of nature, and therefore immutable. The medical model of drives (*Triebe*) suggested that (male) sexuality was a forceful instinct, that had to be released in some way; therefore, many of them argued that their sexual behavior was inevitable and had to be condoned. "Perverts" began to speak for themselves, and they were looking for models with which to identify. Despite the medical bias, many case histories in *Psychopathia sexualis* served as go-betweens, linking painful individual introspection—the self-conscious recognition that one is a deviant kind of person—and social identification—the comforting sense of belonging to a community of like-minded people (see Hansen 1992, 109). Because Krafft-Ebing distinguished himself as an expert who had taken a stand against traditional moral-religious and legal denunciations of sexual deviance, individuals approached him to find understanding, acceptance, and support—as a fragment from a letter by a Belgian Urning to Krafft-Ebing clearly illustrates:

> You will be able to appreciate what it means to lock forever within myself that which touches me by far the deepest, and of not being able to confide in anybody. . . . You are the first to whom I open my heart. Use this letter in any way; maybe one day it will help lighten the fate of future men to whom nature gives the same feelings. (Krafft-Ebing 1890b, 135)

Another Urning, who regretted that he had not read *Psychopathia sexualis* earlier in his life, because this would have prevented a lot of misery, confided to Krafft-Ebing:

> Nobody knows my true nature,—only you, a stranger, you alone know me now, indeed in a more detailed way than father or mother, friend, wife, or [male] lover. It is a real comfort to me to expose, this once, the heavy secret of my own nature. (Krafft-Ebing 1890a, 152)

Krafft-Ebing's humanitarian rhetoric had some real effect. Letters indicate that he had a good relationship with many of his upper-class patients. In a way, they cooperated: "perverts" who wanted to make their voices heard in public depended on sympathetic physicians like Krafft-Ebing because medical science was the only respectable forum available. In turn, Krafft-Ebing had to rely on the confessions of the individuals concerned to validate empirically his theory of sexual pathology. Within the moral climate of his time, Krafft-Ebing showed some open-mindedness and pragmatism. It is true that he experimented with hypnosis to cure perversion, but in general he seems to have applied this remedy only when patients asked for it. Moreover, the endeavor to find a cure for perversions was still of marginal importance in psychiatry then, and Krafft-Ebing (1899) made clear that in the case of inborn perversions a cure was not likely. In fact, many patients did not need a medical cure, because pouring out one's heart was therapeutic in itself. Writing their life history, giving coherence and intelligibility to their torn self, might result in a "catharsis" of comprehension. Evidently, many homosexuals viewed Krafft-Ebing not simply as a doctor treating diseases, but also as an ally embodying an ideal of science as a means for improving their lot. "I recently saw . . . your book *Psychopathia sexualis*," one of them informed Krafft-Ebing:

> I saw from it that you ponder and research without prejudice in the interest of science and humanity. Although I cannot convey much new material to you, I still want to talk about some matters, that you may kindly accept as another contribution to your work, and which I trustingly lay in your hands for our social preservation. (Krafft-Ebing 1890b, 161)

Sexuality and the Narrative of Self

Medical theories such as Krafft-Ebing's have played an important role in the making of sexual categories and identities. However, his sexual pathology was not shaped systematically by the logic of medical science exclusively, and neither was it simply a means of stigmatizing and controlling deviants. Medicalization has to be viewed as a process in which new meanings were attached to existing behaviors and feelings. These new meanings were developed with the collaboration of some of the people concerned as they furnished psychiatrists with the life stories and experiences upon which medical interpretations were grounded. Many of the case reports and autobiographies suggest that new ways of understanding sexuality emerged from a confrontation of medical thinking and individual self-definition. By facilitating greater recognition and discussion of homosexuals, psychiatric accounts did not simply encourage medical treatment, restraint, and repression, but also offered a space in which sexual desire could be articulated in the form of autobiographical narrative. A self-conscious homosexual identity and a sense of community clearly evolved in well-educated, urban, and often cosmopolitan bourgeois and aristocratic circles. Medical knowledge of sexuality could only be successful because it was embedded in society: psychiatrists like Krafft-Ebing and his patients shared the same cultural background and the same bourgeois values.

Both Krafft-Ebing's psychiatric explanations and the (auto)biographical case reports he used as empirical material reflected as well as shaped sexual experiences. In his work, sexuality was not just a biological instinct unmediated by experience. On the contrary, because sexuality played a core part in the narration of self, and because perverse desire was linked to individual identity, it was burdened with significance. The interpretation of the self, as narrated by patients and informants in the form of life histories, was crucial in the development of Krafft-Ebing's sexual pathology. The scientific "will to know" moved forward at the same pace as concern for the authentic and voluble self in late nineteenth-century bourgeois society, particularly in Austria.[9] With the differentiation of the public from the domestic, a sphere of intimacy and privacy had emerged: individual authenticity became a preeminent value and a framework for introspection, self-contemplation, and self-expression. The rise of sexual pathology in psychiatry only magnified the effects of this need for self-comprehension.

It is difficult to ascertain whether the autobiographical accounts of Krafft-Ebing's patients and correspondents are "true" pictures of their lives, in the sense that their stories correspond to the actual events in their lives. Rather than viewing autobiograpies as representations of lives as they have been lived, these life stories should be seen as a particular way people gave meaning to their condition and (re)constructed their selves. They appealed to ideals of authenticity and sincerity to bestow moral value on their sexual identity. However, what was presented as an intricate process of self-discovery was in fact a process of self-creation. Neither scientific nor individual meanings of the sexual self should be considered as reflections of an internal, psychological reality. The way people experienced sexuality and gave meaning to it was determined not so much by given natural or psychological facts, but by cultural codes and symbols as they functioned in social life. Above all, homosexual identity as expressed in Krafft-Ebing's work presumed reflexive awareness, an ability to interrogate the past from the perspective of the present, and to tell a coherent story about one's life history in the light of what might be anticipated for the future. The order autobiographers gave to the facts of their lives is not inherent in them but necessarily of their own devising in order to serve certain needs in the present. Many of Krafft-Ebing's patients had fully developed a sense of themselves as objects of introspection, the more so because they were obliged to keep up appearances in a society in which they felt not well-suited, and because they suffered from their inability to communicate with others about their inner nature—their real self.

Homosexual identity crystallized in patterned narratives, and as such, its content and form were of a social rather than of a psychological origin. It did not appear as a distinctive personal trait or essence, but as a script on which individuals modeled their life history. The psychiatric case history pre-eminently offered a fitting model for self-understanding. In case reports and autobiographies published by Krafft-Ebing, the same elements recur of what was to become a standard "coming-out" narrative: ancestry, family background, the retrospective discovery of a peculiar way of feeling and acting during childhood and puberty, the conviction that one has always felt the same, the first sexual experiences, the struggle with masturbation (which often raised more anxieties than sexual contacts with other individuals did), details about sexual fantasies, dreams, and behavior, the exploration of one's health condition and gender identity in the past and present, the sense of being overwhelmed by irresistible and "natural" drives for which one is not responsible, the (mostly failed) attempts to have "normal" sexual intercourse (usually with a prostitute) in order to "test" the constitutional character of one's sexual preference, the painful knowledge of being different and in conflict with society, the comforting discovery of not being alone, and the endeavor for moral self-justification (compare with Müller 1991, 208–230).

The linking of sexuality with privacy and intimacy and the constitution of desire as the clue to the inner self were not so much a concealment from public view as a reconstitution of the function of sexuality. Anthony Giddens and Niklas Luhmann have explained this change in the experience of sexuality as a consequence of modernity, which Luhmann associates with "functional differentiation" and Giddens with, among other characteristics, increasing "institutional reflexivity," "the regularized use of knowledge about circumstances of social life as a constitutive element in its organization and transformation" (Giddens 1991, 20; compare Giddens 1992; Luhmann 1982). While sexuality as a function of social behavior hardly had a distinct existence before the nineteenth century, the "sequestration of experience" in modern society entailed the increasing dissociation of sexuality from fixed, putatively "natural" patterns of behavior. As a consequence of the rise of the ideal of romantic love, sexuality was gradually differentiated from a transcendental moral order and from its traditional instrumental integration with reproduction, kinship, and social and economic necessities. In the context of romantic love and privacy, sexuality became a separate sphere in human life. To explain changes in (homo)sexual practices and experiences, not only must developments in medical science be taken into account but also changes in the wider social context. Homosexuality as an individual property is only conceivable in a society in which same-sex bonding is not taken for granted any longer, and more or less casual sexuality between men or between women are viewed as short-term diversions from family roles. With the upgrading of romantic love as the foundation of marriage, physical as well as emotional intimacy were exclusively associated with heterosexual bonds. However, the emergence of "perversions" reveals that, in modern experience, human purposes of sexuality began to spread across alternative meanings. The emergence of a separate sexual domain in society, in turn, created the possibility for medical science to define sexuality as a distinct impulse—the sixth, genital sense, as Krafft-Ebing named this instinct—and to discover its internal physical and psychological laws.

Medical explanations of sexuality took shape at the same time as the experience of sexuality in society was transformed and it became a subject for introspection and obsessive self-scrutiny in bourgeois milieux. "The dull drive became conscious perversity," Krafft-Ebing cited one of his female patients as saying (1912, 314); such self-consciousness—shared by many individuals who read his work—was not only facilitated by his psychiatry, but also presumed a "modern" reflexive awareness among individuals in society. Since the modern reflexive project of the self had to be undertaken in the absence of traditional social routines or moral certainties, self-contemplation was a cause for anxiety and uneasiness. Nevertheless, as many of Krafft-Ebing's case histories illustrate, it also created some space for individuality and self-expression.

Krafft-Ebing's sexual pathology reflected the anxieties and the inconsistencies around sexuality in fin-de-siècle culture, especially the bourgeois preoccupation with its dangers and pleasures (compare Birken 1988; Showalter 1991; Eder 1990). His approach fluctuated between the stigmatization of sexual variations as mental illness and the recognition of individuals' particular and unique desires. The way several of his patients and informants read his work illustrates that the sexual domain became a contested field and that it was but one step from the admission of the individual's right to sexual fulfillment. Krafft-Ebing's model of sexuality tended to center on desire instead of reproduction, and many subjects of his case histories appeared as sexual consumers: they were more or less able to pursue their sexual desires as part of a lifestyle. Marking a transition in the urban bourgeois milieu from an ethos of Christianity and productivity (which dictated self-discipline and control of the passions) to a consumerist culture of abundance (which valued the satisfaction of individual desire), *Psychopathia sexualis* was caught in its own contradictory structure. Modern sexuality was suspended between the absolutism of the dichotomy between the normal and the abnormal on the one hand, and the increasing relativization of variance on the other.

Notes

1 Freiherr von R. to Richard von Krafft-Ebing, July 1900. Krafft-Ebing Estate. All original German quotations have been translated by Robert Grimm and Vernon Rosario.

2 Krafft-Ebing's estate is part of the private archive of the Krafft-Ebing family in Graz, Austria.

3 For the so-called essentialist-constructionist controversy, see Stein 1990, Weeks 1985, and Greenberg 1988.

4 On the development of medical sexology, see: Wettley and Leibbrand 1959; Foucault 1976; Lanteri-Laura 1979; Sulloway 1979, 277–319; Weeks 1981 and 1985; Davidson 1987 and 1990; Birken 1988; Greenberg 1988, 397–433; Hekma 1987 and 1989; Bullough 1994.

5 The relative invisibility of women's voices might be explained by the fact that in Germany and Austria a self-defined lesbian identity and subculture did not emerge until the 1920s. See Hacker and Lang 1986, 13–17.

6 The original German subtitle is "Mit besonderer Berücksichtigung der konträren Sexualempfindung," which was rendered in the English translation of *Psychopathia Sexualis* as "With Especial Reference to the Antipathic Sexual Instinct" (Krafft-Ebing 1965).

7 [Robert Grimm's translation note: It is difficult to convey the connotative difference between *krank/Krankheit* versus *krankhaft/Krankhaftigkeit*. The former indicates the state of sickness or disease, while the latter suggests the *mental state* of illness—see Friedrich Köhler's *Dictionary of the English and German Languages*, Third Edition (Leipzig: Verlag von Philip Reclam, 1865). While this distinction is important in the German nineteenth-century literature on sexual perversions, it is difficult to translate; therefore, I have used *sick* or *ill* for *krank*, and *unhealthy* for *krankhaft*.]

8 See *Aufruf an alle gebildeten und edelgesinnten Menschen!*, published in 1899 by the Berlin-based "Comité für Befreiung der Homosexualen vom Strafgesetz." Krafft-Ebing Estate.

9 Cf. Perrot 1990, 453–667; Le Rider 1993; Schorske 1981; Worbs 1983.

References

Birken, Lawrence. 1988. *Consuming Desire. Sexual Science and the Emergence of a Culture of Abundance, 1871–1914*. Ithaca: Cornell University Press.

Brecher, E. M. 1969. *The Sex Researchers*. Boston: Little, Brown.

Bullough, Vern L. 1994. *Science in the Bedroom. A History of Sex Research*. New York: Basic Books.

Davidson, Arnold. 1987. Sex and the emergence of sexuality. *Critical Inquiry* 14:16–48.

———. 1990. Closing up the corpses: Diseases of sexuality and the emergence of the psychiatric style of reasoning. In *Meaning and Method: Essays in Honor of Hilary Putnam*, ed. G. Boolos. Cambridge: Cambridge University Press.

Eder, Franz X. 1990. Erotisierendes Wissen. Zur Geschichte der "Sexualisierung" im Wiener Fin de Siècle. In *Erotik, Versuch einer Annäherung. Ausstellungskatalog des Historischen Museums der Stadt Wien*, 20–28. Vienna.

Foucault, Michel. 1976. *Histoire de la sexualité I. La volonté de savoir*. Paris: Gallimard.

Gay, Peter. 1988. *Freud. A Life for Our Time*. New York: Norton.

Giddens, Anthony. 1991. *Modernity and Self-Identity. Self and Society in the Late Modern Age*. Cambridge: Polity Press.

———. 1992. *The Transformation of Intimacy. Sexuality, Love and Eroticism in Modern Times*. Cambridge: Polity Press.

Greenberg, David F. 1988. *The Construction of Homosexuality*. Chicago: University of Chicago Press.

Hacker, Hanna, and Manfred Lang. 1986. Jenseits der Geschlechter, zwischen ihnen. In *Das lila Wien um 1900*, ed. Neda Bei et al., 8–18. Vienna: Promedia.

Hansen, Bert. 1992. American physicians' "discovery" of homosexuals, 1880–1900: A new diagnosis in a changing society. In *Framing Disease. Studies in Cultural History*, ed. Charles E. Rosenberg and Janet Golden, 104–133. New Brunswick, NJ: Rutgers University Press.

Hauser, Renate I. 1992. Sexuality, neurasthenia and the law: Richard von Krafft-Ebing (1840–1902). Ph.D. diss., University of London.

Hekma, Gert. 1987. *Homoseksualiteit, een medische reputatie. De uitdoktering van de homoseksueel in negentiende-eeuws Nederland.* Amsterdam: Sua.

———. 1989. A history of sexology. Social and historical aspects of sexuality. In *From Sappho to De Sade. Moments in the History of Sexuality*, ed. Jan Bremmer, 173–193. London: Routledge.

Krafft-Ebing, Richard von, Estate of (Nachlass Richard von Krafft-Ebing). Private Krafft-Ebing Family archives, Graz, Austria.

———. 1877. Über gewisse Anomalien des Geschlechtstriebs und die klinisch-forensische Verwerthung derselben als eines wahrscheinlich functionellen Degenerationszeichens des centralen Nervensystems. *Archiv für Psychiatrie und Nervenkrankheiten* 7:291–312.

———. 1879. *Lehrbuch der gerichtlichen Psychopathologie mit Berücksichtigung der Gesetzgebung von Österreich, Deutschland und Frankreich.* Stuttgart: Enke.

———. 1879–1880. *Lehrbuch der Psychiatrie auf klinischer Grundlage für practische Ärzte und Studierende.* Stuttgart: Enke.

———. 1882. Zur "conträren Sexualempfindung" in klinisch-forensischer Hinsicht. *Allgemeine Zeitschrift für Psychiatrie* 38:211–227.

———. 1884. Zur Lehre von der conträren Sexualempfindung. *Irrenfreund* 26:1–14.

———. 1885. Die conträre Sexualempfindung vor dem Forum. *Jahrbücher für Psychiatrie und forensische Psychologie* 6:34–47.

———. 1886. *Psychopathia sexualis. Eine klinisch-forensische Studie.* 1st edition. Stuttgart: Enke.

———. 1887 and 1890b. *Psychopathia sexualis. Mit besonderer Berücksichtigung der konträren Sexualempfindung.* 2nd and 5th editions. Stuttgart: Enke.

———. 1890a. *Neue Forschungen auf dem Gebiete der Psychopathia sexualis. Eine medizinisch-psychologische Studie.* Stuttgart: Enke.

———. 1892a. Epiloge zu: Par. 175 des deutschen Strafgesetzbuches und die Urningsliebe Von Dr. iur. xxx. *Zeitschrift für die gesammte Strafrechtswissenschaft* 12:34–54.

———. 1892b. Zur conträren Sexualempfindung. Autobiographie und strafrechtliche Betrachtungen von einem conträr Sexualen. *Wiener Medizinische Blätter* 15(1): 7–9; 15(3): 42–44.

———. 1894. *Der Conträrsexuale vor dem Strafrichter. De sodomia ratione sexus punienda. De lege lata et de lege ferenda. Eine Denkschrift.* Leipzig and Vienna: Franz Deuticke.

———. 1899. Introduction to *Therapie der Anomalien Vita sexualis bei Männern. Mit specieller Berüchsichtigung der Suggestivbehandlung*, by Alfred Fuchs. Stuttgart: Enke.

———. 1900. Drei Conträrsexuale vor Gericht. *Jahrbücher für Psychiatrie und Neurologie* 19:262–282.

———. 1901. Neue Studien auf dem Gebiete der Homosexualität. *Jahrbuch für sexuelle Zwischenstufen* 3:1–36.

———. 1912. *Psychopathia sexualis. Mit besonderer Berücksichtigung der konträren Sexualempfindung. Eine medizinisch-gerichtliche Studie für Ärzte und Juristen.* 14th edition. Stuttgart: Enke. Photo-reprint, Munich: Matthes & Seitz, 1984.

———. 1965. *Psychopathia Sexualis. With Especial Reference to the Antipathic Sexual Instinct.* Trans. Franklin S. Klaf, from the 12th edition (1903). New York: Bell Publishing.

Lanteri-Laura, Georges. 1979. *La lecture des perversions. Histoire de leur appropriation médicale.* Paris: Masson.

Le Rider, Jacques. 1993. *Modernity and the Crisis of Identity. Culture and Society in Fin-de-Siècle Vienna.* Cambridge: Polity Press.

Luhmann, Niklas. 1982. *Liebe als Passion. Zur Codierung von Intimität.* Frankfurt: Suhrkamp Verlag.

Müller, Klaus. 1991. *Aber in meinem Herzen sprach eine Stimme so laut. Homosexuelle Autobiographien und medizinische Pathographien im neunzehnten Jahrhundert.* Berlin: Verlag rosa Winkel.

Perrot, Michelle, ed. 1990. *A History of Private Life. IV. From the Fires of Revolution to the Great War.* Cambridge: Harvard University Press.

Schorske, Carl. 1981. *Fin-de-Siècle Vienna: Politics and Culture.* New York: Vintage.

Showalter, Elaine. 1991. *Sexual Anarchy. Gender and Culture at the Fin de Siècle.* London: Bloomsbury.

Stein, Edward, ed. 1990. *Forms of Desire. Sexual Orientation and the Social Constructionist Controversy.* New York: Garland.

Sulloway, Frank J. 1979. *Freud, Biologist of the Mind. Beyond the Psychoanalytic Legend.* New York: Basic Books.

Szasz, Thomas. 1980. *Sex by Prescription.* Garden City, NY: Anchor Press/Doubleday.

Weeks, Jeffrey. 1981. *Sex, Politics and Society. The Regulation of Sexuality since 1800.* London: Longman.

———. 1985. *Sexuality and Its Discontents. Meaning, Myths and Modern Sexualities.* London: Routledge and Kegan Paul.

Wettley, Annemarie, and Werner Leibbrand. 1959. *Von der 'Psychopathia sexualis' zur Sexualwissenschaft.* Stuttgart: Enke.

Worbs, Michael. 1983. *Nervenkunst. Literatur und Psychoanalyse im Wien der Jahrhundertwende.* Frankfurt: Europäische Verlagsanstalt.

Inversion's Histories | History's Inversions
Novelizing Fin-de-Siècle Homosexuality

Vernon A. Rosario

> *Monsieur Emile Zola, Paris*
>
> It is to you, Monsieur, who are the greatest novelist of our time and who, with the eye of the savant and the artist, capture and paint so powerfully *all* the failings, all the shame, all the ills that afflict humanity that I send these *human documents* so cherished by the cultivated people of our age.
>
> This confession, which no spiritual advisor has ever learned from my lips, will reveal to you a frightful illness of the soul, a rare case—if not, unfortunately, unique—that has been studied by learned psychologists, but which till now no novelist has dared to stage in a literary work.[1]

So opens a truly unique "human document" of the late 1880s: a bundle of letters and postcards mailed to Emile Zola by a 23-year-old Italian aristocrat. In florid, raunchy detail exuding hubris and shame, the young man recounts his full sexual history: from his early cross-dressing experiences and masturbatory addiction, through to the feverish evolution of his "frightful illness," *an erotic passion for men.* He notes that Zola had briefly referred to the "horrid vice that dishonors humanity" in the person of Baptiste, the groom-loving valet in *La Curée*, but that was a matter of debauchery, not love, the Italian complains: "It is a purely material thing, a question of conformation, which doctors have more than once observed and described. All of that is very *common* and terribly *disgusting* and has nothing to do with the confession which I send you and which may perhaps serve you in some way" (1894, 212).

The young man's aim is to provide an abundance of authentic documentation so that his unusual "deviation" might be represented more extensively and candidly by Zola (1840–1902)—the inventor of the "experimental novel"—who had declared that "the dream of the physiologist and the experimental doctor is also that of the novelist who applies [Claude Bernard's] experimental method to the natural and social study of man" ([1880], 1188). Zola's image as paternal doctor clearly seduced the young Italian, for he wrote, "Please forgive my horrible scribble, but I [write] with my heart on my sleeve, as if I were confessing to a doctor or a friend, and I have not paid attention to the form or the spelling" (Invert 1895, 231).

As it turned out, Zola's mysterious correspondent was indeed confessing to a doctor, in fact, to the whole community of doctors who read the French *Archives of Criminal Anthropology, Criminology, and Normal and Pathological Psychology* where his letters were first published in 1894–1895. What was an erotic confession doing in a medical journal, and how did a novelist, Zola, make such a contribution? In addressing these questions, I will show how the construction of *inversion* and *homosexuality* in fin-de-siècle France was a broad literary and cultural affair beyond the professional confines of medical texts and knowledge.

The importance of late-nineteenth-century medical science in constructing *homosexuality* has been well documented (Foucault 1976; Greenberg 1988; Chauncey 1982–83; Lanteri-Laura 1979). This essay focuses on the significant role of *belles-lettristes*—both medical professionals and scientific dilettantes—in shaping the medical discourse. Some writers, such as Marc-André Raffalovich, were engaged in more or less explicit self-representation and defense of *inversion*. Others, such as Emile Zola and J.-K. Huysmans, were concerned with condemning the epidemic of "perversity." Apologists and censors both argued for the power of fiction in shaping disciplinary knowledges, social stereotypes, and intimate experiences of *inversion*. The ætiology of *homosexuality*—whether it was a product of *biological* "degeneration" or of *social* decay—was of concern to these medical and nonmedical writers who, even as they argued for the congenital "nature" of "inversion of the genital sense," erected novel ontological structures out of old materials and new historical experiences.[2] The oldest association was with *sodomy* (any non–phallo-vaginal sex),[3] but French neurologists of the late nineteenth century recharacterized same-sex passion within a novel narrative of hysterical gender delusion and fictional excess.

Effeminate Sodomites and Novel Hysterics

Ambroise Tardieu (1818–1879) made his fame in forensic medicine with the publication of his *Medico-Legal Study of Crimes Against Public Morals* (1857) in which he described how to identify positively both active and passive sodomites by the anatomical peculiarities of their penises and anuses (Aron & Kempf 1984, 47–52). Tardieu was equally preoccupied with the behavioral deviance of pederasts or sodomites (he used the terms interchangeably). He sketched the following image to illustrate the effeminate façade and psyche of the typical pederast:

> Curled hair, made-up skin, open collar, waist tucked in to highlight the figure; fingers, ears, chest loaded with jewelry, the whole body exuding an odor of the most penetrating perfumes, and in the hand a handkerchief, flowers, or some needlework: such is the strange, revolting and rightfully suspect

physiognomy of the pederast. . . . Hairstyles and dress constitute one of the most constant preoccupations of pederasts. (Tardieu [1857], 216–217)

The physicians who began to describe same-sex erotic attraction in the late 1860s did not equate this *new* phenomenon with the old category of *sodomy* as Tardieu had represented it. For example, neurologist Wilhelm Griesinger (1817–1869) published his observations under the title "On a *Little-Known* Psychopathological State" (1868–69; emphasis added). Other German writers scrambled for an appellation. The Hannoverian lawyer Karl Heinrich Ulrichs (1825–1895), under the pseudonym Numa Numantius, suggested "Urningen" to describe those with female souls caught in a male body (see Kennedy in this volume). Dr. Karl Westphal (1833–1890), editor of the German *Archives of Psychiatry and Nervous Diseases*, proposed the name *conträre Sexualempfindung* (contrary sexual sensation) (1869). In a historical review of the condition, Dr. Richard von Krafft-Ebing (1840–1902) was able to identify only seventeen such cases in all the medical literature through 1877. Given the German dominance of the field, it is no wonder that a French medico-moral novella of 1896 on wicked inverts was subtitled *The German Vice*.[4]

Not to be left out of this hot, new, research agenda, the French entered the arena led by two prominent neurologists: Jean-Martin Charcot (1825–1893) and Valentin Magnan (1835–1916). They were the first to introduce *inversion sexuelle* into French along with their description of the first French invert: a man whose imagination from the age of six was inflamed by the image of naked men. Like the Italian, this French invert had no sensual interest in women, but loved women's clothes and wished he were female so he might dress in ladies' garments—which he confessed he did on occasion. Charcot and Magnan exclaimed, "This patient, what is he?" (1882, 56).

In keeping with the dominant hereditarian, degenerationist theories of the time,[5] they agreed with the Germans that these were cases of psychopathological degeneration, but they rejected the German notion that inverts suffered from gender discordancy between their psyches and their bodies (often called "psychosexual hermaphroditism"). No, Charcot and Magnan argued, inverts were neuro-degenerates of the hysterical kind, and did not differ much from those patients with erotic penchants for boots, buttocks, or bonnets—attractions that would later be labeled *erotic fetishes* by Binet (1887). The invert simply had a delusional attraction to *human* objects of the same sex (Charcot & Magnan 1882, 321–322).

Although Charcot and Magnan tried to portray "inversion of the genital sense" as a new nosological entity, the diagnosis was actually a new hybrid of the older medical descriptions of the sodomite and the male hysteric.[6] The construction of the hysterical male in France in the 1870s (the decade when German physicians were uncovering *contrary sexual sensation*) is particularly interesting because of the numerous associations made between these patients' symptoms and perverse literary production.

Hysteria in the male (although semantically an oxymoron) developed as a credible diagnosis in the nineteenth century because hysteria was increasingly believed to be a neuropsychiatric disorder and not a disease of the uterus (*hystera* in Greek) (Veith 1965;

Micale 1990, 1995). Nonetheless, hysterics of either sex were portrayed as exhibiting characteristics traditionally associated with "femininity": excessive emotionality, hyperexcitability, and impressionability. Furthermore, male hysterics were regularly found to demonstrate physical stigmata of "*féminisme*" (sparse beard, delicate complexions, fine hair, weak constitutions, and underdeveloped genitals) as well as familial histories of degeneration—in particular, hysterical mothers. For example, Paul Fabre, physician at the Vaucluse asylum, noted that "the individuals stricken by this neurosis [male hysteria] offer certain psychological and physical analogies that seem to distance them from the sex to which they belong, to direct them to a new sex, so to speak, whose neutrality [that is, indifference to sex with women] and exaggerated impressionability are the principle attributes" (1875, 365). To illustrate this, he described the case of Mr. X. . . , a "man of letters" whose character "resembles in many ways that of a woman; despite an entirely virile exterior appearance, he cries and laughs easily depending on the circumstances; emotions have the greatest influence on him" (Fabre 1875, 363).

Mr. X. . . , the hysterical writer, was in good company, since novelist Gustave Flaubert (1821–1880) also bore the diagnosis of hysteria.[7] Flaubert wrote to George Sand complaining about his isolation in Croisset:

> The sensibility is unduly exalted in such a milieu. I suffer palpitations for no reason, rather understandable, all told, in an old hysteric like myself. For I maintain that men are hysterical like women and that I am one. When I wrote *Salammbô*, I read "the best authors" on the matter and I recognized all my symptoms. I have the ball [*globus hystericus*] and the nail in the occiput. ([January 12–13, 1867] 1980–91, III:592)

He later wrote to Mme. Roger des Genettes, "Dr. Hardy . . . calls me a hysterical old woman. 'Doctor,' I tell him, 'you are perfectly right'" ([May 1, 1874] 1926–54, 7:134). To his longtime friend, Marie-Sophie Leroyer de Chantepie, he similarly wrote that he had the *nervous irritability* of a kept woman ([March 18, 1857] 1980–91, II:692).

The diagnosis of hysteria stuck to Flaubert even into the twentieth century, when René Dumesnil (editor of the Pléiade edition of Flaubert's works) retrospectively examined Flaubert with the intention of dispelling persistent rumors that the novelist had been epileptic, sexually frigid, and *afraid of women* (Dumesnil 1905, 88). Dumesnil determined—supposedly in Flaubert's defense—that the novelist's nervous crises were the product of "epileptoid hysteria with a strong neuropathic tendency" (94). Flaubert's superior literary abilities could thus be attributed to his neurodegeneracy since "his mania for analysis is pushed to exaggeration, and this is a trait common to all intellectual neuroses and superior mentality" (95). The excessive imaginativeness and hypersensibility of the hystero-epileptic placed Flaubert on the dangerous edge between insanity and literary genius. Fortunately, as the son of the Physician-in-Chief of the Rouen Hôtel-Dieu, Flaubert was endowed with a medical mentality and steely surgical style that prevented him from falling into the abyss (148). Reproducing Third Republic physicians' penchant for degenerationist, hereditary mechanisms of psychopathology, Dumesnil concluded that Flaubert united the ardent imagination and romantic character inherited from his mother with the superior intelligence and scientific spirit of his father, the physician (317).

The image of Flaubert as hysteric was most evident in his first novel, *Madame Bovary* (1856). Baudelaire (1821–1867), in a review of the novel, had even declared that Emma was the female incarnation of Flaubert, and inversely that, "despite all his zeal as an actor,"

> [Flaubert] was unable not to infuse virile blood into the veins of his creature, and that Madame Bovary—for all the energy and ambition she may have in her, and also her dreaminess—Madame Bovary remains a man. Like armed Pallas [Athena], springing from the brain of Zeus, that bizarre androgyne has kept all the seductions of a virile soul in a charming feminine body. (Baudelaire [1857] 652)

The representational brilliance produced by hysterical gender inversion may have seemed like the ultimate in literary genius to Baudelaire, but contemporary physicians were far more wary of the novels of hysterics.

Dr. Ernest Lasègue (1816–1883), in an article on "Hysterics, Their Perversity, Their Lies" (1881), warned colleagues against the willful malevolence and irresistible deceitfulness of the hysteric's imagination. Hysterics and lunatics both told untrue stories, Lasègue noted, but the great danger was that "the latter are unbelievable, whereas *the novels of hysterics* impose themselves by their verisimilitude" (1881, 114; emphasis added). The same principle could be applied more broadly, he observed:

> Do we not have something analogous in the wide field of human inventions? This is the novelist who, commencing with a premise furnished by the imagination, allows himself to be led by this to the point of believing that everything he creates actually happened. (Lasègue 1881, 112)

The novels of hysterics and hysterical novelists would seem to collapse into the same category remarkable for their hypersensibility, over-imaginativeness, deceitfulness, and self-delusion. The same characteristics would hold true of the novels and lives of inverts—those literate fin-de-siècle perverts such as the Italian dandy. Following Lasègue's warnings concerning hysterics, physicians cautioned against the seductions of inverts' narrative productions and these stories' ability to pervert society.

Science, Inverts, and the Flaming Truth

> Whenever my nurse sees me, she always tells me that all the women she knows had named me *the little Madonna*, I was so cute and delicate. . . . I still recall the shiver of joy and pleasure that coursed through my little per-

> son when I went out in my little puffed-up blue piqué dress with blue bows and my big Italian straw hat.
>
> When I was four, they took away my little dresses to put me in trousers and a little jacket. Once they had dressed me as a boy, I experienced profound shame—I remember it as if it were today—and I quickly ran to my nanny's room to hide and cry; to console me, she had to dress me again as a girl. They still laugh whenever recalling my cries of despair in seeing them take away those little white dresses which were my greatest joy.
>
> It seemed as if they were taking away something that I was always destined to wear.
>
> That was my first great sorrow. (Invert 1894, 215)

Zola was impressed by the Italian invert's confessions of effeminacy and same-sex passion, and felt the subject was extremely important. "I was struck by the great physiological and social interest [the confession] offered," Zola wrote, "It touched me by its absolute sincerity, because one senses the flame, I would even say the eloquence of truth. . . . It is a total, naïve, spontaneous confession that very few men would dare make, qualities that render it quite precious from many points of view" (1896, 1). He hoped that its publication might inspire some pity for these "unfortunates," but he found it impossible to utilize the manuscript in his own fiction.

"With each new novel of Zola's," the Italian invert later wrote, "I hoped to finally discover a character who was the reproduction of myself, but I was always disappointed and I was finally convinced that the writer had lacked the *courage* to stage so terrible a passion" (qtd. in Saint-Paul 1930, 115). Zola was hardly one to shy away from controversy. Even before the Dreyfus Affair and his famous essay, "J'accuse!" (1898), his naturalist novels had been condemned for their vulgarity, sensuality, and morbidness. Some of Zola's harshest literary critics were those people he claimed as his colleagues—physicians, who nevertheless considered him a "scientific dilettante." Like Flaubert before him, Zola had been deemed a pathological writer and had been "diagnosed" as an epileptoid degenerate, a "superior degenerate," an olfactory fetishist, and a sexual psychopath (Toulouse 1896; Nordau 1894–95, II:456). Yet Zola had persisted in dramatizing the great spectrum of physical and moral degenerations: alcoholism, prostitution, monomania, adultery, and homicide. Therefore, Zola's literary impotence on the topic of inversion is quite revealing. He could never have edited the Italian's manuscript, he confessed, because:

> I was then in the roughest hours of my literary battle; critics treated me daily as a criminal capable of all vices and all debaucheries. . . . First of all they would have accused me of entirely *inventing* the story from personal corruption. Then I would have been duly condemned for merely having seen in the affair an occasion for base speculation on the most repugnant instincts. And what a clamor if I had permitted myself to say that no other subject is more serious or more tragic; that it is a far more common and

> deep wound than pretended and that still the best thing for healing wounds is to study them, to expose them, and to treat them! (Zola 1896, 2)

The social taint of "inversion" was clearly too much even for the scientific novelist despite Legrand du Saulle's dictum that "Science, like fire, purifies everything it touches"—a claim regularly cited in the introductions to medical works on sexuality. Privately, Zola confessed to a far more personal impediment: "I have encountered [inverts] . . . and in shaking their hand, I experience an instinctive repulsion I can barely overcome" (qtd. in Laupts 1907, 833). And to another correspondent, Zola wrote, "If I am full of pity for those whom you call Uranists, I have no sympathy for them, no doubt because I am different."[8]

So, after pouring his heart out, the poor Italian never saw himself fictionalized by Zola. *Or did he?* Zola had become increasingly fervent over French natality—a concern most clearly voiced in *Fécondité* (1899), the first volume of his *Quatre Evangiles*. Therefore, he was extremely anxious about all forms of nonprocreative sexuality, and once moaned, "How much seed is wasted in one night in Paris—what a shame that all of it does not produce human beings" (quoted in Laupts 1907, 832n). This seminal waste was of equal concern to the medical and anthropological community, particularly after the humiliating French defeat in the Franco-Prussian War (1870–1871). Therefore, Zola delivered the Italian's confession to his medical friend, Dr. Laupts, who was conducting a survey in 1894 on "sexual inversion" for the prestigious French medicolegal journal, the *Archives of Criminal Anthropology, Criminology, and Normal and Pathological Psychology*. Glancing into a bookstore window by chance some years later, the Italian discovered a book entitled *Taints and Poisons. Sexual Perversions and Perversities* (Laupts 1896) in which his own confessions were republished. He immediately wrote to Laupts that he was elated to find himself "printed in *living color*, although I would have much preferred to be reborn in the pages of a novel and not in a medical science treatise" (qtd. in Saint-Paul 1930, 116). Indeed, the Italian dandy repeatedly suggested that he fashioned himself a *belles-lettriste* and likewise envisioned his life itself as a work of art: "I unloaded my soul somewhat [in my confessions to Zola] and I wrote with a retrospective voluptuousness of the abominable and ardent scenes in which I was the actor. . . . I therefore want to complete the study of my person, whom I often consider favored by nature because she made me a creature that even the most audacious poets have been unable to create" (Invert 1895, 231–232). Ironically enough, his "true" confession was printed *verbatim*, but under the title, "The *Novel* of an Invert."

Dr. Laupts, a student of the prominent forensic doctor, Alexandre Lacassagne (1843–1924), introduced the "document" in a style more suited to the back-cover blurb of a racy "true crime" novella: "It is the true story of a man who bore a great name, a very great name in Italy. As exact as a scientific observation, as interesting as a novel, as sincere as a confession, it is perhaps the most complete and most endearing document of this genre" (Laupts 1894, 212). Just like most of Zola's novels, the confession was published serially, and Laupts had a knack for breaking the action at critical moments of sexual climax. For example, in the third installment on "Youth—First Acts," we learn of the Italian's first erotic encounter with a handsome young officer during his military service:

> He was half undressed and seated on my legs right up against me. I spoke to him as if enchanted . . . suddenly he leaned over, embraced me in his arms and applied a long kiss to my cheek; at the same time he plunged his hands under the sheets and seized my flesh with both his hands. I thought I would die and an immense joy suddenly seized me. We remained a few seconds like that, resting one head against the other, our fiery cheeks touching, my mouth in his in the warmth of the pillow. I was never again so happy!!
>
> The lamp on the floor cast faint rays upon the immense dormitory where my companions were sleeping in the distant beds, and left in profound darkness the corner where we two were thus ecstatic. (Invert 1894, 737)

Break! Readers had to cool off for two months before the hard-core action continued.

But is it science or is it fiction? As Zola feared, some foreign writers were convinced it was entirely his own fabrication,[9] and it did not help matters that Laupts labeled it a "novel."

The second half of the title is equally important: "inversion" itself was a novel diagnosis coined just twelve years earlier. Remarkably, the young Italian never applied any label to himself, although he liked comparing himself to Greek heroes. Perhaps he felt the two traditional terms, *pederast* and *sodomite*, were inappropriate in his case. Technically he was not a pederast since he was attracted to virile, adult men. The label *sodomite* also seemed inappropriate because he had only experienced sodomy (anal sex) quite recently since he had believed it too painful. In any case, the Italian dismissed these two designations as old matters of vice and defective genital conformation which had long been examined by doctors. He was quite convinced that his condition was rare and new, and therefore worthy of publication (Invert 1894, 212).

Physicians of the time clearly agreed, since, as we have seen, the diagnoses of "contrary sexual sensation" and "inversion of the genital sense," which had sprung up in the 1870s and 1880s, were considered new disease entities. After the publication of Charcot and Magnan's article introducing into French the terms "inversion of the genital sense" and "sexual perversion" (1882), French medical journals were suddenly pullulating with these queer, new creatures. Just three years later, Chevalier published a whole medical thesis on the matter of *Inversion of the Sexual Instinct from the Medico-Legal Point of View* (1885). Chevalier highlighted the dizzying panoply of designations for the illness:

> contrary, inverse, perverted, [or] inverted genital sense;—contrary, inverse, [or] perverted sexual attractions, impulsions, [or] sensations;—attraction of same sexes;—crossed sensation of sexual individuality; . . .—perversion, [or] interversion of the sexual instinct, [and so on]. (Chevalier 1885, 14)

Some order needed to be brought to this field of confusions; therefore, Dr. Laupts bravely launched a national survey of sexual inversion with a detailed list of questions concerning the heredity, physical and psychological status, and medical and legal history of inverts. It was addressed not only to doctors, but to professors, lawyers, and *novelists* as well (Laupts 1894, 105–106). The first published response was the Italian's manuscript contributed by Zola, who strongly endorsed Laupts's research.

Laupts shared Zola's natality concerns, which were the *raison d'être* of the whole project. In the introduction to his monograph, *Taints and Poisons. Sexual Perversions and Perversity*, Laupts argued for the sympathetic treatment of these "patients," but continued:

> These days, no one doubts that the number of degenerations, of cerebral derailings—expressed by the tendencies towards suicide, by phobias, etc.—result in large part from the fact that in our nation the genital functions are often not accomplished as they should be.
>
> Therefore, it is necessary from the point of view of the vitality, of the future of the race, to study the morbid causes, to discern the dangerous and evil elements, amongst which must be ranked for an appreciable part the creature stricken with sexual perversion: the pervert, the feminiform born-invert. (Laupts 1896, 104–105)

Clearly, for Laupts, sexual inversion was a terrifying nexus of medical, social, and moral deviations and the "feminiform born-invert" was the embodiment of almost all fin-de-siècle social ills.

The second response to Laupts's survey was from Marc-André Raffalovich (1864–1934), who would become the most prolific writer in French on the subject of "unisexuality" (his preferred term) and would eventually accuse Laupts and his colleagues of being far too squeamish and prejudiced to study inversion scientifically. These "fatuous" French scientists, Raffalovich declared in the pages of the *Archives*, discuss inverts "as if they were newly imported savages that had been unknown in Europe" (1895a, 126). Raffalovich was in a privileged position. He kept abreast of the German, French, and English medical literature, and, most significantly, he had insider information since *he* was an invert. But then, so was Dr. Laupts, literally: "Laupts" was a fiction—the inversion of his real name, St-Paul. Even better, he was a fiction writer, under the pseudonym G. Espé de Metz (1907)—a name he began using because bibliographers were cataloguing Laupts's texts with German authors (Saint-Paul 1930, 5).

Raffalovich was also an impostor of sorts. Although he was entrusted with writing the "Annals of Unisexuality" within the *Archives of Criminal Anthropology*, and was the only French writer on homosexuality whom British sexologist Havelock Ellis praised, Raffalovich was not a doctor. He had no degree whatsoever—he was an Oxford dropout. Raffalovich came from a wealthy Russian-Jewish family that had emigrated to France. His mother was an intimate friend of Claude Bernard, who had recommended that Marc-André become a doctor. He was shipped off to Oxford, but he was too sickly to finish his studies. Instead he became a London dandy, published a few novels and collections of maudlin love poems, and established a literary salon frequented by the notable authors of the day: Henry James, Aubrey Beardsley, Stephan Mallarmé, Pierre Louÿs, and the most admired of æsthetes, Oscar Wilde (1854–1900).

Raffalovich and Wilde were intimate friends until a vicious falling out in the early 1890s. At that time Raffalovich was enamored of Wilde's companion, a pretty-boy and budding poet named John Henry Gray (1866–1934) (whom Raffalovich had met in 1892 through their common friend Arthur Symons [1853–1945]). *A Portrait of Dorian Gray*, with its secret dedication to John, was published in 1891, but the next year Wilde met the younger and more angelic Lord Alfred Douglas. Raffalovich got the suicidal Gray on the rebound, and they became inseparable. The *Queensbury v. Wilde* affair of 1895 perturbed Raffalovich and Gray as well as other English homosexuals. Soon thereafter, the two converted to Catholicism and later moved to Rome. Raffalovich paid for Gray's seminary training and for the construction of St. Peter's Church in Edinburgh where Fr. Gray was appointed first parish priest. Raffalovich, in turn, was admitted to the lay order of Dominicans in 1898 under the name Brother Sebastian, and in 1905 moved into a house next to St. Peter's. The two met every day at Raffalovich's home for tea, and Raffalovich's wealth was held in a joint account with Gray. Raffalovich became a great benefactor of the Dominicans, and donated funds for the construction of St. Sebastian's Priory in Pendelton, Manchester. He passed away in his sleep on St. Valentine's Day, 1934; Fr. Gray followed him to the grave four months later.[10]

Perhaps it was through Arthur Symons, a close friend of John Addington Symonds (1840–1893) and Havelock Ellis (1859–1939), that Raffalovich was introduced to the burgeoning scientific study of inversion and to Ellis and Symonds's groundbreaking *Sexual Inversion* (1896). But even before Ellis began to publish his series on *Studies in the Psychology of Sex*, Raffalovich had begun writing a stream of articles on homosexuality for the *Archives*, including a review of the Wilde affair with a spiteful critique of Wilde's pederasty and literary style. Raffalovich inveighed against Wilde's "flaccid" and "unoriginal" writing, which only represented "artificious, superficial, effeminate" homosexuals (Raffalovich 1895b, 450). These were in the minority, Raffalovich controversially argued. Not all inverts were degenerate sodomites, and he mocked doctors who, in the tradition of Tardieu, "search, almost with desperation, for stigmata of degeneracy" (1896b, 429). Most unisexuals were virile and law-abiding, but "pseudoscience," caving in to popular prejudice, had pushed these decent homosexuals into the shadows (1896a, 25–26). Given Raffalovich's conservative position condemning flamboyant "effeminates," it is not surprising that he had even less sympathy for the Italian invert and his "novel" than did Laupts. "This autobiography resembles those of all effeminate Uranists who have gone public," Raffalovich warned. "This novel of an invert will teach nothing to those with experience in psychiatry. . . . Unbridled vanity and lust are especially demonstrated in the relations between the invert of the novel and the Captain [an older pederast who seduces the hero]. . . . Repugnant or dangerous acts will generally occur between people united by debauchery, vanity, or self-interest" (1895c, 333). He cautioned, "It seems to me that one should not dwell on such autobiographies or attach much importance to them" (1895a, 116).

Echoing Lasègue on the novels of hysterics, Raffalovich exhorted doctors and the general public alike to beware of the narratives of artificious, effeminate inverts, not only because their "true confessions" might be deceitful novels, but more seriously, because these novels were noxious. Raffalovich warned that literature reflected the true inner moral state of its creator just as Dorian Gray's portrait and Wilde's novel itself reflected the true corrupt and corrupting soul. Conversely—appropriating Wilde's dictum that "life imitates art"—Raffalovich claimed that literature shaped the moral character of its readers. Doctors since the eighteenth century had repeatedly complained that artistic representations were dangerous to the malleable brains of women and children. Raffalovich, however, argued for their salubrious use in the treatment of the imagination. With poetic grandiloquence, he lectured novelists from the bully pulpit of medicine about the connection between fiction and social hygiene:

> I call upon our French novelists. . . . I would tell them: Because your readers, your admirers permit you to say anything, why not deliver them real observations? You have them. Describe then that passion of the strong for the strong, of Hercules for Colossus, of robust flesh, as they say, for robust flesh; show that it is not only the female but also the effeminate who is of no interest to these virile [homosexuals]; draw back the veils of ignorance and of falsehood . . . the clichés must be shattered. . . . We must contemplate the education of our children, of our grand-children. (Raffalovich 1896b, 431n)

The battle over the moral purity of France became even more feverish and nationalistic after Raffalovich drew another French novelist into the medical literature by anonymously publishing extracts from a letter J. K. Huysmans (1848–1907) had written to Raffalovich about the sordid Parisian sodomitic underworld. "It made me think of Hell," Huysmans wrote:

> Imagine this: the man who has this vice willfully *withdraws* from association with the rest of mankind. He eats in restaurants, has his hair done at a coiffeur, lives in a *hôtel* where the patrons are all old sodomites. It is a life apart, in a narrow corner, a brotherhood recognizing itself by their voice, by a fixed gaze, and that sing-song tone they all affect.
>
> Furthermore, that vice is the *only* one that suppresses the castes, the decent man and the rogue are equal—and speak to each other naturally, animatedly without distinction of education. . . . It is rather strange and disquieting. ([April 19, 1896] Allen 1966, 216)

Raffalovich contrasted this "Sodom of Paris" with Dr. Paul Näcke's descriptions of the gatherings of educated, bourgeois homosexuals and lesbians at a meeting of the Scientific and Philanthropic Committee (a homosexual organization started by Magnus Hirschfeld) and at other social venues in Berlin. Näcke was so moved by the narratives of these homosexuals' sufferings and their struggles with their parents that he wondered, "Why doesn't someone write unisexual novels?" (qtd. in Raffalovich 1904, 931). Raffalovich hoped to indict French society for its general immorality, irreligion, and ignorance of the psychology of *healthy* unisexuals. "Heterosexuals, by their example and behavior," Raffalovich complained, "have created many inverts" (1904, 935).

Näcke promptly responded to the article by complaining that it was totally unbalanced and ill-informed. He imagined that the homosexual worlds of Paris and Berlin were quite similar, and that the number of homosexuals given to vice was a small minority in both cities. He estimated that Paris probably had fifty to a hundred thousand homosexuals and that, while pederasty was not the rule amongst homosexuals, he suspected there was a higher incidence of pederasty in Latin cultures than Teutonic ones (Näcke 1905, 184). In a subsequent article in a *German* journal, Näcke (1908) suggested that the French generally suffered from more degeneration than the Germans.

Dr. Laupts/Saint-Paul immediately took umbrage at these aspersions against French masculinity. He shot back at both Raffalovich and Näcke that the French were no more degenerate that the Germans (Laupts 1908). Furthermore, he insisted, "*I know* that homosexuality does not exist save as a *rare* exception in the entirety of continental . . . France. . . . *I know* that the vast majority of my (non-colonial) compatriots experience an undissimulated and *extreme* disgust for homosexuality" (Laupts 1909, 693, 696; original emphasis). (Laupts was less certain of the sexual normality of France's colonized subjects.) This was in dramatic contrast to the situation in Germany, where notable doctors, such as Westphal, Krafft-Ebing, and Näcke, had taken up the defense of homosexuals and had favored the deletion of anti-sodomy laws from the Penal Code. Laupts feared that homosexuality was contagious and was spreading in both France and Germany precisely "because it is studied, and spoken, and written about" (1909, 694). The very fact that German doctors had done so much work on the subject was proof of (and presumably cause of) the higher incidence of homosexuality in Germany than in France (1908, 741). In retort to Raffalovich's insult that Laupts's work on homosexuality was in "a literary tradition," Laupts accused Raffalovich of being "a bit too literary, too inclined, in any case, to introduce into a scientific debate considerations of a moral nature that have no place there and are . . . a sort of non-sense" (1909, 695–696).

These accusations and counteraccusations that scientific scholarship was merely fictional "literature" continued to be flung across national boundaries thanks to essays by Eugène Wilhelm. A homosexual Alsatian lawyer who had already published several articles on German sexology in the *Mercure de France*, Wilhelm initially joined the debate under the pseudonym, "Dr. Numa Prætorius." If Laupts and his French colleagues were practically ignorant of the existence of homosexuality in France, Wilhelm observed, it was because their old prejudices prevented them from broach-ing the subject with their patients and discovering how many of these, in fact, were homosexual (Prætorius 1909, 201). He chastised French men of science for generally neglecting sexual questions, and flung Laupts's insult of "literariness" back in the face of French physicians. "They seem to want to leave this terrain to literature and superficial popularizers; one could say that a certain false shame, an ill-placed prudishness prevents them from studying these problems in detail and methodically" (Wilhelm 1912, 301). In a way, Wilhelm was right: men of letters, heterosexual and homosexual alike, *did* have an especially significant role in shaping the French discourse on homosexuality, but one can hardly accuse the *belles-lettristes* of having perverted science. On the contrary, they *informed* the very fictions science was dedicated to spinning.

Science Fictions and Inversions

In his scathing critique of degenerate, fin-de-siècle culture, physician Max Nordau (1849–1920) fumed: "Does [Zola] think that his novels are serious documents from which science can borrow facts? What childish folly! Science can have nothing to do with fiction" (Nordau 1894–95, II:437). As we have seen, however, the scientific literature on inversion was especially dedicated to fiction: both the fictions it studied, and the fictions it sponsored. To label the scientific literature on inversion a "fiction" is not, however, to dismiss it as *untruthful.* Foucault has pointed out that "there is the possibility for fiction to function in truth,"

> for a fictional discourse to induce effects of truth, and for bringing it about that a true discourse engenders or "manufactures" something that does not as yet exist, that is, "fictions" it. One "fictions" history on the basis of a political reality that makes it true, one "fictions" a politics not yet in existence on the basis of a historical truth. (Foucault 1980, 193)

The novelizing and fictioning of "homosexuality" served to advance the underlying goals of defenders and derogators of homosexuality alike: on the one hand, to reify the notion of a normal, virile homosexual; on the other hand, to fashion a monster of perversity embodying the degenerations and insecurities that plagued the cultural imagination of fin-de-siècle France.

While perfectly consonant with the latest, scientific, biomedical "truths" of the day, the medical debates on the nature of inversion were, nevertheless, also molded by the cultural and political preoccupations of the time. The nationalistic fires of Franco-German rivalry continued to burn on the terrain of science well after France's defeat in the Franco-Prussian War. The construction and counting of inverts was just one amongst many ideological weapons (just as it is, albeit under different scientific and political conditions, in the United States today).[11] The fictioning of what would later be called "homosexuality"—embellished as it was by associations with effeminacy, hysteria, and deceitfulness—was especially critical in bolstering nationalist myths of strength, in which strength was always figured as masculine (Nye 1989, 1993).

In the case of the history of inversion, fiction and nonfiction were blurred on a stage bustling with novelists in medical drag and physicians passing incognito as novelists or inverts. Inverts and homosexuals found their "true" confessions turned into scientific fictions under the fear that their narrative productions shared in the deceitfulness and self-delusion of their sexual natures. Homosexuals also played an *active* part in the "fictioning" of their experience—not just because they wrote anonymously or under pseudonyms to disguise themselves. Like the medical researchers of "sexual perversions," homosexual correspondents found it necessary to invent a new history for themselves. Manufactured in the political cause of homosexual emancipation and decriminalization, this *histoire homosexuelle* or historical coming-out narrative advanced seemingly contradictory claims of a long tradition beginning with "the Greek vice," and claims of "homosexuality's" historical novelty. Likewise, the scientific *histoires* simultaneously asserted the *congenital* nature of homosexuality and its *acquired*, even contagious, nature (Laupts 1909, 695 and 694 respectively).

In the promiscuous intercourse between doctors and novelists over the societal poison of "sexual perversion," science itself served as a potent but ambiguous elixir. As Derrida (1972) points out in his exegesis of the *pharmakon* in Plato's *Phædrus* (274c–275b), letters and numbers are unmasked as dangerous supplements to "true learning": superficially, written language appears to be a technique for remembering, but ultimately, it produces forgetfulness.[12] Like the female soul disguised in the male body, the mechanism of poisoning is that of inversion. Physicians and littérateurs played a similarly dangerous game with the *pharmakon* of *science*, which—like the novels conceived by Zola, Raffalovich, and the Italian invert—had the seductiveness of a social panacea.

We have seen that the Italian invert was delighted to find his confessions represented by science, and in his letter to Laupts, praised the doctor as a "savant . . . and a kind and indulgent man." The Italian contributed dozens more pages directly to Laupts because, "like every sick person who sees in a doctor a friend . . . , I am filled with friendship and gratitude for those who occupy themselves with the odious illness that haunts me, and . . . I seek to render them service by exhibiting that which they painfully seek, and which I, on the contrary, know so well: *by innate science*" (Saint-Paul 1930, 116). Even while attempting to condemn and contain perversity, the scientific fictions of inversion were embraced by the inverts themselves, who used science to defend their "naturalness," to consolidate an identity, and to disseminate their stories of passion and "robust flesh." Where better than in scientific journals could the Italian invert "cry my [joy] from the rooftops" for finally having been sodomized (Saint-Paul 1930, 115).

In addition to science, I cannot overlook the *pharmakon* of history itself. Of all the human technologies, none is more inherently dependent on *fabricating* and *forgetting* than history. It figured prominently in the fin-de-siècle medical analysis of homosexuality. A patient's individual case history or *anamnesis* (reminiscence), often printed as a confession, was connected to other family histories and a [illegible] supposedly related disorders. Doctors and inverts regularly alluded to [illegible] Greek vice" of antiquity; yet, as Raffalovich astutely noted, these historical connections were un-remembered in the convenient science fiction that "inversion" was a new syndrome of organic degeneration and social disintegration. Inverts were therefore concocted as a terrible social and cultural poison through the conventions of amnesia and anamnesis: the inversions of forgetting and reminiscence, the masquerade of intolerance as sympathy, the travesty of ignorance as knowledge.

Notes

Sections of this essay appeared in a different form in "Pointy Penises, Fashion Crimes, and Hysterical Mollies: The Pederasts' Inversions," in *Homosexuality in Modern France,* eds. Jeffrey W. Merrick and Bryant Ragan, 146–176 (New York: Oxford University Press, 1996). I am enormously grateful to David Halperin, Anne Harrington, and Kent Brintnall for their helpful comments and editorial suggestions. Research for this essay was supported through a National Science Foundation Graduate Research Fellowship and the Henri Lurcy Traveling Fellowship.

1 Invert (1894, 212); original emphasis. As I will explain shortly, the Italian's confession (which I cite as "Invert") was published anonymously in a medical journal in 1894 to 1895. Its date of composition is uncertain. Setz (1991, 82) estimates that it was written in 1887 or 1888 based on the Italian's references to historical events. Alternatively, the document can be approximately dated to 1889, since the Italian author wrote to Dr. Laupts upon encountering the published version of the confession (Laupts 1896), and Laupts notes that this was seven years after the original letters were sent to Zola (Saint-Paul 1930, 115 n. 2). All translations are mine. For convenience and legibility, I have also translated book titles into English in the text. The original titles appear in the References.

2 For a discussion of the contemporary stakes of the "essentialism" versus "social constructionism" debate, see the Introduction to this volume.

3 The word *sodomy* was used quite loosely in eighteenth- and nineteenth-century France to refer to any variety of "unnatural" sexual acts: anal intercourse (no matter what the sex of the participants), oral sex, and penetration by dildos. *Pederasty* (etymologically, the love of boys) was frequently used interchangeably with *sodomy.* Dr. Fournier Pescay struggled to provide a precise definition in the *Dictionary of Medical Sciences*:

> "SODOMY. . . . Under this name is designated the infamous coitus, for the accomplishment of which, the depraved man prefers, instead of the organ destined by nature to receive the fecundating liqueur of the male, that neighboring organ where the most disgusting excretion of the human body occurs. Theologians, as well as legists, define this vile action: *Sodomia, turpitudo masculum facta.* This definition is incomplete and only applies to pederasty. Sodomy is equally well exerted between a man and a person of the other sex as between two men: when it takes place between a

man and a child, and even between two men, it is distinguished under the name of pederasty" (Fournier Pescay 1821, 441).

4 The journalist and traveler, Armand Dubarry, published a whole novel series on the "Déséquilibrés de l'amour" including the volume on *Les Invertis (Le vice allemand)* (Paris: Chamuel, 1895). He eventually succeeded Jules Verne as the popular science journalist for the *Musée des Familles*.

5 The theory of hereditary degeneration had been initially suggested by Prosper Lucas in his *Traité philosophique et physiologique de l'hérédité naturelle* (Paris: Baillière, 1847–1850), but gained almost universal currency in France through Bénédict Morel's *Traité des dégénérescences* (Paris: Baillière, 1857). Morel argued that all varieties of environmental, biological, and psychological insults (from miasmas to alcohol) could be expressed in offspring through almost any form of pathology. The cumulative weight of these hereditary degenerations would eventually lead to idiocy, sterility, and the termination of family lines. For more on the extensive social impact of the theory of degeneration, see Pick (1989).

6 For a detailed development of this argument, see Rosario (1995).

7 Goldstein (1991) argues that Flaubert used his hysteria to gain a subversive, androgynous gender position from which to write of women's experience. While one might interpret hysteria to have been Flaubert's muse, Flaubert instead complained that his hysterical, feminine hypersensitivity—like masturbatory exhaustion—was the cause of his bouts of literary *impotence*: "Each attack . . . was a seminal loss of the picturesque faculty of the brain" (Flaubert to Colet, cited in Dumesnil 1905, 430).

8 Zola to Marc-André Raffalovich, April 16, 1896 (cited in Allen 1966, 221). This was part of Zola's thank-you note for the gift of Raffalovich's *L'Uranisme et l'unisexualité* (1896).

9 Critiques related by Laupts (1907, 837).

10 Sewell (1963, 33–34). See Ellman (1988) and Sewell (1963) for further biographical information on Raffalovich.

11 In the United States—particularly since the wave of "gay liberation" and public visibility sparked by the Stonewall Riot in 1969—fictions of homosexuality have served the nationalist cause. During the Gulf War (1990–1991), Iraq's President, Saddam Hussein, was portrayed as a transvestite, sadistic pederast (*National Examiner*, March 12, 1991). T-shirts sporting an image of a camel with Hussein's face for an anus declared patriotically, "America Will Not be Saddam-ized" (see Goldberg 1992, 1–5). Homosexualizing the enemy and protecting the U.S. nation from homosexual invasion were a unified strategy of defense. The U.S. military feared a homosexual invasion, quite literally, in 1993 when threatened by President Bill Clinton with the open admission of gays into the armed services. U.S. television viewers were treated to grainy footage of enlisted men in the showers as soldiers confessed their fears of being cruised by the impending hoards of queers clamoring to enter the services. These soldiers' anxieties (or fantasies) of homosexual objectification and scopophilic feminization clearly outweighed any concerns about flashing on millions of television screens. Given the incessant mention of AIDS throughout the debate, one imagines that these showering soldiers feared a double contagion: both AIDS and homosexuality. Their generals' paranoid delusions and phobias of the homosexual menace uncannily mirror the very neuropsychiatric unfitness for which homosexuals were originally screened out by the Selective Service in 1940 (Medical Circular No. 1; also see Bérubé 1990, 11–15).

12 In this Platonic dialogue, Socrates tells Phædrus the following story: Theuth (the god of numbers, geometry, letters, and games) offers Thamus, King of Egypt, letters (*grammata*) as

a means of making Egyptians wiser and of improving their memory: it w (*pharmakon*) of memory and wisdom, Theuth promises. Thamus rejects th , predicting that they will produce forgetfulness: people will come to rely on alien marks rather than their own memory. "You have discovered an elixir not of memory," Thamus declares, "but of reminding" (275a). Writing produces merely an appearance of learning rather than true learning. Instead of a cure for forgetfulness, the *pharmakon* of writing (*logos*) is rejected as an artifice of learning: a poison of memory and knowledge. See Derrida's "La pharmacie de Platon" (1972).

References

Allen, Louis, ed. 1966. Letters of Huysmans and Zola to Raffalovich. *Forum for Modern Languages* 2(3):214–221.

Aron, Jean-Paul, and Roger Kempf. 1984. *La bourgeoisie, le sexe, et l'honneur*. Paris: Editions Complexe.

Baudelaire, Charles. [1857] 1961. *Madame Bovary* par Gustave Flaubert. In *Œuvres complètes*, 647–657. Paris: Pléiade. Appeared originally in *l'Artiste*, 18 October 1857.

Bernard, Léopold. 1898. *Les odeurs dans les romans de Zola,* Conférence faite au Cercle Artistique. Montpellier: n.p..

Bérubé, Allan. 1990. *Coming Out Under Fire: The History of Gay Men and Women in World War Two*. New York: Free Press.

Binet, Alfred. 1887. Le fetichisme dans l'amour. *Revue philosophique* 24:143–167, 252–274.

Charcot, Jean-Martin, and Valentin Magnan. 1882. Inversion du sens genital. *Archives de neurologie* 3:53–60, 296–322.

Chauncey, George. 1982–1983. From sexual inversion to homosexuality: Medicine and the changing conceptualization of female deviance. *Salmagundi* 58:114–146.

Chevalier, Julien. 1885. *De l'inversion de l'instinct sexuel au point de vue médico-légale*. Paris: Octave Doin.

Derrida, Jacques. 1972. La pharmacie de Platon. In *La Dissémination*. Paris: Seuil.

Dumesnil, René. 1905. *Flaubert, son hérédité, son milieu, sa méthode*. Geneva: Slatkine Reprints, 1969.

Ellis, Havelock, and John Addington Symonds. 1896. *Das konträre Geschlechstgefühl*. Trans. Hans Kurella. Leipzig: George H. Wiegands Verlag. Published in English as *Sexual Inversion* (Watford: University Press, 1897).

———. 1936. *Studies in the Psychology of Sex*. 4 vols. New York: Random House.

Ellman, Richard. 1988. *Oscar Wilde*. New York: Knopf.

Espé de Metz, G. [Georges Saint-Paul]. 1907. *Plus fort que le mal. Essai sur le mal innomable*. Pièce en quatre actes. Paris: Maloine.

Fabre, Paul. 1875. De l'hystérie chez l'homme. *Annales médico-psychologiques,* 5th series 13:354–373.

Flaubert, Gustave. 1926–54. *Correspondance*. 13 vols. Paris: Editions Louis Conard.

———. 1980–91. *Correspondance*. 3 vols. In *Œuvres complètes*. Paris: Pléiade.

Foucault, Michel. 1976. *Histoire de la sexualité. Vol. 1: La volonté de savoir*. Paris: Gallimard.

———. 1980. *Power/Knowledge. Selected Interviews and Other Writings, 1972–1977*. Ed. Colin Gordon. New York: Pantheon.

Fournier Pescay. 1821. Sodomie. *Dictionnaire des sciences médicales* 51:441–448.

Goldberg, Jonathan. 1992. *Sodometries: Renaissance Texts, Modern Sexualities*. Stanford: Stanford University Press.

Goldstein, Jan. 1991. The uses of male hysteria: Medical and literary discourse in nineteenth-century France. *Representations* 34:134–165.

Greenberg, David F. 1988. *The Construction of Homosexuality*. Chicago: University of Chicago Press.

Griesinger, Wilhelm. 1868–69. Über einen wenig bekannten psychopathischen Zustand. *Archiv für Psychiatrie und Nervenkrankheiten* 1:626–635.

[Invert]. 1894–1895. [Letters to Emile Zola published anonymously as] "Le roman d'un inverti." Ed. Dr. Laupts. *Archives d'anthropologie criminelle* Vol. 9 (1894): 212–215, 367–373, 729–737; Vol. 10 (1895): 131–138, 228–241, 320–325.

Krafft-Ebing, Richard von. 1877. Über gewisse Anomalien des Geschlechtstriebs und die klinisch-forensische Verwerthung derselben als eines wahrscheinlich functionellen Degenerationszeichens des centralen Nerven-Systems. *Archiv für Psychiatrie und Nervenkrankheiten* 7:291–312.

Lanteri-Laura, Georges. 1979. *Lecture des perversions. Histoire de leur appropriation médicale*. Paris: Masson.

Lasègue, Ernest. 1881. Les hystériques, leur perversité, leurs mensonges. *Annales médico-psychologiques*, 6th series 6:111–118.

Dr. Laupts [Georges Saint-Paul]. 1894–95. Enquête sur l'inversion sexuelle (Réponses), [and editorial remarks to "Le roman d'un inverti."] *Archives d'anthropologie criminelle* Vol. 9 (1894): 105–108, 211–215, 367–373, 729–737; Vol. 10 (1895): 131–138, 228–241, 320–325.

———. 1896. *Tares et poisons. Perversions et perversités sexuelles. Une enquête sur l'inversion. Notes et documents. Le roman d'un inverti né. Le procès Wilde. La guérison et la prophylaxie de l'inversion*. Paris: George Carré.

———. 1907. A la mémoire d'Emile Zola. *Archives d'anthropologie criminelle* 22:825–841.

———. 1908. Dégénérescence ou pléthore? *Archives d'anthropologie criminelle* 23:731–749.

———. 1909. Lettre au Professeur Lacassagne en réponse au lettre de M. Raffalovich. *Archives d'anthropologie criminelle* 24:693–696.

Medical Circular No. 1—Revised. 1941. Minimum psychiatric inspection. Reprinted in the *Journal of the American Medical Association* 116(18): 2059–2061.

Micale, Mark S. 1990. Charcot and the idea of hysteria in the male: Gender and mental science, and medical diagnosis in late nineteenth-century France. *Medical History* 34:363–411.

———. 1995. *Approaching Hysteria: Disease and its Interpretations*. Princeton, NJ: Princeton University Press.

Näcke, Paul Adolf. 1905. Le monde homosexuel de Paris. *Archives d'anthropologie criminelle* 20:182–185, 411–414.

———. 1908. Einteilung der Homosexuellen. *Allgemeine Zeitschrift für Psychiatrie* 65:109–128.

Nordau, Max Simon. 1894–95. *Dégénérescence*. 2 vols. Trans. August Dietrich. Paris: Félix Alcan. Originally published as *Entartung*. Berlin: Carl Dunder, 1893.

Nye, Robert A. 1989. Sex difference and male homosexuality in French medical discourse, 1800–1930. *Bulletin of the History of Medicine* 63:32–51.

———. 1993. *Masculinity and Male Codes of Honor in Modern France*. New York: Oxford University Press.

Pick, Daniel. 1989. *Faces of Degeneration: A European Disorder, c.1848–c.1918*. Cambridge: Cambridge University Press.

Plato. 1986. *Phædrus*. Trans. C. J. Rowe. Wiltshire: Aris & Phillips.

Prætorius, Dr. Numa [Eugène Wilhelm]. 1909. A propos de l'article du Dr. Laupts sur l'Homosexualité. *Archives d'anthropologie criminelle* 24:198–207.

Raffalovich, Marc-André. 1895a. L'Uranisme. Inversion sexuelle congénitale. *Archives d'anthropologie criminelle* 10:99–127.

———. 1895b. L'affaire Oscar Wilde. *Archives d'anthropologie criminelle* 10:445–477.

———. 1895c. A propos du roman d'un inverti et de quelques travaux récents sur l'inversion sexuelle. *Archives d'anthropologie criminelle* 10:333–336

———. 1896a. *Uranisme et unisexualité. Etude sur différentes manifestations de l'instinct sexuel.* Paris: Masson.

———. 1896b. Unisexualité anglaise. *Archives d'anthropologie criminelle* 11:429–431.

———. 1904. Les groupes d'uranistes à Paris et à Berlin. *Archives d'anthropologie criminelle* 19:926–936.

Rosario, Vernon A. 1995. Pointy penises, fashion crimes and hysterical mollies: The pederasts' inversions. In *Homosexuality in Modern France.* Ed. Jeffrey Merrick, Bryant Ragan, Jr., 146–176. New York: Oxford University Press.

Saint-Paul, Georges. *See also* Laupts; Espé de Metz, G.

———. 1930. *Thèmes psychologiques. Invertis et homosexuels*. Paris: Vigot.

Sewell, Brocard. 1963. *Two Friends: André Raffalovich and John Gray*. Aylesford, Kent: Saint Albert's.

Setz, Wolfram, ed. 1991. *Der Roman eines Konträrsexuellen*. Berlin: Verlag rosa Winkel. German translation of Invert (1894–95).

Tardieu, Ambroise Auguste. [1857] 1878. *Etude médico-légale sur les attentats aux moeurs*. 7th ed. Paris: J.-B. Baillière.

Toulouse, Edouard. 1896. *Emile Zola*. Paris: Société des Editions Scientifiques.

Veith, Ilza. 1965. *Hysteria. The History of a Disease*. Chicago: University of Chicago Press.

Westphal, Karl Friedrich. 1869. Die conträre Sexualempfindung: Symptom eines neuropathischen (psychopathischen) Zustandes. *Archiv für Psychiatrie und Nervenkrankheiten* 2:73–108.

Wilhelm, Eugène. 1912. Publications allemandes sur les questions sexuelles. *Archives d'anthropologie criminelle* 27:301–309.

Zola, Emile. [1871] 1963. *La Curée*. In *Les Rougon-Macquart*, vol. I. Paris: Pléiade.

———. [1880] 1968. Le Roman expérimental. *Œuvres complètes*, ed. Henri Mitterand, 1145–1203. Lausanne: Cercle du Livre Précieux.

———. 1896. Preface to *Tares et poisons. Perversions et perversités sexuelles,* by Dr. Laupts [Georges Saint-Paul], 1–4. Paris: George Carré.

Clitoral Corruption

Body Metaphors and American Doctors' Constructions of Female Homosexuality, 1870–1900

Margaret Gibson

In the last few decades of the nineteenth century, American doctors gradually eased their way into a debate full of sensationalist and moralistic passions: the analysis and classification of sexual perversion. These physicians were well aware that they were perceived as explorers in a new and possibly dangerous field, and the potential for heroic service permeated their rhetoric: "the 'mightiest of human instincts,' [the sex drive] is too intimately related to the physical basis of human weal and woe for any physician prudishly to ignore any of its phases. . . . Upon the perfection of the reproductive apparatus depends the position of the animal in the scale of evolution" (Kiernan 1891, 188). For these doctors, the study of human sexual behaviors and perversions was vital to the species. The examination of perversion generally took the form of increasingly fine classifications and divisions.[1] A condition that emerged from the larger category of "perversion" was sexual inversion, homosexuality, *conträre Sexualempfindung*, or a variety of other terms designed to connote a sexual attraction between two members of the same sex.[2] Most medical accounts of homosexual activity or inversion were of male subjects, but in the century's final decades, a growing number of female "inverts" made their appearance in the medical literature. In many accounts of female homosexuality, doctors mentioned its link to an abnormal, enlarged clitoris. The inclusion of this apparently minor characteristic was not a random occurrence, or merely evidence of a thorough medical examination. Instead, by attributing an enlarged clitoris to these women, doctors had access to a shorthand system of cultural meanings. Assumptions and associations surrounding the clitoris highlighted and reinforced connections between female inverts and members of other stigmatized groups—drawing on images of race, class, gender, and insanity, and indicating an individual's position on an evolutionary scale. Through these connections, doctors were able to further marginalize and exoticize the female invert or homosexual, and minimize the threat that the existence of such individuals might pose to broader beliefs about sexuality, gender, and intimate relationships.

The contours of a study of late nineteenth-century American medical research on female homosexuality are difficult to define and somewhat artificial. Medical knowledge circulated freely between the United States and Europe, categories and nosologies were in flux, and no particular medical specialty was devoted to the study of sexuality. Neurologists, alienists, and gynecologists competed for the role of "expert" in cases of female mental, nervous, and sexual disorders (*Alienist* 1885a; Lewis 1890; Sligh 1894). Nancy Theriot describes the professional instability of this period as one in which "the boundaries of these specialties were sites of professional conflict" and "a scientific understanding of gender was part of the knowledge each specialty created as its own" (1993, 4–10). These various fields had significantly different definitions and treatments of sexual perversions, and battle lines were often drawn between perceived "therapeutic nihilism" and radical somatic treatments (Scull & Favreau 1986, 246–247). Furthermore, sexuality was an arena that intersected with legal and religious interests, and doctors tried to stake out a collective claim of expertise in competition with these concerns while masking internal professional struggles (Shrady 1884, 71).

Defining the parameters of female sexual deviance was no simple matter for nineteenth-century doctors, let alone a historian grappling today with their writings. Any definition of what can be considered "lesbian" or "homosexual" is clearly arbitrary in some sense, since the terms are particular to the social and historical context in which they are found.[3] However, through an analysis of a broad base of American medical literature from 1850 to 1900 (with an emphasis on the last three decades of the century), certain recurring themes allow us to sketch a medical image of the female invert. In this investigation, aside from articles devoted to female homosexual practices, I include articles about female genitalia, sexuality, and gynecological diseases, as well as about male homosexuality or other "perversions." Since the categories of the day did not coincide neatly with current definitions or terminology, my interpretation of what might be considered "homosexual" is rather broad. I include any material that mentioned "mutual masturbation" between two women or girls, as well as any discussion of women who thought of themselves as male, or who dressed as men, whether or not there was any specific discussion of their sexual preferences. The cases of cross-dressing would have been considered "inversion" by a physician of the time, a diagnosis in which any violation of proper gender role constituted the pivotal element. I also examine discussions of "female" hermaphrodites, which I generally identify as such.

In these sources, not all of the authors were American, nor were they necessarily writing for an American readership. Some of these articles consisted of or included translations, citations, or reviews of works originally published outside the United States. Furthermore, the cases of female inversion that American doctors discussed were limited in number and often taken from European accounts. However, through the doctors' practice of writing summary articles on the subject or including long citations of other studies to support their own work, this limited number of cases was widely circulated and recycled, and reprinted European or American accounts were incorporated into the same lively American discussion of female inversion. Thus, although an enlarged clitoris was specifically connected in the literature with only a few women, it quickly became a characteristic physical anomaly associated with female homosexuality.[4] The ease with which these few cases became generalizations testifies to the immense cultural predetermination of the link between female homosexuality and clitoral hypertrophy.

The interpretation of Victorian sexual ideology and practice has been a source of extensive debate. Certain scholars of women's history emphasize the repressive and oppressive nature of nineteenth-century female sexual ideology, while others, such as Nancy Cott (1978), have argued that female "passionlessness" was a norm that women embraced as a means towards greater social influence. While a more complex understanding of women's participation in the construction of their roles is clearly valid and important, such an "empowering" idea of female asexuality does not explain female deviance from this norm. Were these deviant, sexualized women lacking in opportunities or the desire for empowerment? Were they expressing a different kind of power? Cott and others in this debate have been criticized for assuming that female asexuality was universally recognized. As Foucault (1990), Degler (1984), and others have pointed out, doctors discussed sexuality, including female sexuality, on a regular basis. However, this recognition of sexuality does not nullify the asexual ideal for women in this period. Instead, doctors discussed female sexuality and asexuality simultaneously, through the creation of a broad category of "hypersexual" women. Carol Groneman (1994, 355–357) has argued that the "hypersexual woman" was a label that could be applied to nymphomaniacs, lesbians, and prostitutes, but I would take the argument further. The use of body metaphors such as the hypertrophied clitoris banded together a motley collection of prostitutes, nymphomaniacs, masturbators, insane women, women of nonwhite races, poor women, criminals, and, finally, the female invert.[5] The female invert was the most recent medical category to be placed in this network of associations, and thus her connections to its other members were particularly reinforced by explicit statements and metaphorical associations.

American doctors entered the study of sexual perversion later than those in Europe, but when they did, they brought with them viewpoints and beliefs that were specifically American. The medical profession in late nineteenth-century America was undergoing numerous changes. American doctors were attempting to raise the standards of their practices, unify orthodox medical knowledge, and become more professional (Starr 1982). This trend meant that any morally dubious study, such as the examination of sexual deviation, was an especially risky undertaking. In order to make such research respectable, doctors added frequent moralizing statements about the behavior they observed, and constantly justified their scrutiny of such an "unrefined" subject. These apologias and warnings were not unique to American treatises, but they were especially common and reflected a more cautious tone in the American medical community than in the more securely established European medical profession. Given the concurrent American anti-vice movements, doctors also realized that the public was on the lookout for any obscene or potentially corrupting literature.[6]

Doctors themselves saw their nationality as relevant to the material they published. In one translation of a work by Marc-André Raffalovich on congenital inversion, the American translator added a note explaining that "the social conditions upon which this paper is based are those in Europe and differ widely from those in this country. . . . [European countries] foster forms of vice with which we . . . may be as yet little familiar." The writer, however, complained that such occurrences were bound to increase with immigration (Raffalovich 1895, 65). Some doctors clearly believed that European studies of perversion were not wholly applicable to Americans.[7]

The "problem" of immigration was one among many late nineteenth-century social concerns reflected in the medical discussions of the time. If the body can be a metaphor for the expression of social uncertainty and disruption, the language used in the description of the body as a whole or in parts can indicate specific issues and values. The late nineteenth-century medical classification of sexuality indicated an attempt to order change in a meaningful way. Anita Clair Fellman and Michael Fellman (1981) have suggested that the emphasis on self-restraint in this period represented an attempt to create at least the appearance of social stability and order. Likewise, the medical concern over clitoral hypertrophy highlighted a variety of social and metaphorical fears and issues. "Hypertrophy" was applied to both the body and behavior—Havelock Ellis described "hypertrophied friendship" in his treatise on female sexual inversion (1895, 147), suggesting that these women's relationships and their bodies revealed a pathological expansion that threatened to overwhelm the physical and social body.[8]

There are a variety of reasons for this perceived social threat. A number of historians have identified the rise of women's education and the feminist "New Woman" in the late nineteenth century as a central factor in the boom in medical reports on female homosexuality and the creation of the "mannish lesbian" (Smith-Rosenberg 1989; Duggan 1993; Newton 1989). Under this hypothesis, women's increasing educational and economic power might be represented by clitoral hypertrophy, and "cured" by clitoridectomy or other radical treatments. Clearly, the medical preoccupation with gender roles and with the impact of female homosexuality (or even sexuality) on the family structure and society reflected such social fears. But this explanation cannot fully account for the concerns about "perverted" sexuality in both men and women that formed the initial framework for the discussion of female homosexuality. The general concern about "perversion," male and female, in this period requires further explanation. The factors that brought forth accounts of male inverts, sadists, masochists, fellators, and a host of other "perverts" were necessary precursors to the discussion of female inversion. If the social role of women had been the sole significant factor leading to the proliferation of "perversions" in women, discussions of female inversion should have preceded or at least been concurrent with discussions of male homosexuality and perversion, rather than lagging behind as they did.

The historical impetus for the mushrooming of literature on perversions is clearly a complex system of trends. A significant aspect of this literary expansion was linked to increasing anxiety about the nature of civilization and evolutionary "progress." Social Darwinism and the start of the eugenics movement provided a framework in which to discuss moral issues in an increasingly biological way, using the human body not just as a personal unit, but as a representation of the limits to human progress and of regression into an animal past (Chamberlain & Gilman 1985; Pick 1989). Elaine Showalter (1990) has provided one possible explanation for the degenerationist anxieties. She argues that the end of a century is a sufficiently powerful symbol of an apocalypse that fin-de-siècle society is obsessed with the prospect of its doom. Showalter claims that late nineteenth-century American fears of degeneration could easily be used to support such a hypothesis. Again, this is not a sufficient explanation for all characteristics of these doctors' writings, since many of the movements spawned by such cultural paranoia continued as important social and medical trends well into the following century, as in the case of eugenic theory. However, the pressure of a new century could have been a contributing factor in the rise of degeneration theory and the study of perversion.

In the course of this essay, I will outline late nineteenth-century theories of female sexuality and the important role the clitoris played in them. Then I will discuss the degenerate and marginalized groups who were linked in three ways: to each other through their hypersexuality, to the female invert through explicit associations in medical accounts, and to each other and to the female invert in particular through their association with clitoral abnormalities. Finally, I will discuss the particular image of the female invert that arose in the late nineteenth century and how the clitoris is described and used in her medical examination. Through an understanding of the self-supporting relationships of the medical categories of women, we can better understand the connections between social anxiety, body metaphors, and the impact of categorization and association.

Aneroticism, Nymphomania, Masculinity, and the Pathologies of Female Sexual States

As many historians have noted, the nineteenth century witnessed the peak in the cult of female "asexuality," when "normal" women were expected to have little or no sex drive.[9] The result of this belief was an expansion of the realm of pathology to incorporate the "hypersexual" woman, or the woman whose sexuality was clearly evident. For example, one woman with a clitoral adhesion suddenly became "unwomanly," exhibiting "lascivious" behavior and suffering from "voluptuous dreams" (Hale 1896, 446–447). For a nineteenth-century doctor, such strong sexual desire in a woman was a notable pathological symptom. Although some physicians in the last decades of the century saw "aneroticism," or lack of sexual feeling in women, as a potential problem, the belief in the "naturalness" of female aneroticism persisted. One doctor argued that "instead of encouraging sexual feeling in women, it should rather be repressed, as Nature does it," since "the Lord made them so" (Bernardy 1894, 429–430).[10]

This concept of female sexuality had a number of ramifications. The belief in a stronger male sex drive resulted in a relative tolerance or ignorance of female homosexual relationships, since it was assumed that no meaningful sexual activity could take place without an active, male initiator. Two asexual, passive individuals were presumed incapable of sexual perversion on their own (Chauncey 1982–83, 117; Faderman 1991, 1–36; Smith-Rosenberg 1985, 53–76). Havelock Ellis pointed out this prejudice among his colleagues, past and present: "We are accustomed to much greater familiarity and intimacy between women than between men, and we are less apt to suspect the existence of any abnormal passion" (1895, 142).[11]

When doctors did begin to examine women's sexual relationships in the final decades of the nineteenth century, the stereotype of the passive, asexual woman was slow to change. Instead of instantly replacing the old view of women's sexuality with one that would embrace such new cases of obvious female sexuality, doctors classified these women as pathological, diseased exceptions, and added them to a growing category of hypersexual women.

Although sexuality in and of itself was a focus of medical studies, sexual pathology was directly linked to other spheres of life. For a woman to be adamantly sexual represented more than a bedroom concern. As George Chauncey suggests, how a nineteenth-century woman behaved sexually was equated with how she acted in all other areas of life (1982–83, 119–128). At the same time, Carol Smith-Rosenberg and Charles Rosenberg (1984) argue that women in the nineteenth century were perceived as intimately limited and affected by their bodies, particularly their reproductive functions, in ways that men were not. Such an interconnection of sexuality, social role, and the body made limiting a diagnosis to any one sphere an impossibility. Thus, for a woman to behave in a "masculine" way sexually, by having a strong sex drive or by being attracted to women, she had to be "masculine" in other ways. The ideals of romantic love depended on the union of opposites, and the polarity attributed to male and female behavior satisfied this ideal in a heterosexual relationship.[12] However, if a woman was "masculine" in her sex drive, she still required a passive partner, male or female. Therefore, all hypersexual women could be viewed with similar suspicion, whether they were "homosexual" or not—they were all, in some sense, masculine.

The medical discussion of nymphomaniacs demonstrates this link between hypersexuality and masculinity. Nymphomania represents the clearest case of female sexuality being viewed as pathological: it was a "disease" in which a woman displayed "excessive and inordinate sexual desire" and "lewdness and vulgarity of speech and action" (Lydston 1889, 283–284). Nymphomania was not the sole sexual condition recognized and pathologized in women, but it was the most extreme example, and its loose definition frequently tied it to other perversions, such as inversion. The hypersexual woman in pre-nineteenth-century society was seen as essentially feminine, an image that flowed from the assumption that women were more lustful that men. However, the Victorian nymphomaniac represented a lust that was necessarily masculine to this later society, and the hyperfeminine hypersexual was discarded as an impossibility (Groneman 1994, 345). Nymphomaniacs were described in explicitly masculine terms: one woman complained that the treatments that lessened her nymphomaniacal sex drive "destroyed her virility" and left her "emasculate" (Walton 1857, 50). This masculinity was implied or explicit in accounts of all "hypersexual" groups of women in this period. The female invert's masculinity was her defining characteristic, and her clitoris was a critical element in this construction and in linking it to her "hypersexual" nature.

The female invert made her first medical appearances well within an increasingly somatic gynecological medical tradition in which the advent of antiseptics and anesthesia permitted radical treatments such as clitoridectomies. The emphasis that doctors placed on the invert's clitoris reflected their new professional interests (Theriot 1993; Scull & Favreau 1986). However, the clitoris itself represented more than just a somatic, gynecological focus. It had its own cultural associations that were intertwined with images of female sexuality and gender. The clitoris was widely recognized as directly related to sexual feeling in women. One medical textbook succinctly identified the function of the clitoris as "the chief seat of sexual excitement" (Garrigues 1896, 39).[13] In studying female sexual problems, doctors consistently examined the clitoris. The recognized role of the clitoris in masturbation and nymphomania and their occasional treatment by clitoridectomy demonstrated the general equation of sex drive with this organ.[14] The frequent inclusion of precise clitoral measurements in medical articles demonstrates that the clitoris was especially useful as an "objective" measure of the otherwise amorphous sex drive.

The role of the clitoris in sex was frequently explained or summarized by using an analogy to the male genitals. Physicians identified the clitoris as the homologue of the penis, a belief that was frequently used to assert the importance of the clitoris and to justify its study. The textbooks of the time reflected this emphasis. In Skene's *Diseases of Women*, the anatomical description of the clitoris reads, "The clitoris is analogous to the penis, but possesses neither corpus spongiosum nor urethra" (1898, 78). A female doctor advocating female circumcision to avoid preputial adhesions listed the analogous parts of the clitoris and the penis, and further validated an investigation of the organ by pointing out that, "small as this organ is, compared to the glans penis, it has in proportion to its size four or five times the nerve supply of the latter" (Hassler 1897, 182).[15]

The recognition of the close relationship between the clitoris and the penis led directly to the issue of size. If the two were differentiated mainly by their size, then the next question was: What happened if the clitoris grew especially large, or the penis was especially small? Clitoral growth was linked directly to an increase in sex drive, and therefore to masculinity, and all three led to the discussion of hermaphrodites, a popular subject in medical texts (see Dreger in this volume). Hermaphrodites were divided into categories of "true" or "false": a true hermaphrodite possessed both a testicle and an ovary, while in a "female" pseudohermaphrodite the clitoris was "so hypertrophied as to resemble a penis," yet the individual possessed ovaries and was therefore "female" (Skene 1898, 83–84). The growth of the clitoris could create a male impostor out of a woman, and was thus deceptive and dangerous. Both physical hermaphroditism and "psychic hermaphroditism" (as inversion was frequently labeled) emphasized the connection between a large clitoris and masculinity and formed a basis for the medical discussion of female homosexuality and the clitoris.[16]

The Ranks of the Degenerate: Marginalized Women and Their Clitorises

The medical literature of the late nineteenth century indicates an ever-present awareness of evolutionary theory which served as an especially versatile, scientific, objective model for rationalizing sexual and social values that had previously been regulated by religion and the law. Degeneration, or the slide down the evolutionary ladder, was a common explanation for mental disease in general, and sexual perversion in particular. Edward C. Spitzka expressed a common perspective on human nature in the statement "The wild beast . . . is slumbering in us all" (1888, 778). Traces of humans' animal ancestors lurked within, and any weakening of an individual's nervous system allowed the beast to rush to the surface, wreaking psychological, moral, or physical havoc. This perspective led to a search for incipient insanity or physical signs in a patient indicating any degradation of the civilized elements that might emancipate the animal instincts. The excessive stimulations of civilized living in the modern era were thought to exacerbate any weakness in individuals' nervous systems, especially in women, and to lead to numerous ailments (Chamberlain & Gilman 1985, 121–164; Pick 1989, 208–212). Masturbation or any form of excess sexual stimulation provided this kind of superfluous excitation, or similarly might reflect a degraded nervous system.[17]

Homosexuality was almost invariably labeled a form of degeneration. By placing their investigation within the realm of larger evolutionary and biological trends, doctors gave objective credibility to their belief in the social and moral degradation of inverts. Perhaps the most common use of evolutionary theory with inversion was the assumption that homosexuality represented a regression to a "bi-sexual" past, in which hermaphroditism was the rule. James G. Kiernan, Secretary of the Chicago Academy of Medicine, summarized this view:

> The original bi-sexuality of the ancestors of the race, shown in the rudimentary female organs of the male, could not fail to occasion functional, if not organic, reversions when mental or physical manifestations were interfered with by disease or congenital defect.[18] (1888, 129)

By implying that female homosexuality was a hermaphroditic reversion, Kiernan suggested that the invert occupied an inferior evolutionary rung. Large clitorises were therefore seen as "stigmata," or specific signs of incipient degeneration. The hypertrophy of the clitoris was a significant physical sign of regression, since this organ was particularly sensitive to degenerative forces (Peckham 1891, 1154). Finally, since evolutionary history was assumed to be analogous to ontogeny (individual growth and maturation from embryo to adult), inversion was seen as regressive in terms of both processes: "The clitoris is often found enlarged in the degenerate and the pubescent" (Hughes 1893, 575).[19]

Sexual perverts were both products and producers of degeneration. Detailed reports of female sexual inversion carefully listed the nervous instability and habits of the patient's parents as keys to her degeneracy. Traits such as "eccentricity" or alcoholism in a parent were seen as support for Richard von Krafft-Ebing's classification of sexual inversion as "a result of neuro-psychical degeneration" (1888, 565). "Aberrations of the sexual instinct are among the most striking stigmata of inherited nervous instability," and therefore the presence of sexual inversion was a reliable indication of broader insanity and degeneration (*Medicine* 1899, 527). Under the late nineteenth-century model of heredity, such negative traits would become increasingly fixed and dangerous with each generation, and any evidence of degeneration could be inherited as any other condition or combination of traits. Thus, female inverts were easily classified as degenerate by association with other degenerates, as well as by specific demonstration.[20] In late Victorian American medicine, degeneration theory was an essential element in linking a wide variety of marginalized women. Social and medical condemnations of these individuals were strengthened by their links to each other, forming an interwoven network of "degenerate" groups and classifications.

Masturbators formed one degenerate group that any physician or reader in the late nineteenth century would associate with clitoral hypertrophy. The masturbator was an epic figure in both the public and medical minds, and the female masturbator was believed to be especially ill and degraded; by her embodiment of the perils of sexuality for women, such a person proved the "naturalness" of female asexuality (Bacon 1898, 279). There was a strong intermingling of masturbation and homosexuality, which often placed them under the same definition (see Bullough & Voght 1973). Female-female sexual activity could be seen as a mere subset of masturbation, since masturbation's definition included "venereal orgasm by means of the hand, the tongue, or any kind of body by one's self or another person" (Garrigues 1896, 289). Although this definition was especially broad, since it could include any sexual act to orgasm, many doctors of this period made the links between female inversion, masturbation, clitoral changes, and a host of other negative associations.

Masturbation and female homosexuality were frequently seen as causally related. Doctors believed that "self-abuse" was a degenerative trend that would lead to increasing degrees of vice, particularly sexual excess and, most severely, homosexuality. One doctor warned that "sometimes, in cases of masturbation, perverted sexual feelings, such as forming morbid attachments for persons of the same sex are quite marked" (Mann 1893, 474). The sexual independence from men shared by women who masturbated and those who had sexual relations with other women was also a strong link between the two groups:

> [Sexual perversions are] frequently produced on the neurotic soil of the male and female masturbator. The female masturbator of this type usually becomes excessively prudish, despises and hates the opposite sex, and frequently forms a furious attachment for another woman, to whom she unselfishly devotes herself. (Kiernan 1888, 171)

Medical arguments against female masturbation also commonly emphasized the harm that resulted from the absence of male participation; these same arguments could be used against female inversion. Doctors generally believed that exhaustion and uterine disease could arise from female orgasm in the absence of "a drop of seminal fluid . . . to refresh and protect [women] from disease" (*Medical News* 1884). One doctor argued that women did not orgasm in masturbation, and the "congestion" that accompanied arousal was "unrelieved by the act of consummation." Diseases of the reproductive system, like engorgement and enlargement of the genitals, resulted from this perpetual buildup of sexual excitement (Chapman 1883, 454–455).[21] These examples reinforced the perception that a male presence was necessary for healthy female sexuality.

Masturbation was depicted as a dangerous practice with potentially severe and practically unlimited consequences. "Self-abuse" could lead to changes anywhere in the body, from "circulatory disturbances" to epilepsy, but was especially linked to changes in the reproductive organs (Morris 1892, 294). The medical community generally believed that most female masturbation was clitoral, or at least focused on the external genitalia. This did not mean that internal organs were not affected by the practice, but changes in the external appearance of the genitals were particularly prominent and easy to spot (Beebe 1897; Chapman 1883). One doctor argued that female modesty required that the diagnosis of masturbation in women depend more on identifying genital abnormalities than on the patient's testimony (Chapman 1883, 450). Such arguments indicated doctors' emphasis on genital change as an indicator of masturbation. Even the division of clitoral hypertrophy into various diagnostic categories, such as "congenital malformations, simple hypertrophy and elephantiasis, carcinomatous and benign tumors," did not deny the relationship this condition had to masturbation, since doctors believed that most of these, including clitoral cancer, were potentially a result of the practice (Peckham 1891, 1153; Cumston 1895–96, 268). Throughout the medical literature, clitoral excision was offered as a cure for masturbation and all of its associated ailments, including nymphomania and inversion.[22]

One of the most drastic results of masturbation in women was insanity, a condition that was also linked to homosexuality by more than their common relationship with "self-abuse." Insane women had genital abnormalities similar to those doctors described among inverts and masturbators. One doctor noted the association of "immoderate" (large) genital organs and insanity, and argued that asymmetries of sexual development were also common among the insane (Clark 1888, 292). Another doctor extensively examined the reproductive abnormalities of the insane, which ranged from internal to external to behavioral (Skene 1889, 929–945).

Insane women were frequently classified alongside hypersexual women. Articles warned that excessive sexual activity could cause insanity, which arose "from brain exhaustion produced by prolonged or excessive functional activity of [the reproductive] organs" (Skene 1889, 933). Alternatively, hypersexuality could be a symptom of insanity, since doctors generally acknowledged that there were "high degrees of sexual excitement . . . among the insane," which required little explanation save the extreme degeneration of both madness and female sexual passion (Rosse 1892, 795).

Statements assuming an association between insanity and perversion were even more widespread than those connecting these two with hypersexuality. Doctors believed the insane were especially given to perverse expressions of their strong sexual impulses, often through homosexual activity. Ellis cited an Italian doctor's assertion that "the vice [tribadism] is not peculiar to any disease or age, for nearly all insane women, except in acute forms of insanity, are subject to it" (Ellis 1895, 144). Kiernan found that female homosexual activity was also common in an American insane hospital and was exacerbated by overcrowding (qtd. in Hughes 1893, 575). From medical accounts like these, it appears that female homosexuality was a notorious and anticipated companion to insanity, and therefore the association scarcely needed explaining.

Cases of criminal insanity illuminated the link between homosexuality and madness. Doctors were frequently called to testify as to the responsibility or lack thereof among alleged criminals, and the issue of legal responsibility in cases of sexual perversion was the source of numerous medical articles (Hughes 1893; Mann 1893; Anthony 1898; *Medicine* 1899; Kiernan 1888, 1892). Certain high-profile cases, like the Alice Mitchell–Freda Ward murder case—in which Mitchell sliced her lover's throat—provided the medical community with fodder for generalizations about female homosexuality. A list of traits that one doctor presented as evidence of insanity included Alice Mitchell's "boyish tendencies," "indifference to young men's company," "her intense and peculiar affection for Freda Ward and her earnestness in the irrational idea that she could marry Freda" (Hughes 1893, 555–556). These articles implied that insanity and female homosexuality overlapped extensively, even if they were not necessarily interchangeable.[23]

The female criminal was associated with inversion more broadly than in high-profile cases where inversion was a specific aspect of the crime. Ellis made the link between female homosexuality and criminals clear: "In prisons and lunatic asylums homosexual practices flourish . . . [and] such manifestations are often very morbid, and doubtless often very vicious." He also related an account of lesbian "initiation" in a Spanish prison (Ellis 1895, 144). The legal discussions surrounding the medical analysis of sexual perversion fortified this relationship between criminals and homosexuals, and the growing field of forensic medicine played a prominent role in most discussions of sexual perversion, as doctors waged professional turf battles with the legal profession.

There was also a historical connection between a woman who engaged in homosexual activity and criminality through the tool of the enlarged clitoris. In legal and religious history, the penetration of one woman by the enlarged clitoris or a dildo of another was considered "sodomy" and therefore had much more severe legal ramifications than mere mutual masturbation or "pollution." The sixteenth-century Italian author, Sinistrari, advised that in cases of alleged female homosexuality, the women's clitorises should be examined to see if "sodomy" was possible, and therefore more severe punishment warranted (Faderman 1981, 35–37; Park 1996; Daston & Park 1995). In one of the frequently cited cases of a female invert with an enlarged clitoris, the patient claimed to make use of her clitoris in this manner (Wise 1883, 89–90).

Clearly, such a practice was not an obscure, historical note at this time, but was known by women as well as doctors. In nineteenth-century cultural consciousness, the association of an enlarged, potentially sinful clitoris and a female homosexual implied criminality as well as sexual feelings toward women.

Prostitutes represented a separate class of criminals that was enormously important to the image of female sexuality in the nineteenth century. In her role as the merchant of vice, the prostitute was "the essential sexualized white female of the nineteenth century" (Gilman 1989b, 297). If the nineteenth century represented the height of female "asexuality," then the prostitute was the degenerate demon that defined the ideal by polar opposition. Prostitutes formed an especially strong example of natural female hypersexuality, since "their passions have drawn them" to the profession of continuous sexual activity, and they were somehow particularly suited to sexual work (Bernardy 1894, 431).[24]

A link between prostitution and female inversion was forged throughout the major articles on inversion. Ellis treated the association as well-known and indisputable, since it had "been noted by all who are acquainted with the lives of prostitutes" (1895, 156–157). In a case written by Krafft-Ebing, a woman of high class (a doctor's daughter, no less) ran away to a brothel, in which she entered into a homosexual relationship (Kiernan 1891, 202). The woman's entrance into prostitution and the advent of homosexual activity were almost certainly interpreted as causal or linked. Another case described a prostitute who "from curiosity" visited women who made "a specialty of the vice" and performed oral sex on her. The prostitute had a violent attack as a reaction to the experience, suggesting that even hardened prostitutes could not withstand the debauchery of such activities (Rosse 1892, 807).

In the case of female homosexual activity within prostitution, doctors could blame the male client and preserve a belief in female asexuality. Lydston claimed that female homosexuality usually catered to male perversion: "Women usually fall into perverted sexual habits for the purpose of pandering to the depraved tastes of their patrons rather than from instinctive impulses" (1889, 254). He also recounted a case of sexual perversion and inversion in which the woman "was not a prostitute, but moves in good society" (1889, 254). The phrasing in this case indicates that such an individual was meant to be viewed as the exception to the rule that female perverts or inverts were lower-class prostitutes under the direction of men.[25]

Prostitutes were similarly linked to female inverts through the increased size of their clitorises. Dr. Grace Peckham wrote that "it is the general belief that hypertrophies of this organ [the clitoris] are common among prostitutes"—a claim that Peckham disputed but nonetheless acknowledged (1891, 1153–1154). An increase in the organ's size could suggest a moral judgment and indicate growing corruption and sexuality. The association of prostitution with clitoral hypertrophy was fortified by their shared connection to syphilis, which was a common factor in accounts of clitoral hypertrophy and excision.[26] Female prostitutes were seen as a source of disease and corruption, and syphilis provided a graphic corporeal representation of the moral putrefaction of these "fallen" women.[27] Therefore, the attribution of a syphilitic symptom to the female invert not only associated her with a shady side of female sexuality, but also introduced images of contagion and degradation. The image of infection can be found in various accounts of female homosexuality. The differentiation between "true" inverts and those who could be swayed in either direction cast the former as the disease-carrier and the latter as the infected. An explicit account of contagious female homosexual activity told of the spread of "morbid sexual love for a person of the same sex" in a women's seminary. The author assumed that "some one girl, of a faulty nervous organization," started the "epidemic," which ended in the expulsion of several women. The other women involved were probably "neuropathically endowed," but required the developed insanity of the true invert to lead them into the vice (Mann 1893, 474).

Prostitutes were not the only lower-class women to be portrayed as hypersexual and inclined to perversion; all women from lower social strata were connected to hyper- and homosexuality, directly and through clitoral symbolism. The lower classes were seen as more degenerate and as operating under separate, lower standards than their wealthier counterparts (Chauncey 1982–83, 134–135). It was therefore anticipated that sexual inversion would also be more readily discovered in the working classes. Doctors condemned certain forms of lower-class employment for fostering sexual inversion in women, and claimed that the ideal situation for women was not to work outside the home at all. Thomas Laycock specified that "servants in hotels, seamstresses, lacemakers," and women employed in "large shops and stores" were especially prone to inversion (qtd. in Ellis 1895, 145). Such medical accounts excluded women in higher social positions and linked the lower class to inversion.

Similarly, certain lower-class activities were thought to be excessively stimulating for the clitoris, causing genital abnormalities. The sewing machine was a frequent subject of medical criticisms, and its indirect clitoral stimulation was held responsible for "attacks" of "erections" and "ejaculations." As a form of involuntary masturbation, sewing machine usage led to many degenerative symptoms: loss of appetite, a pale complexion, fatigue, uncontrollable "voluptuous sensations," and, eventually, pain (*Alienist* 1885b). One doctor directly linked clitoral hypertrophy to "the lower class of women"—whether she meant prostitutes or simply the poor is ambiguous, but either implied the working class (Peckham 1891, 1171). The clitoral sensitivity supposedly prevalent among these women reinforced the link between working women and hypersexuality, and tied other sources of clitoral abnormality, such as female inversion, to lower-class women.

Female homosexuality was especially effectively marginalized through the use of racial assumptions common to the medical community and society at large. The evidence of an "unfeminine" sex drive in lesbians linked them to other hypersexual creatures. To many American doctors this meant women of nonwhite races. One doctor summed up the hypersexuality of these races: "Doubtless from an ethnic point of view there is a difference in the erotic constitution, and an Anglo-Saxon may not be capable of so much salaciousness as a Turk, an Arab, or a negro" (Rosse 1892, 801).

Nonwhite races were generally associated with sexual perversion in American medical accounts, and this relationship extended to connect certain racial groups with homosexuality (See Somerville 1994; Carter in this volume). Various "lower races" were thought to be prone to this perversion; Ellis cited evidence of extensive female homosexual activity in New Zealand and South America, and in Egyptian harems (1895, 143). But the black woman was the zenith of all sexuality, normal or perverse. Ellis asserted that lesbian sexual activity was especially common among the "negroes and mulattos of the French Creole countries," and cited an account in which a respectable, beautiful, white woman was forced to avoid certain public places on account of "the excessive admiration of mulatto women and negresses, and the impudent invitations which they dare to address to her." Ellis also cited cases in which black women raped black girls, emphasizing the criminality (and masculinity) of black women's sexuality (1895, 143–144).

The medical discussions of the "imprisoned clitoris" or adhesions of the prepuce (a condition diametrically opposed to clitoral hypertrophy) give one example of how race affected the link between female inversion and clitoral hypertrophy. An "imprisoned clitoris" was covered and pinned by its hood so that it was less sensitive to the touch. In a paper entitled "Is Evolution Trying to Do Away with the Clitoris?" (1892), Dr. Robert T. Morris described this condition as the product of evolutionary processes, a form of degeneration that indicated that the white race was at the evolutionary limit of advances in civilization. He argued that the trait's prevalence indicated that "Nature . . . shows that it is intended to do away with the clitoris as civilization advances," simultaneously eradicating white female sexual desire (288). In comparison, other races were hypersexual. Morris stated that "in negresses the glans clitoriditis is free and the prepuce not adherent, except in a few individuals who probably possess a large admixture of white blood"; black women did not have the sexual restraint of white women, as indicated by their large, "free" clitorises (1892). Just as having smaller, restrained clitorises indicated that a black woman was closer to whites than other blacks, the presumably uninhibited or hypertrophied clitorises of female inverts suggested that they were closer to blacks and the "lower" races than to other whites.[28]

The connection between larger clitorises and blacks or other nonwhite races appeared throughout gynecological and anthropological literature in the late nineteenth century. It was believed that a hotter climate caused hypertrophy of the clitoris, and that the women of exotic continents were more prone to this condition than Europeans or Americans.[29] One writer generalized even further, and stated that writers in "Eastern countries" told of "the enormous hypertrophies of the clitoris as of a common occurrence" (Peckham 1891, 1153). Black women were frequently singled out in eighteenth- and nineteenth-century literature and culture as representatives of a primitive state without sexual control or repression. The "Hottentot Venus"—a southwest African woman whose buttocks and genitals were displayed and discussed throughout Europe in the early nineteenth century—left a strong legacy of the connection between blacks and genital hypertrophy (Gilman 1985, 84–93). Throughout the remainder of the century, people arguing for the separateness of human races commonly used the differences between white and black female genitalia to indicate the vast distance between the "civilized" and "primitive" peoples (Gilman 1989b, 291–294). Therefore, the possible degradation of the barrier between the races also lay in the female genitalia. One doctor, asserting that white female asexuality should not be surgically "cured," used the argument that "in some tribes in Africa the clitoris is said to hang down like a finger, and sometimes really prevent the approach of the male," suggesting that freeing the sexuality of white women might simultaneously lower their racial status, masculinize them through clitoral growth, and prevent "normal" penetration (Bernardy 1894, 430). A white invert's large clitoris could similarly cross the lines between white and black, between the civilized and the savage. Since perversion was believed to flourish among the "lower" races, white women could be dragged down to a similar degree of degeneration if they exhibited similar symptoms, either through homosexual behavior or through large clitorises. If they could be shown to have both conditions, then these women could effectively be excluded from the white race and from the elevated social and evolutionary status it claimed.

The Sexual Diagnoses of the Female Homosexual

Given the wide variety of groups and meanings associated with abnormal, enlarged clitorises, the female invert's assumed enlarged clitoris painted a powerful image of her. However much she was lumped together with other marginalized women, the female invert still had a unique combination of sexual diagnoses; her assigned traits were generally shared with other types of women, but the relative importance of each trait varied between the types. The mental and physical masculinity and the hypersexuality of the invert were more heavily emphasized than with the other degenerate and hypersexual women who also exhibited these traits. The cultural meanings placed on the clitoris and sexuality in nineteenth-century America would predetermine many aspects of this new creature, demonstrating the power of such body metaphors and associations.

According to the nineteenth-century understanding of sexuality and genitalia, the female invert was constructed as masculine for two reasons: first, because she was active in a sexual role with another woman, and therefore could not be classified as an asexual, "normal" woman; second, because her clitoris was larger than the average woman's. An enlarged clitoris, threatening to become or be used as a penis, indicated that the invert could not be considered truly female, and thus underlined her essential masculinity. By placing the female invert outside the world of womanhood, doctors maintained the image of the asexual woman. The medical literature supported these equations by supplying ample evidence of the masculinity of the female invert.

Within the category of "sexual inversion," doctors often described women in terms of the degree of their inversion, rather than simply whether they were inverted or not. In determining an individual's placement on the scale of inversion, doctors relied heavily on the assumption that a true invert was in some sense masculine—she might merit the remark: "such a person 'ought to have been a man' " (Ellis 1895,

153). Ellis identified the final stage in congenital homosexuality as "androgynia . . . in which the general bodily form corresponds in some degree to the abnormal sexual instinct and psychic disposition" (1894, 154). Thus, the progression from less to more inverted culminated in a physical masculinization that would embody the masculinity of the sex drive, possibly through genital abnormalities like clitoral growth.

In their case studies, physicians frequently listed evidence of masculinity in clothing, features, habits, or abilities as relevant facts concerning inversion. Well-developed muscles, a "masculine type of larynx," habits such as smoking, and a distaste for feminine tasks were examples of such elements in the invert's masculine gender role (Ellis 1895, 154). Childhood enjoyment of "masculine pastimes" was a frequent sign of subsequent inversion (Krafft-Ebing 1888, 580). Further evidence of the masculinity of the invert was found in the fact that only feminine men would ever be attracted to her, providing the required "passive" complement to her "active" masculinity (Ellis 1895, 154). This last example demonstrates that "inversion" was not entirely equivalent to the contemporary meaning of "homosexuality," but left room for sexual relations with certain members of the opposite sex. Finally, the patients themselves were often said to view themselves as masculine (Krafft-Ebing 1888, 581).[30]

Female inversion was sometimes attributed to sexual excesses, in itself a "masculine" quality, which had led her to ever increasing levels of perversity in order to gain satisfaction. Homosexuality was the ultimate last resort in this hierarchy, chosen when the sexual sense was too accustomed to other stimulation to be satisfied by anything less depraved: "sexual perversions . . . are sometimes . . . acquired vices being the result of a continual search for new sexual stimuli on the part of voluptuaries" (Dana 1891, 242). As mentioned above, inversion was frequently linked to nymphomania; in some cases there was no distinction between the two in terms of treatment (Kiernan 1888, 171; 1893).

In general, the hypersexuality of the invert was uncontrollable and potentially violent—qualities both attributed to male sexuality (Chauncey 1982–83, 118–119; Duggan 1993). One woman was described as prone to "periodical attacks of sexual furor" (Kiernan 1888, 171). Other accounts suggested that the invert was possibly in danger of raping others. In one such case, the patient "attempted to violate a female relative," while another subject "embraced the female attendant [in a hospital ward] . . . and came near to overpowering her" (Wise 1883, 89–90). Implicit in the description of such violent cases was the idea of female inverts possessing greater, masculine, physical strength. Another account of a dangerous and corrupting invert described "a woman who practices orgies of tribadism with other women after getting them under the influence of drink" (Rosse 1892, 807). The female homosexual, as a "female physically but a male psychically," was out of control, and unlike a "normal female," she "gave in to that sexual thirst" (Kiernan 1892, 210). Once again, the connection between inversion and inevitable criminality and insanity was fortified through the invert's evident lack of sexual self-control.

Such overt masculinity in the female invert presented in medical accounts was further supported by her enlarged clitoris. Clitoral hypertrophy in an invert was not always attributed to a specific cause, and could be congenital, acquired, or possibly both. On the one hand, it could result from lesbian sexual activity involving clitoral stimulation, since "most organs grow by manipulation" (Bernardy 1894, 430). Another doctor argued that "sexual perversions may result in pseudo-hermaphrodism," as indicated by clitoral growth. Women who were not originally pseudohermaphrodites could become so after "experiments" with "pseudohermaphroditic" females (Kiernan 1888, 130). This process demonstrates the feared power of sexual activity to alter the apparent gender of the invert and consequently to disrupt social order as well as swell the ranks of inverts through their contagious encounters with "experimenting" women. On the other hand, some doctors viewed sexual perversion as attributable to genital abnormalities, rather than the other way around. One doctor believed so strongly that sexual perversion needed to have a somatic cause that he claimed the perversion itself was sufficient to prove the genital abnormality, even if it could not be distinguished by examination: genital abnormality "would necessarily be too occult for discovery by any physical means at our command. It is however, but too readily recognized by its results" (Lydston 1889, 256).

Doctors were not the only ones to associate clitoral enlargement and female inversion. In one case, the patient identified her own clitoris as abnormal, and linked this abnormality to increased masculinity: "I may be a woman in one sense, but I have peculiar organs that make me more a man than a woman." The doctor did not notice extreme genital abnormalities, "except an enlarged clitoris covered by a relaxed pudendum." The patient claimed to be able to erect the clitoris for sexual intercourse "in the same way a turtle protrudes its head," and she saw this as a positive trait (Wise 1883, 90). This patient "considered herself a man in all that the name implies," and having abnormal genitals was clearly a significant trait for her, as well as for doctors (Wise 1883, 88–89).

The use of clitoridectomies as a possible cure for homosexuality was a rare outcome of the connection between female inversion and clitoral abnormality. One author counseled against clitoridectomies for sexual perversions, and suggested instead "the use of douches, baths, bromide of potassium, or camphor, acetate of ammonia" as other possible treatments for perversion (Moreau 1884, 383). A colleague believed that "in some cases" surgery could be helpful, but only in the case of "hereditary sexual perverts" (Hughes 1893, 563). The interaction between clitoridectomy and masculinity in the case of the female invert suggests that some doctors viewed removing the clitoris as a way of "feminizing" the patient. Such an association between the very presence or awareness of the clitoris and improper adult female sexuality was to become especially significant for Freud and his followers in the coming decades.[31]

Conclusion

As Thomas Laqueur has observed, "there is nothing natural about how the clitoris is constructed" (1989, 92). In the late nineteenth century, the clitoris was positioned at the intersection of many cultural categories. To a physician of the time, the clitoris was the source of passion, the woman's penis, the source of nervous disorder; its growth was a sign of the masturbator, the insane, the degenerate, the masculine, the savage, the poor, the prostitute, the criminal, the syphilitic—the list is long and intertwined. The complexity of these relationships reflects the frequently conflicting trends of history. The very fact that these relationships were not consciously planned out and universally observed is what lends such richness to the symbolism of what one doctor dismissively called "this little bit of flesh" (Garrigues 1896, 292). The female invert was brought into a medical world full of associations and meanings—there was never any chance of her body being viewed apart from these values.

The application of social and cultural meanings to the clitoris, or to any other part of the body, was not something that died out in the last century. Although the search for genital abnormalities in homosexuals gradually fell out of favor in the early twentieth century, the cultural association of sexual orientation and the body housing it continued. The terms changed to reflect new trends: electroshock, neurophysiology and lobotomy, hormones, and genes.[32] Jennifer Terry's discussion (1990) of the research conducted by the Committee for the Study of Sex Variants in the 1930s indicates the continuity of many of the associations I have discussed here. Although the treatment of sexuality was greatly affected by medical and psychiatric changes (notably the advent of psychoanalysis), the Committee's results, published by George Henry as *Sex Variants: A Study of Homosexual Patterns* (1941), demonstrate that the somatic search for pathognomonic differences between lesbian and heterosexual women, and the assumption that gender role was reversed in homosexuality both remained important factors. Furthermore, the study included genital measurements, and reported larger-than-average clitorises and greater clitoral excitability in the lesbian subjects. Female homosexuality continued to be connected to hypersexuality, and race seemed to be an important factor since one black subject had an especially long clitoris with which she claimed to penetrate her partners (Terry 1990).

The clitoris played an important role in the medical accounts of female homosexuality from the late nineteenth century, and its cultural meanings have been widespread and persistent over time. An interesting and crucial line of future study is the investigation of the patient's perspective, or an analysis of the body image of women who were classified as deviant by the medical world. How much of an impact did this medical model have on these women, and how much influence did these women have on their doctors and on medical theory? An examination of these kinds of questions would clearly complement analyses of medical constructions of sexuality. Without such inquiries, it is especially difficult to analyze the social significance of medical writings. While medicine reflects its society, it also has a specific perspective on and perhaps a limited significance to its broader world.

The web of associations and mutual links that surrounded female homosexual activity and other marginal social groups a century ago lend a perspective to many current issues facing lesbians, gay men, people of color, poor people, women, and other groups that are condemned by the most powerful members of American society. The slippery slope that many politicians, among others, build into their arguments against "rampant" corruption in modern society relies on similar connections. The poor are still linked to hypersexuality (and hyperreproductivity) in debates about welfare and teenage pregnancy. People of color and gays are marginalized through images of contagion in AIDS debates. Lesbians, feminists, and "unnatural" masculinity are seen as synonymous, and are represented as a threat to male power and traditional morality. Lesbians and gays are popularly invested with incredible power to convert (or infect) men and women, girls and boys, to the homosexual "lifestyle" and its associated licentiousness, unless prevented by strong-arm tactics. Likewise, women's sexuality is by no means a settled matter; while women are seen as less sexually driven than men, they are frequently portrayed as the sum of their sexual parts and desires. As Valerie Traub (1995) and Paula Bennett (1993) point out, the clitoris also continues to serve as a powerful symbol in the lesbian and feminist communities, representing either a rejection or a vestige of patriarchal and heterosexual associations and beliefs. To gain a more complete insight into society and sexuality, we need an understanding of how our bodies have been construed, and how they might be reconstructed. As we lose an absolute faith in the "natural" or "objective" elements of anatomy and medicine, we gain innumerable options, and can base our decisions more confidently on our own perspectives and authorities.

Notes

1 The doctors who developed the most prominent classification systems published in American journals were James Kiernan (1892, 197–198), Richard von Krafft-Ebing (1888), Havelock Ellis (1895), and Frank Lydston (1889, 254–255); also Anthony (1898, 288). Also see C. H. Hughes (1893, 531) on the importance of classification.

2 For a more precise and complete discussion of the development and differences between these and other terms see Chauncey (1982–83; 1994, 47–50).

3 Also see Jonathan Ned Katz's discussion of the construction of these categories and the changes such terms have undergone over the past 150 years (1994, 137–174; 1995). Greenberg (1988, 1–25) describes general issues in the definition of sexuality and social construction. Leila Rupp (1984) and Lillian Faderman (1991, 1–9) examine some of these issues in the analysis of women's historical relationships.

4 The most widely reported cases in which clitoral hypertrophy was linked to female inversion were: one from P. M. Wise (1883), which was cited in many of Kiernan's articles; one from Duhousset, cited in Kiernan (1892, 209), along with another case on page 208 of the same article; one case classified as a "female hermaphrodite" in Kiernan (1892, 196; 1891, 196–197). The generalizations connecting the clitoris, or abnormal genitals, with homosexuality were more widespread than specific cases in the literature. It is equally interesting to note the cases in which the clitoris was explicitly denied any direct relationship to female inversion, as if such a relationship was expected but absent in a particular individual (e.g., Ellis 1895, 155; Shaw & Ferris 1883, 188).

5 Elizabeth Lunbeck identifies the creation of the "hypersexual female" as a broad category occurring in early-twentieth-century America. She claims that the discussion of women as pathologically sexual represented a rejection of Victorian sexual ideology (1987, 513–517).

Although medical definitions of female sexuality were undoubtedly in flux in the early twentieth century, the links between a variety of medical subjects who were seen as hypersexual were clearly forged in the preceding century.

6 See Bullough (1994, ch. 4) and Starr (1982, ch. 3) on the American medical profession and the purity campaigns. Also see Walter Kendrick's historical work on pornography (1987, ch. 3) discussing fears of the corruption of youth in the nineteenth century.

7 For a debate on ethnicity and perversions, see *Chicago Medical Journal* (1884, 265).

8 Paula Bennett (1993, 249–251) examines the symbolism of the "castration" of sexually deviant women through clitoridectomies as a clear attempt to control "socially undesirable," excessively "masculine" sexuality, and she identifies clitoridectomy as a precursor to Freud's phallocentric theory of the vaginal orgasm.

9 See Lillian Faderman's work on nineteenth-century views of female sexuality (1981, Part II ch. 1); also see Hays (1964, 224–233), Chauncey (1982–83, 117–119), and Cott (1978) on female asexuality at this time.

10 Another interesting note about the debate in this article is that, in order to convince their colleagues that female desire should be a concern, some doctors argued that female aneroticism caused male ailments (Bernardy 1894).

11 In the first three decades of the twentieth century, British physician Havelock Ellis was to become perhaps the foremost authority on sexuality in the American medical community. He was an honorary member of the Chicago Academy of Medicine, a member of the Medico-Legal Society of New York, and Vice President of the International Medical and Legal Congress of New York in 1895. Published first in American journals before his book on *Sexual Inversion* (1897) appeared briefly in Britain, Ellis's early articles on male and female homosexuality (1894, 1895) were more extensive and frequently more accepting than those of his predecessors. His work, however, did not represent an absolute departure from past authorities. His sympathies were undoubtedly shaped by his many friendships with homosexual artists and writers, and his marriage to a lesbian, Edith Lees (see Grosskurth 1980).

12 Kiernan quotes another writer on the nature of love: "In love the fundamental tome is the sexual relation—the fact that one of the lovers is male, the other female" (1892, 190–191).

13 The clitoris was widely recognized as important for sexual desire, but this theory was by no means uncontested. Dr. Eugene P. Bernardy reflected on this conflict, stating, "But few physicians believe alike regarding the location of the sensitive area which causes sexual orgasm. Some will give the vagina; some the ovaries, while others the uterus; but in my judgment I believe undoubtedly the clitoris is the prime factor" (1896, 51). Notwithstanding some disagreement, most doctors in this period, and many of their predecessors, believed that the clitoris was in some way linked to sexual desire and satisfaction.

14 The most notorious advocate of clitoridectomies, Isaac Baker Brown, was expelled from the London Obstetrical Society in 1867 for his excessive use of the technique (Scull & Favreau 1986). This does not mean that clitoridectomies died out at this time. They continued to be seen as a valid option for a variety of sexual disorders, from clitoral cancer to nymphomania and inversion, especially as antisepsis made operations less risky and surgical branches of the medical community gained power in the final decades of the century.

15 Comparison of the clitoris to the penis was not the only available approach in this period. Paula Bennett points out that there was a well-developed system of clitoral symbolism in the nineteenth century that female poets exploited and claimed as separate from phallocentric symbolism (1993).

16 See Daston and Park (1995), Park (1996), and Laqueur (1990, 134–142) for discussions of hermaphroditism in the early modern period.

17 Interestingly, there was a degree of concern in the medical community that even doctors' articles about perversion would serve, in turn, as a source of overstimulation (*Alienist and Neurologist* 1893, 527).

18 Dr. James Kiernan was a prolific writer on perversion who served as a professor of forensic psychiatry at the Chicago Academy of Medicine in the late nineteenth century. He would become the editor of a sexology column in the *Urologic and Cutaneous Review* in the early twentieth century.

19 A woman's life was seen as passing through many perilous periods, especially puberty and menopause, in which degenerative traits could surface and not only affect her children but also alter her own developmental processes (e.g., a mishandled puberty might lead to difficulties in pregnancy or menopause) (Smith-Rosenberg 1985, 182–196).

20 Bram Dijkstra (1986, 272–332) also notes the intertwining concepts in late nineteenth-century art of female hypersexuality and of degeneration to an animal past.

21 Chapman (1883, 453–455) argued that the use of contraception or withdrawal produced similar effects.

22 On clitoridectomy as a treatment for masturbation and other female ills, see Lydston (1889, 285), Engelmann (1882), Mills (1885), Eyer (1894), and Cooper (1862).

23 See Duggan (1993) on the particulars and historical significance of the Alice Mitchell-Freda Ward case, and on the general association of female inversion with criminality or violence.

24 More on this division between the prostitute and the virtuous woman in Victorian society can be found in H. R. Hays (1964, 228–233).

25 This concept of lesbian sex as a source of pleasure for men rather than something women would initiate is historically persistent. The pornography of the eighteenth and nineteenth (and twentieth) centuries contained numerous references to lesbian sex among prostitutes, accounts written by and for men (Bullough 1979, 120–121). Brothel entertainment in late nineteenth-century America also often included performances of lesbian sex acts (Gilfoyle 1992, 162 and 176–177).

26 On the association between syphilis and clitoral hypertrophy, see Edis (1892, 412), Thomas (1873–84), Wylie (1873–84), and Peckham (1891).

27 Gilman also points out the similarities in the cultural significance of eighteenth-century venereal disease and nineteenth-century masturbation (1989b, 203–210, 306; 1989a, 87–98).

28 Morris also claimed that the clitorises of Semitic women were less given to "imprisonment," and wrote, "I presume that the glans clitoriditis is free in wild tribes generally." He interjected in his discussion of blacks and "wild tribes" a paragraph stating that the clitoris is also free in domestic animals (1892, 291).

29 This belief may have been prompted by knowledge of female circumcision practiced by some African tribes (Laqueur 1989, 114–117; Park 1996; Traub 1995, 88–89).

30 Why women might want to embrace masculinity and adopt the role of the "mannish lesbian" has been the subject of some debate (Smith-Rosenberg 1989; Newton 1989; Vicinus 1993; Duggan 1993).

31 See Traub (1995), Bennett (1993), Laqueur (1989; 1990, 233–243) on the historical trends surrounding Freud's views on the clitoris.

32 See Katz's summary of historical trends in the medical treatment of homosexuality (1992, 129–207).

References

Alienist and Neurologist. 1885a. The sober second thought in gynecology. 6:155–156.

———. 1885b. Clitoridean crisis before the pains of progressive locomotor ataxia. 6:438–439.

———. 1893. Review of *Psychopathia Sexualis* by Richard von Krafft-Ebing. 14:526–527.

Anthony, Francis W. 1898. The question of responsibility in cases of sexual perversion. *Boston Medical and Surgical Journal* 89:288–291.

Bacon, C.S. 1898. Adhesions of the female prepuce. *American Gynæcological and Obstetrical Journal* 1:278–283.

Beebe, H.E. 1897. The clitoris. *Journal of Orificial Surgery* 6:8–12.

Bennett, Paula. 1993. Critical clitoridectomy: Female sexual imagery and feminist psychoanalytic theory. *Signs* 18:235–259.

Bernardy, Eugene P. 1894. One of the causes of aneroticism in women. *Proceedings of the Philadelphia County Medical Society* 15:426–432.

———. 1896. Report of cases of aneroticism in women. *The Medical Council* 1:51–52.

Bullough, Vern L. 1979. *Homosexuality: A History.* New York: New American Library.

———. 1994. *Science in the Bedroom.* New York: Basic Books.

Bullough, Vern L., and Martha Voght. 1973. Homosexuality and its confusion with the "Secret Sin" in pre-Freudian America. *Journal of the History of Medicine* 28:143–155.

Chamberlain, J. Edward, and Sander L. Gilman, eds. 1985. *Degeneration: The Dark Side of Progress.* New York: Columbia University Press.

Chapman, J. Milne. 1883. On masturbation as an etiological factor in the production of gynic diseases. *The American Journal of Obstetrics and Diseases of Women and Children* 16:449–458, 578–598.

Chauncey, George. 1982–83. From sexual inversion to homosexuality: Medicine and the changing conceptualization of female deviance. *Salmagundi* 58:114–146.

———. 1994. *Gay New York: Gender, Urban Culture, and the Making of the Gay Male World, 1890–1940.* New York: Basic Books.

Chicago Medical Journal. 1884. Chicago Medical Society. 48:263–267.

Clark, A. Campbell. 1888. Relations of the sexual and reproductive functions to insanity. *Journal of Insanity* 45:292–297.

Cooper, E.R. 1862. Removing the clitoris in cases of masturbation, accompanied with threatening insanity. *San Francisco Medical Press* 3:17–21.

Cott, Nancy. 1978. Passionlessness: An interpretation of Victorian sexual ideology. *Signs* 4:219–236.

Cumston, Charles Greene. 1895–96. On primary malignant tumors of the clitoris. *Annals of Gynecology and Pædiatry* 9:268–279.

Dana, Charles L. 1891. On certain sexual neuroses. *The Medical and Surgical Reporter* 65:241–245.

Daston, Lorraine, and Katherine Park. 1995. The hermaphrodite and the orders of nature: Sexual ambiguity in early modern France. *G L Q* 2:419–438.

Degler, Carl N. 1984. What ought to be and what was: Women's sexuality in the nineteenth century. In *Women and Health in America*, ed. Judith Walzer Leavitt, 40–56. Madison: University of Wisconsin Press.

Dijkstra, Bram. 1986. *Idols of Perversity: Fantasies of Feminine Evil in Fin-de-Siècle Culture.* New York: Oxford University Press.

Duggan, Lisa. 1993. The trials of Alice Mitchell: Sensationalism, sexology, and the lesbian subject in turn-of-the-century America. *Signs* 18:791–814.
Edis, Arthur W. 1892. *Diseases of Women*. Philadelphia: Henry C. Lea.
Ellis, Havelock. 1894. The study of sexual inversion. *Medico-Legal Journal* 12: 148–157.
———. 1895. Sexual inversion in women. *Alienist and Neurologist* 16:141–158.
Engelmann, George J. 1882. Clitoridectomy. *American Practitioner* 25:1–11.
Eyer, Alvin. 1894. Clitoridectomy for the cure of certain cases of masturbation in young girls. *International Medical Magazine* 3:259–262.
Faderman, Lillian. 1981. *Surpassing the Love of Men*. New York: William Morrow.
———. 1991. *Odd Girls and Twilight Lovers: A History of Lesbian Life in Twentieth-Century America*. New York: Penguin.
Fellman, Anita Clair and Michael Fellman. 1981. The rule of moderation in late nineteenth-century American sexual ideology. *Journal of Sex Research* 17:238–255.
Foucault, Michel. 1990. *The History of Sexuality: An Introduction, Volume 1*. Trans. Robert Hurley. New York: Vintage Books, Random House.
Garrigues, Henry J. 1896. *A Text-Book of the Diseases of Women*. Philadelphia: W. B. Saunders.
Gilfoyle, Timothy J. 1992. *City of Eros: New York City, Prostitution, and the Commercialization of Sex, 1790–1920*. New York: W. W. Norton.
Gilman, Sander L. 1985. *Difference and Pathology*. Ithaca: Cornell University Press.
———. 1989a. AIDS and syphilis: The iconography of disease. In *AIDS: Cultural Analysis/Cultural Activism*, ed. Douglas Crimp, 87–107. Cambridge: MIT Press.
———. 1989b. *Sexuality: An Illustrated History*. New York: Wiley.
Greenberg, David F. 1988. *The Construction of Homosexuality*. Chicago: University of Chicago Press.
Groneman, Carol. 1994. Nymphomania: The historical construction of female sexuality. *Signs* 19:337–367.
Grosskurth, Phyllis. 1980. *Havelock Ellis. A Biography*. New York: Alfred Knopf.
Hale, Edwin M. 1896. Two cases of imprisoned clitoris. *Homeopathic Journal of Obstetrics* 18:446–449.
Hassler, M. Margaret. 1897. Preputial adhesions in little girls. *The Hahnemannian Monthly* 32:182–185.
Hays, H.R. 1964 *The Dangerous Sex: The Myth of Feminine Evil*. New York: G.P. Putnam.
Henry, George W. 1941. *Sex Variants: A Study of Homosexual Patterns*. New York: Hoeber.
Hughes, C.H. 1893. Erotopathia—morbid erotism. *Alienist and Neurologist* 14:531–578.
Katz, Jonathan Ned. 1992. *Gay American History*. New York: Penguin.
———. 1994. *Gay/Lesbian Almanac*. New York: Carroll & Graf.
———. 1995. *The Invention of Heterosexuality*. New York: Dutton.
Kendrick, Walter. 1987. *The Secret Museum*. New York: Viking Penguin.
Kiernan, James. 1888. Sexual perversion, and the Whitechapel murders. *Medical Standard* 4:129–130, 170–172.
———. 1891. Psychological aspects of the sexual appetite. *Alienist and Neurologist* 12:188–219.
———. 1892. Responsibility in sexual perversion. *Chicago Medical Recorder* 8:185–210.
———. 1893. Psychical treatment of congenital sexual inversion. *The Review of Insanity and Nervous Disease* 3–4: 293–295.
Krafft-Ebing, Richard von. 1888. Perversion of the sexual instinct—report of cases. *Alienist and Neurologist* 9:565–581.

Laqueur, Thomas. 1989. "Amor veneris, vel dulcedo appeletur." In *Zone: Fragments for a History of the Human Body.* Part Three. Ed. Michel Feher, 90–131. New York: Zone.

———. 1990. *Making Sex: Body and Gender from the Greeks to Freud.* Cambridge: Harvard University Press.

Lewis, Bransford. 1890. A consideration of sexual neurasthenia. *American Practitioner and News* 9:228–232.

Lunbeck, Elizabeth. 1987. "A new generation of women": Progressive psychiatrists and the hypersexual female. *Feminist Studies* 13:513–543.

Lydston, G. Frank. 1889. Sexual perversion, satyriasis and nymphomania. *Medical and Surgical Reporter* 61:253–258.

Mann, Edward C. 1893. Medico-legal and psychological aspect of the trial of Josephine Mallison Smith. *Alienist and Neurologist* 14:467–477.

Medical News. 1884. Does male copulation without emission injure female health? 45:240–241.

Medicine. 1899. A case of probable *conträre Sexualempfindung.* 5:526–528.

Mills, Charles K. 1885. A case of nymphomania. *Medical Times* 15:534–540.

Moreau (de Tours), Paul. 1884. On the aberrations of the genesic sense. *Alienist and Neurologist* 5:367–385.

Morris, Robert T. 1892. Is evolution trying to do away with the clitoris? *Transactions of the Association of Obstetricians and Gynecologists* 5:288–302.

Newton, Esther. 1989. The mythic mannish lesbian: Radclyffe Hall and the New Woman. In *Hidden From History: Reclaiming the Gay and Lesbian Past,* ed. Martin B. Duberman, Martha Vicinus, and George Chauncey, Jr., 281–293. New York: New American Library.

Park, Katherine. 1996. The rediscovery of the clitoris: French medicine and the *tribade,* 1570–1620. Forthcoming in *The Body in Parts: Discourses and Anatomies in Early Modern Europe,* ed. Carla Mazzio and David Hillman. New York: Routledge.

Peckham, Grace. 1891. Tumors of the clitoris. *The American Journal of Obstetrics* 24:1153–1172.

Pick, Daniel. 1989. *Faces of Degeneration.* Cambridge: Cambridge University Press.

Raffalovich, Marc-André. 1895. Uranism, congenital sexual inversion. *Journal of Comparative Neurology* 5:33–65.

Rosse, Irving C. 1892. Sexual hypochondriasis and perversion of the genesic instinct. *Journal of Nervous and Mental Disease* 17:795–811.

Rupp, Leila. 1984. "Imagine my surprise": Women's relationships in historical perspective. In *Women and Health in America,* ed. Judith Walzer Leavitt, 40–56. Madison: University of Wisconsin Press.

Scull, Andrew, and Diane Favreau. 1986. The clitoridectomy craze. *Social Research* 53:243–260.

Shaw, J.C., and G.N. Ferris. 1883. Perverted sexual instinct. *Journal of Nervous and Mental Disease* 10:185–204.

Showalter, Elaine. 1990. *Sexual Anarchy: Gender and Culture at the Fin de Siècle.* New York: Penguin.

Shrady, George F. 1884. Perverted sexual instinct. *The Medical Record* 26 (July 19): 70–71.

Skene, Alexander J.C. 1889. *Treatise on the Diseases of Women for the Use of Students and Practitioners.* New York: D. Appleton.

———. 1898. *Treatise on the Diseases of Women for the Use of Students and Practitioners.* 3d ed. New York: D. Appleton.

Sligh, J.M. 1894. Adherent prepuce in the female. *Medical Sentinel* 2:215–218.
Smith-Rosenberg, Carroll. 1985. *Disorderly Conduct: Visions of Gender in Victorian America.* New York: Oxford University Press.
———. 1989. Discourses of sexuality and subjectivity: The New Woman, 1870–1936. In *Hidden From History: Reclaiming the Gay and Lesbian Past.* ed. Martin B. Duberman, Martha Vicinus, and George Chauncey, Jr., 264–280. New York: New American Library.
Smith-Rosenberg, Carroll, and Charles Rosenberg. 1984. The female animal: Medical and biological views of woman and her role in nineteenth-century America. In *Women and Health in America,* ed. Judith Walzer Leavitt, 12–27. Madison: University of Wisconsin Press.
Somerville, Siobhan. 1994. Scientific racism and the emergence of the homosexual body. *Journal of the History of Sexuality* 5:243–266
Spitzka, Edward C. 1881. A historical case of sexual perversion. *Chicago Medical Review* 4:378–379.
———. 1888. The Whitechapel murders: Their medico-legal and historical aspects. *Journal of Nervous and Mental Disease* 13:765–778.
Starr, Paul. 1982. *The Social Transformation of American Medicine.* New York: Basic Books.
Terry, Jennifer. 1990. Lesbians under the medical gaze: Scientists search for remarkable differences. *Journal of Sex Research* 27:317–339.
Theriot, Nancy M. 1993. Women's voices in nineteenth-century medical discourse: A step toward deconstructing science. *Signs* 19:1–31.
Thomas, T. G. 1873–74. Case of syphilitic hypertrophy of the clitoris: removal with the electric cautery by Prof. T. G. Thomas; death thirteen days after, from peritonitis due to salpingian dropsy. *American Journal of Obstetrics* 6:43–45.
Traub, Valerie. 1995. The psychomorphology of the clitoris. *G L Q* 2:81–113.
Vicinus, Martha. 1993. "They wonder to which sex I belong": The historical roots of the modern lesbian identity. In *The Lesbian and Gay Studies Reader,* ed. Henry Abelove, Michèle Aina Barale, and David Halperin, 432–452. New York: Routledge.
Walton, John T. 1857. Case of nymphomania sucessfully treated. *American Journal of Medical Science* 33:47–50.
Wise, P. M. 1883. Case of sexual perversion. *Alienist and Neurologist* 4:88–91.
Wylie, W. G. 1873–4. Case of syphilitic hypertrophy of the clitoris. *American Journal of Obstetrics* 6:43–45.

Per scientiam ad justitiam
Magnus Hirschfeld and the Sexual Politics of Innate Homosexuality

James D. Steakley

In November 1930, when Magnus Hirschfeld arrived in New York to begin a four-month lecture tour that would take him to Chicago, Detroit, Los Angeles, and San Francisco, he was hailed in the headlines of the far-flung Hearst newspaper chain as "the Einstein of sex" (Viereck 1931, 1). By invoking the most renowned German Jewish scientist of the times, this bit of journalistic shorthand both suggested Hirschfeld's preeminence within the emerging discipline of sexology and punned on his particular contribution:

> [Hirschfeld] espouses the theory of sex relativity. He is not the first to enunciate this doctrine, but he carries it to its logical conclusion. Hirschfeld looks upon homosexuality and other divergences from standardization not as pathological phenomena but as variations of the sex instinct. A student of eugenics, Hirschfeld attempts to find a scientific basis for love. His experiments are as revolutionary as his conclusions. (Viereck 1930, 285)

Such publicistic puffery will no doubt seem particularly exaggerated to any reader who, in a library or in a secondhand bookstore's "*erotica et curiosa*" section, has perused Hirschfeld's *Sexual Pathology* (1917–1920), *The Sexual History of the World War* (1930d), or *Sexual Anomalies and Perversions* (1936b). For decades the cornerstones of Hirschfeld's quite limited reception in the English-speaking world, these shoddy works were published without his prior knowledge or consent—and without any payment of royalties. In the words of one American colleague familiar with Hirschfeld's works in German, the English versions offered "not a translation, but a mutilation" (Robinson 1934, 151). The first two omit well over half the contents of the German originals, while the third is not by Hirschfeld at all—even though his name appears on the spine—but instead is a posthumous pastiche, thrown together by Arthur Koestler and Norman Haire to turn a quick profit (Koestler 1954, 213). All three either downplay Hirschfeld's views on homosexuality or subject them to outright distortion.

The same is true of the sole extant copy of the film *Different from the Others* (1919b), which Hirschfeld coscripted and in which he appeared. Broadcast on New York television in 1986, this truncated version (one-third the length of the original) shows Hirschfeld sagely observing that homosexuality is a pathological condition, criminalized because of the danger it poses to youth—the very opposite of the standpoint he voiced in the original film and, in an even more perverse twist, precisely the rationale advanced by the German censorship panel that banned the film in 1920.

Until such time as reliable translations of Hirschfeld's works appear—and his thousand page magnum opus, *Homosexuality of Man and Woman* (1914c), is now in preparation for the American press that recently published his *Transvestites: The Erotic Drive to Cross-Dress* ([1910] 1991)—the best access to his thought for readers limited to English will continue to be books by Edward Carpenter (1908), Xavier Mayne ([1908] 1975), and Havelock Ellis (1915), all of whom largely adopted Hirschfeld's views even when they did not expressly acknowledge it.

The Education of a Sexologist

Magnus Hirschfeld was born on May 14, 1868, in Kolberg, a provincial city on the Baltic coast celebrated by nationalists for its unyielding resistance to Napoleon's conquest of Germany in 1806. Until the civil rights reforms brought on by the six-year French occupation, Kolberg had entirely banned Jews from residing within its walls (Stoewer 1927, 19), and Hirschfeld's parents moved there in 1852, when the rising popularity of seashore bathing brought the city new prosperity as Germany's premiere Baltic resort—although it never matched the prestige of those on the North Sea coast, where Jews were unwelcome. His father was originally from Neustettin, where in 1881 the synagogue was burned to the ground (Friedlaender 1919, 17).

As a schoolboy, Hirschfeld was subjected to occasional anti-Semitic slights and harbored a dawning sense of difference based on his homosexual orientation. He was deeply influenced by his father's prominence as a highly respected physician specializing in balneo- or hydrotherapy (H. Hirschfeld 1870), as the founding director of a Jewish hospital (*Festschrift* 1884, 9), as a regular political columnist for the local newspaper, and as a public hygienist, spearheading, for example, the laying of sewage lines to halt contamination of the economically crucial waterfront (Hirschfeld 1925b, 5, 7). In time, Hirschfeld was to hurl himself into each of these four spheres of activity. He grew up reflecting as well on his father's role as a young medical student in the revolution of 1848, when he had treated insurrectionists wounded at the barricades surrounding the royal palace in Berlin; and Hirschfeld would later figure in the revolution of 1918 on the same spot. He affiliated with the Social Democratic Party early on, and he remained a staunch socialist throughout his life.

During his *Gymnasium* (secondary school) years, Hirschfeld's interests focused on language study, and his university studies at Breslau initially concentrated on languages and philosophy. After only one year, however, he acceded to the example of his father—

now deceased—and two older brothers by changing to medicine. He by no means abandoned his interest in languages, however, as documented by the fascinating chapter on "The Name and Terminology of Male and Female Homosexuality" in *Homosexuality of Man and Woman.* As a result of repeated sojourns abroad, he was able to converse, correspond, and lecture in both English and French with considerable fluency.

He carried out his medical studies as a journeyman of sorts, transferring from Breslau to the universities of Strasbourg, Munich, and Heidelberg, before taking his M.D. degree at Berlin in 1893. Study of anatomy, physiology, embryology, neurology, histology, and internal medicine as well as surgery, ophthalmology, and obstetrics briefly brought him into contact with some of the most distinguished German medical professors of the late nineteenth century, including Emil Du Bois-Reymond, Heinrich von Bardeleben, and Rudolf Virchow.

Religious affiliation was duly noted by university bureaucracies of that era, and as a twenty-year-old, Hirschfeld discontinued entering "Jewish" on registration forms (Herzer 1992, 18). This departure from his parents' religion was largely predicated on his exposure to Darwinism, which provided the socialist movement with an all-encompassing alternative to creationism. Denounced by the authorities as a godless challenge to church and crown, the teaching of evolutionary theory was forbidden in German secondary schools until after World War I.

In Germany, it was above all the Jena zoologist Ernst Haeckel who popularized Darwin's notion of sexual selection as the scientific key that unlocked the riddles of nature, and the focus of Hirschfeld's later sexological work was the natural occurrence of variations of sexual dimorphism. Hirschfeld later dedicated his *Natural Laws of Love* (1912a) to the "sage of Jena," who subsequently expressed his confidence that the scientific study of sexuality would destroy "millennia-old religious superstitions and traditional morals" (Hirschfeld 1914b, 282–283), and he was honored when Haeckel contributed an article on hermaphroditism to his *Yearbook of Sexual Intermediates* (Haeckel 1912). He affiliated with the Monist League, founded by Haeckel to advance the scientific education of the general public and to organize Sunday morning gatherings devoted to reverential reflection on nature—an alternative to church services. This spiritual aspect was scarcely coincidental, for monism repudiated the Judeo-Christian dualism of body and soul, postulating instead a unity down to the level of the individual cell. The monistic outlook would eventually lead Hirschfeld to assert an underlying harmony of physical and psychological traits in homosexuals.

Hirschfeld's break with Judaism may also have set the stage for coming to terms with his own homosexual orientation, a process that the study of medicine by no means facilitated. Reflecting on his university years, he recalled an all-pervasive prudishness. He "scarcely ever heard the term 'sexual' from the mouth of a professor," let alone "the word 'love,' which was completely beyond the pale":

> Venereal disease was talked about, to be sure. The hideous Gorgon's head of syphilis was held up before the eyes of students. . . . Professors did speak about normal and abnormal births, described in anatomy the final structure

> and in evolutionary biology the developing structure of sexual organs; and at the end of class they shamefacedly erased any drawing of these organs from the chalkboard so that no unauthorized person would glimpse them. Their functions, to say nothing of sexual feelings and needs, went entirely unmentioned by any professor of physiology and any hygiene textbook; these things were at most mentioned fleetingly by a particularly courageous lecturer in zoology. Such a thing as normal sexual drive [that is, desires and acts] was officially nonexistent, and concerning drive disturbances, which went by the name of "perversities," people only whispered strange and horrible things. ([1922–1923] 1986, 162)

The unnamed zoology instructor bold enough to mention sexuality may well have been Richard Hertwig at Munich, who had studied under Ernst Haeckel and specialized in nuclear plasma and sexual determination. But during Hirschfeld's final year of study, the shroud of silence was briefly lifted:

> The most renowned alienist of Berlin, Professor Emanuel Mendel, offered students of medicine and law a weekly evening lecture on feeble-mindedness with demonstrations. Among the sex offenders brought before us young academics was one pederast. We heard at the outset about the bodily signs of "active" and "passive" pedication—a funnel-shaped anus and a correspondingly pointy penis. These signs, set forth in our forensic medicine textbooks, were declared by our professor to be unreliable proofs, for there were pederasts without them and other persons who presented them but were not given to pederasty. In recent times, he continued, the St. Petersburg neurologist Tarnovsky and the Viennese psychiatrist von Krafft-Ebing had even claimed that some pederasts or homosexuals abhorred the use of the rectum and did not commit pederasty at all, but instead received gratification from lighter contact. These individuals too presented a degeneracy of feeling, even if it was less pronounced than with the "actual pederasts." Their degeneration was either inherited from their parents or a condition acquired through licentiousness, especially excessive onanism. The homosexual malady often took on such a compulsive character that those stricken with it ought to be regarded by the courts as lacking sufficient control of their mental faculties to be held liable for their actions. Many pederasts betrayed themselves by their staring gaze, uncertain gait, shy demeanor, and womanish behavior. ([1922–1923] 1986, 162–163)

After completing his demonstration of the pederast, Mendel presented his audience with two more psychopaths who had been apprehended by the police.

> Throughout the lecture, the pederast, the child-molester, and the exhibitionist were clustered at the front of the auditorium like a three-leaf clover,

> hanging on every word in the presentation of their mental defects with just as much respectful attention as the adulatory throng of students, now enriched by a vividly memorable spectacle. This was the knowledge of sexual pathology with which the future doctors and judges of that era were "turned loose" on mankind. ([1922–1923] 1986, 163)

Of all Hirschfeld's professors, Mendel was far and away the most forthcoming on the subject of homosexuality, which may account for Hirschfeld's selection of Mendel to direct his dissertation on the neurological sequelae of influenza. Despite the tinge of mockery in Hirschfeld's account, we will see that his standpoint on homosexuality by no means constituted a paradigm shift vis-à-vis that set forth in Mendel's lecture. Thanks to Darwin's emphasis on the indispensability of natural variation for the process of evolution, Hirschfeld was able to advance beyond regarding homosexuality as a pathological degeneracy, but at base he remained a product of the nineteenth century, ensnared in the discursive web staked out by the generation of Benjamin Tarnovsky ([1886] 1898) and Richard von Krafft-Ebing ([1886] 1965).

Following completion of his medical studies, Hirschfeld undertook his first journey to the United States. The centerpiece was attending the 1893 Columbian World Exposition in Chicago, and he also visited Milwaukee, where his brother, following in their father's footsteps, had just founded a hydrotherapeutic institute ("Eine Kneippsche" 1893, 1). Hirschfeld later offered some intriguing remarks on his experiences in various American cities:

> In Chicago I was introduced to a Negro girl on Clark Street who turned out to be a male prostitute. I met two other transvestites, conversely, one from San Francisco and one from New York, who were heterosexual. . . . During a visit to Philadelphia and Boston I noticed almost nothing of homosexuality, but visitors from those cities later assured me that there was "an awful lot going on" within private circles in these centers of Quakerism and Puritanism. ([1914d] 1976, 50)

This text is noteworthy in two respects. It documents Hirschfeld's first known encounter not only with homosexuals in a nonclinical setting (that is, beyond Mendel's lecture hall) but also with transvestites—a term not even coined until several years later, and then by Hirschfeld himself ([1910] 1991). In addition, the use of the first person in the account opens up a characteristic oscillation between disinterested observation and the hint of more than purely academic involvement. Hirschfeld's ambiguous status as a participant-observer and his almost conversational tone, hallmarks of his writing, earned him the enmity of many contemporary academics but simultaneously rendered his works a rich source for lay readers of that era and for historians at work today.

Upon returning to Germany in 1894, Hirschfeld opened a practice in Magdeburg and there specialized for two years in naturopathy (Regin 1993, 5–11). A word of explanation may be in order for non-German readers: still quite widely practiced in Central Europe, naturopathy (*Naturheilkunde*) is a holistic form of therapy focusing on preventive measures to fortify the immune system through proper nutrition, open-air exercise, and plenty of water within and without. Its emergence and growing popularity in the late nineteenth century was a cause of consternation for those of the medical mainstream (*Schulmediziner*), who stoutly opposed its lay practitioners and cast a gimlet eye on any certified practitioners. They placed naturopathy only a notch above homeopathy, mesmerism, faith healing, and other practices that relied on the suggestibility of patients suffering from ill-defined, untreatable, or nonexistent conditions. Closely akin to the hydrotherapy practiced by his father and brother, naturopathy schooled Hirschfeld in defying received wisdom, and the naturopathic emphasis on developing a greater awareness of the body's inner resources and one's naturally healthy state of being corresponded with Hirschfeld's monistic outlook. Together, they contributed significantly to his growing conviction that any affliction linked with homosexuality was not inherent to the orientation but a stress response to social opprobrium, and that the best therapy was to grasp fully the fundamental naturalness of one's psychological and physical being.

Beyond meeting the demands of his growing medical practice in Magdeburg, Hirschfeld also became increasingly active as a public lecturer on health matters (Tiemann 1993, 13–32) and began to be significantly involved with the movement for abstinence from alcohol (Hirschfeld 1894). Both prior to and during his eventual specialization in sexology, he made joint cause with naturists (that is, nudists), antivaccinationists, and teetotalers who participated in a broad spectrum of voluntaristic activism termed the "life reform movement" in turn-of-the-century German social history. Hirschfeld's involvement in the naturopathy and temperance wings of this movement provided practical experience in the mobilization of public support for hygienic and political reform that he would apply to the cause of homosexual emancipation a short time later.

Hirschfeld received further impetus to shift his specialization to sexology when he attended an 1894 medical congress in Rome, where he not only witnessed the idolization accorded his countryman and teacher Rudolf Virchow, whose fifty-year career had brilliantly combined medicine and political engagement, but also met Cesare Lombroso and Paolo Mantegazza. Already acquainted with Lombroso's *Criminal Man* (1889) in German translation, Hirschfeld was awed by Lombroso's vast collection of data on the physical and psychological traits of criminals as well as prostitutes and "geniuses"; five years later, he would begin conducting much the same kind of research with homosexuals. He had also read Mantegazza's *Anthropological Studies of Sexual Relations of Mankind* (1886) in German translation and now learned that Mantegazza had established an anthropological museum in Florence, which—like Haeckel's biological museum in Jena—influenced the scope and mission of Hirschfeld's Institute for Sexology, founded twenty-five years later. Both of these anthropologists later contributed to his *Journal of Sexology* (Lombroso 1908; Mantegazza 1908).

A final development that pushed Hirschfeld in the direction of homosexual emancipation was the 1895 trial of Oscar Wilde, which elicited widespread discussion in Germany that at times took on nationalistic undertones. Wilde's fate, it was argued, unmasked the hypocritical prudishness typical of Britain and would be purely impossible in Germany, the land of forthrightness and true appreciation for culture. To Hirschfeld, the time seemed ripe for public enlightenment on homosexuality. In 1896 he gave up his practice in Magdeburg and moved to Charlottenburg, a city just west of Berlin that was later subsumed within the burgeoning metropolis. The same year brought the publication of his first sexological book, *Sappho and Socrates, or How Is the Love of Women and Men for Persons of Their Own Sex to Be Explained?* Treading cautiously, he released the book under a pseudonym but simultaneously instructed the publisher to reveal his identity to anyone who inquired.

The ensuing contacts led in 1897 to the founding of the Scientific-Humanitarian Committee, the world's first homosexual rights organization. In naming this group, Hirschfeld may well have been hearkening back to the words of Rudolf Virchow:

> I have fought many battles in my life but nevertheless I can say that fundamentally I have always been a man of peace, that is of peace between those who represent the same interests. . . . Our interests are none other than those of science and humanity. (Ackerknecht 1953, 35, quoting Virchow 1893)

By including science in the name of this organization, Hirschfeld was not only invoking a touchstone of modernity that rendered moot the traditional argument of sinfulness, but was also pointing to medical and biological research suggesting that homosexuality was not a sickness. His corollary, the invocation of humanitarianism, aimed to address all those everyday forms of intolerance under which homosexuals suffered needlessly—from social discrimination, in all its multifarious forms, to the psychic cost of internalized oppression, such as heightened susceptibility to alcoholism and suicidal depression. While the Scientific-Humanitarian Committee initially formulated as its primary goal the repeal of § 175, the German sodomy statute, Hirschfeld quickly came to recognize that "the elimination of popular prejudice is of greater value than the repeal of laws" (1903a, 1329).

From this point on, his life's work was so tightly meshed with the "organized movement against the persecution of homosexuals" (1914c, 937) that the turning points in his biography were simultaneously milestones in the movement's history, which is adequately chronicled elsewhere (Steakley 1975; Stümke 1989). Up to World War I, Hirschfeld's scientific work and his political activism focused on the homosexual question. His petition to reform § 175 was endorsed by thousands of prominent Germans and received considerable though by no means unanimous support from the Social Democratic Party. Hirschfeld's growing prestige was drastically reduced in 1907 because of his role as an expert court witness in the Eulenburg Affair, which began with the outing of homosexuals in the entourage of Wilhelm II, and resulted in an antihomosexual backlash from pro-monarchist conservatives (Steakley 1989). In the ensuing years, Hirschfeld redoubled his efforts as a writer and also expanded his areas of involvement, collaborating with the left wing of the women's movement, especially Helene Stöcker and the League for the Protection of Mothers, in the campaign to repeal § 218, the abortion statute.

Figure 1. Dr. Magnus Hirschfeld with his longtime companion Karl Giese, photographed in Nice, Franca, ca. 1934. (Courtesy of the Magnus Hirschfeld Society, Berlin.)

Following World War I, he revived his initiative to reform § 175, gaining support from the newly founded German Communist Party as well as the Social Democrats. His widening horizon led in 1919 to establishing the Institute for Sexology, the first such institution in the world. Around the time he founded the institute, Hirschfeld became acquainted with Karl Giese, who became his domestic partner for the remainder of his years in Germany. In 1928 he founded and chaired the World League for Sexual Reform, which held four congresses and lauded the sexual politics of the pre-Stalinist Soviet Union as exemplary.

Brutally assaulted by fascists and left for dead as early as 1922, excoriated in the press of the rising Nazi Party, and challenged by rivals within the homosexual emancipation movement for his biological approach to sexuality, his political leanings, and his Jewish parentage, Hirschfeld departed in 1930 for his lecture tour to the United States and continued across the Pacific and around the world (Hirschfeld 1933 [1935]). By the time he returned to Europe in late 1932, the Nazis were close to taking power in Germany. Warnings he received from colleagues in Berlin led him to take up residence in Paris in 1933, and the following year he moved to Nice (Figure 1), where he died of heart failure on the day of his sixty-seventh birthday. Engraved on his tombstone is the motto he had chosen for his life's work: *Per scientiam ad justitiam* (Through science to justice).

Science and Homosexuality

Although Hirschfeld firmly believed in the advancement of science as the most important vehicle of social reform, and a substantial portion of his prodigious writings dealt with the biological basis of homosexuality, he simultaneously voiced an important reservation about inquiry into homosexuality's etiology:

> The question as to "why" is not always just an indicator of profound learning, but often enough of callow simple-mindedness. If someone wanted to know *why* mammals exist or *why* there are humans, those questions would hardly be deemed worthy of an answer, as rewarding as a description of the various species of mammals or an investigation of the tasks of humankind would be. We simply regard the fact of their existence as a given—and so we should with homosexuality. (1914c, 395)

Convinced as an activist that "science exists not for its own sake, but for the sake of people" (1924), Hirschfeld drew on biology and medicine to develop his sexological theories in pursuit of an overarching social and political objective: eliminating discrimination against homosexual men and women. He regarded homophobia as a deep-seated prejudice that could be effectively combated only by mounting an unceasing campaign to educate the entire populace about homosexuality's fundamental naturalness:

> [This is] the great task, one which—for anyone who has experienced it in its full meaning—must needs be a life's work. Certainly, it does require the patience of a lamb to propound the same teaching year in and year out, with the prospect of having to continue doing so for a long time to come. But happily the area at issue here is such an extensive one, nearly limitless in scope, one permitting so many approaches, among which the sociological and ethnological must be emphasized alongside the biological and psychological, is one which meshes from so many angles with all sorts of practical aspects of life, connects with so many interdisciplinary questions, and continually offers so many new findings and opens up avenues for future study, that a thorough treatment of the homosexual problem can never become one-sided and therefore never monotonous. (1922, 6–7)

He intuitively grasped that the universal legitimacy of heterosexuality was based on an unquestioning acceptance of sexual dimorphism, and indeed that each individual's development of a harmonious sexual and gender identity took the body as its starting point. He therefore set about legitimating homosexual desire by focusing attention on the sexually intermediate body.

In his first publication on homosexuality, Hirschfeld proposed regarding it as akin to hermaphroditism, the incomplete differentiation of genitalia. Neither homosexuality nor hermaphroditism was "a sickness in the customary sense," he argued, but instead a congenital "impediment of evolution" (1896, 14). Because he went on to characterize "harelip, or cleft palate" as analogous impediments (1896, 14), he was upbraided by homosexuals stung by any likening of their condition to a deformity, and in subsequent publications he instead compared homosexuality to the less offensive anomaly of color blindness (1914c, 372).

Congenital sexual intermediacy was to remain the foundation of all his subsequent research, undergoing modification only to the extent of constantly integrating new findings that bolstered his position. He later remarked that his paradigm was initially regarded by most contemporaries as a sort of "grotesque eccentricity," and he calmly attributed this to its far-sightedness: it was advanced prior to the belated recognition of Gregor Mendel's experiments on heredity, before Charles-Edouard Brown-Séquard's work on endocrinology was taken seriously, and in advance of Franz von Neugebauer's study of the morphology of hermaphrodites—to say nothing of the "sensational" speculations of Sigmund Freud and Otto Weininger (Hirschfeld 1923, 8). As a scientist, Hirschfeld had come of age in a generation that was virtually unanimous in designating homosexuality as a type of "degeneracy," a term that was popular precisely because its meaning was subject to slippage, eliding easily between moral judgmentalism and biological objectivism. Moreover, the key debate of Hirschfeld's lifetime was whether homosexuality was a product of nature or nurture, innate or acquired; a middle ground was apparently unthinkable. Hirschfeld's position within this discursive framework was similarly unambiguous: "Homosexuality is neither a disease nor degeneracy, . . . but rather represents a piece of the natural order, a sexual variation like numerous, analogous sexual modifications in the animal and plant kingdoms" (1914c, 395).

From the outset he did acknowledge as estimable precursors the alienist Johann Ludwig Casper and the polymath Karl Heinrich Ulrichs (Hirschfeld 1896, 27), whose investigations in the 1860s had led them to regard homosexuality as a sort of "spiritual" or psychological hermaphroditism, and in 1898 he saw to it that Ulrichs's scattered writings on homosexual emancipation were brought back into print (Ulrichs [1864–79] 1994). Such early observers as Ulrichs and Casper, having determined that the male homosexual manifested a discordance between body ("male") and sexual drive ("female"), had "deduced—what could be more obvious—that one ought to seek the central location of these drives and traits . . . in his soul" (Hirschfeld 1914c, 348). At work a generation later, after considerable progress in the field of neurology, Hirschfeld firmly biologized their hypotheses by locating the homosexual drive in the "central nervous system" (1914c, 385), specifically in a "brain constitution characterized by a special mixed relationship of male and female hereditary matter" (1914c, 394). While receptive to advances in neurological research from the time of his earliest writings, he rejected out of hand Valentin Magnan's simplistic hypothesis that the male homosexual had a female brain (Hirschfeld 1896, 27; see Magnan 1892).

To disseminate the notion of sexual intermediacy as broadly as possible, Hirschfeld authored a twenty-six-page brochure entitled *What Should the People Know about the Third Sex?* ([1901b] 1915), of which some fifty thousand copies were in circulation within a decade. The title hearkened back not only to the use of the term "third sex" to designate homosexuals in Plato's *Symposium* and Vatsyayana's *Kama-sutra*, classical texts that bridged the Occident and Orient (Hirschfeld 1919a, 22), but also to the adoption of the term by Ulrichs, who had moreover coined the term *Urning* to designate the male homosexual. The very title of his second monographic study of homosexuality, *The Uranian Person*, was an homage to Ulrichs (Figure 2), and here Hirschfeld argued that male and female homosexuals were "neither men nor women in the traditional sense, but a different, singular, third sex" (1903b, 68). Yet as early as one year later, he noted that the term was only a "metaphor," and "not entirely apt" at that (1904a, 3). He grew increasingly dissatisfied with the third-sex terminology and would soon drop it entirely, for he was coming to regard it as both scientifically inaccurate and tactically counterproductive to minoritize homosexuals in a world populated entirely, as he ultimately saw it, by sexual intermediates.

Figure 2. "Metatropic Transvestism. The woman is a feminine man, the man a virile woman with a glued-on moustache." (From Hirschfeld [1930b], Plate 927. Courtesy of the Magnus Hirschfeld Society, Berlin.)

To bolster his position, Hirschfeld cited no less an authority than Carl von Linnaeus (who himself had echoed Georg Wilhelm Leibniz and Amos Comenius): "Nature does not make leaps" (Hirschfeld 1905, 17). Extending this to the domain of sex, Hirschfeld argued that nature itself proceeded by gradual transitions between male and female. He also quoted Charles Darwin, who had written: "We thus see that in many, probably all cases, the secondary characters of each sex lie dormant or latent in the opposite sex, ready to be evolved under peculiar circumstances" (Darwin 1868, 2:52). What Darwin had observed with regard to secondary sexual characteristics, Hirschfeld extended to "primary and tertiary sexual differences" (1905, 18). Challenging the supposed sexual unambiguity of the body, he emphasized the sexual significance of all body parts and of habitus (that is, comportment and bodily constitution). Finally, he positioned his paradigm in the tradition of Ernst Haeckel's law stating that "ontogeny recapitulates phylogeny." Haeckel himself wrote:

> We may conclude, in accordance with the universally valid biogenetic law, that the older precursors of vertebrates were hermaphroditic and that over the course of phylogenesis, a sexual division of labor led gradually to the gonochorism that now prevails. (Haeckel 1912, 287)

Hirschfeld noted that the human embryo underwent a process of sexual differentiation, which entailed a stage of "ontogenetic bisexuality" (1914c, 351). He combined the axioms of Linnaeus, Darwin, and Haeckel to formulate what he termed "genogenetic laws" of sexual intermediacy, culminating in this observation: "In every living being produced by the union of two sexes, there are to be found, alongside signs of the one sex, those of the other, often far beyond the rudimentary stage and in quite varied gradations" (Hirschfeld 1905, 18).

Over time, he became convinced that "further study of endocrine secretions [was] the most promising way to arrive at even greater clarity about the ultimate causes of homosexuality" (1914c, 378). Twenty-seven years before Leopold Ružička was awarded the 1939 Nobel Prize in chemistry for identifying the structure of testosterone and synthesizing sex hormones, Hirschfeld hypothesized the existence of "andrin" and "gynecin" (1912a, 179). Attributing particular importance to the ductless glands, he held that whenever a female gonad took shape in an embryo, a female individual came into being; *mutatis mutandi*, the same was true of males. If, on the other hand, "this differentiation is not carried out so clearly in that male and female gonadal cells coexist and have their effects, intersexual variants come about" (Hirschfeld 1926, 422).

The theory of sexual intermediacy, as Hirschfeld emphasized repeatedly, was not at all a theory in the strict sense of the word, but instead simply a type of systematics that made it possible to order the multiplicity of individual cases (1926, 548). To order the gradations between the sexes, he investigated sexual differentiation along four lines: "I. the sex organs, II. other bodily qualities, III. the sexual drive, IV. other psychological qualities" (1914c, 357). These corresponded to four distinct domains of sexual intermediacy (1926, 548):

I. Hermaphroditism as an intersexual formation of the sex organs
II. Androgyny as an intersexually mixed form of other bodily qualities
III. Metatropism, homosexuality, and bisexuality as intersexual variants of sexuality
IV. Transvestism as an intersexually mixed form of other psychological qualities

(Hirschfeld's coinage "metatropism" designated a reversal of the sex drive in terms of gender, as, for example, in a heterosexual relationship between a dominant female and a passive male.)

These domains of sexual differentiation could be approached in various ways. First, each of the four allowed for a full range of gradations, from the most fully developed to the most intermediate manifestation (a notion familiar to us, at least on a purely behavioral level, in the Kinsey scale). In Category III, for example, gradations existed between the bisexual at the center and the homosexual and the heterosexual at the two extremes, while in Category I, there were gradations between hermaphroditism at the center and the imaginary poles of the "full male" (*Vollmann*) and the "full female" (*Vollweib*) at the two extremes (Figures 3 and 4). Concerning the "full male" and the "full female," Hirschfeld cautioned that they were "constructed abstractions; in reality they have never been observed in such extreme forms; instead, it has been possible to demonstrate signs, however minor, of every man's descent from a woman and with every woman corresponding traces of male descent" (1914c, 357).

Second, individuals could be examined to determine their distinctive positions within each of the four domains of sexual intermediacy. Doing so revealed a stagger-

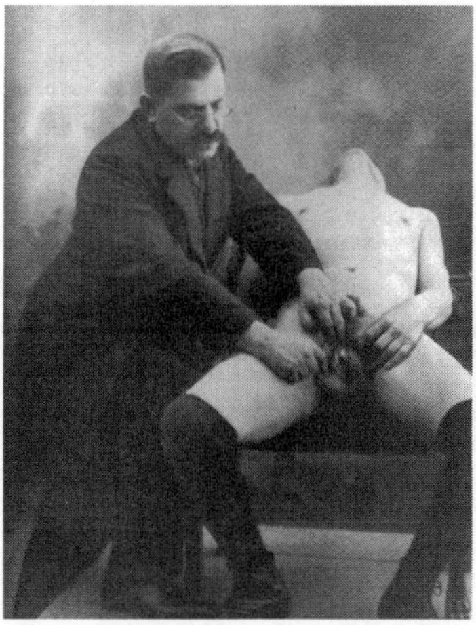

Figure 3. Hirschfeld demonstrating a case of "erroneous sex determination," the pseudohermaphrodite Friederike Schmidt. (From Hirschfeld [1930b], Plate 684. Courtesy of the Magnus Hirschfeld Society, Berlin.)

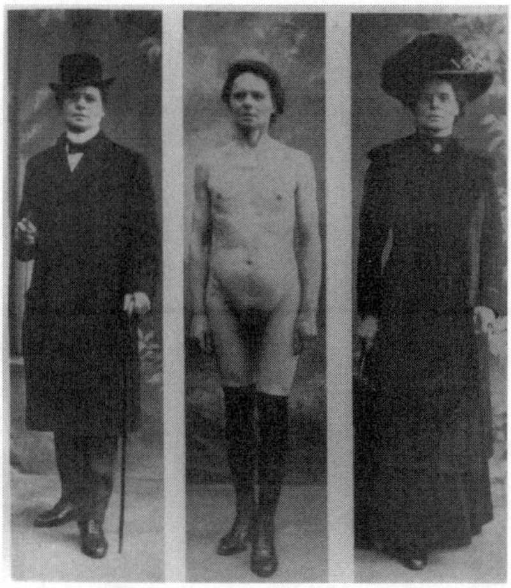

Figure 4. "Friederike Schmidt as a man, naked, and as a woman in customary garb." A case of *pseudohermaphroditismus masculinus*. (From Hirschfeld [1930b], Plate 685. Courtesy of the Magnus Hirschfeld Society, Berlin.)

ing number of ways that the four categories could interface in various combinations (Figure 5). As a mathematical exercise to demonstrate the wealth of natural possibilities, Hirschfeld calculated that there were 3^{16} or 43,046,721 sexual types ([1910] 1991, 219–227). In later publications, he went even further and postulated that there was "absolutely no such thing as two individuals identical in their sexuality" (1918, 206). Each person was a sexual intermediate of his/her own type, subject to his/her "own nature and law" (1923, 23). All people—including so-called normal heterosexuals—were only more or less strongly developed intermediates:

> To be sure, observing nature in the realm of sexual variants requires an especially sharp eye, extremely trained for fine nuances. Let me just recall the infinitesimally small but never coincidental differences in the attributes and ordering of the sexes, the boundless but never groundless variability of body proportions. (1923, 9)

Comparing sexual variability to the distinctiveness of a fingerprint, he finally declared sexual unambiguity itself to be a fiction. (1926, 546, 596)

Hirschfeld hypothesized that the nonprocreativity of homosexuality was a part of nature's plan. Extensive studies of the parents, siblings, and offspring of homosexuals convinced him that their genetic material was compromised, as evidenced in a range

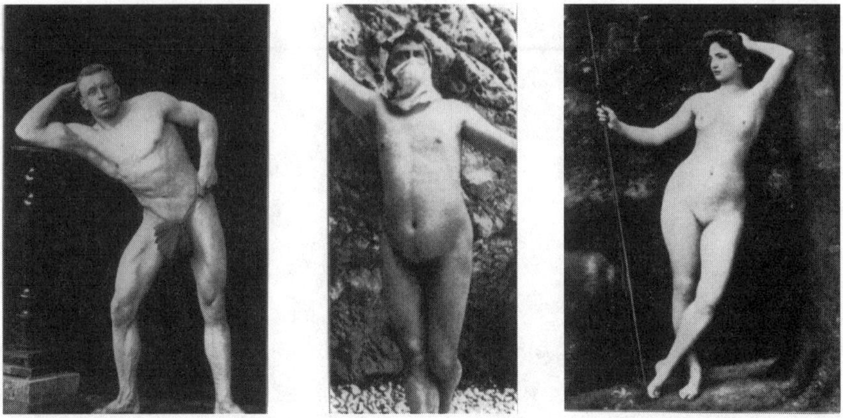

Figures 5, 6, and 7. "Proportions of shoulders to hips in the male type, the 'Uranian' [homosexual] type, and the female type." (From Hirschfeld [1903b]. Courtesy of the Magnus Hirschfeld Society, Berlin.)

of neurasthenic conditions. While homosexuals themselves could by no means be categorized as degenerate, their progeny were at risk of degeneracy, and a sort of evolutionary teleology intervened to prevent homosexuals from reproducing (1901a, 55). Hirschfeld felt that he was backing up nature by counseling lesbians and male homosexuals not to enter into heterosexual marriage and not to bear or beget children (1914c, 402–414). This consideration evidently seemed so important to him that he also declared it valid for heterosexual transvestites, even though he added that they were as a rule healthy and produced entirely healthy offspring (1910, 235). During Hirschfeld's lifetime, evolutionary and eugenic thought was indebted to both Charles Darwin and Jean Baptiste de Lamarck, who differed on the question whether the environment affected genetic material. Perhaps because of the embrace of Lamarckianism by the left, especially in the Soviet Union (which Hirschfeld visited in 1926), he rather quaintly regarded it as inadvisable to produce offspring immediately after a typically exhausting wedding celebration (1926, 330). Intriguingly, however, he suggested that his own homosexuality could be explained in Darwinian terms: he noted that his fraternal grandfather and maternal great-grandmother were siblings, attributing to this ancestral inbreeding the "limited reproductive capacity" of his own generation ([1922–1923] 1986, 158).

Hirschfeld took a dim view of attempts to alter homosexuality, and he noted with a certain satisfaction the consistent failure of hypnotherapy. He nonetheless spoke out against therapy only cautiously and at times deferred to the wishes of homosexuals desperate to change, provided he was unable to alleviate their dysphoria through intensive counseling. For two male transvestites who were in a frame of mind that suggested the probability of self-mutilation with possibly fatal complications, sex-reassignment surgery was performed under the direction of Dr. Ludwig Levy-Lenz of the Institute for Sexology, involving castration, penis amputation, and construction of a vagina (Abraham 1931). These cases may be the first transsexuals in history, although Hirschfeld himself employed the term differently (1923, 14), and it was not applied to individuals who underwent such procedures until considerably later (Benjamin 1954). Hirschfeld proved willing to refer homosexuals not only to the Berlin psychoanalyst Isidor Sadger but even, on one occasion, to Eugen Steinach, a Viennese neurologist who aimed to transmute homosexuality by removing the patient's testes and replacing them with those from a heterosexual (Steinach & Lichtenstern 1918). Steinach's radical transplant procedure derived from the gonadal "organotherapy" pioneered in late nineteenth-century France (Brown-Séquard 1889), and Hirschfeld anticipated that continuing endocrinological research would confirm the hypothesis that homosexuality was hormonally based. Because he fully expected Steinach's experiment to succeed, he did not speak of its failure in the same triumphant tone he adopted toward the "pointlessness" of psychoanalytic efforts to eradicate homosexuality (1925a, 117), which he interpreted as evidence of homosexuality's innateness (1914c, 433–444).

The only approach that Hirschfeld regarded as truly appropriate was his own "adjustment therapy," a talking cure that guided homosexual patients to accept their difference with dignity, indeed to embrace and affirm their orientation, and to experience love by overcoming guilt and isolation and associating as freely as possible with like-minded people ([1914a] 1976). This therapeutic method, which in many respects anticipated the later development of gay consciousness-raising and self-help groups, may have developed from his experiences in the homosexual subculture and his awareness of its importance for the lives of homosexuals.

At heart, Hirschfeld was no theorist but an empiricist; he regarded phenomena in the realm of sexuality and gender like a new world, which he was eager to explore and map. In doing so, he assembled data to an extent that was unparalleled in his day and age. He claimed to have personally examined thirty five thousand sexual intermediates (1928, 641). His most important research instrument was a voluminous questionnaire, of which he printed the first version in 1898. Initially, he aimed to use it solely to investigate homosexuality, but he later revised and expanded it so that it could also be used for the anamnesis of heterosexuals as well. An effort to gain Freud's support led him to entitle it *Psychoanalytic Questionnaire* in 1909, but it was definitively retitled *Psychobiological Questionnaire* two years later. It was eventually filled out by more than ten thousand people, many of them nonpatients, and Hirschfeld rightly emphasized that he was in the exceptional position of being able to write about hetero- and homosexuality without relying on clinical records (1914c, vii).

In 1903, he launched a major empirical study on the question of sexual orientation. He began by sending a letter to three thousand students of the Polytechnic Academy of Charlottenburg, asking them to mark anonymously on an enclosed card whether their sexuality was directed toward men, toward women, or toward both. He directed the same request to 5,721 men affiliated with a metalworkers' union the following year. Responses were mailed in by some 56 percent of the students and 33 percent of the workers. Homosexual desire was indicated by 1.5 percent of the students and 1.1 percent of the workers; a bisexual response came from 4.5 percent of the students and 3.2 percent of the workers (Hirschfeld 1904b). These figures startled his contemporaries, who had heretofore assumed a far lower number. Homosexuals were no longer some rare curiosity in a medical lecture hall, but 1.2 million citizens of "our German fatherland" (1904b, 170). It should be added that he did not carry out any such statistical investigation on the sexual orientation of women. Considering that he was brought to court by offended Charlottenburg students and sentenced to pay a substantial fine (Hirschfeld 1904c, 691), one can imagine what the outcome would have been had he ventured to direct the same questions to associations of women.

In fact, Hirschfeld felt no need to survey women, for he assumed, however naively, that his statistical findings on male sexuality were equally valid for females. This tacit transposition was based on more than tactical considerations: the inner logic of the theory of sexual intermediacy compelled him to treat both sexes equivalently, if only for the sake of complementarity and completeness. The hypothesis of an infinite spectrum between the two imaginary poles of absolute maleness and absolute femaleness placed Hirschfeld in an exceptional position: when referring to homosexuality without any additional qualifiers, he consistently meant both male and female homosexuality. But this even-handedness was evident only when Hirschfeld dealt with homosexuality in the broader framework of sexual intermediacy. Whenever he supplemented his systematic presentations with case studies and quotations, it quickly became apparent that he found male homosexuality more accessible. The sole, but significant exception is his monumental *Homosexuality of Man and Woman*, which contains the voices of lesbians and homosexual men in approximately equal measure.

Hirschfeld's writings contain virtually no statements about an essential nature of homosexuality going beyond its characterization as a form of sexual intermediacy. Fascinated by the sheer diversity of homosexuals and the heterogeneity of lifestyles they developed across time and space, he was more inclined to document the untenability of generalizations with counterexamples. He nonetheless aimed to prove the naturalness of homosexuality by setting forth a number of features of homosexuality that demonstrated its innateness, including homosexuality's spontaneous emergence in the child, the content of sexual dreams, its ineradicability through external influences, and the affective parallelism between heterosexuality and homosexuality (1912b; see also 1936a). These findings allowed him to postulate that love of one's own sex was just as natural a phenomenon as that of the other sex, and that both ways of loving were therefore equally legitimate. His argumentation at times took on overtones of natural law, particularly in his criticism of the penal code. When homosexuals demanded decriminalization, they were asking not for "mercy but . . . [a] fundamental right" (1896, 31). They were entitled to live freely because their sexuality, no less than that of heterosexuals, was "entirely beyond free will" and "impels enactment with untamable ardor" (1896, 17).

In contrast to modern science, which defines a person's sex by the body (anatomical categories), the sexologists of his era also looked to the individual's "sex drive" (comprising desires and deeds). They therefore regarded homosexuality as paradoxical, for to desire one's own sex meant having the drive of the other sex (Hirschfeld 1903b, 152). Fraught with this inherent contradiction, homosexuals were preordained to lack harmonious unity as sexual beings. Hirschfeld challenged this standpoint by insisting that homosexuals not be reduced to their sexuality, for "sexual inclinations and disinclinations are only symptoms, secondary side effects; primary importance attaches to the psyche and to the habitus in their entirety" (1899, 4). A holistic approach would inevitably lead to recognition of "the homosexual personality's harmony" (Hirschfeld 1903b, 67).

To counter the standpoint that same-sex practices were unnatural because they failed to "correspond with the bodily structure" (Bloch [1907] 1925, 531), Hirschfeld followed the example of Lombroso by conducting extensive physical comparisons of hundreds of male heterosexuals and homosexuals. Contrary to received medical opinion, Hirschfeld found no differences in penis size or shape, but he did report statistically significant disparities in larynx dimensions, hair growth and dentition patterns, and the proportions of trunk/leg length as well as shoulder/pelvis dimensions (1914c, 125–147). Because homosexual men and women manifested psychological and physical traces of the other sex, there was no contradiction between genitalia and sex drive. If the lesbian were a "full female" and the homosexual man a "full male," they indeed "would present something discordant, monstrous" (1903b, 68). But on the contrary, they were harmonious within themselves: Hirschfeld postulated that body, psyche, and sex drive were just as closely attuned for homosexuals as for heterosexuals, and a change of sex drive would only destroy this harmony, which was the overall indicator of homosexuality's innateness and naturalness (1914c, 115–117).

By insisting on the existence of a harmonious homosexual nature, Hirschfeld aimed to refute the argument that genitalia properly serve only reproductive ends as an aesthetic value judgment based on conventional taste. The disqualification of homosexual practices as unnatural sprang from a simplistic and prejudiced "understanding of nature" (Hirschfeld 1903b, 68). Homosexuals could be regarded as pathological only by those who failed to judge them according to their own "law" (1923, 23). It followed from this law that the love of homosexuals was entirely equal to that of heterosexuals and fundamentally the same (1914c, 40). Hirschfeld devoted the opening chapters of *Homosexuality of Man and Woman* to arguing that homosexuals love just as passionately, deeply, and abidingly as heterosexuals, quoting extensively from his questionnaire findings and thereby allowing homosexual men and women to affirm their view of homosexuality in their own words. From his perspective, the inner harmony of individuals was possible only when they fit into an overarching totality. For heterosexuals, this was the succession of generations, which positioned each individual within a greater filiative whole. In their affiliative relationships to others, homosexuals could carry out an analogous task and find the same fulfillment as heterosexuals (1903b, 93).

Hirschfeld's greatest achievement was to challenge the rigid nineteenth-century paradigm of sexual polarity with a new and far more generous theory of sexual pluralism. But as human sexuality has increasingly come to be understood in terms of the social construction of gender and sexual identity, Hirschfeld's unquestioning adherence to biological essentialism—his occasional forays into sociology and ethics notwithstanding—has become ever more apparent. The concept of sexual intermediacy was formulated in response to, and remained haunted by, the sexological debates that dominated Hirschfeld's era—most centrally, whether or not homosexuality ought to be seen as a form of degeneration. His theory now has an unmistakably antiquated and defensive tinge. Even so, his notion of habitus—a holistic view of bodily constitution and comportment—may be closer to widely accepted, commonsense views of the body than many scientific or academic approaches circulating today, be they modern or postmodern. This raises the question, as relevant today as during Hirschfeld's lifetime, of how the stigmatization of lesbians and gay men is linked with a widespread belief in the "full male" and "full female" sexual body. A critical discussion of Hirschfeld along these lines may become increasingly possible as the humanities and social sciences expand their purview beyond sexuality and gender by attending to the body, claiming it as their own rather than simply yielding it to the natural sciences.

References

Abraham, Felix. 1931. Genitalumwandlung an zwei männlichen Transvestiten. *Zeitschrift für Sexualwissenschaft* 18.4:223–226.

Ackerknecht, Erwin H. 1953. *Rudolf Virchow: Doctor, Statesman, Anthropologist.* Madison: University of Wisconsin Press.

Benjamin, Harry. 1954. Transsexualism and transvestism as psychosomatic and somato-psychic syndromes. *American Journal of Psychotherapy* 8:210–230.

Bloch, Iwan. [1907] 1925. *The Sexual Life of Our Time in Its Relation to Modern Civilization.* Trans. M. Eden Paul. New York: Allied. Appeared originally as *Das Sexualleben unserer Zeit in seinen Beziehungen zur modernen Kultur.* Berlin: Louis Marcus, 1907.

Brown-Séquard, Charles-Edouard. 1889. Des effets produits chez l'homme par des injections sous-cutanées d'un liquide retiré des testicules frais de cobaye et de chien. *Comptes rendus hebdomadaires des séances et mémoires de la Société de Biologie* 41:415–419.

Carpenter, Edward. 1908. *The Intermediate Sex: A Study of Some Transitional Types of Men and Women.* London: Sonnenschein.

Darwin, Charles R. 1868. *The Variation of Plants and Animals under Domestication.* 2 vols. London: John Murray.

Eine Kneipp'sche Heil-Anstalt. 1893. *Milwaukee Abend-Post* (December 19): 5.

Ellis, Havelock. 1915. *Sexual Inversion.* 3rd rev. ed. Philadelphia: F. A. Davis.

Festschrift zur Feier des zehnjährigen Bestehens des jüdischen Kurhospitals im See-, Sool- und Moorbade Colberg am 20. Juli 1884. 1884. Kolberg: C. F. Post.

Friedlaender, Hugo. 1919. Der Synagogenbrand von Neustettin. In *Interessante Kriminal-Prozesse von kulturhistorischer Bedeutung,* 9:13–134. Berlin: Hermann Barsdorf.

Haeckel, Ernst. 1912. Gonochorismus und Hermaphroditismus. *Jahrbuch für sexuelle Zwischenstufen* 13:259–287.

Herzer, Manfred. 1992. *Magnus Hirschfeld. Leben und Werk eines jüdischen, schwulen und sozialistischen Sexologen.* Frankfurt am Main: Campus.

Hirschfeld, [Hermann]. 1870. *Was leisten Bäder überhaupt und was Colberg insbesondere?* Kolberg: C. F. Post.

Hirschfeld, Magnus. 1894. *Der Weg zur Gesundheit. Ein Mahnruf zur Verhinderung des körperlichen Niederganges des deutschen Volkes. A. Richtige Ernährung, das Brot. B. Gesamt-Ernährung. C. Alkohol-Mißbrauch und Statistik.* Hagen: H. Risel.

———. 1896. T. Ramien, pseud. *Sappho und Sokrates, oder Wie erklärt sich die Liebe der Männer und Frauen zu Personen des eigenen Geschlechts?* Leipzig: Max Spohr. 2nd ed., under his own name, 1902; 3rd rev. ed., 1922.

———. [1898] 1962. Questionnaire No. _____. In *Minutes of the Vienna Psychoanalytic Society*, vol. 1: *1906–1908*, eds. Herman Nunberg and Ernst Federn, 379–388. New York: International Universities Press. Appeared originally as *Fragebogen No.* _____. [Berlin: by the author, 1898.] Revised as *Psychoanalytischer Fragebogen.* [Berlin: by the author, 1909.] Revised as *Psychobiologischer Fragebogen.* [Berlin: by the author,] 1911. 7th ed., 1930.

———. 1899. Die objektive Diagnose der Homosexualität. *Jahrbuch für sexuelle Zwischenstufen* 1:4–35.

———. 1901a. Sind sexuelle Zwischenstufen zur Ehe geeignet? *Jahrbuch für sexuelle Zwischenstufen* 3:37–71.

———. [1901b] 1915. *The Social Problem of Sexual Inversion.* London: C. W. Beaumont. Reprinted in *A Homosexual Emancipation Miscellany, c. 1835–1952.* New York: Arno, 1975. Revised and abridged translation of *Was soll das Volk vom dritten Geschlecht wissen? Eine Aufklärungsschrift über gleichgeschlechtlich (homosexuell) empfindende Menschen.* Leipzig: Max Spohr, 1901.

———. 1903a. Jahresbericht 1902/3. *Jahrbuch für sexuelle Zwischenstufen* 5:1292–1354.

———. 1903b. Ursachen und Wesen des Uranismus. *Jahrbuch für sexuelle Zwischenstufen* 5:1–193. Also appeared under the title *Der urnische Mensch.* Leipzig: Max Spohr, 1903.

———. 1904a. *Berlins drittes Geschlecht.* Berlin and Leipzig: H. Seemann.

———. 1904b. Das Ergebnis der statistischen Untersuchungen über den Prozentsatz der Homosexuellen. *Jahrbuch für sexuelle Zwischenstufen* 6:109–178.

———. 1904c. Jahresbericht 1903–1904. *Jahrbuch für sexuelle Zwischenstufen* 6:647–728.

———. 1905. *Geschlechtsübergänge. Mischungen männlicher und weiblicher Geschlechtscharaktere.* Leipzig: Verlag der Monatsschrift für Harnkrankheiten und sexuelle Hygiene, W. Malende.

———. [1910] 1991. *Transvestites: The Erotic Drive to Cross-Dress.* Trans. Michael A. Lombardi-Nash. Buffalo: Prometheus. Appeared originally as *Die Transvestiten. Eine Untersuchung über den erotischen Verkleidungstrieb.* Berlin: A. Pulvermacher; Leipzig: Max Spohr, 1910.

———. 1912a. *Naturgesetze der Liebe. Eine gemeinsverständliche Untersuchung über den Liebes-Eindruck, Liebes-Drang und Liebes-Ausdruck.* Berlin: Alfred Pulvermacher; Leipzig: Max Spohr (Ferdinand Spohr).

———. 1912b. Die zwölf Hauptgründe für das Angeborensein der Homosexualität. *Jahrbuch für sexuelle Zwischenstufen* 12:404–418.

———. [1914a] 1976. Adjustment therapy. In Jonathan Katz, *Gay American History*, 151–153. New York: Thomas Y. Crowell. Appeared originally in 1914c, 439–461.

———. 1914b. Ernst Haeckel und die Sexualwissenschaft. In *Was wir Ernst Haeckel verdanken—Ein Buch der Verehrung und Dankbarkeit*, ed. Heinrich Schmidt, 2:282–284. Leipzig: Unesma; Hamburg: Paul Hartung.

———. 1914c. *Die Homosexualität des Mannes und des Weibes*. Berlin: Louis Marcus.

———. [1914d] 1976. Homosexuality in Philadelphia, Boston, Chicago, Denver, and New York. In Jonathan Katz, *Gay American History*, 49–51. New York: Thomas Y. Crowell. Appeared originally in 1914c, 550–554.

———. [1917–1920] 1932. *Sexual Pathology*. Trans. Jerome Gibbs. Newark: Julian. Abridged version of *Sexualpathologie*. 3 vols. Bonn: A. Marcus & E. Weber, 1917–1920.

———. 1918. *Sexualpathologie*, vol. 2: *Sexuelle Zwischenstufen. Das männliche Weib und der weibliche Mann*. Bonn: A. Marcus & E. Weber.

———. 1919a. Das angeblich dritte Geschlecht des Menschen. *Zeitschrift für Sexualwissenschaft* 6:22–27.

———. 1919b. *Anders als die Andern. 6 Akte mit wissenschaftlicher Unterstützung und Mitarbeit von Herrn Dr. Magnus Hirschfeld. Regie: Richard Oswald*. Berlin: Richard Oswald-Film-G.m.b.H.

———. 1922. Zum 25. Geburtstage des Wissenschaftlich-humanitären Komitees. *Jahrbuch für sexuelle Zwischenstufen* 22:5–15.

———. [1922–1923] 1986. *Von einst bis jetzt. Geschichte einer homosexuellen Bewegung 1897–1922*. Ed. Manfred Herzer and James Steakley. Berlin: Verlag rosa Winkel. Appeared originally as: Von einst bis jetzt. Eine Rückschau, Umschau und Ausschau zum 25jährigen Bestehen des Wissenschaftlich-humanitären Komitees. *Die Freundschaft* 4.1–52 (1922), 5.1–3 (1923).

———. 1923. Die intersexuelle Konstitution. *Jahrbuch für sexuelle Zwischenstufen* 23:3–27.

———. 1924. Leitgedanken und Sinnsprüche im Institut für Sexualwissenschaft. *Die Fanfare* (Berlin) 1.46:3.

———. 1925a. Discussion of H. Zondek, "Hypophyse und Keimdrüse," a lecture before the Ärztliche Gesellschaft für Sexualwissenschaft und Konstitutionsforschung in Berlin. *Archiv für Frauenheilkunde und Konstitutionsforschung* 11:117–118.

———. 1925b. *Zum 100. Geburtstag von S.-R. Dr. Hermann Hirschfeld*, coauthor Franziska Mann, née Hirschfeld. Kolberg: C. F. Post.

———. 1926. *Geschlechtskunde*, vol. 1: *Die körperseelischen Grundlagen*. Stuttgart: Julius Püttmann.

———. 1928. *Geschlechtskunde*, vol. 2: *Folgen und Folgerungen*. Stuttgart: Julius Püttmann.

———. 1930a. *Geschlechtskunde*, vol. 3: *Einblicke und Ausblicke*. Stuttgart: Julius Püttmann.

———. 1930b. *Geschlechtskunde*, vol. 4: *Bilderteil*. Stuttgart: Julius Püttmann.

———. 1930c. *Geschlechtskunde*, vol. 5: *Registerteil*. Stuttgart: Julius Püttmann.

———. [1930d] 1934. *The Sexual History of the World War*. New York: Panurge. Appeared originally as *Sittengeschichte des Weltkrieges*, co-ed. Andreas Gaspar. 2 vols. Leipzig and Vienna: Verlag für Sexualwissenschaft Schneider, 1930.

———. [1933] 1935. *Men and Women: The World Journey of a Sexologist*. Trans. O. P. Green. New York: G. P. Putnam's Sons. Appeared originally as *Die Weltreise eines Sexualforschers*. Brugg, Switzerland: Bözberg, 1933.

———. 1936a. Homosexuality. In *Encyclopaedia Sexualis*, ed. Victor Robinson, 321–334. New York: Dingwall-Rock.

———. 1936b. *Sexual Anomalies and Perversions: Physical and Psychological Development and Treatment*. London: Francis Aldor.

Koestler, Arthur. 1954. *The Invisible Writing*. New York: Macmillan.

Krafft-Ebing, Richard von. [1886] 1965. *Psychopathia Sexualis, with Especial Reference to the Antipathic Sexual Instinct: A Medico-Forensic Study*. Ed. Franklin S. Klaf. New York: Stein & Day. Appeared originally as *Psychopathia sexualis. Eine klinisch-forensische Studie*. Stuttgart: Enke, 1886.

Lombroso, Cesare. [1889] 1911. *Criminal Man*. New York: Putnam. Appeared originally as *L'uomo delinquente in rapporto all'antropologia, alla giurisprudenza e alla psichiatria*. 3 vols. Turin: Bocca, 1889.

———. 1908. Liebe, Selbstmord und Verbrechen. *Zeitschrift für Sexualwissenschaft* 1:409–434.

Magnan, Valentin. 1892. *Psychiatrische Störungen. Über die Geistesstörungen der Entarteten*. Leipzig: Enke.

Mantegazza, Paolo. [1886] 1932. *Anthropological Studies of the Sexual Relations of Mankind*. Trans. James Bruce. New York: Anthropological Press. Appeared originally as *Gli amori degli uomini: saggio di una etnologia dell'amore*. Milan: n.p., 1886.

———. 1908. Idiogamie. *Zeitschrift für Sexualwissenschaft* 1:223–227.

Mayne, Xavier [Edward I. Prime-Stevenson]. 1908. *The Intersexes: A History of Similsexualism as a Problem in Social Life*. [Naples]: by the author. Reprint New York: Arno, 1975.

Regin, Cornelia. 1993. Die Naturheilbewegung im Deutschen Kaiserreich und das Wirken Magnus Hirschfelds. Ein Überblick. *Mitteilungen der Magnus-Hirschfeld-Gesellschaft* 18:5–11.

Robinson, William J. 1934. Sexological literature pirates. *Medical Critic and Guide* 32:151–152.

Steakley, James D. 1975. *The Homosexual Emancipation Movement in Germany*. New York: Arno.

———. 1989. Iconography of a scandal: Political cartoons and the Eulenburg Affair. In *Hidden from History: Reclaiming the Gay and Lesbian Past*, ed. Martin Duberman et al., 233–263. New York: New American Library.

Steinach, Eugen, and R. Lichtenstern. 1918. Umstimmung der Homosexualität durch Austausch der Pubertätsdrüsen. *Münchener medizinische Wochenschrift* 65:145–148.

Stoewer, Rudolf. 1927. *Geschichte der Stadt Kolberg*. Kolberg: C. F. Post.

Stümke, Hans-Georg. 1989. *Homosexuelle in Deutschland. Eine politische Geschichte*. Munich: C. H. Beck.

Tarnovsky, Benjamin M. [1886] 1898. *The Sexual Instinct and Its Morbid Manifestations from the Double Standpoint of Jurisprudence and Psychiatry*. Trans. W. C. Costello and Alfred Allison. Paris: Charles Carrington. Appeared originally as *Die krankhaften Erscheinungen des Geschlechtssinnes. Eine forensisch-psychiatrische Studie*. Berlin: Hirschwald, 1886.

Tiemann, Klaus-Harro. 1993. Hirschfelds Wirken als Naturarzt in Magdeburg (1894–1896)—eine Dokumentation. *Mitteilungen der Magnus-Hirschfeld-Gesellschaft* 18:13–32.

Ulrichs, Karl Heinrich. (1864–79) 1994. *The Riddle of "Man-Manly Love."* 2 vols. Trans. Michael A. Lombardi-Nash. Buffalo: Prometheus. Appeared originally as *Forschungen über das Räthsel der mannmännlichen Liebe*. 12 vols., various publishers, 1864–79; reprint in 4 vols. Berlin: Verlag rosa Winkel, 1994. 2nd ed., ed. Magnus Hirschfeld. Leipzig: Max Spohr, 1898; reprint New York: Arno, 1975.

Viereck, George Sylvester. 1930. Hirschfeld: The Einstein of sex. In idem, *Glimpses of the Great*, 285–309. New York: Macaulay.

———. 1931. "Dr. Einstein" of sex not so favorably impressed by U.S. *Wisconsin News* (February 2): 1, 4. Also appeared in other Hearst newspapers, including *Albany Times-Union, Chicago Herald and Examiner, Detroit Times, Los Angeles Examiner, Pittsburgh Sun-Telegraph, San Francisco Examiner, Seattle Post-Intelligencer, Washington Herald.*

Virchow, Rudolf. 1893. Festsitzung der Berliner medicinischen Gesellschaft am 25. Oktober 1893. 50jähriges Doktorjubiläum. *Berliner klinische Wochenschrift* 30:1127.

Normality, Whiteness, Authorship
Evolutionary Sexology and the Primitive Pervert

Julian Carter

Internationally renowned sexologist Havelock Ellis announced *A Thousand Marriages: A Medical Study of Sex Adjustment* with his usual earnestness, praising it as a "searching and comprehensive" investigation of "sex activities and sex relations among fairly normal people" (Ellis 1931, xi, ix).[1] Only the third English-language work to address what Ellis called "normal civilized conditions" of erotic life, *A Thousand Marriages* broke new ground by basing its arguments on extensive clinical observations of the sexual body (ix).[2] The racial body was of concern to him as well; in the same breath, Ellis noted that all three studies in the emerging sexology of the normal were carried out by Anglo-Saxons.[3]

Sexual normality, whiteness, and authorship were more than incidentally juxtaposed here. In the first forty years of the twentieth century, scores of people wrote about modern marriage as a triumph of evolution. In such accounts, "primitive" reproductive arrangements developed, across ages of natural selection, into romantic and sexual love between spouses. These socioevolutionary narratives focused on sex as the means by which races evolved, devolved, or committed suicide. Thus, early twentieth-century studies of "normal" sex among "civilized" people often contained a eugenic element—that is, they sought to aid evolutionary progress by encouraging reproduction among white, middle-class Americans. As such studies forged connections between Anglo-Saxon civilization, evolutionary progress, and normal marital sex, they also linked sexual perversion to primitivism and savagery. In turn, the sexology of the normal was undertaken by people whose legitimacy as scientists and as writers was assured by their own presumed normality, signaled, in Ellis's observation, by their racial heritage.

The atavistic qualities of sexual perversion were not unique to homosexuality; fetishists, adulterers, sadists, masochists, and prostitutes were all explained as evolutionary failures, throwbacks, and threats. However, the sexological construction of homosexuality offers insight into the relationship between race degeneracy and sexual abnormality as it was developed in American sexological writing of the early twentieth century. Homosexuality was usually explained as the outcome of an "arrested development" at a stage prior to full differentiation of the sexes, either physically, psychically, or both. The precise nature of the arrest varied as different authors offered their theories, but the developmental goal that the homosexual had not reached remained constant: modern adulthood, symbolized by the orgasmic and eugenically reproductive heterosexuality lauded in contemporary marriage manuals.

The homosexual's failure to achieve full adulthood in modern, civilized marriage was sometimes accompanied in sexological texts by allegations of homosexuality's literary or linguistic peculiarities. As I will show, it is fairly common to find homosexuality understood as a perversion of interpretation and expression. The ability to use language properly and the corollary ability to tell coherent stories appear in these texts as the property of the sexologists, whose Anglo-Saxon normality is the source of their authorial capacity. While this arrogation of literary power clearly served to establish the authority of the investigating scientist, it also suggested an important connection between modern civilized normality and coherent narrative development. Truthful representation of sexuality's normal *and* abnormal phases was a capacity only of those who had achieved the perspective afforded by successful completion of the grand narrative of sexual development: The evolution of sexual reproduction was recapitulated in the scientist's individual growth, from the moment his mother's egg was fertilized to that in which he conceived the next generation. Sex itself is figured as language, and sexual development—like evolution—as an orderly sequence from one event to the next. Perversion, therefore, introduces an element of confusion or disordering of the tale that ought to climax in marriage and the "happily ever after" of eugenically sound babies.

Early twentieth-century newlyweds of Anglo-Saxon descent had no excuse for ignorance about the importance of their sexual pleasure. Beginning in the second decade of the century, scores of handbooks, manuals, works of philosophy, religion, and physiology were written explaining full sexual union as the cornerstone of modern civilization. Quite frequently, the young couple was told it had a duty to learn how to enjoy sex for the good of the race. Charlotte Perkins Gilman stated flatly that "there is no more necessary step to preserve and promote race progress than the recognition of the right purpose and power of sex and its full use" (1929, 122). Another writer trumpeted alarm over the "failure in propagation among our most intelligent, influential and advanced classes," which, he said, was the result of a system of "education and culture" that made pleasure in eroticism seem animalistic and uncivilized. J.F. Hayden warned that the potential result was race suicide: "As the race is elevating itself in other particulars, it is at the same time, sterilizing itself by prudery, and thus all is lost" (1926, 187–188). Mutually pleasurable sexual intercourse and effective contraception were presented as complex activities requiring considerable technical instruction, and some marriage manuals insisted that education in both erotics and eugenics was crucial to the continuation of evolutionary progress.[4]

But what education? The desirability of reproducing the "most intelligent, influential and advanced classes" seemed obvious, but by what means should that reproduction be achieved? What ought normal Anglo-Saxons to know, and knowing, do in bed with one another? The new sexology of the normal existed in large part to answer exactly these questions. Studying "the actual sex life and endowment of socially normal persons" was intended to establish the nature of normality, so that those who should breed would know how they should do so (Dickinson & Beam 1934, v).

Knowing what was normal was also a potent weapon against shame. Education to combat guilty secrecy about sex was the marriage advisors' major resource in the fight against a dysgenic future of Anglo-Saxon sterility and racial degeneration. The prudishness of American sex mores, they argued, had disastrous results:

> We see our numbers constantly increasing so that most of the gains we make in industrial technology are eaten up by uncontrolled breeding. And we permit the lowest classes of people, even mental defectives, to contribute the largest share of the racial stock that will make up succeeding generations, because our sex morality . . . has prevented our legislators from providing the opportunity for birth control to those classes most in need of it, or from taking a commonsense attitude toward . . . eugenical sterilization. (Everett 1932, 26)

Authors of marriage manuals advocated less prudery among middle-class Anglo-Saxons in part as a result of the writers' fear that the urban working classes, the New Immigrants from Southern and Eastern Europe and from Asia and the Pacific Islands, were becoming the dominant racial stock in the United States. One writer worried that prudery was so powerful it could appropriate eugenical sterilization laws for its own ends, leading to the final elimination of sexual desire among native-born, middle-class, white Americans. Prudery put into law would guarantee the extinction of the "better" classes:

> It is feared that the judges . . . would sterilize the well-sexed persons for some violation of the code of sex morals; and would thus soon breed an indolent race of meek sexual weaklings, which would either fail to reproduce itself or would be overrun and exterminated by some vigorous foreign stock. (Hayden 1926, 166)

This passage implies that "vigorous" (working-class) foreigners could reproduce themselves well enough to replace Anglo-Saxons, but the real challenge to white racial dominance is middle-class white prudery, not primitive potency. The sexual contest evoked here is the struggle that determines the survival of the fittest. Hayden seems to suggest that foreign peasants were not serious contenders in the genetic arena. Dark-skinned immigrants—Italians, Slavs, Jews, Chinese, and Japanese—could only "win" if the naturally superior Anglo-Saxons were handicapped by unnatural laws. The New Immigrants may have been "vigorous," but they were often depicted as too coarse to be profoundly moved by eroticism. Because "lower" races had not undergone the long evolutionary processes that refined the nervous system, and thereby the "nervous and psychic reflexes," these unevolved races could not experience romance and sexual bliss with the sharp joy felt by Anglo-Saxons. Book after book on sexuality includes passages or entire chapters explaining the development of the richly satisfying modern love union in contrast to the "sensory and motor sluggishness," erotic inadequacy, and emotional poverty of relationships among "primitive" peoples (Lydston 1904, 47). In this context, the perceived vigor and fecundity of New Immigrants indicated not a eugenically desirable state of sexual health and normality, such as middle-class Anglo-Saxons would exhibit in the absence of prudery, but a clumsy, coarse excitability untempered by intelligence, social responsibility, or love.

Thus, allegations of sexual vigor among the foreign-born working classes resemble allegations of sexual impotence in primitive people. The erotic inadequacy of savages was the result of their closeness to the animal realm. To Progressive-era sexologists, animality meant not passion, but rather simple, shallow desires, felt in seasonal cycles and unmixed with affection. Havelock Ellis argued in an essay on "The Sexual Instinct in Savages" that the savage "sexual impulse is habitually weak, and only aroused to strength under the impetus of powerful stimuli, often acting periodically" (1903b, 265). One of the more commonly cited differences between "higher" apes and "lower" humans was the "continual sexual readiness" or fertility of human females. When Ellis maintained that savage desire was periodic, he implied that primitive people were more like apes than like humans. He also implied that primitives were not strongly differentiated into two distinct sexes. The generic savage Ellis discusses could be a female, roused into heat by the "powerful stimuli" of the changing seasons; but it could just as easily be a male, lifted out of winter torpor by the sight and scent of female sexual availability.

Like animals, then, primitive men and women are alike in that both experience minimal passion in seasonal cycles. This low level of differentiation between the sexes is one of the most important ways in which savages are unevolved in comparison to civilized Anglo-Saxons, a point to which I will return. Primitive peoples are underdifferentiated in another sense: they are lumped together in sexological works as a more or less unified category of the not-civilized. The sexual and marital practices of Tierra del Fuegans, Trobriand Islanders, Central Australians, American Indians, Samoans, African Negroes, Eskimos, and others are offered as illustrations of the stages through which civilized European-Americans passed in ancient times. But while nineteenth-century anthropology made careful distinctions between grades of progress from savagery, through barbarism, to civilization, modernist sexology reduces all "archaic" cultures and peoples to equivalences. Contemporary South American Indians and the ancient peoples of India are identical, for sexological purposes, because neither is modern. Different citations blur together, and the people they purport to represent merge into a mass of brown bodies, which are continuously displaying themselves without shame while developing modesty, enjoying frequent sex without conflict and observing strict taboos on permissible times and candidates for intercourse, allowing girls free license and abusing women, revering sex as magic and rutting as casually as animals. The contradictory ethnographic assertions that litter this literature resolve themselves into the definition of civilized marriage as that which is not savage. Middle-class white Americans pair off decently and at home, in sharp contrast to the swirling textual orgy of brown flesh. And to underscore the contrast, there is one thing that savages do *not* do in sexological representations: they never make love.

This does not mean primitive peoples do not have intercourse.[5] Instead, it literally means that primitive sex and primitive marriage are not expressions of affection and emotional commitment. The distinction between modern civilized lovemaking and savage intercourse is one of mind and heart, attitude and perception: "if modern marriages are to be better than the more primitive types, couples must be prepared to see in their intimate associations something more than [the primitive states of] blind compulsion of physical mating . . . or . . . apathetic resignation. . . . The more intelligent modern couple sees beyond the instinctive impulses, and beyond the need of food and shelter to the equally important needs of comradeship and mutual inspiration" (Butterfield 1937, 32). The way that modern spouses care for one another deepens and broadens perception: they *see* beyond instinct and bodily drives. The source of inspiration—civilized marriage—provides the context for the emergence of literatures and arts of love.

In contrast, the "sensory and motor sluggishness" of savages means that "the weakness of the physical sexual impulse among savages is reflected in the psychic sphere. . . . Love plays but a small part in their lives. They practice few endearments; they often only kiss children; . . . love-poems are among some primitive peoples few (mostly originating with the women), and their literature often gives little or no attention to passion" (Ellis 1903b, 265; see also Lydston 1904, 47). Modern civilized people embarking on a marriage are at a distinctly different stage of development, and the most notable difference is affectional. In Ellis's account, one of the measurements of civilized affect is its expression in literary form; savage indifference to love reflects itself in indifference to verbal art.

The love that leads to literature may be harder to find than fleeting outlets for mild arousal, however. Occasionally, an author declares that savage marriage had its benefits, that civilized people undergo emotional torments unimaginable to less complex, less passionate people. The greater pressures upon modern marriages sometimes lead to a degree of unhappiness unknown to primitive peoples who have not evolved sufficiently to have added "the psycho-sexual to the purely animal" elements of "matrimonial selection": "The savage does not prate of incompatibility; the question with him is altogether a physical one" (Lydston 1904, 351). Correspondingly, the savage does not need to elaborate his love into literature. In the absence of love and its attendant frustrations, there is no movement through a plot, no peaks of feeling to be resolved, no dramatic tension.

Savagery's preliterary, plotless ease of physiologic functioning also makes initiation into sexual adulthood much simpler than it is for moderns. One researcher explains that among some Indian tribes of South America, mothers "artificially destroy their young daughters' hymens, 'to free their children from the shame of virginity'." This custom, he tells us, is similar to that carried out "among some ancient peoples" who celebrated first menstruation by "the forcible penetration of . . . the young girl's vagina" by "a male idol, carven in stone, sculptured, with an erect penis." He goes on to say that "according to the frank and simple views of such primitive peoples, woman was a symbol of fertility, her one and only function being to bear children, and thus guard against an extinction of the tribe." This view, he explains, frees savage girls from the "inhibitions, deliberations and struggles which trouble the civilized young woman at the time of love's awakenings." Yet, lest the savage practices he describes so pornographically seem too appealing, we are reminded that "such primitive peoples have absolutely no idea of love in our sense of the term. . . . For them, sexuality is nothing other than what it is for irrational animals—an urgent desire for the fulfillment of the sexual impulse" (Bauer 1927, 33). Civilization's inhibitions, deliberations, and struggles are balanced by love and the evolution of emotional and rational elements in sex.

In sum, much early twentieth-century sexology represented primitive people as phasic, erratic, and impulsive in their desires; as apparently overactive but actually undersexed; as physically undeveloped; as not firmly individuated and not well differentiated from one another; as selfish in the pleasures they did take, and unable to feel much love; and as untroubled by inhibition, conscience, or second thoughts. Since the point of writing about these savages was to establish how different they were from Anglo-Saxons, we can infer that normal civilized adults were constant, steady, and rational in desire; discreet, but passionate; physically mature; firmly distinct from one another (especially along the axis of sex difference); generous and loving in relationships; and restrained by morality. In all these ways, civilized adults seemed like excellent candidates for long-term, stable relationships held together by mutual "comradeship and inspiration." They also seemed admirably well-balanced, judicious people whose rule over the less advanced was reasonable and kindly: the sexological description of normal civilized people was, among its other functions, an argument for the inevitability and correctness of white supremacy. The adult status of the "normal" and "civilized" sexologist/authors is easily conflated with their Anglo-Saxon racial heritages; in turn, Anglo-Saxon adult normality slides into the power to define, to interpret, and to circumscribe the lives of abnormal, uncivilized, brown-skinned peoples. The authorial skills of definition, interpretation, and circumscription (literally, writing around) thus are achievements of evolution—the skills of those who have progressed furthest from the animality and insensitivity of the savage state.

The ability to wax literary about passion is not only a gesture of mastery, but also a sign of the flowering of civilization. Bringing language into sex becomes a mark of evolution in the sexological texts, so that writing and normal civilized lovemaking are deeply intertwined. The coincident development of emotion and rationality produces not only civilized love, but also literature. While authorship and normal, marital "mate-love" are modern manifestations of evolutionary growth, sexual perversion and literary incoherence or confusion are the result of arrested development, a failure to evolve past a state of savagery. Indeed, evolution itself is a story, a master narrative that encompasses and confirms the small stories of the sexological investigators. The sexual instinct is the motor for plot development; the genre is eugenic romance, where boy meets girl and they perpetuate the race. A bad choice of mate, or social circumstances that prevent the best mating, shifts the tone to dysgenic tragedy: the "lusty foreigners" take over—the Huns invade Rome—"all is lost." One author described this as "the epic drama of sexual selection" (Dell 1930, 329). The drama plays out simultaneously on small personal stages and on the larger, racial one, so that individual maturation, the achievement of adult normality, is indistinguishable from racial growth and change. Hence the "arrested development" of sex perversion is both a personal failure to grow and a mark of a potentially racial failure to evolve. Arrested development is also a dramatic frustration—the tale does not build to a satisfying climax and resolution of tension; it does not conform to the outline imposed by the master narrative of evolution. Thus, individually arrested development in the form of sex perversion could actually halt the development of the race and, rather than evolution, degeneration or decadence could set in.

The development of the race is like the development of character in literature in that both are recognizable by the increasing distinctness of the characters in the story. The connection between individual sexual "immaturity" and evolutionary failure was made through Ernst Haeckel's theory that ontogeny recapitulates phylogeny, which posited that an individual person's life repeated the drama of evolutionary development. This tale is one of increasing differentiation of types. The original and "lowest type of procreative action," in this story, was "the primal segmentation of the cell"—each organism was complete and sexless, and reproduced by dividing itself in two (Lydston 1904, 377). Later, more advanced yet still primitive forms were truly hermaphroditic (Ellis 1903a, 34). Only with the appearance of the vertebrates did distinctly different sexes evolve. One writer explained that "the difference in gender, and the very definite contrast between the *normal* male and the *normal* female merely results from the orderly processes of evolution"; moreover, each person "must pass through many of these evolutionary cycles during the period of utero-gestation—as the study of embryology confirms" (Potter 1933, 59). Potter was referring to the fact that vertebrates are hermaphroditic in their "embryonic disposition" (Ellis 1897, 312). Given early twentieth-century sexology's emphasis on normality and the firm differentiation of the sexes in modern civilization, such discussion of universal, original hermaphroditism requires some explanation. Primary hermaphroditism helps tie the stories of sexual normality, individual maturity, and white racial superiority together under the larger plot of evolution, by (literally) providing a single point from which all differentiation proceeds. Fetal life functions in these sexological accounts as a sort of preface to the main story of sexual development. Once the prehistory of vertebrate sexuality has been ritually retold, the individual *Homo sapiens* can begin evolving from the stage of infant animality, through childish savagery, to civilized adulthood.

Civilized adults find the early stages of development less interesting than the last; these stages are, after all, a retelling of a story already told countless times, and the real drama and significance lie in the generation of a new and modern race. Hence, like the blurring of the stages of development from savagery to civilization in the marriage manuals, Progressive-era sexology of the normal tended to summarize the evolutionary chapters prior to puberty. The hermaphroditic slug or embryo, the "lower" mammal or infant, the savage or the child are all jumbled together, while the nuances of the sexual life of civilized adults receive loving attention in volume upon volume. The difference between evolving and recapitulating is precisely the brevity and teleology of the latter compared to the former: the *New Shorter OED* defines "recapitulate" as "go briefly through again, go over the main points of (an argument, statement, etc.)." Recapitulation is interesting and important only because it provides background for the present pinnacles of adult civilized sexuality in their eugenical, loving productivity.

Because each individual recapitulates species development in its own growth, the caresses of the normal married couple are a recapitulation of the development of eroticism—they retell the story of the couple's sexual development from autoeroticism and polymorphous perversity through to mutual genital orgasm in coitus. Perversion is not inherent in acts, but in their falling out of sequence. The "stages of the sexual response," one author explained, follow one another "logically," yet do not always do so in "actual life, except in the animal world, where there are no inhibitions. . . . Hence the stages . . . may occur out of order and sometimes simultaneously instead of in sequence" (Everett 1932, 69). This is normal (since civilized adults are not animals) as long as the stages appropriate to animals, children, and savages are touched on only briefly, and then left behind. These "pre-pleasures" form a sort of introduction to the modern ecstasy of intercourse: "Indulgences in various forms of perversities as a presexual act cannot be viewed as abnormal. . . . Such indulgences in normal men and women . . . culminate in normal coitus" (Chideckel 1935, 10). Only when the preamble becomes the main tale, when the "abnormal intercourse is substituted for normal sexual relationship," can such indulgences be called perverse (Chideckel 1935, 10).

Sexual perversion is, then, an error in recapitulation which forecloses the possibility of attaining civilized adult normality. "Abnormalities of sexual expression may arise through either a fixation on one of the steps in the series of reactions, or a fixation on a particular type of external stimulus which does not happen to be biologically normal, i.e., which does not permit the instinct to express itself through all its logical stages" (Everett 1932, 71). The problem here is partly one of the ability to perceive logic and order—"capitulate" means not only submit, but also "draw up in chapters or under heads," that is, organize into a coherent and scribable outline (*New Shorter OED*, s.v. "capitulate"). This is why differentiation or discrimination between different kinds and types is so important as a mark of evolutionary progress, which is here inseparable from authorial capacity. Havelock Ellis's introduction to a collection of essays called *Sex in Civilization* (1929) explains the unique nature of modern sexological writing by establishing that the essential difference between savagery and civilization lies in the primitive inability to draw distinctions: "Where we differ from the savage, and in so differing also differ indeed from ourselves of yesterday, is that to-day we seek to contemplate sex objectively and impersonally, to disentangle it from the felted textures in which it was so tightly woven that we hardly ever saw it naked" (Ellis 1929, 20). Really modern civilized adults can look at sex naked and see it rather than feel its textures, engage with it and yet keep a distance from it. In particular, the sexologist can dispense with the coverings inspired by shame because he is protected by the distance imposed by the visual imperative of focused criticism. That distance, which is the source of differentiations in Ellis's account, constitutes the difference between himself and his ancestor, the savage who could not write sexology—that is, differentiation is the nature of Anglo-Saxon normality and authorship. The sexology of the normal, the achievements of civilization beyond its prehistorical stages, and the ability to make distinctions are here linked in ways that help to entangle savagery and perversion with the tendency to confuse separate entities.

Failure to perceive difference correctly makes organization impossible, so that sex cannot proceed through its "logical stages," and the race remains stuck somewhere prior to civilization. Perversion raises the specter of racial arrest and the lack of perspective that makes for limping or interrupted narratives. Badly organized sex is barely distinguished from texts or stories that do not flow smoothly, as in the description of perversion as "the accidental stopping places" in sexual development (Dell 1930, 83). It is in this sense that certain tendencies and movements of late nineteenth- and early twentieth-century literature were described as "degenerate" and "decadent," stylistic judgments that foregrounded fragmentary, confused narratives and failures of civilized perspective as symptoms of their authors' "arrested development" and atavistic perversity.

To degenerate is to "lose the qualities that are normal and desirable or appropriate to the kind or type; revert to a lower type" (New Shorter *OED*, s.v. "degenerate"). A degenerate writer, then, is one who falls from the heights represented by Ellis and his fellow normal sexologists. Such a writer does not extricate herself or himself from "felted textures," and perhaps does not privilege vision over touch; he or she does not capitulate to the master narrative's demand for differentiations and orderly progress. Worse, a decadent author is one (whose text is) in a state of decay, the reverse of differentiation, in which elements, once distinct, rot together, lose their form and outline. Vision falters as a source of information when confronted with putrescence, still more when one is, oneself, putrid, since the eyes go early. Loss of perspective and the resulting confusion about the nature of separate entities are thus fundamental characteristics of decadent writing.

Indeed, some of Ellis's contemporaries refused to value normal civilized authorship and critical distance, embraced their failures of differentiation, and named themselves Decadents. Though the Decadents were French poets and novelists, and might seem only peripherally related to the Anglo-American sexology under consideration here, it is worth noting that anti-Decadent critics described decadent texts in the same terms that normal civilized sexologists used to describe savage perverts. Like primitive types, Decadents were characterized by failures of perspective that made it impossible for them to recognize, construct, and maintain the crucial differences between sickness and health, evolution and degeneration, men and women, art and symptom, fiction and scientific diagnosis, truncated fragment and organic whole (Spackman 1989, 5, 30, 79, 131–132, 198). The decadent writers' inability to make such fundamental distinctions is reflected in their complex textual structures, the fabulous images that make up their books, and their lavishly symbolic and sensory use of language. Anti-Decadent critics responded to these textual and stylistic characteristics as symptoms of eviration, which, on the part of apparently male writers, is a diagnosis of Decadent failure to maintain the distinction between the sexes. As Barbara Spackman has argued, degeneration becomes "degenderation" (1989, 25, viii f.).

"Degenderation" is also an apt description of contemporary theories of homosexuality as a failure to develop the capacity for discrimination, on the physical, perceptual or imaginary, and narrative or linguistic levels. Recapitulation of the stages of sexual development, when it was halted prior to mature civilized eroticism, resulted in the appearance of atavistic survivals of primitive stages, such as the inadequate differentiation between the sexes characteristic of unicellular organisms, embryonic vertebrates, and savages. Ellis cited a string of eminent authorities—Darwin, Haeckel, Kiernan, Lydston, and so on for more than two pages—in support of this view of homosexuality as a form of hermaphroditism, that is, a "reversion to the primitive ancestral phase in which bisexualism was the normal disposition" (Shattock & Seligman, qtd. in Ellis 1897, 313).[6]

Some critics believed that homosexuality was unnatural, and therefore a vice of "the aesthete, the lover of luxury, and the dilettante"—that is, a decadent sexual style derived from the artificial conditions imposed on human animals by civilization. To such critics, scientists replied that there was evidence of homosexuality among savages (Ellis 1897, 204–205; Potter 1933, 35). Under this paradigm, homosexuals were racially immature people who had developed neither the psychic nor the physical capacity to separate males from females as firmly as a civilized adult could have done. "At an early stage of development the sexes are indistinguishable, and throughout life the traces of this early community of sex remain. . . . Among mammals the male possesses useless nipples, which occasionally even develop into breasts, and the female possesses a clitoris, which is merely a rudimentary penis, and may also develop" (Ellis 1897, 310). The somatic remnants of primary hermaphroditism even in normal people provide the organic grounds for homosexuality understood as "aberrant differentiation" (Lydston 1904, 376). However, in "the maturely developed individual only a few aborted germs of the opposite sex are left," while "in the homosexual . . . the process has not proceeded normally" (Ellis 1897, 311). Homosexuality is a blending of the sexes understood in terms of dynamic organization, or process. Here the central developmental problem is not that development is arrested (though note that the homosexual is in contrast to the mature person) but rather that development is *disorganized.* Breasts or penises may develop on the homosexual body at any moment, for the unidirectional, logical sequence of growth, building through the ages toward full differentiation between the sexes who meet in normal civilized coitus, has gone awry.

Similarly, an American doctor wrote to Ellis that inversion was "far more prevalent" among "American negroes . . . than among the white people of any nation." While Ellis's correspondent believed that homosexuality was obviously atavistic—a survival of ancient undifferentiation of sex—he also considered the possibility that it was a degeneration caused by disruption of the normal sequence and pace of development. He thought that homosexuality in the American Negro might result from the fact that "his civilization has been thrust upon him, and not acquired through the long throes of evolution" (Ellis 1897, 19–20 n. 3). In this view, sexual perversion was a consequence of either halting or overaccelerating development; in either case, Negroes were predisposed to sex perversion, and sex perverts predisposed to racial primitivism.

The organizational aspects of this developmental failure to proceed normally through the evolutionary narrative meant that aberrant differentiation in homosexuals was also a perceptual flaw. Several sources explained that true physical inversion of sexes, "gross exaggeration of [the] signs of community with the opposite sex," is rare in comparison to "more subtle approximations" (Ellis 1897, 310; see also Chideckel 1935, 13; Dickinson & Beam 1934, 214). These "approximations" centrally include an inability to conform to conventional gender expectations, but more interestingly, they describe homosexuality as a problem of perception and interpretation of reality. Like the illiterate savages against whom Ellis defined modern sexological writers, homosexuals were too "entangled in the felted textures" of undifferentiation to recognize their own perceptual limitations. Their deviance from the master narrative of racial and sexual development, their failure to organize bodies and ideas into rationally distinct categories, disqualified them simultaneously from the status of normality and from authorship. For instance, one academic anthropologist dismissed Edward Carpenter's discussions of homosexual roles in primitive society thus: "A quaint fantasy this—homosexual men and women as culture heroes of mankind! And it has a delightfully primitive flare [*sic*] about it. Primitives think this way. . . . The Indian, Australian and African Negro would readily accept Carpenter's theory as a creation myth" (Goldenweiser 1929, 62).[7] In this evaluation, Carpenter's own homosexuality seems reflected in the "primitive flare" of his thinking. The product is not scientific writing but myth, a literature appropriate to savages and, quite significantly, more oral than inscribed.

Clearly, writing about homosexuality is the province of the normal sexologist, who alone can be trusted to maintain the critical clarity that makes for good texts. Morton Prince objected to using homosexuals' autobiographies even as sexological sources in part because any appearance of narrative coherence in a pervert's sexual story or writing was necessarily illusory: "if the pervert was . . . examined by an independent observer, instead of being allowed to tell his own story without interruption, a different tale would be told, or great gaps would be found, which are now nicely bridged" (Prince 1891, 92). Because perverse sexuality was the result of interruptions and "artificial stopping places" in the erotic recapitulation of the evolutionary narrative, the true story of homosexuality's development was necessarily full of holes.

Prince believed that a coherent narrative of perversion was impossible and that a pervert's attempt to produce one was a sign of mendacity. Other authors argued that homosexuals mistake the recapitulation of "preliminary" eroticism for the main story at hand. Images of perceptual failure abound: "immature sex interests," for instance, are called "early blind gropings of sex," which constitute perversion only when a person fails to realize that s/he can and should move on to mature normality. Homosexuality is the result of "tricks which the mind has unconsciously played upon" an otherwise normal person. Cure is thus a question of "understanding the true nature of these fixations," that is, not investing them with the central dramatic importance of mature normality (Everett 1932, 73, 77).

Frequently, misunderstanding of the "true nature of these fixations" was so severe that the homosexual failed to recognize the fact of his or her perversion. For instance, one rather sensational work explained that most female homosexuality believes itself to be heterosexuality. Lesbianism in this argument is the result of a sincere attempt to follow the normal narrative path to reproductive orgasm, thwarted by the lesbian's confusion about the nature of sexual difference: She has invested some part of her body or mind with an imaginary phallus which she cannot understand as different from a penis. Such a woman will choose another woman as her lover because "when people have intercourse they must be of different sexes" (Chideckel 1935, 97). In this view, perversion is both a failure to distinguish between the sexes, and a failure to perceive the distinction between real and imitation normality.

Although physiology dictates that homosexual lovemaking must of necessity halt with the recapitulation of eroticism and before "normal" coitus, the lesbian lovers in this account may not be aware of the difference between genuinely heterosexual intercourse and their "psychological coitus." Indeed, there is some justification for their confusion, since only the absence of the penis keeps them from normality. Chideckel described tribades as engaging in missionary-position intercourse: One partner lies on top of the other and "simulates normal sexual relations. . . . The process is exactly as in normal coitus" (115). Their perversion is in the mind, not the act.

Allegations that perversion is in the mind should not be taken as evidence that the racial aspects of sexual aberration had become unimportant to these sexologists. Indeed, the focus on intellect, perception, and differentiation as signs of sexual deviation derives in large part from earlier sciences of racial normality and their endless fascination with the size and shape of the skull as the index of racial progress. In nineteenth-century anthropometry, cranial formation and capacity explained the inferiority of subjugated races by reference to their low level of development; intellectual inferiority and savage social forms were alike the result of primitive head formation. As Siobhan Somerville has demonstrated, the science of physical measurements—providing a somatic ground for contemporary hierarchies of racial difference—had a profound impact on late nineteenth-century sexology. In the sources she explores, African women's genital formation is represented as ambiguous and excessive to the point of intersexuality. Later examinations of lesbian women follow both the methodology of measurement and the diagnostic evaluation of the findings (Somerville 1994, 251–255). The metonymic relationship between lesbian and Bushwoman genitalia was credible because the primitive body of both African and pervert was understood to be hermaphroditically undeveloped, and undifferentiated by sex in contrast to the modern, civilized, fully heterosexual body.

Yet neither the original racial anthropometry nor its sexological adaptation presented the somatic aspects of perversity as entirely or even primarily genital. The immensely influential Italian criminologist, Cesare Lombroso, included in his *La donna delinquente, la prostituta e la donna normale* (1893) an elaborate image of the famous "Hottentot apron," or hypertrophied labia of certain Bushwomen, but also dozens upon dozens of drawings, engravings, and photographs of skulls, heads, and faces. In 1904, an important American physician-criminologist limited reference to the subcranial body to an offhand assertion that "many female inverts" were "women of perfect physique, moving in good society" (Lydston 1904, 375). In contrast, he was elaborately careful in his description of the cranial basis of desire. Paraphrasing Lombroso, Lydston included "masculinity of type in the female" in a list of "atavistic features frequently noted in a large series of criminal crania" (Lydston 1904, 163). White women with unambiguous genitalia might still be sexually and socially primitive, that is, lustful but not loving: the evidence of arrested development was in the head. Lydston went on to explain that the capacities for lust and affection were in different parts of the brain, and that "the sex attraction of normal civilized man" depended on "a proper balance" between these portions (1904, 178). A woman with too much cerebellar sexuality and too little occipital affection was closer to the male norm than was consistent with her apparently "perfect physique." She was also closer to savagery, or sex prior to the development of love, than her standing in "good society" might indicate. In short, cranial contours indicated a primitive lack of differentiation that manifested itself in the contours of desire.

While cranial measurements could tell you things about a woman's sexual development that the color of her skin and the formation of her clitoris might conceal, the shape of the skull was important because of its relationship to the capacities of the brain it housed. "If distorted skulls mean anything . . . they imply correspondingly aberrant development of the brain beneath, with resulting perversions of the intellectual and moral faculties" (Lydston 1904, 160). One could surmise the shape of a skull, and hence the evolutionary status of its possessor, by analyzing the intellect and especially its literary productions. And so we return to the relations between primitive perversity, authorship, and perceptual failures of differentiation and organization. Primitive lack of differentiation, in some sexological texts, slides into a charge of intellectual unconcern with the difference between homosexuality and heterosexuality: "the evidence shows that among lower races homosexual practices are regarded with considerable indifference. . . . In this matter, as folklore shows in so many other matters, the uncultured man of civilization is linked to the savage" (Ellis 1897, 21). The use of folklore as evidence about the uncivilized reiterates the connection between primitive forms of literature and primitive indifference to proper separation of distinct entities.

Another form of simple literature, the short note, provided evidence that failure to maintain conceptual separation of the sexes could be accompanied by failure to distinguish the nature of racial difference. Margaret Otis's investigation of interracial homosexual affairs among institutionalized girls described the affairs as largely matters of writing: "A white girl . . . would receive a lock of hair and a note from a colored girl asking her to be her love. The girl sending the note would be pointed out, and if her appearance was satisfactory, a note would be sent in reply and the love accepted" (1913, 113).

Writing is the origin of the relationship, and the act of initiating correspondence bears the (heterosexually) gendered significance of initiating courtship. The girl who wrote first slides into a masculine position in Otis's prose. Because the colored girls are inherently closer to a state of primitive sexual undifferentiation than the white girls are, Otis summarizes inmate courtship in terms that represent the colored girls as more "like men" than the white girls. Otis's own normal, civilized ability to organize hierarchical progressions allows her to draw the conclusion that the colored girls take "the man's role," a conclusion contrary to her own evidence. After Otis explains the normal pattern as one in which the colored girl sends the first note, she goes on to say: "Opinions differ as to which one starts the affair. Sometimes the white girls write first. . . . 'It might be either way,' said one colored girl. One white girl, however, admitted that the colored girl she loved seemed the man, and thought it was so in the case of the others" (114). The colored girl's statement that "it might be either way" is not presented as meaningful evidence about the origin of romantic correspondences so much as evidence of her own primitive indifference to proper distinctions of sex and race, a doubling of the lack of discrimination that leads to homosexual note-passing in the first place.

Lack of discrimination in sexual partners was in fact the usual reason girls in the Progressive era found themselves labeled "delinquent" and confined to institutions such as Otis's (Ford 1929, 443). Promiscuous girls, prostitutes, and lesbians were frequently discussed together, as in James Kiernan's observation that Zola's fictional protagonist, Nana, seemed, "like many harlots, to prefer women" (Kiernan 1923, 292). Women who pursued sexual desire outside of marriage shared, in sexological literature, an atavistic tendency to masculinity. At the turn of the century that masculinity was cranial—prostitutes and other female criminals had male skull formations. Lombroso assumed that prostitution indicated fundamentally archaic masculinity: "our female criminals are closer to ancient females and closer yet to ancient males," he wrote; "they are crude masculine types, and sometimes masculine clothing, on female bodies" (qtd. in Spackman 1989, 25). Sometimes there is a suggestion that desire for other women followed more or less naturally from such cranial masculinity, whether or not it manifested itself in cross-dressing. Lydston included his brief discussion of female homosexuality in his chapter on prostitution, and claimed that "female criminals are, on the average, of a masculine type, and excessive hairy development is frequent among them" (1904, 483). In another decade, the skull's formation dropped out of discussion, but the shape of perception remained at issue. Margaret Otis's note-passing girls exhibited what Lydston had called "perversions of the intellectual and moral faculties," both in their preinstitutional delinquencies and in their interracial homosexual affairs while incarcerated. The lack of romance and literary quality in their love notes provided further evidence of their rather primitive intellects. The notes "show the expression of a passionate love of low order, many coarse expressions are used and the animal instinct is seen to be paramount" (Otis 1913, 114). Such stylistic atavisms are hardly surprising in girls who exhibit the reversionary inability to differentiate between sexual partners to a degree that permits them to accept "the difference in color . . . [in] the place of difference in sex" (113).

Fifteen years after Otis's article appeared, Charles Ford published a sort of sequel, describing "The Homosexual Practices of Institutionalized Females" (1929). Although these practices did include "mutual masturbation and cunnilinctus [*sic*]," Ford's focus is on "note passing and attendant imaginary homosexuality" (443). Ford explained that "in the notes" one girl "assumes the role of husband and the other of wife," a comment that underscores a certain graphic voyeurism in the subsequent paragraph's duplication of "uncorrected copies of actual notes passed between a colored girl and a white girl." Unsurprisingly, the colored girl is the "husband," and "her note is presented first" (444).

The steamy but vague promises in Ford's prose continue in the reproduced notes themselves, so that husband Ocean promises wife Gloria that "if I could sleep with you I would not only hough and kiss you. But I will not take the time to write it for I guess you can read between lines" (444). The "homosexual practices" of this institutionalized female are *textual* ones. Ocean, as a good husband, pulls out her note and presents it to Gloria. Ocean writes, Gloria reads. This appears to follow the outline of ordinary, heterosexual courtship between author and reader; but Ocean and Gloria are delinquent girls, that is, they are not good at maintaining firm boundaries between the sexes. Their innate perceptual flaws make it possible for them to confuse the real with the imaginary, sex with race, and so makes their "imaginary homosexuality" across racial boundaries possible. Their primitive thinking also disrupts the straightforward communication pattern between writer and reader. Ocean's advance consists of *not* writing "it"; Gloria's reception, in reading "between lines."

Though he offered Ocean and Gloria's notes as "illustrative of style and content," Ford did not expand on what he thought they illustrated except in one apparently peripheral detail. Both notes had headings in the upper right-hand corner, Ocean's reading:

> You can take my tie
> You can take my coller
> But I'll jazze you
> 'Till you holler.

Ford duplicates five more examples from other notes. These headings are important to him because they are "a perversion of the usual address, place, date, idea" (445). Ford's most direct commentary on the "homosexual practices of institutionalized females" thus addresses deviance from a literary convention.

Ford does discuss the existence of "actual physical contact" between girls who live in the same cottage, between whom, he says, "the relationships are not so imaginary" (446). Yet almost immediately the notes surface again. Ford states that the girls lose interest when they can touch: "the relationships not involving physical contact are more durable than those that do" (447). The perversion of perception and imagination characteristic of delinquent girls, primitives, and sex perverts leads Ford's subjects to find more significant pleasure in caresses of the mind than in those of the body.

Another sexologist, a few years later, went even further than Ford in describing lesbianism in institutions as a linguistic perversion resulting from atavistic lack of differentiation. Maurice Chideckel explains that, because they cannot touch one another, "The inmates talk about sex until gratification is acquired" (1935, 136). In Chideckel's account, this talking merges into writing, especially the writing of clumsy verse, which becomes one of the marks both of interracial liaisons and of communication between tribades. Quoting from the "perverted headings" in Charles Ford's article, Chideckel alleges that "the notes . . . are in rhyme, and the language of violent obscene character" (136). He explains that, just as interracial lesbian liaisons continue outside institutions, "rhyming . . . is a favorite method of communication among most homosexuals, especially among those who practice tribadism" (136, 121). Tribades, he comments, "hold the palm for foul mouthedness" (119).

Chideckel's tribades are conceptually close to Otis's and Ford's colored girls, both in their use of vulgar and rhyming language and in the "mental masculinization" that it reveals (Chideckel 1935, 122). The colored girls were, by virtue of their putative innate primitivism, less differentiated from men than the white girls; the tribadists' butchness made them seem more primitive, less white, than more feminine lesbians. This blurring of intersexuality with interraciality was sometimes supposed to be physical as well as psychic. Perry Lichtenstein mentioned that "both white and colored women" engage in "bull diking," or tribadism, and claimed that "an abnormally prominent clitoris" was common in tribades. He added, "This is particularly so in colored women" (1921, 372–373). Chideckel alleged that the tribade often "succeeded in elongating her clitoris to such an extent that she could easily use it as a penis" (1935, 117), and told a story about a tribadistic couple who communicated by playing recordings of "Negro blues [which] are all of a sexual nature, of very marked . . . significance in man-woman relations." He quoted one of these records:

> Mamma's got something sho' gonna surprise you
> Mamma's got something gonna hypnotize you
> Mamma's got something I know you want. (Chideckel 1935, 123)

The suggestion is that the tribadistic woman has a penis—or, which will do just as well for a sex pervert, she has a rhyme created by a "colored girl."

The linguistic and somatic peculiarities of sex perverts are not clearly distinguished from one another. The sexologists are concerned by the way in which tribadists and colored "husbands" resemble men, both in their bodies and in their aggressive aspirations to authorship. Yet Otis, Ford, and Chideckel's rhyming note-writers are not civilized, literate men, but arrested, mentally hermaphroditic perverts. Their versifying is doggerel, their prose brief, staggering, unanalytic, full of strange lust but without character or plot or development. Only someone suffering from serious perceptual failures—a savage or a pervert—could fail to distinguish such degenerate writing from real poetic art. Fritz, one of Chideckel's tribadists, made assignations with rhyming notes sent to her "wife"; the analyst explained that he could reprint one because Fritz "always kept a copy of her 'poetry' " (Chideckel 1935, 121). Chideckel's scare quotes show his contempt for this overvaluation of what he calls "outrageous ditties" (121).

This stylistic judgment about sex perverts' writing is very close to that which literary critics launched against Decadent authors such as Baudelaire and Huysmans, but Chideckel's image of homosexuality is less one of decay or decline from a previous eminence than it is of an original failure to evolve. He argues that the rhymes of tribades and colored girls, rhythmic and ritual, are primitive forms, intellectual manifestations of arrested development:

> The homosexual unconsciously finds a magnetic quality in words, and derives gratification from utterances. Modern psychologists maintain that this speech and sex have a definite relation to the incantations of primitive peoples. . . . The magical efficacy of words begins in the period when the small child is learning to speak. . . . Among the vulgar homosexuals, and sometimes even among the intelligent, obscene words form one of their chief pleasures. . . . Many homosexual women need nothing more than a sexualized language. (Chideckel 1935, 99)

Unable to differentiate between language and touch, between the linguistic and the real, homosexuals, children, and savages slide together into the general category of those who are not civilized modern adults. None of them have anything to contribute to the future growth of the race, for they are all too busy toying with words, and too confused about who should make love and how.

But why did the sexologists attach such importance to perverts who wrote poetry, or at least rhyming verses? In "The Significance of Sex in Modern Literature," James Kiernan focused almost exclusively on narrative fiction, explaining in a brief aside that poetry was relevant only when it portrayed "living human interest" and so approximated the function of fiction (1923, 294). As I have shown, the living human interest of sex to sexologists (Kiernan among them) lay in the story of its development from undifferentiated embryo to civilized adult coitus, culminating in the creation of new life. Lyric verse is generally less concerned with development of character and plot across time than is narrative, tending instead to explore feeling in fragments of experience or vivid imagery, rather than in the accumulation of events and gradual changes resulting from them.

When Kiernan wrote, modernist verse was increasingly oriented toward this counternarrative material and treatment. Arthur Davidson Ficke claimed in 1929 that truly modern poetry, especially the poetry of love and sex, addressed the ephemeral and above all the emotional, without concern for the duration or unfolding of experience (658–660, 664, 655–656). Many sexologists would have responded to this claim with the judgment that modernism was, then, not real literature, but an example of decadence, degeneration, literary and moral perversion. The threat that this kind of fragmented literature posed is well illustrated by Paul Bourget's definitive 1886 explanation of decadence as not only stylistic, but also social and somatic devolution:

> The term decadence designates the state of society that produces too great a number of individuals unsuited to the work of communal living. Society should be understood as an organism. . . . If the energy of the cells becomes independent, the organisms that compose the whole organism cease subordinating their energy to the energy of the whole, and the anarchy that breaks out constitutes the decadence of the whole. . . . A decadent style is one where the book's unity breaks down to give way to the independence of the page, where the page decomposes to give way to the independence of the sentence, and the sentence breaks down to give way to the independence of the word. (Bourget 1886, 24–25)

Even before Ficke's literary modernism began to flourish, poetry struck Max Nordau as antithetical to science, and therefore as distinctly primitive. The evolution of mental life, he wrote, was away from "erroneous personal interpretations of the universe"—that is, imaginative literature of all kinds—and toward "observation . . . of the laws of Nature." Verse, Nordau believed, appealed because its meter recalled "its origin in the stimulations of rhythmically functioning subordinate organs." Poetry was a symptom, indicating an archaic emotionalism felt in the flesh and unorganized by reason: "Today it is only employed for purely emotional portrayal; for all other purposes it has been conquered by prose, and indeed, has almost passed into the condition of an atavistic language" (Nordau 1895, 543). Though love was an evolutionary attainment, so was rationality, and emotion in fully civilized adult writers should be firmly dominated by reason, logic, and the orderly developmental progressions that logic imposes. Lingering too long on fragments of feeling was a symptom of arrested development in a writer, for although poetry was "originally the only form of literature," that time was long gone, and scientific prose was the literature of the twentieth century (Nordau 1895, 543). Perhaps, then, the decadent tendency of lyric was one element of the sexological allegation that perverts of a particularly primitive type—intersexed, interraced lesbians—were drawn to rhyming.

Although perverts lacked the perspective that would enable them to evaluate their own place in the evolutionary narrative, the objective scientific observer could see clearly that all this talking, versifying, scribbling autobiographies, and confusion, was anarchically hostile to all the ties that held civilization together: "The impulses of the perverts are of a destructive type; they tend to disintegrate humanity, instead of binding it. Imagine a whole world consisting of homosexuals. In a generation or so there would not be enough homosexuals to go around" (Chideckel 1935, 12). The decadence of perverts was sterile. Words said "even among the intelligent" homosexuals would not bear fruit—neither books nor babies. Civilized sexology, in contrast to the futile "incantations" of the primitive and the perverted, could hope to shape the future as it taught the eugenically significant difference between the savage perverse and the civilized normal. Anglo-Saxon sexual normality is once again the precondition for proper use of language to convey real (rather than magical) meaning, and for the arrangement of erotic episodes into stories. In the end, it is the requirement of Nature, driving the race to better itself.

Notes

1 Havelock Ellis (1859–1939) was a British physician and man of letters. He was and is best known for his sexological works, especially those collected into the seven-volume *Studies in the Psychology of Sex* (1897–1928); in addition, he published more than thirty monographs, edited the Mermaid series of Elizabethan dramatists and the Contemporary Science series, and wrote introductions to many works on sex, marriage, censorship, birth control, and social hygiene. His influence on sexology was considerable. See Grosskurth (1980).

2 *A Thousand Marriages* was written by Lura Beam (b. 1887) from the case records of the well-known gynecologist and contraception campaigner, Robert Latou Dickinson (1861–1950). The earlier two works to which Ellis referred were Katherine Bement Davis's *Factors in the Sex Life of Twenty-Two Hundred Women* (1929) (a sociological study financed by the Bureau of Social Hygiene), and primatologist Gilbert Van Tassel Hamilton's *A Research in Marriage* (1929). Both Davis (1860–1935) and Hamilton (1877–1943) obtained their material from questionnaires about sex life and experience. Dickinson's and Beam's material originated in Dickinson's clinical practice, and hence addressed the somatic aspects of sex experience more directly than the earlier studies.

3 The "race" of interest to Ellis and his contemporaries was a complicated category; depending on the context and purpose of its use, the word could indicate a person's nationality of origin, skin color, religion, membership in the species *Homo sapiens*, and, sometimes, class. These meanings were often intertwined, as in Ellis's comment that the authors of the new sexology of the normal were Anglo-Saxons: he meant that they were Caucasian Americans of the educated classes, whose cultural if not literal ancestry was derived from an English inheritance. Whiteness, as I discuss it in this essay, is not only a matter of generally light and pink skin. In turn, the opposite of whiteness is not blackness, but (for my purposes here) primitivism or archaism, which sometimes describes skin color but often does not. The people against whom Anglo-Saxon normality and civilization were defined might be of Irish working-class background, or of the black bourgeoisie; they might be French noblemen and women, since the French were ancient antagonists of the English and were often believed to be lascivious; they might be Jewish; or perhaps they might be blonde and blue-eyed but feebleminded, German, poor or sexually perverse. The complexities of racial definitions and identities in the Progressive era need further study, but see Bederman (1995) and Stocking (1968).

4 On the need for education in erotics and eugenics see especially Hayden (1926, 15–16, 40) and Everett (1932, 73, 131, 155–156).

5 Allegations that savages frequently have "comparatively undeveloped" sexual organs suggest that there might be a somatic foundation for their shallow passions (Ellis 1903b, 263). Genital underdevelopment in and of itself indicates savages' lack of interest in sexual pleasure, since the genitals, like other parts of the body, were believed to develop in size and strength through manipulation and exercise. See also Hayden (1926, 81) on the physical culture of the genitals. Ellis (1905, 157) contains the standard discussion of the enlargement of the nymphæ called the "Hottentot apron." Robert Latou Dickinson devoted much of his career to demonstrating the impact of arousal and manipulation on the genital formation of women. See especially Dickinson and Beam (1931, chap. 4). In each of these cases, enlarged genitals were described as the result of their manipulation. Therefore, Ellis's allegation that savages' genitals were undeveloped could indicate that they were not used much.

It should also be noted that "undeveloped" genitalia—in the sense of being small—were clinically described as "infantile" in medical literature of this period. The understanding that savagery was the "childhood of the race," and that children were recapitulating the evolution of man from primitivism to civilization as they matured, was thus encapsulated in Ellis's comment as well. At the same time, underdevelopment was not always the same thing as small size. In a woman, undeveloped genitalia might be larger than "normal"—her development might have stopped at a hermaphroditic stage characteristic of embryos, whose genital forms are complexly intersexual. In this use of the charge of underdevelopment, perverts were understood not as the children but as the fetuses of the race.

6 On primitive bisexualism, see also Bauer (1927, 255); Lydston (1904, 377); Potter (1933, 59–60).

7 Edward Carpenter (1844–1929) was an English invert and author who coined the term "intermediate sex" to describe the gender inversion he believed to be at the root of homosexuality. The work to which Goldenweiser referred is *Intermediate Types among Primitive Folk* (1914), which argued that deviations from culturally prescribed gender roles were important in the development of religion and art.

References

Bauer, Bernhard A. [1927] 1949. *Woman and Love*. New York: Liveright.

Bederman, Gail. 1995. *Manliness and Civilization: A Cultural History of Gender and Race in the United States, 1880–1917*. Chicago: University of Chicago Press.

Bourget, Paul. 1886. *Essais de psychologie contemporaine*. Paris: Alphonse Lemerre.

Butterfield, Oliver M. [1937] 1946. *Sex Life in Marriage*. New York: Emerson Books.

Carpenter, Edward. 1914. *Intermediate Types among Primitive Folk: A Study in Social Evolution*. New York: Mitchell Kennerley.

Chideckel, Maurice. 1935. *Female Sex Perversion: The Sexually Aberrated Woman as She Is*. New York: Eugenics Publishing Company.

Davis, Katherine Bement. 1929. *Factors in the Sex Life of Twenty-Two Hundred Women*. New York: Harper.

Dell, Floyd. 1930. *Love in the Machine Age: A Psychological Study of the Transition from Patriarchal Society*. New York: Farrar & Rinehard.

Dickinson, Robert Latou, and Lura Beam. 1931. *A Thousand Marriages: A Medical Study of Sex Adjustment*. Baltimore: Williams & Wilkins.

———. 1934. *The Single Woman: A Medical Study in Sex Education*. Baltimore: Williams & Wilkins.

Ellis, Havelock. [1894] 1911. *Man and Woman: A Study of Human Secondary Sexual Characters*. New York: Scribners.

———. [1897] 1936. *Sexual Inversion*. In *Studies in the Psychology of Sex*, Vol. 2, Part 2. New York: Random House.

———. [1897–1928] 1936. *Studies in the Psychology of Sex*. New York: Random House.

———. [1903a] 1936. *Analysis of the Sexual Impulse*. In *Studies in the Psychology of Sex*, Vol. 1, Part 2: 1–65. New York: Random House.

———. [1903b] 1936. The sexual instinct in savages. In *Studies in the Psychology of Sex*, Vol. 1, Part 2: 259–276. New York: Random House.

———. [1905] 1936. *Sexual Selection in Man*. In *Studies in the Psychology of Sex*, Vol. 2, Part 1. New York: Random House.

———. 1929. Introduction to *Sex in Civilization*, ed. V .F. Calverton and S. D. Schmalhausen, 15–28. Garden City, NY: Garden City Publishing.

———. 1931. Introduction to *A Thousand Marriages: A Medical Study of Sex Adjustment* by Robert Latou Dickinson and Lura Beam. Baltimore: Williams & Wilkins.

Everett, Millard S. 1932. *The Hygiene of Marriage: A Detailed Consideration of Sex and Marriage*. New York: Vanguard Press.

Ficke, Arthur Davidson. 1929. A note on the poetry of sex. In *Sex in Civilization*, ed. V .F. Calverton and S. D. Schmalhausen, 649–666. Garden City, NY: Garden City Publishing.

Ford, Charles. 1929. Homosexual practices of institutionalized females. *Journal of Abnormal and Social Psychology* 23:442–448.

Gilman, Charlotte Perkins. 1929. Sex and race progress. In *Sex in Civilization*, ed. V. F. Calverton and S. D. Schmalhausen, 109–126. Garden City, NY: Garden City Publishing.

Goldenweiser, Alexander. 1929. Sex and primitive society. In *Sex in Civilization*, ed. V. F. Calverton and S. D. Schmalhausen, 53–66. Garden City, NY: Garden City Publishing.

Grosskurth, Phyllis. 1980. *Havelock Ellis: A Biography*. New York: Knopf.

Hamilton, G.V. 1929. *A Research in Marriage*. New York: Lear Publishers.

Hayden, Jesse F. [1926] 1936. *The Art of Marriage: A Scientific Treatise*. High Point, NC: Book Sales Agency.

Kiernan, James. 1923. The significance of sex in modern literature. *Urologic and Cutaneous Review* 27:285–295.

Lichtenstein, Perry M. 1921. The 'Fairy' and the lady lover. *Medical Review of Reviews* 27:369–374.

Lombroso, Cesare. [1893] 1923. *La donna delinquente, la prostituta e la donna normale*. New York: Italian Book Company.

Lydston, G. Frank. 1904. *The Diseases of Society: The Vice and Crime Problem*. Philadelphia: J. B. Lippincott.

Nordau, Max. [1895] 1968. *Degeneration*. Translated from the 2nd ed. Lincoln: University of Nebraska Press.

Otis, Margaret. 1913. A perversion not commonly noted. *Journal of Abnormal Psychology* 8:113–116.

Potter, La Forest. 1933. *Strange Loves*. New York: n.p.

Prince, Morton. [1891] 1975. *Psychotherapy and Multiple Personality: Selected Essays.* Ed. Nathan G. Hale, Jr. Cambridge: Harvard University Press.
Somerville, Siobhan. 1994. Scientific racism and the emergence of the homosexual body. *Journal of the History of Sexuality* 5:243–266.
Spackman, Barbara. 1989. *Decadent Genealogies: The Rhetoric of Sickness from Baudelaire to D'Annunzio.* Ithaca: Cornell University Press.
Stocking, George. 1968. *Race, Culture and Evolution: Essays in the History of Anthropology.* New York: Free Press.

"A Finer Differentiation"
Female Homosexuality and the American Medical Community, 1926–1940

Erin G. Carlston

Historians have documented the medical community's promotion, beginning in the late nineteenth century, of a concept of homosexuality as pathological and abnormal, and have suggested how damaging the internalization of this concept could be to people with homoerotic feelings or in homosexual relations.[1] At the same time, at least one scholar has warned against attributing too much power to ideology by assuming "that people uncritically internalized the new medical models" as they arose (Chauncey 1989, 87). In this essay, I examine early twentieth-century U.S. medical literature on homosexuality, particularly lesbianism, and argue that it would be wrong not only to assign medical ideology a determinative role in shaping the lives and identities of homosexuals, but also to characterize that ideology as monolithic.[2]

In fact, the medical discourse on homosexuality was never uniform: while there were many who characterized homosexuality as a disease, there were others who emphatically did not. There were disagreements even among the first sexologists in the late nineteenth century, and by the 1930s, the period on which I concentrate here, medical and psychiatric thinking about homosexuality had proliferated wildly, dividing and subdividing into myriad conflicting schools and viewpoints as doctors struggled to map out and colonize the newly defined territories of human sexual behavior. My intention is not to claim that medical and psychiatric discourses about homosexuality were really, if properly interpreted, emancipatory; rather, I will argue here that in measuring the force of medical ideology—or of any ideology—in the U.S. between 1926 and 1940, we must look at the ways in which it undermines and contradicts itself, lays itself open to (mis)interpretation, and/or makes itself available to strategies of resistance.

Beginning in about 1929, there was a marked increase in the quantity of medical writing about female homosexuality in both the United States and Europe that continued throughout the 1930s, and that was self-consciously demarcated from the earlier work of sexologists such as Havelock Ellis, Magnus Hirschfeld, Richard von Krafft-Ebing, and Albert Moll.[3] At precisely the same time, there seems to have been a surge of popular interest in the subject; this is evident in the increasing number of explicit references to lesbianism in sources such as the *New York Times* (see Katz 1983). In 1929 the first published sociological survey on female sexuality appeared—Katharine Bement Davis's *Factors in the Sex Lives of Twenty-Two Hundred Women*—which revealed that fully one quarter of the white, college-educated women Davis interviewed during the 1920s had at least one sexual relationship with another woman (1929, 238–328). Between 1927 and 1929 a number of major novels that treated the subject of lesbianism were published, notably Radclyffe Hall's celebrated *The Well of Loneliness* (1928), whose publication was followed by widely publicized censorship trials both in Britain and, in 1929, in the U.S.[4]

The material in Katz's *Almanac* and Davis's survey, and the themes of the novels, suggest that the reasons for this intensified popular and scientific interest probably included the increasingly wide dissemination of Freud's work; the influence of a new generation of university-educated women who had formed or witnessed lesbian relationships in college; the national "coming-out" experience in England of women who had served in the war effort; the establishment of openly lesbian, monied, and literate communities in Europe; and a general expansion of public discussion about, and the highly visible commercialization of, sex and sexuality in many forms. In addition, changes in gender norms after World War I certainly influenced medical thinking about gender identity and sexual behavior. In the late nineteenth century, the female invert had often been described as a hermaphrodite, characterized by gender-reversed body type, identity, and behavior; this model had served reasonably well, with modifications, for several decades. But during the 1920s a new model of *heterosexual* womanhood appeared in the person of the flapper, who was thin-hipped and small-breasted, wore androgynous clothes and bobbed her hair, smoked and drank publicly, and enjoyed sports—who, in other words, closely resembled many of the old stereotypes of the invert. Thus medical writers concerned with female deviance were obliged to transfer their attention from mannerisms, dress, and body type to the more threatening behaviors that such stereotypes had originally identified and contained. For example, by the 1930s gender reversal or dysphoria was, as we will see below, more often linked to "inappropriate" behavior—like political activism—than to hermaphroditic body type.

World War II, of course, also precipitated dramatic changes in gender roles and relations, the psychiatric profession, homosexual communities, and concepts of homosexual identity. I have, then, chosen 1940—perhaps a bit arbitrarily—to mark the beginning of the war era and the end of the period under investigation. I would like now to turn to that period and take a closer look at some of the medical and psychiatric literature on (female) homosexuality.

Any discussion of psychiatric theory in the U.S. of the 1930s must take into account the decisive influence of Freud, whose work had been widely disseminated since the 1910s. A thorough examination of Freud's monumental and often-revised work on sexuality lies outside the scope of this essay, and has in any case been extensively discussed elsewhere.[5] For my purposes, I would like to recall the significant points of two of his essays—significant because of the ways they were cited, distorted, or ignored in later work on the subject. In his *Three Essays on the Theory of Sexuality* (1905), Freud introduced his theory of bisexuality. He particularly challenged certain biologically grounded explanations of sexual deviance. Referring to Krafft-Ebing's hypothesis of bisexual brain centers, Freud wrote: "There is neither need nor justification for replacing the psychological problem by the anatomical one" (1905, 142). In his 1920 essay on "The Psychogenesis of a Case of Homosexuality in a Woman," he made this point more explicit: in response to what he considered the reader's expectation that he would define this case as either "inherited" or "acquired," Freud said that the question itself was "fruitless and inapposite" (1920, 154).

In this essay, Freud came close to expressing the aspect of his theory of sexuality that is potentially most radical and perhaps most frequently suppressed in other work, including his own: the admission of the possibility that "masculinity" and "femininity" are culturally constructed concepts. After stating that the young woman in the case showed no physical hermaphroditism, he wrote that she did display objectivity and an acute comprehension that could be characterized as masculine, "but these distinctions are conventional rather than scientific" (1920, 154). And in a footnote he added to the *Three Essays* in 1915, he had opened up the way for a discussion of sexual object-choice as the same sort of cultural construct, arguing that:

> Psycho-analytic research is most decidedly opposed to any attempt at separating off homosexuals from the rest of mankind as a group of a special character. . . . From the point of view of psycho-analysis the exclusive sexual interest felt by men for women is also a problem that needs elucidating and is not a self-evident fact based upon an attraction that is ultimately of a chemical nature. (Freud 1905, 145–146n)

If Freud wrote, often prescriptively, of what constituted "normal" sexuality, particularly for women, he nonetheless did so within the context of an œuvre that dramatically called into question a value-laden concept of normality. "No healthy person," he wrote in *Three Essays*, "can fail to make some addition that might be called perverse to the normal sexual aim; and the universality of this finding is in itself enough to show how inappropriate it is to use the word perversion as a term of reproach" (1905, 160).

Jeffrey Weeks has argued that while Freud attempted to extend "perversion" into the realm of the ordinary and common, problematizing heterosexuality as well as homosexuality, he retained a concept of "perversion" based on a normative idea of development, which sees homosexuality as an "inhibition" along the route to full heterosexual development. "In the end, therefore," writes Weeks, "a heterosexual and reproductive imperative is reinserted into Freud's account. Once a goal-directed version of sexuality is introduced, however surreptitiously, then the whole laboriously constructed edifice of sexual variety begins to totter" (1986, 71–73). The reverse is also true, however: once the recognition of sexual variability has been introduced, a goal-directed version of sexuality is, if not undermined, then certainly complicated.

An emphasis on the multiplicity of sexual aims and choices, and the universality of behavior that is not directed toward heterosexual intercourse, makes progress toward the goal of reproductive heterosexuality seem, at least, a good deal more hazardous, less "normal" or self-evident. In the end, neither concept entirely negates the ideological force of the other, and the tension between them was evident in the 1930s.

Other writers tried to ignore Freud's concept of sexuality as a cultural construct. Instead, they took up his equation of masculinity with activity and femininity with passivity and turned it into an injunction, often justified by biological determinism. Influenced by this crude Freudianism, some writers of the 1920s and 1930s came to characterize deviance from traditional gender roles as a failure to adhere to a newly sexualized model of heterosociality and marriage, and depreciated female homosexuality as an immature or regressive phase of feminine psychosexual development. Freud and the European Freudians viewed polymorphous perversity and oral sadism as infantile stages, in contrast to genitally organized adult sexuality (Jones 1927). American writers explicitly reframed this argument in the context of the patriarchal logic that, it could be argued, implicitly motivated it anyway, and thus posited female homosexuality as a retreat not only from adult female sexuality but from the maternal and marital roles and responsibilities conventionally attached to it.

Although the tone of American physicians was usually patronizing rather than overtly hostile, there is no doubt that in the 1930s some doctors perceived lesbianism as a menace. Christina Simmons (1979, 54–59) has described the condemnation of female homosexuality by medical writers during this period and the manipulation of "the lesbian threat" in the service of a normative heterosexual ideal. Medical advice books and marriage manuals proliferated, offering information about the correct ways to have sexual relations, and enforcing heterosexual norms.[6] While the literature was not as uniformly negative as Simmons implies, it is true that, in the drive to recuperate female sexuality by any means possible in support of the ideal of heterosociality, many earlier ideas on inversion were rephrased as explicitly antifeminist polemic.

Dr. Sandor Lorand, for example, suggested that women who had difficulty adjusting to a feminine role might be struggling with unconscious homosexuality: "Although they may seem extremely feminine, their attractive womanly qualities may be no more than a mask . . . these women are unhappy in relations as women with men, and unable to achieve real sexual gratification" (1939, 179). In a sexual advice book, W. Béran Wolfe wrote that the normal adolescent stage of homosexuality could become an evasion of the responsibilities of marriage and motherhood. He added that if "mature" women formed lesbian relationships *after* having been wives and mothers, he would consider it "a reasonable sublimation of sex," making it clear that he was not so much concerned with repressing female sexual and affective relations entirely as with making sure both that women would reproduce and that they would be sexually available to men during what men considered their most attractive years (Wolfe 1935, 158–159).

An article written by Dr. John W. Meagher in 1929 for the *Urologic and Cutaneous Review* has been cited at length by Simmons and others, probably because

Meagher summarized, in their most quotable and exaggerated form, many of the charges made against homosexuals in the literature of this decade. The tone of his writing was histrionic in the extreme, and his argument crammed with contradictions that resulted, in part, from the attempt to incorporate every available indictment of homosexuality and lesbianism into one essay. As both causes and proofs of female homosexuality, for instance, Meagher offered nymphomania, hatred toward men, an attraction to boys, a "morbid addiction" to enemas and douches, fear of penises, unprovoked trouble with female domestics, shame in the presence of women, excitement in the presence of women, lack of the "natural impulse to preserve the species," unsatisfied libido, a craving to see breasts, "refusal" to orgasm in marital intercourse, and a taste for same-sex massage, among other things.

Like Lorand, Meagher claimed that reluctance to adjust to a feminine role, manifested as feminism, might be evidence of repressed homosexuality:

> The driving force in many agitators and militant women who are always after their rights, is often an unsatisfied sex impulse, with a homosexual aim. Married women with a completely satisfied libido rarely take an active interest in militant movements. They have other interests, family and social, with which to use up their energy. . . . [S]o-called emancipated women are usually frigid, and usually have little unselfish maternal feelings [*sic*]. The best biological and social assets to society are the complete she-women, and the complete he-men. (Meagher 1929, 511–512)

We see here the assimilation, typical of this period, of Freudian terminology to a strongly normative and quite un-Freudian rhetoric of heterosexuality, insistently reinforced by statements such as "happily married persons are not neurotic . . . only neurotic women are anesthetic" (that is, inorgasmic) (Meagher 1929, 513). To become normal, Meagher insisted, the frigid/homosexual woman must give up her narcissism and clitoral sensibility for vaginal sensibility and an interest in men. Meagher also warned parents to protect their daughters from older women and to encourage girls' heterosexual socialization. He asserted that homosexuality was much more prevalent than realized and that seduction by older women was frequently the means by which young girls were initiated and their development permanently "interfered with" (1929, 506 and 510).

In judging the significance of this article, it is important to realize that it was published alongside two other pieces in the same journal that offered differing viewpoints; thus it obviously cannot be taken as representative even of one periodical, let alone a decade. Meagher himself explicitly opposed a contemporary and more tolerant school of thought at several points. His theories were extreme, even when judged by the standards of the time, and I did not find his work cited by any of his contemporaries. Most of the other writing of the period presents a more complex vision of homosexuality. Because more subtle, it is perhaps more insidious; but it is also more open to diverse interpretations.

One highly overdetermined theme in medical work of the period, for example, is the belief that repressing sexual desire could cause neuroses and somatic disorders of all kinds. The idea itself predated Freud; Katz (1983, 156) traces it at least as far back as the 1880s. Freud, however, provided the vocabulary of "repression," "sublimation," and "neurosis" so frequently found in the work of later writers. Samuel Schmalhausen, a liberal/socialist psychoanalyst, credited Freud in 1931 for making people realize how dangerous sexual repression was (see Simmons 1989, 161). Even Meagher, who characterized homosexuals as "ethical" or "pervert" according to whether or not they sublimated their sexual energy, felt that repression could lead to neuroses and psychoses (1929, 506). Not surprisingly, he considered the resultant psychopathology the lesser of two evils, and insisted that congenital homosexuals, since they could not be cured, should cultivate chastity:

> If the pervert homosexual insists on not following advice [to remain celibate], he knows society's attitude and must bear the responsibility for his conduct. For inasmuch as boys or girls are often involved in their pervert conduct, society has its own duties, and will perform them. We note some writers say that perversions have neither a social nor a forensic value, if the public is not injured; that they are only biological variations. But society and the law have a different viewpoint. The social must always prevail over the individual attitude. It might be interesting to note here that many homosexual kleptomaniac women are prone to steal silk underwear. (Meagher 1929, 518)

Another writer, Donald M. Hamilton, while considerably more sympathetic to homosexuals than Meagher, also suggested that (male) homosexuals should try to sublimate their sexual energies in art, or organizations like the Boy Scouts and Y.M.C.A. (1939, 234).[7] Meagher and Hamilton represented something of a minority position, however. It is more common to find articles that implied that neither repression nor sublimation was a reasonable option, and that an open admission of homosexuality was healthiest. John R. Ernst, for instance, cited the repression of homosexual feelings in a discussion of the formation of psychoses:

> The homosexual complex results from a refusal of an introverted individual to admit frankly to himself that he is homosexual and an inability to make a satisfactory adjustment. The moral, religious, and social censors which have subtlely [*sic*] arisen within him, are directly responsible for the violent emotional and mental conflicts that result. Lack of frankness with himself leads to constant repression of instinctive urges and a resultant failure to make proper adaptations. (Ernst 1928, 384)

Aaron Rosanoff, a Los Angeles psychiatrist, felt strongly that homosexuals should be allowed an outlet for their sexual desires, although he also thought that repression was easier for women than for men because they were "less sexed" (1929, 529). While he credited both environmental and inborn factors in the etiology of homosexuality, he felt that in adults it was largely a fixed trait, and could be hereditary. In view of this, he proposed a rather extraordinary eugenic "solution" to the problem of homosexuality, or at least male homosexuality, in an article written for the same issue of the *Urologic and Cutaneous Review* in which Meagher's piece appeared:

> The conventional attitude toward homosexual behavior is quite irrational. It is regarded as a sin and a crime, and homosexuals, like heterosexuals, are officially permitted no other outlet for their sexual energies than through marriage. This results not only in untold misery to the patients and their wives, but also in the perpetuation by heredity of homosexual traits—the very thing that conventional society would wish to avoid.
>
> It would seem more rational not only to ignore homosexual behavior, as being a matter of concern only to the individual, but also actually to encourage it, on eugenic grounds, to the full extent of the tendencies in that direction existing in the subjects concerned. (Rosanoff 1929, 530)

We must note that—in pointed contrast to Meagher—Rosanoff was not concerned about the threat homosexuals posed to society, partly because he, unlike many of his contemporaries, believed that heterosexuals could not be "turned into" homosexuals, and partly because he felt that even in the case of the seduction of minors by homosexuals, "there is no occasion for emotional pyrotechnics. Heterosexual practices are fraught with the greater danger" because of the risk of venereal disease and pregnancy (1929, 530).

Some medical writers went so far as to rank celibacy as a perversion on a level with homosexuality, illustrating how much attitudes had changed since the late nineteenth century. For example, while Abraham Wolbarst acknowledged that celibacy was held "in high esteem in our moral and religious codes," he felt that it "runs counter to the natural and normal sex life" (1931, 64). Thus, while some doctors certainly characterized homosexual behavior as pathological, we also find an increasing emphasis in the literature of the 1930s on the psychopathology of sexual "repression" that potentially legitimates an open expression of homosexual feelings.

Changing definitions of normality also provoked perplexity and contradiction in the medical writing on deviance. One transition in concepts of sexual normality had already taken place in the late Victorian era, when we find a shift from a procreation-based ideal of sexual normality to a statistically defined one; the "normal" began to be defined as whatever the majority of people felt and did, whether it was procreative or not (Katz 1983, 143). But in the 1930s, this definition was also in flux, as by then, Freudianism had problematized even the concept of a "majority" sexuality—for if everyone was either consciously or unconsciously perverse, then who *were* the members of the normal majority? It is worth noting that even the more conservative writers of the 1930s, apparently mindful of Freud, often put the word "normal" in quotation marks, or prefaced the words "perversion" and "normality" with a cautious "so-called." Though few of these writers cared to examine the more radical possibilities suggested by Freud's work, many still manifested an obvious discomfort with morally grounded definitions of the normal, and struggled with alternatives. In 1938, for example, Clifford A. Wright, an endocrinologist, attempted to resolve the question in purely statistical, biological terms, drawing on his studies of the hormone balance in the urine of homosexuals and heterosexuals (see Kenen in this volume). Analyzing the distribution of his results, he asked, "Are we then dealing with an abnormal or pathological condition or a normal infrequent variation—a Mendelian recessive, perhaps?" (1938, 452).

For more psychoanalytically oriented doctors, finding a satisfactory definition of normalcy was more difficult. Wolbarst discussed this difficulty at some length, beginning his article by saying: "What may be considered normal for one individual may be decidedly abnormal for another; and who is there among us who can decide which of the two is normal and which abnormal?" (1931, 5). Wolbarst was hardly an apologist for sexual deviance; while he condemned doctors who judged perversion ethically instead of scientifically, he himself used words like "unpleasant," "obnoxious," and "repulsive" in describing a wide variety of sexual acts. At the same time, however, his concept of sexual morality was so extremely relativistic as to allow latitude for almost any moral stance:

> Essentially, we cannot say that any act *per se* is either right or wrong; the time, the place, the circumstances and the underlying conditions which motivated the act must be taken into consideration. . . . If, on the one hand, the individual is an intelligent, emotionally disciplined and self-controlled normal adult, it is quite reasonable to assume that he may indulge in his pet variations and sexual whims with safety to himself and without injury to the community. While the interests of society as a whole may require that these particular acts to be considered normal should contribute to the higher, larger emotional expansion of the individual concerned, we nevertheless must concede the right of such an individual to live his own life in his own way so long as he does not do anything that makes him feel degraded or that degrades others. (Wolbarst 1931, 64)

It could be argued that by using a term like "self-controlled normal adult," Wolbarst was by definition excluding homosexuals from this generous judgment. But by the end of his article, he still had not managed to describe "normality," and could say only that "[w]e may possibly find ourselves on the correct road if we act on the theory that any sexual deviation which has always given satisfaction without injury to any particular individual must be considered normal for that individual" (1931, 65).

In addition to the concepts of "repression" and "normality," a third area in the medical literature that left room for a range of interpretations was the discussion of the historical and cultural universality of homosexuality and other perversions. It is common in the medical writing from this period to find references to the prevalence of sapphism and pederasty among the ancient Greeks; some articles provided lists of well-known historical personages thought to have been homosexual (see, for example, Wolbarst 1931, 6–7; "Literature and Sexual Inversion" 1933; Hamilton 1939, 229–230). There is a decided tension in this literature between descriptions of the valorization of homosexuality by the ancients, and the insistence that in contemporary society it is an illness or a neurosis; for the difference between classical and contemporary attitudes necessarily marked the specific social construction of sexual mores even as medical writers struggled to affirm the universal applicability of their own theories of sexuality. It is incongruous, to say the least, to find an account of the flourishing of homosexual practices in Greek and Renaissance cultures—both supposed to represent the height of human æsthetic and intellectual development—side by side with the observation that homosexuality is an immature, adolescent stage that is generally outgrown, as we do in Hamilton's article (1939, 229–230).

Similarly, Wolbarst was capable of inserting a negative judgment about sexual practices into an account of the cultural construction of such judgments. "History records that what we speak of as perversions have always been practiced and at certain epochs in human history have been considered perfectly proper and conventional," he wrote, before sliding, in one paragraph, from calling anal intercourse "the most obnoxious type of perversion" to citing its practice among the Greeks as "a respectable and honorable custom" (Wolbarst 1931, 7, 62). This type of inconsistency is most striking in the work of doctors with a strongly psychoanalytic orientation, for a discourse that has drawn its most powerful paradigms from Greek literature could hardly invoke the Greeks' distinctive deployment of sexuality without implicitly jeopardizing its own claim to an historically static explanation of the psychic structures of desire.

In all the works cited above, ambiguities or outright contradictions in medical writings signal inconsistencies and interruptions in the tendency toward the pathologization of homosexuality. But some texts hardly required this sort of subversive reinterpretation. A handful of doctors went further than positing universal deviance, warning against the ill effects of sexual repression or questioning conventional standards of normality; they explicitly criticized social attitudes toward homosexuals, even characterizing what we now call homophobia as a pathology itself. Though their comments generally addressed attitudes towards male homosexuality, they could be and were applied to lesbians.

Rosanoff, for example, acknowledged that for the homosexual, conflicts arose between the individual's instincts and societal mores; a more integrated society, he claimed, would dispose of its "scientifically unsound mores" and establish harmony. In view of the opinions he expressed in his other work, there can be little doubt that by "harmony" he meant acceptance of homosexuality, and not its elimination (Rosanoff 1935, 39). Even more strikingly, in two companion pieces published in the *Medical Journal and Record*, Dr. Harry Benjamin attacked New York vice squad investigations of prostitution and homosexuality.[8] Benjamin blamed criminalization of heterosexual prostitution for fostering male homosexuality, as boys or "bisexual men" without access to prostitutes might turn to homosexual men for gratification. This was, he said, a "misfortune" to be avoided; but he considered it unfortunate because of contemporary social attitudes, rather than because there was something inherently wrong with homosexuality. "[I]t is after all," he wrote, "the lesser evil to visit a prostitute once in a while than to become a homosexual *in our present time of intolerance* against this deviation from the norm" (1931a, 382; my emphasis). Benjamin also criticized sharply those who would pride themselves on their own sexual normality: "'Vicious' desires are part of human nature and anyone boasting to be free of vices, is either a hypocritical liar or a neurotic" (1931a, 380). Furthermore, he described "Puritanism" as "a sex perversion" in itself (1931a, 382).

In his second article, Benjamin expanded on the argument of the first by criticizing legal discrimination against homosexuality and offering a vigorous defense of homosexual relationships and the homosexual's right to privacy and sexual fulfillment—a defense that implicitly extended to homosexual women:

> The law takes a peculiar inconsistent attitude toward homosexuality. In most countries only acts between men but not between women are punished. In Switzerland a law against homosexual practices exists in one canton but not in another. In several countries, for instance, Germany, an energetic and partly successful reform movement is being carried on to abolish any legal differentiation between homo and heterosexual relations. The understanding seems to be gaining ground that the law should indeed make no such differentiation, as long as they take place between adults and with their mutual consent. A homosexual love can be as strong, as fine, as altruistic as any other love. A physical gratification of the homosexual urge is just as essential for the well-being and happiness of the individual as that of the so-called "normal" urge, and both are equally purely private affairs with which no law has any logical right to interfere. (Benjamin 1931b, 119)

Like Rosanoff, Benjamin pointed to society's role in creating conflict for the congenital homosexual: "It could hardly be possible that . . . an 'endocrine homosexual' should endure the friction with the prejudices of our present-day society, without becoming more or less neurotic" (1931b, 119).

It is important to note that both Benjamin and Rosanoff subscribed to the idea that most homosexuality was congenital or hormonally based, although they acknowledged the existence of "acquired" homosexuality and "various infantile fixations and influences" on psychosexual development (Benjamin 1931b, 118–119). Thus they were both firmly on what was often the more liberal side of the great debate between "congenital" and "anti-congenital" theories that intensified during the 1930s, even as those clear, binary categories became increasingly complicated.

In 1926, psychoanalysts Irene Case Sherman and Mandel Sherman had confidently asserted that "observers at the present time are very skeptical of the inheritance of 'tendencies' to particular types of human behavior. The diagnosis of 'innate homosexual' is no doubt often made because of a failure to find the psychogenic factors of significance in producing the behavior" (1926, 37). A few years later, and with equal confidence, George W. Henry and Hugh M. Galbraith prefaced their 1934 study on "Constitutional Factors in Homosexuality" by saying that the constitutional and physiological components of homosexuality had recently been wrongly ignored in favor of psychogenic explanations. A talk given in New York in 1934 by George S. Sprague was followed by an open debate between what might be called "pro- and anti-congenital" forces, which occupied four pages in the published version of the paper.

The heated, confused battles raged throughout the 1930s. The passion of the debates derived from the crucial question, for liberals, of which stance led to greater tolerance, or, for conservatives, which would act as a more effective measure of control over homosexuality; the confusion resulted from the fact that the political valences of the two positions were profoundly unstable. In the early thirties, certainly, liberals such as Rosanoff and Benjamin tended to espouse congenitalism, arguing that as an inborn, immutable condition, homosexuality could not be cured, and that the congenital homosexual was not to blame for her condition. Homosexuals themselves had adopted these arguments, notably Radclyffe Hall. In *The Well of Loneliness*, Hall's plea for tolerance of the invert rested on the premises that inversion is innate and unchangeable, that social stigma compounds the invert's suffering and hastens her degradation, and that for the invert to repress her sexual desires is bad for her health and her work. Esther Newton sees in this argument not only a powerful strategy for emphasizing and legitimating lesbians' sexuality, but a way to "counter demands that they undergo punishing 'therapies'" (1984, 575).

The Well's impact on medical writers was immediate; I found the first reference to it in Oberndorf's 1929 article, the year after the novel was published in England. Those who inclined towards congenital theories and tolerance themselves reviewed the novel favorably; Wolbarst called it "an excellent description of the female invert" (1931, 63). Reaction against the book and congenitalism came, significantly, from Freudians, anxious to shift the blame for homosexuality back onto the individual and into the domain of psychotherapy. In his advice book, Wolfe showed clearly how complicitous Freudian theory could be with anti-homosexual attitudes when he wrote about *The Well* that

> Homosexuality is not, as is popularly supposed, a product of pre-natal influences, of congenital predispositions, or of hereditary taint. . . . Any girl with the usual homosexual tendencies of adolescence may be led to believe that she is condemned and dedicated to a life of homosexuality reading such pseudo-scientific hocus-pocus [i.e., *The Well*] . . . homosexuality in women, as in men, is an acquired neurosis whose causes root . . . in easily demonstrable economic, sociological and psychological determinants. (Wolfe 1935, 157)

At the end of the 1930s, A. A. Brill, the pre-eminent Freudian in the U.S., continued to insist that homosexual neuroses were the fault of the individual, and not society:

> That even so-called classical inverts are not entirely free from some paranoid traits is quite obvious on even superficial observation. Having encountered hundreds of homosexuals, some of whom were prominent in artistic, philanthropic and other fields, I have never found one who, on closer observation, did not show paranoid traits. They are all oversuspicious, "shadowy," and mistrustful. Most of them are unreliable, intriguing, picayune and impetuous. . . . I have felt for years that this behavior was engendered by our civilization, where homosexuals are treated as outcasts. However I am convinced that this is only partially true. Most of these traits are due to anal-sadistic fixations and regressions. (Brill 1940, 13)

Yet, as we have seen, Freudianism could equally well be used to problematize such normative moral judgments, to argue against societal prejudices and for tolerance of homosexuality. Freud himself, as is well known, refused to treat patients for homosexuality *per se*, since he did not consider homosexuals sick (Abelove 1993). This was, therefore, the dilemma confronting those conservative doctors in the mid-1930s who believed that homosexual behavior posed a threat to society and who hoped to eradicate it. Congenitalism could be and had been easily adapted by homosexuals and reformers; psychoanalytically oriented theories, though indeterminate and flexible enough to be turned to almost any purpose, were, for that very reason, too unstable and malleable to support a determined campaign against homosexuality.

Significantly, after 1935 there was an increasing interest among more conservative, anti-homosexual medical practitioners in the new field of endocrinology, and there appeared a trend back toward somatically based theories and therapies, many of them brutally invasive. Armed with theories of eugenics, increasing knowledge about chromosomes, and endocrinological research, anti-homosexual doctors of the 1930s found a way to recuperate congenitalism. Homosexuality might be an innate physiological condition, caused by defective chromosomes or hormonal imbalances; but it might, nevertheless, be treatable thanks to therapies at least as punishing as those Hall and her contemporaries had wanted to avoid.

These therapies, the same that were used during this period on many other patients judged biologically defective or socially unfit, included insulin-induced shock; the use of Metrazol, a cardiac stimulant, to provoke grand mal seizures; and castration of male homosexuals (Grob 1983, 296–308; Kopp 1938; Owensby 1940). To the vehemently anti-homosexual doctor, mutilating homosexuals' bodies must have seemed a far more promising solution than the "talking cure"—which always allowed for the possibility that the patient might talk back. With somatic therapies, the doctor could inscribe his "reading" of the case on the body of the patient, finally and irrevocably establishing himself as the only legitimate interpreter of the meaning of "disease."

Innovations like endocrinological testing also added to doctors' prestige and reinforced their authority to "treat" social and legal problems. Katz cites a 1935 *New York Times* report on hormone treatments that shows that the media were presenting such treatments "as a 'cure' for gender nonconformity, including homosexuality" (1983, 510). Clifford Wright's faith in the infallibility of his urine hormone tests was such that he could claim that "[h]ormone assays of the urine are important in helping to disprove homosexuality in a normal individual where arrest has been made because of an alleged overt act, or for some other important reason" (1939, 400).

By the end of the 1930s, even some psychoanalysts had jumped on the biologistic bandwagon, going so far as to try to wed biologism to an analytic approach, and inventing a history of origins that "rediscovered" Freud's biologistic orientation. It was surely as a defensive reaction to the new dominance of congenitalism and somatic therapies that Brill, who for three decades had promoted Freud's "radically mental" theories in the U.S., asserted in 1940 that Freud had "never ignored the physical element in the neuroses" (Brill 1940, 9). In an extreme instance, the rhetoric of Freudian psychology was employed to justify a brutally somatic "therapy" for homosexuality—the use of Metrazol to induce epileptic seizures:

> [H]omosexuality and lesbianism are symptoms of an underdeveloped schizophrenia which was arrested at the particular phase in its psychosexual development where the libido becomes fixated. . . . [M]etrazol liberates this previous fixation of the libido and the psychosexual energy becomes free once more to flow through regular physiological channels. (Owensby 1940, 65)

Violent somatic treatments of homosexuality, while by no means universally practiced, were perhaps the most extreme manifestation of the anxiety sexual deviance provoked in the psychiatric profession in general. The decade saw a number of "definitional crises" in medical discourse about homosexuality, a series of unsuccessful efforts to elaborate taxonomies of sexualities that would accommodate the wide variety of data accumulated on homosexuality (Richardson 1983, 82). Doctors invented more and more categories of homosexual identity as they tried to contain the contradiction between positing homosexuality as an essential *state*, whether biological or psychological, and recognizing the prevalence and variety of homosexual *behaviors*.

Henry and Galbraith, for instance, described a complicated array of physiological differences between 228 male and female, hetero- and homosexual patients (1934, 1250–1251). Rosanoff, too, in an attempt to account for psychosexual variability in strictly biological terms, eventually made up fifteen possible chromosome permutations to distinguish six "male types" and nine "female types" (1935, 39). Arguing from a psychoanalytic viewpoint, Clarence P. Oberndorf first affirmed that everyone was organically and psychologically bisexual, and then meticulously catalogued a plethora of possible combinations of gender identity, object choice, and sexual behavior: conscious versus unconscious, psychic versus overt, continuous versus intermittent, and deliberate versus compulsive homosexuality; a conscious preference or a choice made in the absence of heterosexual objects; a fixation at an early stage of psychological development or a regression from the heterosexual stage (1929, 520). Other doctors, trying to take a middle course between strictly organic and strictly psychogenic interpretations, devised equally complex, and equally confused, schemas.

In the 1934 paper that provoked, as I mentioned, a heated debate, Sprague summed up the contemporary confusion, arguing that Magnus Hirschfeld's characterization of homosexuality as a clear-cut and rare condition had been superseded by the recognition that it was instead a complicated and varying problem with various manifestations, so that doctors now had to ask themselves not whether a patient was homosexual, but rather, whether "[h]is homosexuality is evidenced in what ways, and under which conditions?" Homosexuality, Sprague concluded, "may be regarded as a pulsing, fluctuating coloring of an individual's way of living his life" (1934, 143–144, 150).

As Sprague almost explicitly stated, none of these theoretical accounts could quite hold together; the neat categories were constantly disrupted and rearranged by recurrent theoretical anxieties. Those who insisted on the primacy of environmental factors, and denied biology any role in the etiology of psychosexual organization, still occasionally spoke of homosexuality as if it were an essential, defining property of an individual, and then had to try to reconcile this essentialism with their belief in the social construction of sexualities. Inversely, biological determinists, who argued for genetic differences between homosexuals and heterosexuals, nonetheless expressed the fear that an undifferentiated and powerful sex instinct might, if heterosexual channels were closed, surface in homosexuality (see Simmons 1989, 167).

The centrality of these debates to the medical enterprise was underlined in 1936 by Dr. Ben Karpman, who announced suggestively, if cryptically, that "the problem of psychiatry will not be solved until we solve the problem of homosexuality" (qtd. in Henry 1937, 906). A watertight, coherent theory of homosexuality obviously seemed essential to the medical profession's unity, prestige, and consolidation of power, but that theory refused to materialize. Meanwhile, best-sellers about lesbianism were published, evidence of widespread homosexual behavior accumulated, homosexual subcultures continued to grow. If recognizing a wide variety of homosexual types and behaviors spurred medical professionals into a frantic endeavor to catalogue these types in ever-increasing detail, and thus gain control over them, it also forced the doctors to confront the possibility that this variety was inexhaustible and might continually escape their efforts to label and subordinate it. Karpman remarked pointedly that "[t]o group all these people together merely on the basis of homosexuality is, for the present at least, fictitious. We need a finer differentiation and sub-grouping": thus tacitly confessing not only the inadequacy of the medical profession's existing vocabulary for explaining sexuality, but the fictional status of all such classification (qtd. in Henry 1937, 906).

One final point about the medical literature of the 1930s deserves consideration, and that is what it can tell us about the relation of homosexuals themselves to medical discourse. My desire here is not to recap information provided by homosexuals and available in autobiographies, oral histories, and works of fiction, but to look briefly at the doctors' testimony about their patients, which hints at patient-doctor complicity in some cases, and at struggle in others. Wolbarst implied that the very diversity of opinions among professionals alienated homosexuals (and, we might speculate, made them suspicious of these supposed authorities): "[T]he alienist associates [homosexuality] with some form of mental disturbance; the endocrinologist with an imbalance of the internal secretions, while the invert himself stands bewildered and unable to agree with any of them" (1931, 63). Other medical texts indicate that homosexual patients were not only bewildered but stubborn, often defending the "normality" of their own behavior and vigorously resisting negative medical theories, regardless of the attitude of their personal physician.

For instance, nearly every writer who mentioned patients' feelings stated, in tones varying from detached observation to pronounced irritation, that many homosexual patients did not consider their condition abnormal and/or did not wish to be cured. Over and over this theme is repeated: "We must not confound those who justify their position and do not desire to change, with ethical acquired homosexuals, who desire and are amenable to treatment for their condition" (Meagher 1929, 518); "[i]t is to be expected, of course, that those who find enjoyment and satisfaction in their perversion and have adjusted themselves to their abnormal sexual status, will remain indifferent to the prospects of changing it" (Wolbarst 1931, 65); "[n]ot all who practice sexual perversions want to be treated" (London 1933, 97). George Henry said that the individuals who joined a study of his did so "because of their interest in a scientific investigation of a human relationship which they believe is unjustly frowned upon by society" (1937, 889–890). Louis S. London noted that Havelock Ellis and Albert Moll had tried to prove that homosexuals considered themselves normal, implying that the situation had not changed by the time he was writing (1933, 93).

In some instances, a doctor writing up a case history apparently could not avoid reporting a patient's contentment with her homosexuality, despite his own obvious desire to gloss over it. In one case study, Henry attributed what he called elsewhere a woman's "homosexual compromise" to her unhappy marital life and unsatisfied sex drive. The patient herself said that if her marriages had been happy she would not have become involved with a woman, but described her current homosexual relationship as "a very great love" and stated that she had no regrets (Henry 1937, 896–898, 900–901). We must remember that this case, like the others cited here, represented only people whose desire for medical or psychiatric treatment of some condition brought them to the attention of the doctors in the first place.

Another indication that homosexuals resisted negative stereotypes is found in the book, *The Single Woman* (1934), in which Lura Beam recorded twenty-eight case histories of homosexual women seen, for other conditions, by gynecologist Robert L. Dickinson. The type of questions Beam and Dickinson asked the patients presumably reflected contemporary ideas about homosexuality, and the patients' answers definitely refuted many prevailing stereotypes. Beam and Dickinson stated that they did not find organic differences, exceptional athletic activity (particularly masculine occupations), or unusual manners or attire in their patients. The patients reported that their homosexual activities took place within their age group, in contrast to the popular view that lesbians were particularly inclined to seduce young girls. And when, in twenty-one cases, "the patient was asked whether she or the other person took the male part . . . she always answered that it was not she and the typical reply was that they did not think of it in that way" (Dickinson & Beam 1934, 211–212).

Undoubtedly the medicalization of female-female relationships *did* stigmatize and oppress some women, as some scholars have claimed (Faderman 1978); certainly the "Boston marriages" of the nineteenth century came under critical scrutiny, as did the phenomenon of working-class "passing women." At the same time we must admit, as Newton points out, that the discourse of medicalization gave other women a language to define and celebrate lesbian eroticism and to form identities and communities on the basis of their shared sexuality. And finally, we should consider the possibility that large numbers of homosexual women (and men) may have managed to live their lives more or less untroubled by medical theories, dictates, and practices. The fact that even anti-homosexual doctors, treating only people sufficiently unhappy to seek medical help, reported such great resistance to negative stereotyping strongly suggests that many homosexuals managed to avoid internalizing images of themselves as sick, pathological, or disturbed, even when those images were promoted and reinforced by medical authorities. Judging from the articles described above, the discourses of medicalization in this century have been, variously, oppressive, useful, or even liberating for some homosexuals; they have never been monovalent, and the evidence is that they have not been determinative in forming homosexual identity.

In conclusion, we find that in the medical and psychiatric literature of the late 1920s and 1930s a number of gaps were opening up and inviting reinterpretation; some conceptual loose ends were beginning to unravel; a structure of theoretical beliefs and therapeutic practices was simultaneously expanding and weakening under the strain of conflicts within the medical community. The changes taking place set the stage for developments in scientific and popular thinking about homosexuality during the following decades.

A quantitative definition of normality, as Katz (1983, 143) has pointed out, would culminate in, and begin to disintegrate with, Kinsey's startling revelations about the extent of "perverse" behaviors among "average" white Americans. While Freudian theory could motivate highly normative and repressive approaches to nonconformity, in a broader sense it is also clear that the dissemination of potentially radicalizing elements of Freud's work contributed to the upheaval in contemporary thinking about sexuality and gender. Positing the universality of homosexual libidinal attachments and stressing their culturally variant deployments made it possible to ask why—in contemporary, bourgeois, Western culture—it was usually homosexual rather than heterosexual object-choice that was repressed. This, is turn, helped provide the ideological basis for a cultural critique and a political analysis of institutionalized heterosexuality, such as those undertaken by the gay liberation movement in the early 1970s.

The general acceptance of Freud's theory of the bisexuality of infantile psychological organization was also a crucial step away from the biologically attributed gender dichotomies of the nineteenth century. By moving debate about femininity and masculinity into a field of inquiry that invited diverse interpretations, psychoanalysis problematized these concepts in rather the same way that medical science had already done in wresting them from the domain of religion (D'Emilio 1983, 18–19). It could be argued, in fact, that the transfer of authority over the discourse on gender and sexual behavior onto ever more uncertain and relativistic territory has frequently had emancipatory effects. (Inversely, the sometimes dire consequences for homosexuals of the reversion from psychoanalysis to somaticism in the 1930s may suggest that homosexuals today ought to be wary of any theory of sexuality purporting to be empirically verifiable and grounded in biological "facts.")

A great deal more research will be necessary to illuminate the relationship during this period between medical literature on homosexuality, mainstream ideologies, popular and literary discourses, and the self-images and lifestyles of homosexuals. It is indisputable that some medical theories about homosexuality contributed to the oppression of homosexuals by their families and communities, and to their own self-condemnation and loss of self-respect. But both the diversity of and conflicts in opinion among doctors, and the recasting of the basic terms of the discourse on sexuality after the nineteenth century, helped to create spaces for resistance to the prescriptions of medical theory. I have tried here to trace the outlines of those conflicts, and to suggest some of the strategies of resistance devised by the people who were subjected to this massive and fiercely debated inquiry.

Notes

1 I will use the term "homosexual" as a convenient shorthand for "people with homoerotic feelings, or engaging in homosexual behavior, or identifying themselves as homosexual," while acknowledging, of course, that the use of such a term involves me in the highly problematic reification of sexualities that is described in this essay.

2 While I focus here on the medical writing on lesbianism, I must add the caveat that although many medical writers dealt exclusively or mostly with male homosexuality, they did not always specify that they were doing so. They used the masculine forms generically, which makes it difficult to distinguish which articles or sections in an article might concern women. I have tried, however, to include general comments on homosexuality only when I judged they were at least potentially applicable to women.

3 I should note that while examining the attitudes of doctors in the U.S. toward homosexuality, I have drawn on some European material that was circulated in the U.S. and presumably influenced American doctors.

4 The novels include, in addition to *The Well of Loneliness,* Rosamund Lehmann's *Dusty Answer* (1927), Dorothy Sayers's *Unnatural Death* (1927), Elizabeth Bowen's *The Hotel* (1928), Compton Mackenzie's *Extraordinary Women* (1928), Wanda Fraiken Neff's *We Sing Diana* (1928), and Virginia Woolf's *Orlando* (1928).

5 On Freud and homosexuality, see especially Abelove (1993) and Davidson (1987).

6 Oddly enough, writers of this period did not generally deny women's capacity to achieve complete physical satisfaction in homosexual relations, which we might expect to be a logical correlate of the denigration of affective relationships between women and the increasing emphasis in the 1930s on the role of mutually satisfying sexual relations in cementing the marital bond. The influence of Freudian theory may explain what seems like a curious omission from the range of arguments used against lesbianism. If doctors believed, with Freud, that a shift from clitoral to vaginal sensitivity accompanies a girl's successful transition to adulthood, then they could acknowledge "clitoral orgasms" and still dismiss them as immature. It would only have been with Kinsey's demonstration that "clitoral orgasms" did not differ physiologically from "vaginal orgasms," and that, furthermore, lesbians reached orgasm more often than heterosexual women, that female homoerotic pleasure might have begun to seem a serious threat to phallic primacy, in the bedroom and elsewhere (Henry 1937, 901; Wolfe 1935, 158–160).

7 Given the Y.M.C.A.'s notoriety as a meeting place for homosexual men, it is interesting to ask whether Hamilton was, intentionally or not, providing a cue for homosexual men in the same way that pulp fiction of the 1950s and '60s alerted lesbians to the existence of a lesbian subculture in certain urban areas. (See, for example, D'Emilio and Freedman 1988, 290; D'Emilio 1983, 12, 25–27, 135; The Village People, ca. 1978.) It is possible that some homosexuals read medical literature in the hope of finding information about subcultural codes and communities; it is even possible that some (homosexual?) doctors deliberately included suggestions like Hamilton's in their writing for that reason. This, however, is sheer speculation.

8 Benjamin later dedicated himself professionally to transsexualism, and eventually founded the Harry Benjamin International Gender Dysphoria Association (see Rosario 1995).

References

Abelove, Henry. 1993. Freud, male homosexuality, and the Americans. In *The Lesbian and Gay Studies Reader*, ed. Henry Abelove, Michèle Aina Barale, and David M. Halperin, 381–393. New York: Routledge.

Allen, Frederick H. 1940. Homosexuality in relation to the problem of human difference. *American Journal of Orthopsychiatry* 10:129–135.

Appel, Kenneth E., and James A. Flaherty. 1937. Endocrine studies in cases of homosexuality. *Archives of Neurology and Psychiatry* 37:1206–1207.

Baur, Julius. 1940. Homosexuality as an endocrinological, psychological, and genetic problem. *Journal of Criminal Psychopathology* 2:188–197.

Benjamin, Harry. 1931a. For the sake of morality. *Medical Journal and Record* 133:380–382.

———. 1931b. An echo of and an addendum to "For the sake of morality." *Medical Journal and Record* 134:118–120.

Brill, A. A. 1933. Homoerotism and paranoia. *American Journal of Psychiatry* 13:957–974.

———. 1940. Sexual manifestations in neurotic and psychotic symptoms. *Psychiatric Quarterly* 14:9–16.

Chauncey, George, Jr. 1989. From sexual inversion to homosexuality: Medicine and the changing conceptualization of female deviance. In *Passion and Power*, ed. Kathy Peiss and Christina Simmons, 87–117. Philadelphia: Temple University Press.

Davidson, Arnold. 1987. How to do the history of psychoanalysis: A reading of Freud's *Three Essays on the Theory of Sexuality*. *Critical Inquiry* 13:252–277.

Davis, Katharine Bement. 1929. *Factors in the Sex Life of Twenty-Two Hundred Women*. New York: Harper & Bros.

D'Emilio, John. 1983. *Sexual Politics, Sexual Communities: The Making of a Homosexual Minority in the United States, 1940–1970*. Chicago: University of Chicago Press.

D'Emilio, John, and Estelle B. Freedman. 1988. *Intimate Matters: A History of Sexuality in America*. New York: Harper & Row.

Dickinson, Robert Latou, and Lura Beam. 1934. *The Single Woman: A Medical Study in Sex Education*. London: Williams & Norgate.

Ernst, John R. 1928. Dementia praecox complexes. *Medical Journal and Record* 128:381–386.

Faderman, Lillian. 1978. The morbidification of love between women by nineteenth-century sexologists. *Journal of Homosexuality* 4:73–90.

Ford, Charles A. 1929. Homosexual practices of institutionalized females. *Journal of Abnormal and Social Psychology* 23:442–448.

Freud, Sigmund. [1905] 1953. *Three Essays on the Theory of Sexuality*. *Standard Edition*, 7:125–245. London: Hogarth Press.

———. [1920] 1955. The psychogenesis of a case of homosexuality in a woman. *Standard Edition* 18:146–172. London: Hogarth Press.

Grob, Gerald. 1983. *Mental Illness and American Society, 1875–1940*. Princeton: Princeton University Press.

Hall, Radclyffe. [1928] 1981. *The Well of Loneliness*. New York: Avon.

Hamilton, Donald M. 1939. Some aspects of homosexuality in relation to total personality development. *Psychiatric Quarterly* 13:229–244.

Henry, George W. 1934. Psychogenic and constitutional factors in homosexuality; their relation to personality disorders. *Psychiatric Quarterly* 8:243–264.

———. 1937. Psychogenic factors in overt homosexuality. *American Journal of Psychiatry* 93:889–908.

Henry, George W., and Hugh M. Galbraith. 1934. Constitutional factors in homosexuality. *American Journal of Psychiatry* 90:1249–1270.

Jones, Ernest. 1927. The early development of female sexuality. *International Journal of Psycho-Analysis* 8:459–472.

Katz, Jonathan. 1983. *Gay/Lesbian Almanac: A New Documentary*. New York: Harper & Row.

Kopp, Marie E. 1938. Surgical treatment as sex crime prevention measure. *Journal of Criminal Law and Criminology* 28:692–706.

LaBarre, Weston. 1939. The psychopathology of drinking songs: a study of the content of the "normal" unconscious. *Psychiatry* 2: 203–212.

Literature and sexual inversion. 1933. *Urologic and Cutaneous Review* 37:820–821.

London, Louis S. 1933. Analysis of a homosexual neurosis. *Urologic and Cutaneous Review* 37:93–97.

Lorand, Sandor. 1939. Perverse tendencies and fantasies: their influence on personality. *Psychoanalytic Review* 26:178–190.

Meagher, John F. W. 1929. Homosexuality: Its psychobiological and psychopathological significance. *Urologic and Cutaneous Review* 33:505–518.

Newton, Esther. 1984. The mythic mannish lesbian: Radclyffe Hall and the New Woman. *Signs: The Lesbian Issue* 9:557–575.

Oberndorf, Clarence P. 1929. Diverse forms of homosexuality. *Urologic and Cutaneous Review* 33:518–523.

Owensby, N. M. 1940. Homosexuality and lesbianism treated with Metrazol. *Journal of Nervous and Mental Disease* 92:65–66.

Richardson, Diane. 1983. The dilemma of essentiality in homosexual theory. *Journal of Homosexuality* 9:79–90.

Robie, Theodore R. 1927–1928. The investigation of the Oedipus and homosexual complexes in schizophrenia. *Psychiatric Quarterly* 1–2:231–241.

Rosanoff, Aaron J. 1929. Human sexuality, normal and abnormal, from a psychiatric standpoint. *Urologic and Cutaneous Review* 33:523–530.

———. 1935. A theory of chaotic sexuality. *American Journal of Psychiatry* 92:35–41.

Rosario, Vernon A. 1995. Trans [homo] sexuality? Double inversion, psychiatric confusion and hetero-hegemony. In *Queer Studies: A Lesbian, Gay, Bisexual, and Transgender Anthology*, ed. Brett Beemyn and Mickey Eliason, ch. 2. New York: New York University Press.

Schilder, Paul. 1929. On homosexuality. *Psychoanalytic Review* 16:377–389.

Sherman, Irene Case, and Mandel Sherman. 1926. The factor of parental attachment in homosexuality. *Psychoanalytic Review* 13:32–37.

Simmons, Christina. 1979. Companionate marriage and the lesbian threat. *Frontiers* 4:54–59.

———. 1989. Modern sexuality and the myth of Victorian repression. In *Passion and Power*, ed. Kathy Peiss and Christina Simmons, 157–177. Philadelphia: Temple University Press.

Sprague, George S. 1934. Varieties of homosexual manifestations. *American Journal of Psychiatry* 92:143–154.

Stekel, Wilhelm. 1930. Is homosexuality curable? Trans. Bertrand S. Frohman. *Psychoanalytic Review* 17:443–451.

Weeks, Jeffrey. 1986. *Sexuality*. Chichester: Ellis Horwood Ltd.

Wolbarst, Abraham L. 1931. Sexual perversions: their medical and social implications. *Medical Journal and Record* 134:5–9, 62–65.

Wolfe, W. Béran. [1935] 1946. *A Woman's Best Years*. Garden City, New York: Garden City Publishing.

Wright, Clifford A. 1938. Further studies of endocrine aspects of homosexuality. *Medical Record* 147:449–452.

———. 1939. The sex offender's endocrines. *Medical Record* 149:399–402.

Who Counts When You're Counting Homosexuals?
Hormones and Homosexuality in Mid-Twentieth-Century America

Stephanie H. Kenen

In July 1993, the journal *Science* published an article about a scientific study linking homosexuality with a specific site on the X chromosome (Hamer et al. 1993; Angier 1993). As Garland Allen discusses elsewhere in this volume, the "gay gene," as it was dubbed, or the "gay brain," which preceded it by a few years (LeVay 1991), were not the first hypotheses of a biological cause of homosexuality, nor, I suspect, will they be the last. Both studies, however, have shared the limelight: they have been praised and condemned for their scientific merits, and they have been hailed and vilified for their political implications. One locus of criticism has been the delineation of the subject population (see, for example, Gorman 1994; Byne 1994): LeVay (1991) examined brain tissue of thirty-five males who had died of AIDS (nineteen of whom were retrospectively classified as homosexual); Hamer's group (1993) studied forty families with pairs of self-identified gay brothers. The question underlying the critiques pertains to the definition of homosexuality itself: Who counts when you're counting homosexuals? (See also Hamer and Copeland 1994, 52–73.)

In studies like these, a type of circular reasoning often follows the delineation of the subject population: scientific research on homosexuality does not begin with random populations, but rather with groups of people who are defined as homosexual to begin with (by themselves, by scientists, or both); then, researchers search for a biological (or social) marker common to the group (whether it be a gene, a portion of the brain, or an overbearing mother); finally, if such a marker is found, homosexuality is redefined by the presence of the marker itself. In a curious way, then, each study can be said to reinvent its own object.

Much of this criticism echoes older controversies, not specifically about genetics or neurobiology but about the relative merits of searching for the biological basis of sexual identity and behavior, and about some of the methodological limitations of such attempts. In this essay I examine an analogous debate from the decade before World War II, analyzing some of the assumptions common to many scientific studies of homosexuality in the American context. I describe a series of articles by Clifford A. Wright from the late 1930s about the relationship between sex hormones and homosexuality, and contrast them with Alfred Kinsey's first publication on the issue, in which he forcefully rebutted the endocrinological work. By focusing on the assumptions these authors made about the cause, characteristics, and "cure" of homosexuality and, perhaps most importantly, about who counted as a homosexual subject of investigation, I illustrate the ways in which researchers have constructed legitimated knowledge and categories about certain groups of people.

It is not my intention in this paper to support or deny biological components of complex human traits, nor to stake out a particular political position. Rather, by contrasting recent scientific and political debates about sexual orientation with historical ones, I try to show that there are no *necessary* political valences to "nature" versus "nurture." Furthermore, my aim is to highlight the fundamental roles that cultural assumptions, social contexts, and historical precedents *necessarily* play in scientific studies of human behavior, and to argue that no investigation of sexuality *can* be politically neutral, at least as long as human sexual behavior is socially significant and politically contested.

Hormonal Inversion and the "True" Homosexual

The modern scientific study of sex has its roots in social reform movements. Many late-nineteenth- and early-twentieth-century American reformers focused their attention on sexual issues, especially urban prostitution, believing them to be destructive to the moral fabric of society (Bullough 1994, 97–98). In the 1910s, some reformers (especially those associated with the Rockefeller-sponsored Bureau of Social Hygiene in New York City) became increasingly concerned with the study of sexually related social issues (including prostitution, divorce, venereal disease, illegitimacy, birth control, and homosexuality), hoping that better knowledge would lead to better solutions to unsettling social problems. In the early 1920s, a small number of scientific researchers formed the Committee for Research on Problems of Sex under the auspices of the National Research Council in order to study the biological and psychological basis of human sexual behavior (although most of the committee's early work was concerned with the physiology of lower animals) (Aberle & Corner 1953; Bugos 1989). Many reformers believed that social change depended directly on the biological and social scientific understanding of human behavior, and many social scientists, psychologists, and physicians concurred.

Physicians have long viewed social problems (including sexual ones) as the collective effects of diseased individuals—a position that has had the dual effect of pathologizing classes of people while at the same broadening the social authority of the medical profession (Conrad & Schneider 1980; Foucault 1978; Nye 1984). Since the nineteenth century, homosexuality, for example, has been viewed by many as a biological anomaly or a disease to be cured by doctors, rather than a crime to be punished by the courts. This view was especially prevalent among scientists and physicians in the mid-1930s when, according to historian George Chauncey, an "anti-gay reaction gained force . . . as it became part of a more general reaction to the cultural experimentation of the Prohibition years and to the disruption of the gender arrangements by the Depression" (1994, 331). In the context of new legal attacks on homosexuals, many physicians viewed themselves as especially humane and progressive because, they believed, their actions were based on sound, objective knowledge, rather than on moral traditions and legal anachronisms that no longer corresponded with the complexities of the new urban world (Bullough 1994, 112–118). Thus, like many of his contemporaries, Dr. Clifford A. Wright (1882–1961) felt that homosexuality was either a vice (a moral issue) or a pathology, but not a crime, and that it should be treated as a social and medical problem rather than a legal one (1935, 407; 1939, 400).[1]

Wright was Associate Professor of Clinical Medicine at the College of Medical Evangelists (*Directory* 1940, 102), and senior attending physician at the Los Angeles County General Hospital's Psychoendocrine Clinic, which was established in 1925 by Wright and his associate E. H. Williams. According to the founders, "the Clinic was a free public institution established for the purposes of making scientific, laboratory, and clinical studies of cases of all kinds that show psychotic and endocrine gland symptoms." In the first sixteen years of operation, over 66,000 patient visits were recorded: some patients sought help at the clinic on their own initiative, some were referred by physicians, others by juvenile or criminal courts (Williams & Wright 1941, 302, 307.) Based on his experience at the Clinic, Wright wrote or co-wrote five articles between 1935 and 1941 about the relationship between hormonal balance and homosexuality in which he claimed that "true" homosexuality was a result of a reversal in the proportion of sex hormones and that, with proper treatment, the condition could be reversed (Wright 1935, 1938, 1939, 1941; Glass et al. 1940).

As a hospital clinician, not an academic researcher, Wright made no grandiose claims about the production of scientific knowledge. While many sex researchers were emphasizing the objective and quantitative aspects of their work, Wright merely reported what he found (or perhaps what he was looking for) and what he thought it meant. His ideas about homosexuality were based on certain widely held assumptions concerning the relation between biological sex, psychological gender, and the direction of sexual desire. Furthermore, like most empirical studies of homosexuality before Kinsey, his research predominantly utilized male subjects,[2] the majority of whom had found their way into the criminal justice system, the medical-psychiatric system, or both.

Wright suggested that society rethink its attitudes toward homosexuals, especially because most of them "if left alone[,] will create no disturbance, preferring to live what they consider a normal existence and not take chances of arrest" (1935, 408). Furthermore, Wright suggested that endocrinological treatment could "control" or "rehabilitate" those homosexuals who did cause "disturbances," and thus homosexuality should be viewed as a medical condition, rather than a crime, "particularly when three percent at least of all persons are homosexuals" (1939, 402).[3] The "congenital" homosexual, then, deserved a certain modicum of compassion because his sexual desire was biologically determined: "It is no more logical to expect to cure a homosexual's abnormal sex instinct by eighteen months' stay in jail," Wright argued, "than it would be to change the normal sex instinct of a normal man or woman" (1939, 400).

Wright's theory of the etiology and treatment of homosexuals was quite simple, and remained remarkably consistent through six years of work. According to Wright, all humans are bisexual (that is, they are part male and part female), but in the homosexual the proper proportions are reversed.[4] Although Freud and others were beginning to use the term "bisexual" in the current sense (that is, erotic attraction to both sexes), Wright's use of the word was *not* a statement about the character of sexual behavior or the direction of sexual desire in humans. Rather, it was a reflection of contemporary theories about the biological processes of sex determination and sex differentiation in embryological development.

As Anne Fausto-Sterling points out in this volume, by the late nineteenth century it was well known that the fetal tissue that would develop into either male or female sexual organs remained undifferentiated until about the sixth or seventh week of gestation. "Bisexuality," then, referred to the bipotentiality of development—to the common, sexually neutral (or hermaphroditic) origins of human organisms.[5] Furthermore, several nineteenth-century theorists linked homosexuality to a disturbance in this aspect of somatic development, and even Havelock Ellis, the famed English sexologist of the early twentieth century, suggested that homosexuality might be linked to some abnormality in the process of sexual differentiation, probably having "a fundamental source . . . in the stimulating and inhibiting play of the internal secretions" (1928, 310–311, 316). Freud was highly critical of these theories, but still speculated that future biological research might cast light on the role of internal secretions in somatic and psychodynamic sexuality (1905, 141–144, 144–147 n. 1, 215–216).

At the turn of the twentieth century, biological and medical researchers began to search for and study biochemical agents that were crucial to bodily function. Hormones, as these agents were named in 1905, were thought to control a variety of physiological systems, including digestion, metabolism, and reproduction. Following the successful isolation of hormones from the pancreas and thyroid, some scientists turned to the chemically complex physiology of sexual reproduction. In the late 1920s and 1930s, while studying the development of secondary sex characteristics and the reproductive cycle of females, endocrinologists discovered and subsequently synthesized female and, later, male sex hormones (Borell 1985; Oudshoorn 1990a, 1993, 1994).

According to Nelly Oudshoorn, scientific ideas about sex hormones were embedded in a cultural context of gender:

> The chemical substances believed to originate in the sex glands were designated sex hormones. . . . Sex hormones were conceptualized as the chemical agents of masculinity and femininity, thus emphasizing the ancient folk-wisdom that femininity and masculinity resided in the gonads. (Oudshoorn 1990a, 7)

However, in 1927, Dutch endocrinologist Ernst Laqueur discovered so-called female hormones in the urine of males, and thus, Oudshoorn argues, set off a reconceptualization of the endocrinology of sex, from an idea of mutual exclusivity to one of the relative *ratio* of maleness and femaleness in a single organism (Laqueur & de Jongh 1928; Oudshoorn 1990b; Oudshoorn 1994, 22–39). The "bisexual" debate was thus recast in endocrinological terms: the role of hormones in sex differentiation, in sex differences in personality, and in sexual behavior seemed to hold the key to understanding the relation between the sexes.[6] Wright, therefore, pursued his studies on the hormonal "imbalance" of homosexuality in a broader context of new endocrinological theories and discoveries.

Sex hormones were central to the sexual impulse, according to Wright's theory of "normal" sexuality, and were implicitly complementary:

> The sex urge, one of the strongest influences in life . . . undoubtedly depends largely, if not entirely, on the sex hormones and hormonal attraction. The usual sex attraction between the normal male and the normal female is undoubtedly caused by the predominance of the male hormone in the former and the female hormone in the latter. (Wright 1935, 408; see also Wright 1939, 399)

Since, according to Wright, heterosexuality was the result of a particular endocrinological balance, homosexuality was a result of an abnormal ratio of sex hormones: "In the [homosexual] male . . . there is a predominance of the female element and in the homosexual woman a dominance of the male factor" (1938, 449). It was not necessary for the *absolute* amount of androgens in the male or estrogens in the female to be less than normal, just for the *proportion* or balance to be reversed.[7] Furthermore, because of his inverted hormonal balance, "the sex attraction of the true congenital [male] homosexual . . . is as logical in regard to his hormone balance or physiology as is the normal sex attraction" (Wright 1938, 449). "From records now available," Wright explained, "it appears that true homosexuality is congenital in most cases and probably originates in fetal life at the time of sex determination and sex differentiation, and is markedly influenced by the endocrine glands, and, as would be expected, most of these individuals regard homosexual interest as the natural one" (1939, 400).

Finally, like many of his contemporaries, Wright believed in the "probable" relationship between hormones, homosexuality, and hermaphroditism. This view was rooted in the theory of the bisexuality of development, which resurrected and reformulated older explanations of homosexuality such as "inversion" or "psychic hermaphroditism" (Young 1937; Witschi & Mengert 1942). While his patients, Wright wrote, "exhibit[ed] rather definite feminine characteristics, . . . [they] . . . fail[ed] to show the marked body changes seen in hermaphroditism and virilism," which indicated that "homosexuality seem[ed] to be an irregularity of function rather than morphological make up" (1938, 452). He explained the absence of these morphological markers of intersexuality in homosexuals as an effect of developmental timing: "the interference with [sexual] differentiation occurs late enough [in that process] not to produce anatomical changes" (Wright 1941, 60).

The "naturalness" of congenital homosexuality, however, was not considered a reason to ignore it: Wright proposed a treatment for homosexuals using a combination of a gonadotropic factor (a substance that stimulates sex glands) and a male or female hormone corresponding to the anatomical sex of the patient.[8] The idea behind Wright's treatment was to stimulate the production of testosterone in the body of a male homosexual or estrogens in the body of a female, thus bringing the body's hormonal balance back into line.

While Wright never explicitly defined homosexuality in his writings, a working definition can be found in his classification of clinical subjects: first, he distinguished "true" (or "congenital") homosexuality from the "acquired" or "latent" type; second, he focused on the "feminine" attributes of his homosexual subjects. In this scheme, the "true," "innate," or "congenital" homosexual had *always* and *only* been attracted to members of the same sex, and the "acquired" or "latent" type developed or exhibited his or her sexual tastes later in life. Furthermore, homosexual desire was usually characterized as "inverted," that is, a feminine characteristic of a male body. These distinctions did not originate with Wright; rather, they emerged from the late nineteenth-century German medical writings of Magnus Hirschfeld, Carl Westphal, Albert Moll, and Richard von Krafft-Ebing, among others.[9]

In the early part of the twentieth century, both Havelock Ellis and Sigmund Freud discussed, and dismissed, the distinction between "true" and "acquired" homosexuality. Ellis, for example, preferred a tripartite division of homosexual, bisexual (in its modern usage), and heterosexual, while stipulating that it was "a useful superficial division . . . [not] a scientific classification" (1928, 88). However, he believed in the congenital nature of all homosexuality (even those cases that appeared on the surface to be of the "acquired" type), positing a congenital predisposition for inversion, which would manifest itself earlier or later in life, if at all (Ellis 1928, 308–311, 322–324; Robinson 1976, 4–11).

In his *Three Essays on the Theory of Sexuality*, Freud discussed three types of homosexuals: the "absolute" type (corresponding with Wright's "true" homosexual); the "amphigenic" (who would today qualify as a "bisexual" or, in Freud's terms, a "psychosexual hermaphrodite"); and the "contingent," for whom external circumstances constrain heterosexual contact and allow the possibility of pleasure in and consummation of homosexual acts, a pleasure that, for some, could become psychologically fixed (1905, 135–137, 140). However, he expressed "suspicion" that the distinction "between 'innate' and 'acquired' [was] not an exclusive one [and] that it [did] not cover all the issues involved in inversion" (1905, 140). Furthermore, Freud vehemently opposed placing homosexuals in a category apart from the rest of humanity because, as Henry Abelove has pointed out, "to do so would be to reject, in fact to repress, the psychoanalytic theory of sex," which provided equal explanatory power for the sex lives of men, women, heterosexuals, homosexuals, fetishists, and neurotics

(1993, 390). Instead, Freud interpreted homosexuality in terms of his broader theories of the deviations of sexual aim and sexual object (1905, 136–160).

Despite the theoretical rejection of the distinction between "true" and "acquired" homosexuality by such eminent students of sexuality as Freud and Ellis, it continued to play a crucial role in the scientific study of homosexuality in the United States, and was especially apparent in Wright's work on the endocrinology of homosexual males. However, while Wright frequently used these terms, he never explicitly defined them nor indicated their origins; instead, he assumed his readers' familiarity with the technical nomenclature (1935, 407; 1939, 399–400).

When referring to his "true" homosexual male patients, Wright routinely described "effeminate" homosexual males. But emphasizing the feminine nature of male homosexuals was certainly nothing new: twentieth-century medical writers often evoked and reinscribed nineteenth-century ideas about sexual "inversion," wherein a homosexual's psychology and behavior (what we now might call gender) was thought to be inverted or reversed from his or her anatomical and genital sex.[10] A binary vision of sex, gender, and sexuality underlay medical, psychological, and psychoanalytical literature, in which two individuals (one male and one female) were supposed to couple in heterosexual reproductive union. The implicit reasoning behind this view went as follows: if two men were having sexual contact, one of them had to be "feminine" in some respect. The scientific definition of the homosexual thus rested largely on the premise of a cross-sex (that is, "feminine") personality and the behavior that was thought to go along with it. A "feminine" male—in dress,[11] mannerisms, or position in sexual acts (that is, "passive")—was, in effect, the primary criterion for a diagnosis of "true" homosexuality. Wright's ideas about the character of homosexuality were not novel, but his ideas about its etiology were. He provided a new twist on an old theme—effeminate male homosexuals in this picture became *hormonal* inverts.

Again, for Wright, the ostensible "femininity" of a male patient was the defining characteristic of inversion, a trait that implicitly included sexual desire for men: a male subject who exhibited feminine traits or mannerisms *and* exhibited the identifying hormonal imbalance would be diagnosed as a "true" homosexual, *whether or not the subject had ever engaged in sexual activity with another man.* Case 2 from Wright's 1935 article is an excellent example: here was a twenty-four-year-old male with "no actual abnormal or normal sex experiences, but [who] had in several instances almost uncontrollable desire toward his own sex. He . . . frequently took girls' parts in school plays and always enjoyed dressing up in girls' clothes." After being treated with a gonadotropic substance combined with a male hormone, the subject showed "clinically marked improvement" and reported that he "felt no fear of any consequences of [male] associations." On the basis of his hormone levels and a certain definition of "femininity" (which included cross-dressing and sexual desire for men), but *despite the absence of any overt homosexual (or heterosexual) experiences,* Wright conceptually viewed this subject as identical to other males who claimed to have been homosexual all their lives (1935, 408).

Wright increasingly came to define "true" homosexuality by the hormonal fingerprint itself. In 1938, for example, he divided his subjects into three classes: "positive cases," whose "history, examination, and behavior" were indicative of "true" homosexuality, and who exhibited the telltale hormonal reversal; "negative cases," who did not show a hormonal imbalance (but who were examined at the direction of the court system); and miscellaneous cases, who were examined for other reasons (such as male impotence or breast enlargement) and were subsequently diagnosed as "true" or "congenital" homosexuals because "hormone assays significant of homosexuality ha[d] been found" (1938, 449). His impotent patients, for example, all "showed homosexual [hormonal] formulae," and he believed that their impotence with women was a result of their hormonally defined homosexual status (1938, 451).

At times, Wright argued that hormonal assays should be used to diagnose "true" homosexuality as distinct from the "latent" or "acquired" type. In some cases, he went so far as to argue that an individual's guilt or innocence, if criminally accused of homosexual acts, could and should be determined by hormone levels (Wright 1939, 400; Glass et al. 1940, 593). At the same time, his classificatory system became complicated by social and criminal categories, and he began to distinguish the white, middle-class, law-abiding homosexual from the so-called criminal type, who was poor, uneducated, and usually an immigrant. The homosexual "good citizen" rarely committed crimes (other than adult, consensual, homosexual acts) unless his situation was complicated by alcoholism, psychosis, or feeblemindedness. The criminal type came in two varieties: "obtrusive" homosexuals, who made advances to other men (and got caught), and those who "contribute[d] to the delinquency of minor boys." Nevertheless, Wright believed that many homosexuals who displayed the hormonal marker could be "rehabilitated" with the appropriate endocrinological treatment (1939, 400–402).[12]

Although Wright proclaimed his treatment program a success, "improvement" usually meant a more "normal" hormonal assay and the subjective accounts of any combination of the following libidinal changes: development of sexual attraction for the opposite sex, reduction in sexual desire for the same sex, abatement of anxiety about sexual matters (1935, 408–409; 1938, 451). Wright's final publication on homosexuality reported the results of his year-long treatment of fourteen congenital homosexual men who were "well controlled under custodial care," all but one of whom reported "improvement." Even Wright admitted the "questionable value" of his patients' "subjective evidence," especially when it came from an institutionalized group that was informed that "all supervision from the legal authorities was finished" after the last specimens had been collected (1941, 60). Ironically, several of these patients reported that their "improvement [was] not due to treatment" (1941, 61). Wright, however, remained conspicuously silent about these last remarks.

Finally, I would like to point out a conceptual problem with Wright's work that was common to many studies of homosexuals in this period. Wright stressed the "wifely" role that a number of his subjects played in their relationships, dressing in women's clothes and "keeping house" for another man (1935, 408–409). But what about the implicitly masculine partners of these effeminate men? How could their hormonal balance possibly account for the direction of their desire? The only possible answer, which Wright never explicitly investigated, is that the "active," "masculine" "husbands" of the effeminate, cross-dressing "wives" were not "true" homosexuals, but rather belonged to the "latent" or "acquired" type. Wright's hormone reversal could provide a plausible explanation only for the "passive" invert, not for his "active" partner.[13] The absence of any discussion of this issue in Wright's work is an interpretative problem for the historian. It is possible, but unlikely, that Wright reserved his compassion only for the "congenital" homosexual and left the acquired type to his fate at the hands of the criminal courts, or that he believed "acquired" homosexuality was not a social or medical problem. Unfortunately, he did not leave us his opinions on the matter.

Wright's silence on the theoretical explanation and social significance of the "acquired" type, however, leads to a crucial question in the analysis of scientific studies of homosexuality: Who counts when you're counting homosexuals? For Wright, only "inverted" men, who had (or might) play the "passive" or "feminine" role in the sexual act with another man, *and* who exhibited telltale hormone levels, counted as homosexual. The issues underlying this question are generalizable to any study of human behavior, whether historical (as in the case of Clifford Wright's work) or contemporary (as in the case of the "gay gene" or the "gay brain"): What sample was used, according to what criteria, and how were the criteria justified? It was precisely these questions that Alfred Kinsey addressed in his article, "Criteria for a Hormonal Explanation of the Homosexual" (1941).

Kinsey's article was a scathing critique of Wright's work, challenging his assumptions and his methodology. Seven years before the appearance of his landmark *Sexual Behavior in the Human Male* (1948), Kinsey redefined sexuality solely on the basis of behavior, and posited a continuum of such behavior from exclusively heterosexual to exclusively homosexual, with most people falling somewhere in between. Committed to the belief that all sexual behavior was "natural," and therefore "normal," Kinsey effectively and intentionally blurred the traditional boundaries between the categories of sexual practice.

Orgasm versus Identity: Kinsey's Redefinition of Homosexuality

Alfred C. Kinsey (1894–1956) is famous for his two books on human sexual behavior—the first exhaustive studies of the sex lives of Americans (1948, 1953). The books included data gathered from face-to-face interviews with over 18,000 white American men and women about the nature and frequency of their sexual activities. Almost fifty years later, Kinsey's works are still cited as authoritative texts, and remain the standard by which more recent sex surveys judge themselves (Laumann et al. 1994, 35). Kinsey himself was trained as a biological taxonomist at Harvard University, and received his doctorate in 1920. He spent his entire professional career at Indiana University in Bloomington, the first twenty years of which were devoted to teaching biology and continuing his exhaustive research on the gall wasp. Kinsey's early reputation as a scientist was based on his taxonomical rigor: he collected over 300,000 specimens of this particular creature in order to analyze, evaluate, and improve the taxonomic system on which their classification was based. This experience of collecting and classifying, several historians have argued, profoundly influenced his later work on human sexuality (Pomeroy 1982, 37–51; Gould 1985; Robinson, 1976, 51–54; Morantz 1977; Christenson 1971, 95, 109).

Kinsey's intellectual shift from "wasps to WASPs" (Gould 1985) ostensibly began when he was invited to coordinate an interdisciplinary course on marriage (which was, in effect, a sex education course) at Indiana University in 1938. According to his biographer and colleague, Wardell Pomeroy, when Kinsey began to put together materials on human sexuality for the class, "he discovered almost at once that there was little adequate research material in the field, and it was quickly obvious that he would have to do his own" (Pomeroy 1982, 52). He began collecting data on the sexual behavior of Americans by interviewing students in his classes, and quickly expanded his database to the broader campus community and to the Bloomington community at large, then to the entire state, and eventually to the entire country. Within two years, Kinsey resigned from the marriage course that had stimulated his interest in this field, and devoted himself full-time to the study of human sexuality (Christenson 1971, 95–124; Pomeroy 1982, 52–79).

Kinsey's first publication on the subject was a direct attack on the work that Wright and his colleagues were publishing on the relation between hormones and homosexuality (Christenson 1971, 118–119; Robinson 1976, 71–72). For Kinsey, it was especially important to analyze the methods and assumptions of Wright's work, because

> [his results] are in line with wide-spread and long-standing popular opinion that homosexual behavior depended on some inherent abnormality which, since the time of the discovery of the sex hormones, is often supposed to be glandular in origin. This assumption is offered as specific explanation in some of the psychology and sociology texts, and some of the psychiatrists are treating homosexuality as an organic disease which is to be cured . . . by endocrinologic adjustments. Since [Wright's] . . . studies are . . . the first to test the validity of the current opinion, they are likely to attract some attention; and it is, therefore, desirable to examine the bases of the conclusions. (Kinsey 1941, 424)

Kinsey's early interviews convinced him of the futility of this hormonal approach for a number of reasons, and his critique of Wright's methods was quite succinct: Wright's sample sizes were too small; there were more significant variations between the hormone levels of individuals *within* the same group than there were between the averages of the two distinct groups; and the variations in separate samples of a single individual often exceeded the average difference between the homosexuals and the heterosexuals. Finally, the methods for collecting data were not standardized between, or even within, sample populations. In conclusion, Kinsey wrote, "little significance can be attached to the results" (1941, 424–425).

After challenging the validity of Wright's findings on purely methodological grounds, he moved on to more conceptual issues. By undermining the category of "homosexual" as an identity, he tried to demonstrate the futility of searching for the causes of homosexuality. Kinsey argued that all previous studies of homosexuality posited homosexuals as fundamentally different from "normals" (that is, heterosexuals). This, for Kinsey, was a false assumption:

> More basic than any error brought out in the analysis of [Wright's] data is the assumption that homosexuality and heterosexuality are two mutually exclusive phenomena emanating from fundamentally and, at least in some cases, inherently different types of individuals. (Kinsey 1941, 425)

Basically, Kinsey claimed that there was no adequate physiological, psychological, or behavioral basis for distinguishing homosexuals from "normals." He further found no discrete distinctions between the so-called true (or "passive") homosexual and the so-called acquired (or "active") type (1941, 427). According to his preliminary study (which was based on a sample of 1,600 male case histories, about half of whom were of college age), one-third to one-half of all American men had *at least one orgasmic homosexual contact* in the course of their lifetime (1941, 425). By this standard, it would be very hard indeed to identify exactly what constituted a "homosexual," and how he would differ from a heterosexual. Kinsey tried to discredit the use of the word "homosexual" as a noun, and to restrict its use to that of an adjective. In other words, behavior could be homosexual, but people could not (Robinson 1976, 67).

Kinsey's point was masterfully argued. First, he precisely defined homosexual experience as same-sex contact resulting in orgasm. This did not include homoerotic attraction, desire, or even sexual contact that did not culminate in ejaculation. Despite this restricted definition, Kinsey's preliminary studies still showed that 35 percent of American men had participated in at least one homosexual encounter during their adult lives. Second, he wrote about homosexuality as a behavior, not a personality or an identity. It was a behavior that was just as "normal" as anything else; it was not a crime to be punished, a vice to be prevented, or a disease to be cured. For Kinsey, it was *not* a transgressive act. Homosexual contact was simply a "natural" and frequent variant of human behavior, and could not be deemed "rare and therefore abnormal or unnatural" (Kinsey et al. 1948, 659).[14] Third, Kinsey represented the relative proportion of heterosexual to homosexual experiences as a continuum of behavior in which it was impossible to define what a homosexual person was and how he would have differed from a heterosexual one, except in degree of certain behaviors (1941, 425).[15] In the end, Kinsey dismissed Wright by arguing that the homosexual as a distinct species could not really be distinguished from anyone else, and therefore no study could prove the biological basis of an identity that, for Kinsey, did not exist.

Kinsey's later work on male homosexuality extended and elaborated these ideas.[16] He continued to challenge the legitimacy of previous studies of homosexuality in the adult male population for their problematic definitions of the phenomenon, which, he claimed, were based either on the misapplication of animal data to humans or on social stereotypes of "inverts" (1948, 610–617). "Inversion and homosexuality," Kinsey argued, "are two distinct and not always correlated types of behavior" (1948, 615). Furthermore, he claimed earlier estimates of the incidence of homosexuality were plagued by statistical and sampling problems. Ironically, these were the same issues for which Kinsey's own work was most vehemently criticized (Terman 1948; Cochran et al. 1954). He also disparaged the search for the causes of homosexuality—be they biological, psychological, or both—by highlighting again the inadequacy of definitions of the phenomenon (1948, 659–663). Finally, Kinsey challenged the social stigma and legal prosecution of individuals labeled as homosexual (1948, 663–666). Behind all these critiques lay Kinsey's continued insistence that homosexuality was a description of sexual contact between individuals of the same sex, not a distinct physiological or psychological type (1948, 617, 638–639). However, as Robinson has pointed out, Kinsey "followed the awkward practice of referring to manifestations of homosexuality as 'the homosexual,' indicating that, for all his theoretical objections, he found it syntactically impossible" to do otherwise (Robinson 1976, 67 n. 61, also 71).

In an attempt to address the complexities of human sexual behavior, Kinsey developed his famous "heterosexual-homosexual rating scale." The scale ranged from 0 (exclusively heterosexual) to 6 (exclusively homosexual), with various shades of overlap in between. The ratings, however, included erotic response as well as physical contact in its classificatory criteria: a rating of 4, for example, described an individual who had "more overt [homosexual] activity *and/or psychic reactions*" but who concurrently had a "fair amount" of heterosexual activity and responses (Kinsey et al. 1948, 641, emphasis added; Robinson 1976, 73). The scale was designed to eliminate the distinction between heterosexuality and homosexuality as mutually exclusive categories, yet they still remained as binarily opposed terms. In addition, Kinsey hoped to replace the use of the term "bisexual" as a description for individuals who engaged in sexual activity with both males and females, because of its specific meaning in biological contexts (that is, the existence of male and female structures in a single organism), and the confusion that it thus caused when applied to human sexual behavior. He also objected to the use of "bisexual" because, like the word "homosexual," it implied the existence of a distinct personality or identity, and did not reflect the complexity of the hetero-homosexual "continuum" of behavior (Kinsey et al. 1948, 656–659). Ironically, Kinsey's rating scale shared a basic feature with Wright's theory of homosexuality: a bipolar scale of sexual difference that was expressed as a ratio or proportion. In this case, however, the relevant poles were heterosexual and homosexual behavior and desire, rather than degree of (endocrinological) "maleness" and "femaleness."

Kinsey's rating scale was not a resounding success. Robinson has called the famous construction "the most pathetic manifestation of Kinsey's philosophical naïveté," because it differed in no significant way from the homosexual/bisexual/heterosexual distinction it was supposed to replace: the two schemes shared "the same basic assumption . . . that at some point differences of degree became differences of kind" (Robinson, 1976, 73–74). In more recent contexts, the ratings themselves have become reified categories of identity, and references to "Kinsey 4s" and "Kinsey 6s" are not uncommon in popular parlance or scientific literature, including the "gay gene" study (Hamer et al. 1993; see also Irvine 1990, 53–54).

Finally, Kinsey is perhaps most famous for the estimate that 10 percent of the adult population is homosexual. However, depending on the specific definition of homosexual activity (such as a particular rating on the hetero-homosexual scale), the numbers came out very differently. For example, in the adult, white, male population, Kinsey found that 50 percent of men who did not marry before the age of 35 had "overt homosexual experience to the point of orgasm" since puberty; 25 percent had "more than incidental homosexual experiences or reactions (i.e., rates 2–6)" during a three-year period or longer; and 4 percent were "exclusively homosexual" for their entire lives. "Ten percent" referred only to males who were "more or less exclusively homosexual (that is, rate 5 or 6) for at least three years" of their adult lives (Kinsey et al. 1948, 650–651). Kinsey's parallel estimate for unmarried women between the ages of 25 and 35 (who rated 5 or 6 on the hetero-homosexual scale) was 2 to 6 percent, and only 1 percent for married women in the same age range (1953, 473–474). The 10 percent figure, therefore, was a specifically defined estimate of the frequency of certain behaviors and erotic response in adult, American, white males in the 1930s and 1940s. While the estimate has been frequently invoked in popular and political discussions of gay rights in contemporary America (most recently in the debates about homosexuals in the military and about same-sex marriage), the percentage of homosexuals in the general population can be dramatically higher or lower, depending on how one defines the category. Despite Kinsey's zealous commitment to the decriminalization and depathologization of homosexual behavior, he did *not* use his statistical findings as support for a gay rights movement based on the existence of a separate and delineable homosexual identity (Chauncey 1994, 70–71; Irvine 1990, 48).

In sum, Kinsey had his own set of assumptions about homosexual activity, and he was as interested as Wright in defining homosexuality in a certain way (in Kinsey's case, according to behavior rather than biochemistry). His intent to undermine the traditional distinctions between normal and abnormal sexuality in general (and the specific distinction between homosexuality and heterosexuality as discrete personality types), and the simultaneous commitment to reforming antiquated sexual laws and cultural values were themselves basic operating principles that influenced the ways in which Kinsey collected, interpreted, and presented his data. While Christenson has argued that "Kinsey came to the study of human sex behavior as a biologist, not a social reformer" (1971, 95), Morantz has countered that Kinsey's determination to study human sexuality free from the traditions of prudish social and puritanical legal contexts went above and beyond the call of scientific duty: "cloaked in the unbiased empiricism of the dispassionate scientist," Morantz claims, "lay the emotional preferences of a moral crusader" (1977, 566).

While Kinsey forever changed the discursive field in which scientific studies of homosexuality have taken place (and despite his searing attack on Wright and others), he did not greatly impact contemporary biological research on the subject. Wright and his colleagues largely ignored Kinsey's 1941 article, or dismissed it outright. Myerson and Neustadt (1942, 954–955), for example, supported Wright's findings, "in spite of the criticism accorded [his] figures from the mathematical viewpoint by Kinsey." However, they agreed with Kinsey (without acknowledging his contribution) by rejecting the typology of homosexuals based on their purported femininity, whether in mannerism or sexual position. Glass and Johnson (1944, 542) counterattacked Kinsey on methodological grounds by challenging his statistical methods, and by ridiculing his criticism of sexual categorization, arguing that "if intergradation were to be thought of as vitiating classification, the medical sciences would require revolution."

In general, Kinsey's work was very controversial in its own time: some scientists attacked his statistical methods, others praised his objectivity and courage; some social commentators were shocked and offended by his sexual liberalism (or libertinism); others found legitimation, hope, and encouragement for social and legal reforms.[17] In any case, Kinsey's pair of tomes, laden with statistics, charts and tables, analyses of biological, sociological, and psychological literature on sex and sexuality, and dry (although often wry) descriptions of the sexual behavior of white Americans, were best-sellers among the general public, and have remained controversial cultural reference points in the social, political, and scientific discourses of sex in America.

Science, Sex, and the Social Order: Or, Gay Genes, Gay Brains, and Gay Scientists

According to many historians, the idea of homosexuality as an identity developed in the nineteenth century, alongside the elaboration of biomedical explanations of homosexuality as moral failing, crime, hereditary degeneration, constitutional anomaly, disease, neurosis, lifestyle, orientation, or genetic trait (Foucault 1978; Greenberg 1988; Bullough 1976; Conrad & Schneider 1980, 172–213). In Wright's work of the mid-1930s, a biological explanation was, in certain ways, socially "progressive" and part of the medicalization of so-called deviant behavior. In other words, attempting to "cure" homosexuals was seen by many (including Wright) as preferable to, and more humane than, incarcerating them. Kinsey attempted to render the entire question moot. For him, all sexual behavior, including homosexual contact, was "natural," and therefore within the range of the "normal." He attempted to undermine the category of "homosexual" as a distinct type of individual and thereby remove the justification for differential treatment, whether punitive or "progressive." Kinsey's denial of the existence of homosexuality as an identity (and implicitly, therefore, as a political category) makes him an especially unlikely hero for gay rights advocates, who base their politics on the fundamental assumption of just such an identity.

Despite Kinsey's critiques, scientific research into hormonal influences on sexual orientation has continued almost unabated from the 1930s to the present, although the particular theories have changed dramatically and now concentrate primarily on the effects of sex hormones on the pre- and neonatal brain (Meyer-Bahlburg 1977, 1984). Furthermore, although neither LeVay (1991) nor Hamer et al. (1993) focuses explicitly on hormonal aspects of homosexuality, or posits simple causative explanations for complex human traits, the "gay brain" and "gay gene" are only the most recent examples in the long tradition of the search for the biological basis of human sexuality.

Detailed analyses of the methods and assumptions in LeVay's and Hamer's work have been skillfully performed by others (Gorman 1994; Byne 1994; Allen, this volume), and are beyond the scope of this paper. However, many of the basic questions that Kinsey asked of Wright's work could be asked of the most recent research as well: Who counts when you're counting homosexuals? Who doesn't? And, finally: Who does the counting? Today, it is gay scientists like Hamer and LeVay who are researching and advocating biological explanations of sexuality, and are being challenged by the religious right (which has co-opted the terminology of "sexual preference" to attack so-called sinful lifestyles), and the liberal left (which is systematically wary of biological arguments suspected of oppressing women and people of color).

Historically, biological markers of difference have served the politics of exclusion and oppression rather than of liberation (see, for example, Schiebinger 1993; Gilman 1985). Twenty years ago, biological explanations of homosexuality would have been anathema to those opposing homophobic political and social campaigns, which have often been laced with eugenic and medical undertones. Now, however, many (though by no means all) advocates of homosexual rights look to biological or genetic explanations as a means of extending the legal umbrella of anti-discrimination to the gay community. In the 1990s, in the age of AIDS and the concurrent expansion of religious right-wing political movements, the political stakes regarding homosexuality have been raised once again, and we are seeing a reconfiguration of the relationship between the epistemological and the political.

Notes

1 The position that homosexuality is *both* a medical and a social "problem" is an interesting one. It can be read as a territorial strategy, promoting one type of expertise over another (in this case the medical/social over the legal). In the end, however, the position becomes paradoxical: the medical or social *treatment* of the problem is most likely to be based on conflicting ideas of the origin of homosexuality—thus the nature/nurture dichotomy. It is the definition of homosexuality *as a problem* (whether criminal, social, or medical) that leads to the debate about causation. Why would it be impor-

tant whether a behavior is environmentally or biologically determined if there were no desire to "fix," alter, or eliminate it? Alternatively, however, the eugenics movement was originally concerned with the promotion of positive traits (such as "genius") rather than the elimination of negative ones. Either way, the "nature/nurture" debate has continued to frame many social policies aimed at "improving" society by the eradication of certain "problems" or the promotion of certain "assets." For further discussion of these issues, see the introduction to this volume.

2 Homosexuality in women received much less scientific and medical attention than in men. This was usually explained and justified in two ways: first, women were thought to have different modes of intimacy with each other, which made the detection of specifically homosexual relations difficult to distinguish from close friendships. Second, the assumed general domesticity of women made lesbians seem less of a social and criminal threat than gay men, who had carved out institutional niches in the public sphere, such as bars and baths (Kinsey et al. 1953, 475–471).

The most significant exception to the general exclusion of homosexual women from medical concerns was the massive, two-volume work sponsored by the Committee for the Study of Sex Variants in New York City (Henry 1941)—volume 2 was about lesbians. Other studies of female sexuality that included chapters on lesbianism include: Davis (1929), Landis (1940), and Kinsey et al. (1953). For discussions of medical sexology and lesbianism, see Terry (1990); Chauncey (1982–3); Faderman (1981, 239–253, 314–331); Faderman (1991, 37–61); Smith-Rosenberg (1985).

Of the sixty cases summarized in Wright's 1938 article, only five were women (1938, 451). However, none of the cases supported his theory about the relationship between homosexuality and hormonal imbalance.

3 See also Wright (1938, 452). Wright did not specify the source of this estimate of frequency, but it concurred with a number of other studies from the same period. Lewis Terman, for example, estimated about 4 percent of the male population to be homosexual (Terman & Miles 1936, 467). The estimate probably comes from Hirschfeld. Kinsey devoted several pages to challenging these sorts of estimates in the scientific literature (1948, 617–622).

4 Wright (1935, 407), Wright (1938, 449), Wright (1939, 399), Glass et al. (1940, 590), Wright (1941, 60).

5 For example, Witschi (1932) described the state of knowledge about sexual differentiation and sex reversal in lower animals; Miles (1936, 688–694) provided a brief survey of contemporary ideas about sexual differentiation (and sex differences) in humans. The term "bisexual" was used by Wright as well as many of his colleagues: Wright (1938, 452); Myerson and Neustadt (1942). Alfred Kinsey and colleagues (1948, 656–659) rejected the use of the term "bisexual" for describing human behavior specifically because of its precise usage in biological literature. For a psychoanalytic critique of the idea of physiological bisexuality, see Rado (1940).

For historical discussions of eighteenth- and nineteenth-century theories and discoveries about the embryological origins of male and female sexual organs, see Laqueur (1990, 169–171); Moscucci (1990, 17–18).

6 As the specific chemical substances were isolated and synthesized, much research focused on the physiological origins of so-called cross-sex hormones as well as their multifarious functions. A few of the most important articles in the field include: Allen and Doisy (1923); Laqueur and de Jongh (1928); Lillie (1917); Moore (1930); Stockard

and Papanicolaou (1917). The Rockefeller-sponsored Committee for Research on Problems of Sex (CRPS) funded a significant portion of American research in the field and supported the publication of the first American surveys on sex endocrinology (see Allen 1932, 1939). For an in-house history of the committee, see Aberle and Corner (1953). For the most recent historical analysis of sex endocrinology, see Oudshoorn (1994).

7 Wright (1935, 407), Wright (1938, 449), Wright (1939, 399), Glass et al. (1940, 593). The measurement of hormone levels was performed using biological assays, which functioned roughly as follows: a researcher isolated the chemical substances under study from the blood or urine of a patient, and injected them into an animal whose gonads had been surgically removed. If the injected substance reproduced the same physiological effects that had disappeared when the sex glands were removed, the assay was considered positive. For example, the comb of a castrated rooster would grow when the animal was injected with male sex hormones. Measurements were calculated by the amount of hormone required to produce the physiological reaction. See Oudshoorn (1990a, 27 n. 8; 1994, 42–64).

8 Wright (1935, 409), Wright (1938, 452), Wright (1939, 402), Wright (1941, 61). The scientific and commercial nomenclature for the newly discovered sex hormones was confusing and complex. Wright usually used antuitrin S (manufactured by Parke-Davis) and follutein (manufactured by Squibb) as his gonadotropic hormones, and androsterone and perandren (both manufactured by Ciba) for his testosterone injections (Glass et al. 1940, 594; Wright 1941, 61). It is not clear that Wright ever treated any women in the same manner, but he suggested that the use of various estrogenic substances (progynon, theelin, amniotin, estrin, etc.) "would be advisable" for female homosexuals (Wright 1935, 409; Wright 1938, 452; Wright 1939, 402). For more on the role of pharmaceutical companies in the development of sex hormones, see Oudshoorn (1993, 1994).

Wright's treatment was in direct contrast to the "chemical castration" of the 1950s, in which male homosexuals were given female hormones to reduce or eliminate the sex drive.

9 For more on late nineteenth-century German sexology, see Greenberg (1988, 408–415); Bullough (1994, 34–72); Oosterhuis and Steakley (this volume).

10 For contemporary psychological and medical writings which evoked images of "inversion," see Ellis (1928); Terman and Miles (1936); Henry (1941); Witschi and Mengert (1942). For historical treatments, see Minton (1986); Terry (1990).

11 Wright especially emphasized the femininity of those subjects who liked to dress in women's clothes. For a recent and provocative analysis of cross-dressing, see Garber (1992). See also Bullough and Bullough (1993).

12 George Chauncey has written an excellent and provocative history of gay life in New York City during this period, in which he analyzes the contemporaneous categories of homosexual identities that, he argues, differ dramatically from those most commonly recognized by the dominant culture today (1994, 12–23, 47–127). For other contemporary classificatory schemes of homosexuality, based on economic or educational class, as well as sexual practices, see Henry and Gross (1938, 1941); Henry (1941).

One of Kinsey's most significant, and controversial, conclusions was the differential sexual behavior of what he called "social level." See Kinsey et al. (1948, chap. 10); Robinson (1976, 92–99). Economic and educational class, as well as immigrant status, were central factors in early-twentieth-century American sexological studies, and stemmed from the legacy of eugenic interests in controlling the population of the lower classes. Unfortunately these factors have been largely ignored by historians of sex research.

13 Chauncey makes a strong argument for the existence of a cultural space for masculine-identified men to have sexual relations with other men without seeing themselves, or being seen by others, as anything other than "normal," especially in certain early twentieth-century working-class and immigrant communities (1994, 12–23, 65–97; see also Chauncey 1982–83 and 1985). However, I doubt that most professional middle-class physicians concurred: the category of "acquired" homosexuality was not a medical description of "normality."

14 On Kinsey's ideas about variation and taxonomy in biological populations and their relation to his thinking about human sexuality, see Kinsey et al. (1948, 16–21), Gould (1985, 155–166), Robinson (1976, 51–56).

15 Kinsey described a few cases of predominantly heterosexual men who had more homosexual experiences than some of those who had exclusively homosexual relations, and vice versa. Thus the *proportion* of sexual experiences was more important to Kinsey than their absolute number. This discussion of the proportion of different types of sexual activity prefigures Kinsey's later six-point scale of homosexuality, to which I will return.

16 Paul Robinson (1976, 66–75) has done an excellent job of summarizing this aspect of Kinsey's work, and Kinsey's own chapter on the subject is relatively short and very readable (1948, 610–666).

17 For historical discussions of the response to Kinsey's work, see Morantz (1977, 575–582), Pomeroy (1982, 251–259, 283–306, 339–372), Christenson (1971, 143–146), Robinson (1976, 115–119). Cochran, et al. (1954) includes a summary of reviews of Kinsey's work. Geddes (1954) is a collection of essays by eleven contemporary commentators.

References

Abelove, Henry. 1993. Freud, male homosexuality, and the Americans. In *The Lesbian and Gay Studies Reader*, ed. Henry Abelove, Michèle Aina Barale, and David M. Halperin, 381–393. New York: Routledge.

Aberle, Sophie D., and George W. Corner. 1953. *Twenty-Five Years of Sex Research. History of the National Research Council Committee for Research in Problems of Sex, 1922–1947.* Philadelphia: Saunders.

Allen, Edgar, and Edward Doisy. 1923. An ovarian hormone. *Journal of the American Medical Association* 81:819–821.

Allen, Edgar, ed. 1932. *Sex and Internal Secretions. A Survey of Recent Research.* Baltimore: Williams and Wilkins.

———. 1939. *Sex and Internal Secretions. A Survey of Recent Research.* 2d ed. Revised. Baltimore: Williams and Wilkins.

Angier, Natalie. 1993. Report suggests homosexuality is linked to genes. *New York Times* (July 16), A1:2, A12:2.

Borell, Merriley. 1985. Organotherapy and the emergence of reproductive endocrinology. *Journal of the History of Biology* 18:1–30.
Bugos, Glenn. 1989. Managing cooperative research and borderland science in the National Research Council, 1922–1942. *Historical Studies in the Physical and Biological Sciences* 20:1–32.
Bullough, Vern. 1976. *Sex Variance in Society and History.* New York: Wiley.
———. 1994. *Science in the Bedroom.* New York: Basic Books.
Bullough, Vern L., and Bonnie Bullough. 1993. *Cross Dressing, Sex, and Gender.* Philadelphia: University of Pennsylvania Press.
Byne, William. 1994. The biological evidence challenged. *Scientific American* 270:50–55.
Chauncey, George. 1982–83. From sexual inversion to homosexuality: Medicine and the changing conceptualization of female deviance. *Salmagundi* 58–59:114–146.
———. 1985. Christian brotherhood or sexual perversion? Homosexual identities and the construction of sexual boundaries in the World War One era. *Journal of Social History* 19:189–211.
———. 1994. *Gay New York. Gender, Urban Culture, and the Making of the Gay Male World, 1890–1940.* New York: Basic Books.
Christenson, Cornelia V. 1971. *Kinsey. A Biography.* Bloomington: Indiana University Press.
Cochran, William G., Frederick Mosteller, and John W. Tukey. 1954. *Statistical Problems of the Kinsey Report.* Washington, DC: American Statistical Association.
Conrad, Peter, and Joseph W. Schneider. 1980. *Deviance and Medicalization: From Badness to Sickness.* St. Louis: Mosby.
Davis, Katherine B. 1929. *Factors in the Sex Life of Twenty-Two Hundred Women.* New York: Harper.
Directory of Medical Specialties: 1939. 1940. New York: Columbia University Press.
Ellis, Havelock. 1928. *Studies in the Psychology of Sex. Vol. II. Sexual Inversion.* 3d ed. Philadelphia: Davis.
Faderman, Lillian. 1981. *Surpassing the Love of Men. Romantic Friendship and Love Between Women from the Renaissance to the Present.* New York: William Morrow.
———. 1991. *Odd Girls and Twilight Lovers. A History of Lesbian Life in Twentieth-Century America.* New York: Columbia University Press.
Foucault, Michel. 1978. *The History of Sexuality. Volume 1. An Introduction.* New York: Pantheon.
Freud, Sigmund. [1905] 1953. *Three Essays on the Theory of Sexuality.* In *Standard Edition,* ed. and trans. James Strachey et al., 7:123–245. London: Hogarth.
Garber, Marjorie. 1992. *Vested Interests. Cross-Dressing and Cultural Anxiety.* New York: Routledge.
Geddes, Donald Porter, ed. 1954. *An Analysis of the Kinsey Reports.* New York: Mentor.
Gilman, Sander L. 1985. *Difference and Pathology: Stereotypes of Sexuality, Race, and Madness.* Ithaca: Cornell University Press.
Glass, Samuel J., H. J. Deuel, and Clifford A. Wright. 1940. Sex hormone studies in male homosexuality. *Endocrinology* 26:590–594.
Glass, Samuel J., and Roswell H. Johnson. 1944. Limitations and complications of organotherapy in male homosexuals. *Journal of Clinical Endocrinology* 4:540–544.
Glass, Samuel J., and B. J. McKennon. 1937. The hormonal aspects of sex reversal states. *Western Journal of Surgery, Obstetrics and Gynecology* 45:467–473.

Gorman, Michael R. 1994. Male homosexual desire: neurological investigations and scientific bias. *Perspectives in Biology and Medicine* 38:61–81.
Gould, Stephen J. 1981. *The Mismeasure of Man*. New York: Norton.
———. 1985. Of Wasps and WASPs. In *The Flamingo's Smile. Reflections in Natural History*, 155–166. New York: Norton.
Greenberg, David F. 1988. *The Construction of Homosexuality*. Chicago: University of Chicago Press.
Halley, Janet. 1994. Sexual orientation and the politics of biology: A critique of the argument from immutability. *Stanford Law Review* 46:503–568.
Hamer, Dean H., et al. 1993. A linkage between DNA markers on the X chromosome and male sexual orientation. *Science* 261:321–327.
Hamer, Dean, and Peter Copeland. 1994. *The Science of Desire. The Search for the Gay Gene and the Biology of Behavior*. New York: Simon & Schuster.
Henry, George W. 1937. Psychogenic factors in overt homosexuality. *American Journal of Psychiatry* 93:889–908.
———. 1941. *Sex Variants. A Study of Homosexual Patterns*. New York: Hoeber.
Henry, George W., and Alfred A. Gross. 1938. Social factors in the case histories of one hundred underprivileged homosexuals. *Mental Hygiene* 22:591–611.
———. 1941. The homosexual delinquent. *Mental Hygiene* 25:420–42.
Irvine, Janice M. 1990. *Disorders of Desire. Sex and Gender in Modern American Sexology*. Philadelphia: Temple University Press.
Kinsey, Alfred C. 1941. Criteria for a hormonal explanation of the homosexual. *Journal of Clinical Endocrinology and Metabolism* 1:424–428.
Kinsey, Alfred C., Wardell B. Pomeroy, and Clyde E. Martin, 1948. *Sexual Behavior in the Human Male*. Philadelphia: W. B. Saunders.
Kinsey, Alfred C., Wardell B. Pomeroy, Clyde E. Martin and Paul H. Gebhard. 1953. *Sexual Behavior in the Human Female*. Philadelphia: W. B. Saunders.
Landis, Carney. 1940. *Sex in Development*. New York: Hoeber.
Laqueur, Ernst, and S. E. de Jongh. 1928. A female (sexual) hormone. *Journal of the American Medical Association* 91:1169–1172.
Laqueur, Thomas. 1990. *Making Sex. Body and Gender from the Greeks to Freud*. Cambridge: Harvard University Press.
Laumann, Edward O., John H. Gagnon, Robert T. Michael, and Stuart Michaels. 1994. *The Social Organization of Sexuality*. Chicago: University of Chicago Press.
LeVay, Simon. 1991. A difference in hypothalamic structure between heterosexual and homosexual men. *Science* 253:1034–1037.
———. 1993. *The Sexual Brain*. Cambridge: MIT Press.
LeVay, Simon, and Dean H. Hamer. 1994. Evidence for a biological influence in male homosexuality. *Scientific American* 270:44–49.
Lillie, Frank R. 1917. The free martin: A study of the action of sex hormones in the foetal life of cattle. *Journal of Experimental Zoology* 23:371–452.
Meyer-Bahlburg, Heino F. L. 1977. Sex hormones and male homosexuality in comparative perspective. *Archives of Sexual Behavior* 6:297–325.
———. 1984. Psychoendocrine research on sexual orientation: Current status and future options. *Progress in Brain Research* 61:375–398.
Miles, C. C. 1936. Sex in social psychology. In *A Handbook of Social Psychology*., ed. C. Murchison, 683–797. Worcester, Mass.: Clark University Press.

Minton, Henry L. 1986. Femininity in men and masculinity in women: American psychiatry and psychology portray homosexuality in the 1930s. *Journal of Homosexuality* 13:1–21.
———. 1988. American psychology and the study of human sexuality. *Journal of Psychology and Human Sexuality* 1:17–34.
Moore, Carl R. 1930. A critique of sex-hormone antagonism. *Proceedings of the Second International Congress for Sex Research,* 293–303.
Moore, Carl R., and Dorothy Price. 1932. Gonad hormone functions. *American Journal of Anatomy* 50:3–71.
Morantz, Regina Markell. 1977. The scientist as sex crusader. Alfred C. Kinsey and American culture. *American Quarterly* 29:563–589.
Moscucci, Ornella. 1990. *The Science of Woman. Gynaecology and Gender in England, 1800–1929.* Cambridge: Cambridge University Press.
Myerson, A., and R. Neustadt. 1942.The bisexuality of man. *Journal of Mt. Sinai Hospital* 9:668–678.
———. 1942–1943. Bisexuality and male homosexuality; their biologic and medical aspects. *Clinics* 1:932–957.
———. 1940. Quantitative sex hormone studies in homosexuality, childhood, and various neuropsychiatric disturbances. *American Journal Psychiatry* 97:524–551.
Nye, Robert, A. 1984. *Crime, Madness, and Politics in Modern France. The Medical Concept of National Decline.* Princeton: Princeton University Press.
Oudshoorn, Nelly. 1990a. On the making of sex hormones. Research materials and the production of knowledge. *Social Studies of Science* 20:5–33.
———. 1990b. Endocrinologists and the conceptualization of sex, 1920–1940. *Journal of the History of Biology* 23:163–186.
———. 1993. United we stand: The pharmaceutical industry, laboratory, and clinic in the development of sex hormones into scientific drugs, 1920–1940. *Science, Technology, and Human Values* 18:5–24.
———. 1994. *Beyond the Natural Body: An Archaeology of Sex Hormones.* New York: Routledge.
Pomeroy, Wardell B. 1982. *Dr. Kinsey and the Institute for Sex Research.* New Haven: Yale University Press.
Rado, Sandor. 1940. A critical examination of the concept of bisexuality. *Psychosomatic Medicine* 11:459–467.
Robinson, Paul. 1976. *The Modernization of Sex.* New York: Harper & Row.
Schiebinger, Londa. 1993. *Nature's Body. Gender in the Making of Modern Science.* Boston: Beacon.
Smith-Rosenberg, Carroll. 1985. The New Woman as androgyne: Social disorder and gender crisis, 1870–1936. In *Disorderly Conduct: Visions of Gender in Victorian America,* 245–296. New York: Knopf.
Stockard, C. R., and G. N. Papanicolaou. 1917. The existence of a typical oestrous cycle in the guinea-pig. *American Journal of Anatomy* 22:225–284.
Terman, Lewis M. 1948. Kinsey's *Sexual Behavior in the Human Male*: Some comments and criticisms. *Psychological Bulletin* 45:443–459.
Terman, Lewis M., and Catherine Cox Miles. 1936. *Sex and Personality. Studies in Masculinity and Femininity.* New York: McGraw-Hill.
Terry, Jennifer. 1990. Lesbians under the medical gaze: Scientists search for remarkable differences. *The Journal of Sex Research* 27:317–339.

Williams, Edward Huntington, and Clifford A. Wright. 1941. Endocrine patterns in some psychoses. *Medical Record, NY* 154: 302–307.

Witschi, Emil. 1932. Sex deviations, inversions, and parabiosis. In *Sex and Internal Secretions. A Survey of Recent Research*, ed. Edgar Allen, 160–245. Baltimore: Williams and Wilkins.

Witschi, E., and W. F. Mengert. 1942. Endocrine studies on human hermaphrodites and their bearing on the interpretation of homosexuality. *Journal of Clinical Endocrinology* 2:279–286.

Wright, Clifford A. 1935. Endocrine aspects of homosexuality. A preliminary report. *Medical Record, NY* 142:407–410.

———. 1938. Further studies of endocrine aspects of homosexuality. *Medical Record, NY* 147:449–452.

———. 1939. The sex offender's endocrines. *Medical Record, NY* 149:399–402.

———. 1941. Results of endocrine treatment in a controlled group of homosexual men. *Medical Record, NY* 154:60–61.

Young, Hugh Hampton. 1937. *Genital Abnormalities, Hermaphroditism, and Related Adrenal Diseases*. Baltimore: Williams and Wilkins.

How to Build a Man

Anne Fausto-Sterling

How does one become a man? Although poets, novelists, and playwrights long past answered with discussions of morality and honor, these days scholars deliberate the same question using a metaphor—that of social construction. In the current intellectual fashion, men are made, not born. We construct masculinity through social discourse—that array of happenings that covers everything from the visuals on MTV, rap lyrics, and poetry to sports, beer commercials, and psychotherapy. But underlying all of this clever carpentry is the sneaking suspicion that one must start with a blueprint—or, to stretch the metaphor yet a bit more, that buildings must have foundations. Within the soul of even the most die-hard constructionist lurks a doubt. It is called the body.

In contrast, biological and medical scientists feel quite certain about their world. For them the body tells the truth. (Never mind that postmodern scholarship has questioned the very meaning of the word *truth.*) My task in this essay is to consider the truths that biologists extract from bodies, human and otherwise, to examine scientific accounts—some might even say constructions—of masculinity. To do this, I treat the scientific/medical literature as yet another set of texts open to scholarly analysis and interpretation.

What are little boys made of? While the nursery rhyme suggests "snips and snails and puppy dog tails," during the past seventy years medical scientists have built a rather more concrete and certainly less fanciful account. Perhaps the single most influential voice during this period has been that of psychologist John Money. At least since the 1920s, embryologists have understood that during fetal development a single embryonic primordium, the indifferent fetal gonad, can give rise to either an ovary or a testis. In a similar fashion, both male and female external genitalia arise from a single set of structures. Only the internal sex organs—uteri, fallopian tubes, prostates, sperm transport ducts—arise during embryonic development from separate sets of structures. In the 1950s, John Money extended these embryological understandings into the realm of psychological development.[1] He envisioned that while all humans start on the same road, the path rapidly begins to fork. Potential males take a series of turns in one direction, potential females in another. In real time the road begins at fertilization and ends during late adolescence. If all goes as it should, then there are two and only two possible destinations: male and female.

But of course all does not always go as it should. Money identified the various forks in the road by studying individuals who took one or more wrong turns. From them he came up with a map of the normal. This is, in fact, one of the very interesting things about biological investigators. They use the infrequent to illuminate the common. The former they call abnormal, the latter, normal. Often, as is the case for Money and others in the medical world, the abnormal requires management. In the examples I will discuss, management means conversion to the normal. Thus we have a profound irony. Biologists and physicians use natural biological variation to define normality. Once armed with the description, they then set out to eliminate the natural variation that gave them their definitions in the first place.

How does all this apply to the construction of masculinity? Money lists ten road signs directing a person along the path to male or female. In most cases these indicators are clear, but as in any large city these days, sometimes graffiti makes them hard to read, and the traveler ends up taking a wrong turn. The first sign is *chromosomal sex*: the presence of an X or a Y. The second is *gonadal sex*: when there is no graffiti, the Y or the X instructs the fetal gonad to develop into a testis or an ovary. *Fetal hormonal sex* marks the third fork: the embryonic testis must make hormones that influence events to come—most especially the fourth (*internal morphologic sex*), fifth (*external morphologic sex*), and sixth (*brain sex*) branches in the road. All of these, but most especially external morphologic sex at birth, illuminate the road sign for step number seven: *sex of assignment and rearing*. Finally, to become, in John Money's world, either a true male or a true female, one must produce the right hormones at puberty (*pubertal hormonal sex*), acquire and express a consistent gender identity and role, and, to complete the picture, must be able to reproduce in the appropriate fashion (*procreative sex*) (see Money & Tucker 1975; Money & Ehrhardt 1972).

Many medical texts reproduce this neat little scheme, suggesting that it is a literal account of the scientific truth, but neglecting to point out how, at each step, scientists have woven into the fabric their own deeply social preexisting understandings of what it means to be male or female. Let me illustrate this for several of the branches in the road. Why is it that usually XX babies grow up to be female while XYs become male? Geneticists say that it is because of a specific Y chromosome gene, often abbreviated SDY for "sex-determining gene on the Y chromosome." Biologists also refer to the SDY as the Master Sex Determining gene, and say that in its *presence*, a male is formed. Females, on the other hand, are said to be the default sex. In the *absence* of the master gene, they just naturally happen. The story of the SDY begins an account of maleness which continues throughout development. A male embryo must activate its master gene and seize its developmental pathway from the underlying female ground plan.

When the SDY gene starts working, it turns the indifferent gonad into a functional testis. One of the first things the testis does is to induce hormone synthesis. It is these molecules that take control of subsequent developmental steps. The first hormone to hit the decks (MIS or Müllerian Inhibiting Substance) suppresses the development of the internal female organs, which otherwise lie in wait ready to unveil their feminine presence. The next, fetal testosterone, manfully pushes other embryonic primordia to develop both the internal and external trappings of physical masculinity. Again, medical texts offer the presence/absence hypothesis: Maleness requires the presence of special hormones; in their absence, femaleness just happens.[2]

At this point two themes emerge. First, masculinity is an active presence that forces itself onto a feminine foundation. Money (1992) calls this "The Adam Principle—adding something to make a male." Second, the male is in constant danger. At any point, male development can be derailed: a failure to activate SDY, and the gonad becomes an ovary; a failure to make MIS, and the fetus can end up with fallopian tubes and a uterus superimposed on an otherwise male body; fail to make fetal testosterone, and, despite the presence of a testis, the embryo develops the external trappings of a baby girl. One fascinating contradiction in the scientific literature illustrates my point. Most texts write that femaleness results from the absence of male hormones,[3] yet, at the same time, scientists worry about how male fetuses protect themselves from being feminized by the sea of maternal (female) hormones in which they grow. This fear suggests, of course, that female hormones play an active role after all; but most scientists do not pick up on that bit of logic. Instead they hunt for special proteins the male embryo makes in order to protect itself from maternally induced feminization. (It seems that mother is to blame even before birth.)

Consider now the birth of a boy-child. He is perfect—Y chromosomes, testes descended into their sweet little scrotal sacs, a beautifully formed penis. He is perfect—except that the penis is very tiny. What happens next? Some medical texts refer to a situation such as this as a social emergency; others, as a surgical one. The parents want to tell everyone about the birth of their baby boy; the physicians fear he cannot continue developing along the road to masculinity. They decide that creating a female is best. Females are imperfect by nature, and if this child cannot be a perfect or near-perfect male, then being an imperfect female is the best choice. What do physicians' criteria for making such choices tell us about the construction of masculinity?

Medical managers use the following rule of thumb: "Genetic females should always be raised as females, preserving reproductive potential, regardless of how severely the patients are virilized. In the genetic male, however, the gender of assignment is based on the infant's anatomy, predominantly the size of the phallus" (Donahue, Powell, & Lee 1991, 527). Only a few reports on penile size at birth exist in the scientific literature, and it seems that birth size, in and of itself, is not a particularly good indicator of size and function at puberty. The average phallus at birth measures 3.5 cm (1–1.5 in.) long. A baby boy born with a penis measuring only 0.9 inches raises some eyebrows, while medical practitioners do not permit one born with a penis less than 0.6 inches long to remain as a male (Danish et al. 1980). (The medical name for this condition is "micropenis.") Despite the fact that the intact organ may provide orgasmic pleasure to the future adult, it is surgically removed (along with the testes), and replaced by a much smaller clitoris, which may or may not retain orgasmic function. When surgeons turn "Sammy" into "Suzanna," they also build her a vagina. Her primary sexual activity is to be the recipient of a penis during heterosexual intercourse. As one surgeon recently commented, "It's easier to poke a hole than build a pole."

All this surgical activity goes on to ensure a congruous and certain sex of assignment and sex of rearing. During childhood, the medical literature insists, boys must have a phallus large enough to permit them to pee standing up, thus allowing them to "feel normal" when they play in little boys' peeing contests. In adulthood the penis must become large enough for vaginal penetration during sexual intercourse. By and large, physicians use the standard of reproductive potential for making females and phallus size for making males, although Kessler (1990) reports one case of a physician choosing to reassign as male a potentially reproductive genetic female infant rather than remove a well-formed penis.

At birth, then, masculinity becomes a social phenomenon. For proper masculine socialization to occur, the little boy must have a sufficiently large penis. There must be no doubt in the boy's mind, in the minds of his parents and other adult relatives, or in the minds of his male peers about the legitimacy of male identification. In childhood all that is required is that he be able to pee in a standing position. In adulthood he must engage in vaginal heterosexual intercourse. The discourse of sexual pleasure, even for males, is totally absent from this medical literature. In fact, male infants who receive extensive penile surgery often end up with badly scarred and thus physically insensitive members. While no surgeon considers this to be a desirable outcome, in assigning sex to an intersexual infant or to a boy with micropenis, sexual pleasure clearly takes a back seat to ensuring heterosexual conventions. Penetration in the absence of pleasure takes precedence over pleasure in the absence of penetration.

In the world of John Money and other managers of intersexuality, men are made, not born. Proper socialization becomes more important than genetics. Hence, Money and Ehrhardt (1972, 118–123) have a simple solution to accidents as terrible as accidental penile amputation following infant circumcision: raise the boy as a girl. If both the parents and child remain confident of his new-found female identity, all will be well. But what counts as good mental health for boys and girls? Here Money and coworkers focus primarily on female development, which becomes the mirror from which we can reflect the truth about males. Money has published extensively on observations of XX infants born with masculinized genitalia (Money, Schwartz, & Lewis 1984; Money & Daléry 1976, 1977). Usually such children are raised as girls, and receive surgery and hormonal treatments to feminize their genitalia and ensure a feminine puberty. He notes that frequently such children have a harder time than usual achieving clarity about their femininity. The signs of trouble include: engaging in rough-and-tumble play, and hitting more often than other toddler girls; thinking more about having a career, and fantasizing less about marriage than other adolescent girls; and having lesbian relationships as an adolescent and young adult.

The homologue to these developmental variations can be found in Richard

Green's description of the "Sissy Boy Syndrome" (1987). Green studied little boys who develop feminine interests—playing with dolls, dressing in girls' clothing, not engaging in enough rough-and-tumble play. These boys, he argued, are at high risk for becoming homosexuals. Money's and Green's ideas work together to present a picture of normality. And—surprise, surprise—there is no room in the scheme for a normal homosexual. Money makes a remarkable claim: Genetics and even hormones count less in making a man or a woman than does socialization. In sustaining that claim his strongest evidence, his trump card, is that the child born a male but raised a female becomes a heterosexual female. In fact, Milton Diamond (1995) has followed up on Money's early case histories and found the outcomes to be far more complex. In their accounts of the power of socialization, Money, Hampson, and Hampson (1955b) define heterosexual in terms of the sex of rearing. Thus a child raised as a female (even if biologically male) who prefers male lovers is psychologically heterosexual, although genetically she is not.

Again, we can parse out the construction of masculinity. To begin with, normally developing little boys must be active and willing to push one another around; maleness and aggression go together. Eventually little boys become socialized into appropriate adult behavior, which includes heterosexual fantasy and activity. Adolescent boys do not dream of marriage, but of careers and a professional future. A healthy adolescent girl, in contrast, must fantasize about falling in love, marrying, and raising children. Only a masculinized girl dreams of a professional future. Of course, we know already that for men the true mark of heterosexuality involves vaginal penetration with the penis. Other activities, even if they are with a woman, do not really count.

This might be the end of the story, except for one thing: accounts of normal development drawn from the study of intersexuals contain internal inconsistencies. How does Money explain the higher-than-normal percentage of lesbianism or the more frequent aggressive behavior among masculinized children raised as girls? One could imagine elaborating on the socialization theme: parents aware of the uncertain sex of their children subconsciously socialize them in some intermediary fashion. Shockingly for a psychologist, however, Money denies the possibility of subconsciously driven behavior (Money, Hampson, & Hampson 1955b). Instead, he and the many others who interpret the development of intersexual children resort to hormonal explanations. If an XX girl born with a penis, surgically "corrected" shortly after birth and raised as a girl, subsequently becomes a lesbian, Money and others do not look to socialization. Instead they explain this failure to become heterosexual by appealing to hormones present in the fetal environment. Excess fetal testosterone caused the masculinization of the genitalia; similarly, fetal testosterone must have altered the developing brain, readying it to view females as appropriate sexual objects. Here, then, we have the last bit of the picture painted by biologists. By implication, normal males become sexually attracted to females because testosterone affects their brain during embryonic development. Socialization reinforces this inclination.

Biologists, therefore, write texts about human development. These documents, which take the form of research papers, texts, review articles, and popular books, grow from interpretations of scientific data. Often written in neutral, abstract language, the texts have the ring of authority. Because they represent scientific findings, one might imagine that they contain no preconceptions, no culturally instigated belief systems. But this turns out not to be the case. Although based on evidence, scientific writing can be seen as a particular kind of cultural interpretation—the enculturated scientist interprets nature. In the process, he or she also uses that interpretation to reinforce old or build new sets of social beliefs. Thus scientific work contributes to the construction of masculinity, and masculine constructs are among the building blocks for particular kinds of scientific knowledge. One of the jobs of the science critic is to illuminate this interaction. Once such illumination has occurred, it becomes possible to discuss change.

Notes

1 See Money (1952 and 1957); Money and Hampson (1955); Money, Hampson and Hampson (1955a).

2 The data do not actually match the presence/absence model, but this seems not to bother most people. For a discussion of this point, see Fausto-Sterling (1987, 1989, 1992).

3 I use the phrases "male hormones" and "female hormones" as shorthand. There are, in fact, no such categories. Males and females have the same hormones, albeit in different quantities and sometimes with different tissue distributions.

References

Danish, Robert H., Peter A. Lee, Thomas Mazur, James A. Amrhein, and Claude J. Migeon. 1980. Micropenis II. Hypogonadotropic hypogonadism. *Johns Hopkins Medical Journal* 146:177–184.

Diamond, Milton. 1995. Presentation at meeting of the Society for the Scientific Study of Sex, San Francisco.

Donahue, Patricia, David M. Powell, and Mary M. Lee. 1991. Clinical management of intersex abnormalities. *Current Problems in Surgery* 28:513–579.

Fausto-Sterling, Anne. 1987. Society writes biology/biology constructs gender. *Dædalus* 116:61–76.

———. 1989. Life in the XY Corral. *Women's Studies International Forum* 12:319–331.

———. 1992. *Myths of Gender: Biological Theories About Women and Men*. New York: Basic.

Green, Richard. 1987. *The "Sissy Boy" Syndrome and the Development of Homosexuality*. New Haven: Yale University Press.

Kessler, Suzanne J. 1990. The medical construction of gender: Case management of intersexed infants. *Signs* 16:3–26.

Money, John. 1952. Hermaphroditism: An inquiry into the nature of a human paradox. Ph.D. diss., Harvard University, Cambridge.

———. 1957. *The Psychologic Study of Man*. Springfield, IL: Charles C. Thomas.

———. 1992. *The Adam Principle*. Elmhurst, NY: Global Academic Publishers.

Money, John, and J. Daléry. 1976. Iatrogenic homosexuality: Gender identity in seven 46, XX chromosomal females with hyperadrenocortical hermaphroditism born with a penis. *Journal of Homosexuality* 1:357–371.

———. 1977. Hyperadrenocortical 46, XX hermaphroditism with penile urethra. In *Congenital Adrenal Hyperplasia*, ed. P. A. Lee, L. P. Plotnick, A. A. Kowarski, and C. J. Migeon. Baltimore: University Park Press.

Money, John, and Anke A. Ehrhardt. 1972. *Man and Woman, Boy and Girl: The Differentiation and Dimorphism of Gender Identity from Conception to Maturity*. Baltimore: Johns Hopkins University Press.

Money, John, and J. G. Hampson. 1955. Idiopathic sexual precocity in the male. *Psychosomatic Medicine* 17:1–15.

Money, John, J. G. Hampson, and J. L. Hampson. 1955a. An examination of some basic sexual concepts: The evidence of human hermaphroditism. *Bulletin of the Johns Hopkins Hospital* 97:301–319.

———. 1955b. Hermaphroditism: Recommendations concerning assignment of sex, change of sex, and psychological management. *Bulletin of the Johns Hopkins Hospital* 97:284–300.

Money, John, M. Schwartz, and V. G. Lewis. 1984. Adult erotosexual status and fetal hormonal masculinization and demasculinization: 46, XX congenital virilizing hyperplasia and 46, XX androgen-insensitivity syndrome compared. *Psychoneuroendocrinology* 9:405–414.

Money, John, and Patricia Tucker. 1975. *Sexual Signatures: On Being a Man or a Woman*. Boston: Little, Brown and Co.

The Search for a Genetic Influence on Sexual Orientation

Richard C. Pillard

Reflections about human nature have been marked by controversy over how much of our personality is preordained, and how much is shaped by what happens to us in the course of living. Philosophers in the nativist tradition, such as Kant, supposed that mental properties unfold independently of experience (a "destiny that shapes our ends"), while the empiricists, Locke, Hume, and Condillac for example, imagined the mind as a blank slate, a *tabula rasa*, upon which individual experience writes. This controversy is older than genetics, older indeed than the science of psychology. Behavioral scientists in the hundred or more years of our discipline have contended between these two camps.

Homosexuality and Psychiatry: Some Background

During the 1960s, when I was training in psychiatry, the formative influence of early life events was the primary object of study. Mental disorders were thought to be "psychogenic," that is, the result of unfortunate experiences early in life. Homosexuality had its place among these disorders. In the first two editions of the American Psychiatric Association's *Diagnostic and Statistical Manual* (1952, 1968), homosexuality was designated as a *Sociopathic Personality Disturbance* and subsequently a *Personality Disorder* (in the same neighborhood as sadism, fetishism, and sexual intercourse with domestic animals). These classifications were justified by diagnosticians of the time because of the distress many gays/lesbians experienced as a result of their sexual orientation. Few clinicians from this era reflected on the suffering necessarily visited on gay people by the unrelenting homophobia of pre-Stonewall society.

A more fundamental reason to "diagnose" homosexuality, however, was the then current view of its origins. The debate about causes was dominated by psychoanalytically trained psychiatrists, most of whom regarded homosexuality as the result of "hidden but incapacitating fears of the opposite sex" (Rado 1940). Etiologic theories had many nuances, some emphasizing a detached and hostile father, others, a seductive, overwhelming mother. Still others debated whether psychological traumas occurred during the pre-Oedipal, Oedipal, or pre-adolescent phases of development. Classifications such as "true," "latent," and "obligatory" homosexuality were proposed. The leading psychodynamic theory of the time (roughly, the thirty years between Sigmund Freud's death in 1939 and the Stonewall riots in 1969) was articulated by Irving Bieber: "Adult homosexuality is a psychopathologic state. . . . Heterosexuality is the *biologic* norm and . . . unless interfered with all individuals are heterosexual" (Bieber et al. 1962, 319). One psychiatrist took the trouble to calculate that, given the number of gays and lesbians estimated by the Kinsey survey, homosexuality was *the* most widespread mental disorder in the United States.

An important implication of the "incapacitating fears" theory was that a homosexual orientation, having been acquired by traumatic events in early life, might be reversed by reparative ones during treatment, a position endorsed by Bieber et al. (1962), Charles Socarides (1978), Lawrence Hatterer (1970), Edmund Bergler (1956), and their colleagues in the New York Society of Medical Psychoanalysis. Bieber wrote that "homosexuals do not bypass heterosexual developmental phases and all remain potentially heterosexual. . . . [Thus] psychoanalysts may well orient themselves to a heterosexual objective . . . rather than 'adjust' even the more recalcitrant patient to a homosexual destiny" (Bieber et al. 1962, 319). The possibility of a "cure," that is, a sexual orientation change, was said to be a function of the motivation of the patient. Thus, the prescribed course for the homosexually oriented person was to undertake the long, uncertain, and expensive treatment of psychoanalysis. Therapeutic failures were implicitly the result of the patient's deficient motivation rather than the misguided assumptions of the treatment. (For critical reviews, see Pillard 1982; Lewes 1988; Duberman 1991; Gonsiorek & Weinrich 1991.)

Sigmund Freud, on the contrary, appears to have been rather puzzled by the homosexual phenomenon. He proposed a theory of "constitutional bisexuality" that essentially argued that libidinal attachments to one or both genders are fundamentally a matter of biological predisposition (Freud 1922). On several occasions, Freud expressed personal support for homosexuals, for example:

> I am of the firm conviction that homosexuals must not be treated as sick people for a perverse orientation is far from being a sickness. Homosexual persons are not sick, but they also do not belong in a court of law! (Freud 1903)

He also argued that homosexuality should not be an automatic bar to membership in a psychoanalytic training institute, a position only recently adopted by U.S. psychoanalytic institutes. Most leading sexologists of the early part of this century similarly regarded a homosexual orientation benignly, as neither a crime nor an illness (see for example, Ellis 1897; Hirschfeld 1936).[1]

It may be more than coincidence that denigrating attitudes from official psychiatry surfaced only after Freud's death in 1939: the era when psychoanalysts began to occupy positions of power in the U.S. medical establishment as well as in legal theory and the popular media. Sandor Rado's 1940 paper was a harbinger breaking sharply with Freud by rejecting the theory of constitutional bisexuality. Rado's paper was cited by the following psychiatrists, whose personal abhorrence toward gays was blatant:

> The passive homosexual is trying to extinguish the race. . . . Society is justified in its violent feeling towards him and in taking steps against him. (Silverberg 1938)

> Homosexuals are essentially disagreeable people . . . [displaying] a mixture of superciliousness, false aggression, and whimpering. (Bergler 1956)

> Every homosexual encounter first concerns itself with disarming the partner through one's seductiveness, appeal, power, prestige, effeminacy, or "masculinity" and then taking advantage from the vanquished. To disarm in order to defeat is the motif. (Socarides 1972)

The above were not merely sound bites for the benefit of the media, but statements in professional publications by psychiatrists presuming to have expert knowledge about the diagnosis and treatment of a mental disorder. No wonder that Barbara Gittings, a lesbian activist and founder of the New York Daughters of Bilitis, was moved to write:

> The homosexual community . . . increasingly sees psychiatry as *the* major enemy in a battle against deeply rooted societal prejudice, and sees psychiatrists as singularly insensitive and obtuse to the destruction which they are wreaking upon homosexuals. . . . The homosexual community looks upon efforts to change homosexuals into heterosexuality . . . as an assault upon our people comparable in its way to genocide. (Gittings 1973)

It was in this atmosphere of polarized opinion, superimposed on a national consciousness tense over the Vietnam War, the recent invasion of Cambodia, and the shootings at Kent State, that the American; Psychiatric Association (APA); held its 116th annual meeting. The year was 1970; Stonewall had galvanized the gay community: Student Homophile Leagues and more radical organizations such as the Gay Activists Alliance were forming on many college campuses. A reexamination of professional thinking about sexual orientation was, for many newly politicized gays and lesbians, a high priority.

The APA's annual meeting took place that year in San Francisco, giving the gay activists positional advantage. During two panels on sexuality, they "zapped" the presenting speakers and demanded time to present their own views. What impressed many of those present, more than the assertiveness of the gay activists, was the response of some psychiatrists in the audience. Pandemonium erupted! The protesters were denounced as "maniacs," "paranoid fools," and "bitches." One physician is said to have shouted for police to shoot the protesters (Bayer 1981, 103). That such a deluge of hatred could explode against persons who were, by the Association's own official rubric, suffering from a mental disorder, caused the more sober minds at the meeting to realize the need for a reappraisal.

Fortunately, a desire for rational discourse prevailed. Gay advocates were invited to the next annual meeting. Gay and lesbian psychiatrists started "coming out," formed their own caucus within the APA, entered the association's political process, and sponsored their own scientific programs. Redefinitions of mental disorders during the preparation of DSM-III resulted, a little more than three years later, in dropping homosexuality from the diagnostic nomenclature (Bayer 1981).

I give this background to suggest the context in which a re-evaluation of theories of sexual orientation began to take place. Paradigms that undergo sudden shifts prompt new research questions. Do lesbians and gays always or even usually have "hostile fathers" and "seductive mothers," and do these parents in fact bring about an alteration of their child's sexual orientation? Is homosexuality caused by "incapacitating fears of the opposite sex"? If it is not a mental disorder, is it then a "normal" behavior? What does it mean to assert that heterosexuality is the "biologic norm"? And of course, the origin of heterosexuality itself is as little understood as that of homosexuality. These issues began to occupy the thinking of therapists and sex researchers alike (Green 1972; APA 1973; Bayer 1981).

Lovemaps

The questions just posed suggest that the study of homosexuality as a form of "psychopathologic deviance" should be superseded by a study of sexual desire more broadly considered. Recently, the term "lovemap" has come into use (Money 1986). A lovemap is the set of desires and activities that an individual finds most erotically stimulating. Thumbnail descriptions of lovemaps can be found in the Personals section of many newspapers. Personal ads seek individuals with features that, one assumes, would satisfy the erotic ideal, the lovemap, of the seeker. Variables such as gender, age, body size, distribution of body hair (for gay men), socioeconomic status (marked by education and vocation), personality, and preferred sexual activity seem to be salient variables in the lovemap of many, judging from the attributes often mentioned in advertisements. We await studies that will provide specific information about the frequency, durability, factor coherence, and cultural specificity or universality of various lovemaps. Until then we must rest with the impression that the gender of the partner is a salient feature of most individuals' sexual hierarchy of desire, although, to be sure, only one such feature.

Alfred Kinsey and his colleagues (1948, 1953) proposed that sexual orientation forms a continuum from heterosexual, through bisexual, to homosexual. Kinsey marked the continuum at seven arbitrary points beginning at 0 for those with exclusively heterosexual desire and behavior, and ending at 6, indicating exclusive homosexuality. Five intermediate points defined various degrees of bisexuality. Kinsey ratings capture the *relative* amount of homo/heterosexual behavior/activity during a defined period, for example, "past year," "adolescence," "lifetime," and so on. Kinsey scale ratings provide a simple way to indicate relative degrees of gender preference, the aspect of the lovemap referred to as "sexual orientation."

The frequency with which individuals fall at different points on the Kinsey scale has been estimated in several population surveys, including Kinsey's own massive project, which collected some 18,000 individual sex histories. Beyond adolescence, the great majority of men and women are exclusively heterosexual in fantasy and behavior; a minority are homosexual (perhaps 3 or 4 percent of men, and 1 or 2 percent of women); and a very small minority self-identify as bisexual, that is, they are attracted, in some proportion, to members of both sexes.[2] Thus, sexual orientation appears best described by a J-shaped frequency distribution, a fact bearing on genetic studies, to which I will return.

The Kinsey scale has become a standard metric in sex research, but Kinsey himself regarded homosexuality specifically as something people *do*, not something they *are*. He was, therefore, at pains to argue against orientation as an innate quality. Kinsey was a scrupulous worker, but his graphics are, in my opinion, misleading because they show *cumulative* frequencies, thus obscuring the true shape of the frequency distribution (see, for example, Figure 169, in Kinsey et al. 1948, 656).

Genes and Environment

Before presenting specific evidence favoring a genetic component to sexual orientation, some qualifications are in order. Few sex researchers believe that sexual orientation is entirely the product of genetic endowment. Among the facts that undercut a pure genetic hypothesis: many identical (monozygotic [MZ]) twins who presumably have identical genes also unquestionably have different orientations (one gay, one straight). This observation alone would require the inclusion of environment variables as part of a causal scheme. Further, we know examples from both human and animal research in which the effect of specific genes is modified by the presence of other genes as well as by the environment.

An example of gene/environment interaction in animals is provided by psychiatrist Myron Hofer (1994). Hofer's target is Herrnstein and Murray's *The Bell Curve*, but his comment is generally relevant:

> Novel environments can redefine even well-established genetic relationships. For example, when rats are selectively bred over 5 to 10 generations to perform a series of complex learning tasks poorly or well, the genetic contribution to the difference in the two groups on this measure of general intelligence is extremely high. But when the rearing environment is sub-

> stantially changed for both groups by increasing interaction and by providing a varied habitat, their differences in performance virtually disappear. . . . The enriched environment has led to remarkable increases in brain size—and in more recent studies, substantial increases in areas of nerve cells crucial for learning and memory. . . . Individual genes in the cells of the developing brain are in effect turned on and off in a complex pattern by signals from their immediate and distant environments. Genes in action, we have learned, are more like an information network than the static blueprints they were once likened to. (Hofer 1994)

Hofer reminds us that simply finding a gene or two associated with a particular trait is likely to be only one piece of the complex of genes, prenatal biology, and postnatal environment that sum or interact to form the final product: the individual phenotype.

Gender Atypicality

A good place to start the study of any behavior is with its natural history. A gay/lesbian or heterosexual orientation is often recognized by the individual in childhood. Many gays and lesbians recall their first same-sex attraction at an early age, often well before puberty. A comment from the sexual history of one gay man is typical: "I always knew I was different but I didn't understand how. I had feelings of attraction to other boys that my friends didn't seem to have. For a long time, I thought these feelings would go away and I'd start feeling sexual to girls but somehow—and it really worried me—that never happened." Accounts of same-sex erotic attraction beginning spontaneously at an early age and persisting through adolescence despite overwhelming negative reinforcement are found again and again in the sexual histories of gays and lesbians. For most people, sexual orientation *feels* innate.

A related observation is that many gay men and lesbian women were "gender atypical" in childhood. Descriptively, this means that gay men were often considered to be "sissy boys," and lesbian women were more often tomboys than their heterosexual counterparts. This relationship has been confirmed in prospective and retrospective studies (Green 1987; Bailey, Miller, Wilerman 1993; Bailey & Zucker 1995) as well as across cultures (Whitam 1983). Anyone observing gender-atypical children at play is struck by the pervasive and tenacious nature of this trait. Moreover, some gender-atypical children even *look* different. Kenneth Zucker and his colleagues gave photographs of gender-typical and atypical boys (Zucker et al. 1993) and girls (Fridell et al. 1996) to raters blind to any information about the children's behavior. The raters were simply asked to rate the children by their looks. They described the gender-atypical boys as "cuter," "prettier," and "more attractive" than the gender-typical boys, the obverse for the atypical girls. Apparently, in addition to their behavior, something in the physiognomy of these children marked them early as gender atypical. While a follow-up of these children has yet to be reported, what we know about the natural history of gender atypicality suggests they will be over-represented among gay and lesbian adults.

The term "gender atypicality" is chosen to avoid pre-judging whether the behaviors at issue are typically those of the other sex, and of course there are all sorts of gender atypicality, many ways that a child can feel "different" from other children. Still, the many studies of childhood gender behavior make clear that this trait is not just a matter of feeling lonely, isolated, different, or depressed. The feelings and behaviors are often strikingly and specifically those of the other sex (Pillard 1991).[3] A theory of the development of sexual orientation must take account of the robust and frequently replicated data on the coincidence of gender-atypical behavior in early childhood followed by same-sex attraction in adolescence and adulthood (for a skeptical view, see Bem 1996).

Sexual Orientation across Time and Culture

If sexual orientation were formed in response to reinforcements in the social milieu, one would expect that the incidence of homosexuality would be dramatically increasing during the past thirty years as it has become more widely known and better tolerated. Homophobia remains a powerful disincentive, but no one can argue that being lesbian or gay is not more acceptable now than a decade ago and far more accepted then than it was before Stonewall. From a demographic point of view, the stability of population prevalence rates across the Kinsey scale is striking. Despite differences in definition and methodology, recent estimates of gay/lesbian behavior are very close to the Kinsey survey a half century ago (Rogers & Turner 1991; Diamond 1993; Seidman & Rieder 1994; Laumann et al. 1994). One can cite any number of behaviors that fluctuate with the times: cigarette smoking falls, teenage pregnancies rise. Social influence is surely powerful in many domains, but apparently not in this one; there is simply no evidence that social approval or disapproval has affected the rate of homosexuality in the U.S.

Stoller and Herdt's 1985 study of ritual fellatio among the Sambia people of New Guinea adds another dimension. Sambian pre-adolescent boys are required to perform fellatio on older members of the tribe and imbibe quantities of semen so as to grow to virile manhood. If sexual orientation developed as a conditional response to contexts of teenage orgasm, Sambian men should be mostly gay. But they are not. Boys grow up, leave the boys' hut, court and marry women, have erotic desire for women even though their early sexual activity had been exclusively homosexual. Any clinician can find in her/his practice examples, perhaps less dramatic, of men and women whose early sexual activity was confined to members of one sex, yet who later found their truest erotic fulfillment with the other sex. A simple learning or conditioning paradigm cannot account for these observations.

Homosexual behavior among animals is frequently observed but difficult to integrate with the human data. For many years, such behavior was thought to be the product of a caged, restricted environment, to be play behavior, or to be directed toward non-sexual aims, such as to establish dominance. But as more observations come from the wild, it is clear that same-sex interactions are part of the natural repertoire of many species. Animals may show unambiguous homosexual partner choice and even compete for same-sex partners. Vasey (1995) proposes that homosexual adaptations may have a long evolutionary history, though their precise function remains unknown.

In summary, the comments above are offered to bolster the thesis that human sexual orientation has a "built-in" quality. There seems to be a fundamental bias toward either a heterosexual or a homosexual developmental path, prefigured early in life, neither taught nor learned, and profoundly resistant to modification. It exists recognizably in a variety of animal species and human cultures from diverse times and places. There are stylistic variations of course, and they are properly of great interest to social scientists, but looking broadly, one is also struck by the universal features in accounts of same-sex desire from pre-Christian Greece (Lucian 1931) to nineteenth-century Germany (Ulrichs 1994), from the Plains Indians of the western U.S. (Williams 1986) to China (Ruan 1991) and Japan (Hinsch 1990)). Call me a reductionist, but read the cited accounts before you do.

Genetic Evidence

I now review more traditional genetic evidence from family, twin, and adoptee studies. Families with unusual numbers of gay members were described by Magnus Hirschfeld (1936) more than sixty years ago, but systematic family studies are only a decade old. A genetic hypothesis virtually requires that being gay and lesbian should run in families. All modern family studies show that this is true. Randomly recruited gay men have from two to five times as many gay brothers as a similar group of heterosexual men (Pillard et al. 1981, 1982; Pillard & Weinrich 1986; Hamer et al. 1993; Bailey & Bell 1993). Family studies of lesbian probands also find unusual numbers of lesbian sisters (Pillard 1988; Bailey & Benishay 1993; Bailey & Bell 1993). Cross-gender familiality, that is, families with an excess of both gay brothers and lesbian sisters, is a subject needing more investigation.

Critics will note that many behavior characteristics—going to mass, wearing an obi, eating feijoada—are familial more for cultural than for genetic reasons. And indeed, heritability calculations will show that those habits are attributable to the shared environment, not to genes. The relative genetic and environmental contributions to a behavioral trait can be estimated from twin/adoptee studies, to which we now turn.

Research comparing the concordance of a trait in MZ twins, fraternal (dizygotic [DZ]) twins, non-twin siblings, and adoptees into the family at an early age, permit an estimate of the relative amounts of variance accounted for by genes and by environment—at least for the sample under study. The logic is straightforward. If the variance due to genetic endowment is large, MZ twins will frequently be concordant (both possessing the trait), DZ twins will be concordant only as often as non-twin brothers (something like half as often as MZ twins), while adopted siblings will share the trait no more often than a random draw of the population. If the intrauterine environment is influential (a congenital as opposed to a genetic influence), DZ twins will be more often concordant than non-twin siblings.

Environment variance, in turn, can be partitioned into "shared" and "unshared" portions. The shared environment includes everything the siblings have in common: same town, same parents, same school, and so on. Unshared environment, on the other hand, encompasses events that the siblings do not share: one takes piano lessons, the other goes to summer camp. A shared environment influence is reflected in the degree to which all members of a family share the trait in question. Realistically, one expects each source of variance—genes, shared and unshared environment—to exert some influence. Calculations derived from trait concordance frequencies in twins, non-twin siblings, and adoptees, permit us to assign a portion of variance to each category. In the cited twin/adoptee studies, *about half* the variance in sexual orientation for both sexes was attributable to genes, the rest to environment, and, of that, almost all to the *unshared* environment (Bailey & Pillard 1991; Bailey, Pillard, et al. 1993).

The reader should be warned that heritability is a tricky concept. One might think that having two arms and two legs would be a strongly heritable trait, but a heritability calculation does not support that intuition. This is because there is hardly any variance in "limbedness," and what there is tends to be due to events in the environment, such as accidents, rather than to genes.

It might, however, be true that the heritability of sexual orientation is inflated by an artifact: a failure of the "equal environments" assumption. Heritability calculations arbitrarily assume that members of the same family share an environment to about the same extent. But MZ twins, sometimes nearly indistinguishable, are more likely to be treated by friends and family almost as one person, in contrast to the more differentiated treatment accorded other siblings; thus, the observed concordance of MZ twins could be due not to their identical genes, but to the extraordinary sameness of their social milieu. The equal environments assumption has been tested for a variety of traits, though not for sexual orientation. Twins treated alike (same dress, same schools, similar names) have been compared with twins whose families made a conscious effort to individuate them. It turns out that on a variety of traits, the "treated alike" twins and the "treated differently" twins have the same concordance rates. The similar sexual orientation of many MZ twin pairs might still result from some unguessed and uncontrolled similarity in their milieu, but the evidence to support that contention is lacking.

A more persuasive test of gene effects would be to examine MZ twins separated at or near birth and raised apart in radically different environments. This research is being done in the Minnesota Twin Study (Bouchard et al. 1990). The Minnesota twins, as is now widely known, though raised apart, were found to share many astonishing similarities, from details of personal adornment (same hairstyles, type of eye glasses, number of rings, type and color of clothing) to personal quirks (flushing the toilet before urinating, wearing rubber bands on the wrist) to similar personality traits.

The sexual orientation of separated MZ twins has been examined in those few examples of twins separated in infancy where at least one has become a gay adult. Eckert et al. (1986) identified two male MZ pairs raised apart and reunited for the Minnesota study. One pair was remarkably alike. Both twins had an almost exclusive homosexual orientation as well as other similar personality traits. A second pair included one substantially homosexual twin (Kinsey 5), and the other, though married and labeling himself heterosexual, had engaged in more than casual homosexual experience (Kinsey 2). Whitam et al. (1993) added two male pairs raised apart, one pair concordant (both gay) and one discordant. Altogether, only these four pairs have been reported, but two were concordant for homosexuality, one mixed, and one discordant—about the same outcome that we observed among the MZ twins raised together. On the other hand, Eckert et al. (1986) also reported four pairs of female twins, all of whom were *discordant.*

Even these unusual examples of separated twins, as persuasive as they may be, are not perfect experiments of nature. The best "experiment" requires random assignment of environments; however, adoption agencies try to do the opposite, to place adoptees in families as alike as possible to their biological parents. Who knows whether some subtle feature of the environment, relevant to sexual orientation, is thereby imperfectly controlled?

Another powerful strategy to identify genetic components in behavior is the cross-fostering study. Traits known to pass down the generations can be identified in children adopted away from their biological parents. Both the adoptive and biological parents must then be assessed. If the trait is found more often in the adoptive parents, cultural transmission is implicated; if in the biological parents, a genetic influence is suggested. The study of half-siblings also helps to identify traits carried in the maternal versus the paternal line. Cross-fostering studies are labor intensive, and so far, none has been done for sexual orientation.

Gene Linkage

The research strategies so far mentioned may be useful to judge whether a given trait has a probability of being genetically transmitted, and perhaps something can be guessed about the nature of the gene, whether dominant or recessive, sex-linked or autosomal, highly penetrant or not. But family studies neither implicate a particular gene nor define its mode of action. Molecular biologists now have the means to locate a gene using linkage with gene markers. Linkage is simply a statistical relationship between a stretch of polymorphic DNA (a marker) and a physical or psychological trait of interest to the researcher. DNA is obtained in blood samples from informative family members, gay brothers for example. The marker can be any piece of DNA that is sufficiently variable from person to person; pieces of DNA that are the same in everybody cannot, of course, be informative as markers. The task is to sort through hundreds (or thousands) of markers to find those the gay brothers share and, ideally, that heterosexual brothers do not share. Two brothers, gay or not, will share a lot of markers, a random half of them in fact, but when gay brother pairs are cumulated, the researcher may discover "hot spots": DNA segments that the gay brothers have in common more often than chance predicts. Heterosexual brothers are useful too in that they ought *not* to share with the gay brother a marker at the putative linkage site. Markers are not the genes of interest, but if they are close enough, the researcher can employ more specific methods to sequence the gene region.

If a trait is known to be transmitted in the maternal lineage, so-called "enate" transmission, it may be sex-linked. Genes for sex-linked traits reside on the X chromosome (as contrasted with a sex-limited trait that resides on an autosome but is expressed only in one sex), so the search for them is greatly simplified. The possibility that some instances of male homosexuality could be sex-linked was suggested by data from the volume *Sex Variants* published by George Henry (1941). He presented pedigrees of "sex variants," many of whom appear to be gay men. The identified gay relatives were more often on the mother's side of the family. Our study of sexual orientation in families produced similar data (Pillard et al. 1981).

Dean Hamer and his colleagues (1993) independently observed enate transmission. The Hamer team examined DNA from families with two gay brothers and looked along the X chromosome for DNA markers common to both brothers. Each son gets one of mother's X chromosomes at random, so the chance of both brothers getting the same chromosome (or the piece of it containing the relevant gene) is 50 percent. The chance of a second pair of gay brothers sharing a marker at the same locus is one in four (one half times one half), the probability generated by flipping pairs of coins. To build a statistically convincing case, the pairs of coins (markers) need to be the same (both heads or both tails) more often than chance predicts, a binomial probability function. Hamer's sample included 40 pairs of brothers: 33 of these brother pairs had similar DNA markers in the Xq28 region while 7 had different markers—a highly significant outcome. Hu et al. (1995) replicated the study and included some heterosexual brothers who ought to have *different* DNA markers in the Xq28 region, and in most cases, they did. No linkage at Xq28 was found for pairs of lesbian sisters. A "gay gene" has, therefore, not been found. At most, a marker has been identified in the neighborhood of that gene. Also note that only families with a prior probability of enate transmission were studied. Further replication is needed; one report *excluded* linkage everywhere on the X chromosome (Rice et al. 1995).

A molecular biology approach has appeal as a rational way to sort behavior. The identification of a gene predisposing to a particular sexual behavior would help us to understand, for example, whether the ten-year-old Mohave boy seeking to become a berdache is expressing in his behavior the same genetic prompting as an eighteenth-century London sapphist (Herdt 1994). To achieve this research objective, many subjects and their informative family members must be recruited to generate the statistical power to locate a candidate gene. Once found, the gene must be cloned and its location and the mechanism of its expression discovered. Similar traits may arise from different genes, that is, similar phenotypes from different genotypes. Linkage findings are often not replicated and, at this writing, no one has come close to finding or cloning a "gay gene." Interacting environmental influences, presumably substantial in any behavior trait, are unknown for sexual orientation and difficult to study since the relevant influences may be active early in life while the outcome, a defined sexual orientation, may not appear for decades.

There is, however, at least one advantage for the geneticist who wishes to study sexual orientation and its relatively binary nature as mentioned above. Most personality traits follow bell-shaped distribution (that is, are normally distributed). In order to maximize the chance of finding a contrast, the researcher studying intelligence, aggressiveness, shyness, and so on, will probably choose those subjects lying at the distribution tails; unfortunately for the researcher, these are low frequency individuals. Sexual orientation, on the other hand, tends to be bimodal; it comes closer to being an either/or trait. Yes, there are bisexuals, but *most* adults are pretty clearly either gay or straight. Working with an unambiguously defined phenotype is a huge advantage to any research endeavor (for an extended discussion, see Bailey, in press).

The Future of Sexual Orientation Research

The genetic analysis of behavior will prove to be, in my opinion, the most important advance in the behavioral sciences in my lifetime. A major impetus in this direction has been the study of drug effects on mental disorders. Psychiatric symptoms such as dysphoric moods and disordered thinking have been related to alterations in brain neurochemistry. Some of these alterations have been found to be familial and, ultimately, genetic. More complex "normal" behavior patterns are now the subject of similar study. As one example, Jerome Kagan and his colleagues (1988) studied extremely shy children and their counterparts, children who were relaxed extroverts. This trait continuum can be identified in the earliest months of infancy; it persists through childhood and into adulthood with remarkable consistency. Kagan found familial patterns and he suggests a genetic basis for the shyness-extroversion axis. Treatment trials now show that medication may alter the expression of the shyness trait, although social therapies may be effective as well. Most researchers now think that there is a "wired in" component to much of what we used to believe were wholly learned behaviors. Language acquisition, musical ability, attention, memory, addictive drug seeking (a behavior with an excellent analogue in laboratory animals), intelligence, and the predisposition to impulsive violence are some of the traits for which there is evidence for an innate predisposition.

It seems plausible to me that human sexual attraction, a trait that must have been subject to strong evolutionary pressure, is also likely to be powerfully influenced by an innate, inherited predisposition. The data presented above support this hypothesis. Social influences are not dismissed; indeed, the fascination of this research is precisely to study a trait across levels of organization, from intracellular events to the formation of nuclei and neuronal pathways (including the effect of the prenatal environment), to familial and societal influences, all contributing to shape the final product, in this case, the lovemap of each individual.

This view of human behavior may seem pessimistic inasmuch as it reserves a large place for biologic forces, over which we do not have much control. On the other hand, as we become able to control genetic outcomes, will we put this knowledge to wise use? I suppose most parents would not choose to have a gay child if they could choose otherwise. Fortunately, that choice is not at hand, but similar choices are. Deafness will soon be an example. Deafness is frequently genetic; approximately thirty different genetic loci for deafness have been hypothesized. Many people see deafness simply as a "handicap" and could not imagine the slightest objection to reducing or eliminating it. But those born deaf have a linguistic and cultural community, as precious to them as the gay community is to gays. The deaf, not surprisingly, want control of their culture and resent the imperialistic assumptions of the hearing majority (Lane 1992).

One problem with the exercise of genetic choice is that we do not know how to do so in a manner beneficial to long-term survival. As an example, if prospective parents were allowed to choose one attribute for their children, that attribute might well be "intelligence." A high IQ surely predicts wealth and status, but nobody can argue that being brainy is, *a priori*, a survival trait for our species. If intelligence predicted survival, gorillas would be flourishing and cockroaches would be on the verge of extinction. Lovejoy (1981) argues that humans evolved a unique pattern of sexual bonding and parenting that accounts for the proliferation of *homo sapiens* in contrast to our dwindling primate cousins. Many of us believe this proliferation has itself become our greatest potential hazard. It may be that genetic research in sexuality will provide an understanding of the dynamics of population growth and promote our long-term survival by guiding us to avoid reckless reproductive competition.

I have said nothing about the presumed evolutionary implications of "gay genes" because, given the uncertainty of their existence, one can hardly speculate about what they do. Yet here, I think, may be the antidote to a Luddite rejection of genetic technology. Everything we know about the survival of living things points to the advantage of flexible adaptation to an ever-changing environment (Williams 1975). Genetic variability is the substrate of adaptation and conversely, genetic homogeneity is a ticket to extinction—as the fate of the wild cheetah may now be illustrating.[4] Therefore, our present understanding of genetics suggests this axiom: Preserve genetic diversity wherever we can. The hope is that this point of view will take root before the exploitation of gene technology plunges us into an orgy of unthinking destruction of genetic potential.

Notes

[1] Freud's daughter, Anna Freud, herself a distinguished psychoanalyst and her father's alter ego and intellectual heir, never married and never had a romantic attachment with a man. In 1925, she met an American divorcee, Dorothy Burlingham, daughter of Louis Comfort Tiffany. The two women worked and lived together for more than fifty years.

[2] Women appear to be bisexual relatively more often than men.

[3] Though with some interesting exceptions: gender-*atypical* boys do not often show the interest in "mothering" younger children seen in gender-*typical* girls.

[4] Inbreeding depression results from loss of heterozygote superiority as well as the exposure of deleterious recessives.

References

American Psychiatric Association. 1952. *Diagnostic and Statistical Manual of Mental Disorders.* Washington.

———. 1968. *Diagnostic and Statistical Manual of Mental Disorders. DSM-II.* Washington.

———. 1973. Symposium: Should homosexuality be in the APA nomenclature? *American Journal of Psychiatry* 130:1207–1216.

Bailey, J. M. (In press). Can behavior contribute to evolutionary behavioral science? In *Evolution and Human Behavior: Ideas, Issues, and Applications*, ed. Crawford and Krebs. Mahwah, NH: Lawrence Erlbaum.

Bailey, J. M., and A. P. Bell. 1993. Familiality of female and male homosexuality. *Behavior Genetics* 23:313–720.

Bailey, J. M., and D. Benishay. 1993. Familial aggregation of female sexual orientation. *American Journal of Psychiatry* 150:272–277.

———. 1993. Familial aggregation of female sexual orientation. *American Journal of Psychiatry* 150:272–277.

Bailey, J. M., J. S. Miller, and L. Willerman. 1993. Maternally rated childhood gender nonconformity in homosexuals and heterosexuals. *Archives of Sexual Behavior* 22:461–469.

Bailey, J. M., and R. C. Pillard. 1991. A genetic study of male sexual orientation. *Archives of General Psychiatry* 48:1089–1096.

Bailey, J. M., R. C. Pillard, M. C. Neale, and M. A. Agyei. 1993. Heritable factors influence sexual orientation in women. *Archives of General Psychiatry* 50:217–223.

Bailey, J. M., and K. J. Zucker. 1995. Childhood sex-typed behavior and sexual orientation: A conceptual analysis and quantitative review. *Developmental Psychology* 31:43–45.

Bayer, R. 1981. *Homosexuality and American Psychiatry.* New York: Basic.

Bem, D. J. 1996. Exotic becomes erotic: A developmental theory of sexual orientation. *Psychological Review* 103:320–335.

Bergler, E. 1956. *Homosexuality: Disease or Way of Life.* New York: Hill & Wang.

Bieber, I., H. Dain, P. Dince, M. G. Drellich, H. G. Grand, R. H. Grundlach, M. W. Kremer, A. H. Rifkin, C. B. Wilbur, and T. B. Bieber. 1962. *Homosexuality: A Psychoanalytic Study of Male Homosexuals.* New York: Basic.

Bouchard, T. J., D. T. Lykken, M. McGue, N. L. Segal, and A. Tellegen. 1990. Sources of human psychological differences: The Minnesota study of twins reared apart. *Science* 250:223–228.

Diamond, M. 1993. Homosexuality and bisexuality in different populations. *Archives of Sexual Behavior* 32:291–310.

Duberman, M. 1991. *Cures: A Gay Man's Odyssey*. New York: Dutton.

Eckert, E. D., T. J. Bouchard, J. Bohler, L. L. Heston. 1986. Homosexuality in monozygotic twins reared apart. *British Journal of Psychiatry* 148:421–425.

Ellis, H. [1897] 1922. *Studies in the Psychology of Sex*. Vol. II. *Sexual Inversion*. Philadelphia: F. A. Davis.

Freud, S. 1903. Letter. *Die Zeit* (Vienna) (27 October): 5.

———. [1922] 1959. The pathogenesis of a case of homosexuality in a woman. In *Collected Papers*, ed. J. Rivière, II:202–231. New York: Basic.

Fridell, S. R., K. J. Zucker, S. J. Bradley, and D. M. Maing. 1996. Physical attractiveness of girls with gender identity disorder. *Archives of Sexual Behavior* 25:17–31.

Gittings, B. 1973. *Gay, Proud and Healthy*. Philadelphia: Gay Activists Alliance.

Gonsiorek, J. C., and J. D. Weinrich, eds. 1991. *Homosexuality: Research Implications for Public Policy*. Newbury Park: Sage.

Green, R. 1972. Homosexuality as a mental illness. *International Journal of Psychiatry* 10:77–98.

———. 1987. *The "Sissy Boy Syndrome" and the Development of Homosexuality*. New Haven: Yale University Press.

Hamer, D. H., S. Hu, V. L. Magnuson, N. Hu, and A. M. L. Pattatucci. 1993. A linkage between DNA markers on the X chromosome and male sexual orientation. *Science* 261:321–327.

Hatterer, L. 1970. *Changing Homosexuality in the Male*. New York: McGraw-Hill.

Herdt, G., ed. 1994. *Third Sex, Third Gender: Beyond Sexual Dimorphism in Culture and History*. New York: Zone.

Henry, G. W. 1941. *Sex Variants: A Study of Homosexual Patterns*. New York: Paul B. Hoeber.

Hinch, B. 1990. *Passions of the Cut Sleeve*. Berkeley: University of California Press.

Hirschfeld, M. 1936. Homosexuality. In *Encyclopædia Sexualis*, ed. I. Bloch and M. Hirschfeld, 321–334. New York: Dingwall-Rock.

Hofer, M. A. 1994. Behind the curve. *New York Times* (26 December): 39.

Hu, S., A. M. L. Pattatucci, C. Patterson, L. Li, D. W. Fulker, S. S. Cherny, L. Kruglyak, and D. H. Hamer. 1995. Linkage between Xq28 and sexual orientation in males but not in females. *Nature Genetics* 11:248–256.

Kagan, R., J. S. Reznick, and N. Snidman. 1988. Biological basis of childhood shyness. *Science* 240:167–171.

Kinsey, A. C., W. B. Pomeroy, and C. E. Martin. 1948. *Sexual Behavior in the Human Male*. Philadelphia: W. B. Saunders.

Kinsey, A. C., W. B. Pomeroy, C. E. Martin, and P. H. Gebhard. 1953. *Sexual Behavior in the Human Female*. Philadelphia: W. B. Saunders.

Lane, Harlan. 1992. *The Mask of Benevolence. Disabling the Deaf Community*. New York: Knopf.

Laumann, E. O., J. H. Gagnon, R. T. Michael, and S. Michaels. 1994. *The Social Organization of Sexuality: Sexual Practices in the United States*. Chicago: University of Chicago Press.

Lewes, Kenneth. 1988. *The Psychoanalytic Theory of Male Homosexuality*. New York: Simon & Schuster.

Lovejoy, C. O. 1981. The origin of man. *Science* 211:341–350.

Lucian. 1931. *The Mimes of the Courtesans*. New York: Rarity Press.

Money, J. 1986. *Lovemaps*. New York: Irvington.

Pillard, R. C. 1982. Psychotherapeutic treatment for the invisible minority. In *Homosexuality: Social, Psychological, and Biological Issues*, ed. W. Paul, J. D. Weinrich, J. C. Gonsiorek, and M. E. Hotvedt. Beverly Hills: Sage.

———. 1988. Sexual orientation and mental disorders. *Psychiatric Annals* 18:52–56.

———. 1991. Masculinity and femininity in homosexuality: "Inversion" revisited. In *Homosexuality: Research Findings for Public Policy*, ed. J. C. Gonsiorek and J. D. Weinrich, 32–43. Newbury Park: Sage.

Pillard, R. C., J. Poumadere, and R. A. Caretta. 1981. Is homosexuality familial? A review, some data, and a suggestion. *Archives of Sexual Behavior* 10:465–475.

———. 1982. A familial study of sexual orientation. *Archives of Sexual Behavior* 11:511–520.

Pillard, R. C., and J. D. Weinrich. 1986. Evidence of familial nature of male homosexuality. *Archives of General Psychiatry* 43:808–812.

Rado, S. 1940. A critical examination of the concept of bisexuality. *Psychosomatic Medicine* 2:459–467.

Rice, G., C. Anderson, N. Risch, and G. Ebers. 1995. Male homosexuality: Absence of linkage to micro satellite markers on the X-chromosome in a Canadian study. Abstract. International Academy of Sex Research, Annual Meeting, Provincetown.

Rogers, S. M., and C. F. Turner. 1991. Male-male sexual contact in the U.S.A.: Findings from five sample surveys, 1970–1990. *Journal of Sex Research* 28:491–519.

Ruan, F.-F. 1991. *Sex in China*. New York: Plenum.

Seidman, S. N., and R. O. Rieder. 1994. Review of *Sexual Behavior in the United States*. *American Journal of Psychiatry* 151:330–341.

Silverberg, W. 1938. The personal basis and significance of passive male homosexuality. *Psychiatry* 1:41–53.

Socarides, C. 1972. A masquerade of life. *International Journal of Psychiatry* 10:18.

———. 1978. *Homosexuality*. New York: Aronson.

Stoller, R. J., G. Herdt. 1985. Theories of the origins of male homosexuality: A cross-cultural look. *Archives of General Psychiatry* 42:399–404.

Ulrichs, K. H. [1864–79] 1994. *The Riddle of "Man-Manly" Love*. 2 vols. Buffalo: Prometheus.

Vasey, P. L. 1995. Homosexual behavior in primates: A review of evidence and theory. *International Journal of Primatology* 16:173–204.

Voth, H. 1971. Homosexuality. *Psychiatric News* (17 March).

Whitam, F. L. 1983. Culturally invariable properties of male homosexuality: Tentative conclusions from cross-cultural research. *Archives of Sexual Behavior* 12:207–226.

Whitam, F. L., M. Diamond, and J. Martin. 1993. Homosexual orientation in twins: A report of 61 pairs and three triplet sets. *Archives of Sexual Behavior* 22:187–206.

Williams, G. C. 1975. *Sex and Evolution*. Princeton: Princeton University Press.

Williams, W. L. 1986. *The Spirit and the Flesh: Sexual Diversity in American Indian Culture*. Boston: Beacon.

Zucker, K. J., J. Wild, S. J. Bradley, and C. B. Lowry. 1993. Physical attractiveness of boys with gender identity disorder. *Archives of Sexual Behavior* 22:23–36.

The Double-Edged Sword of Genetic Determinism

Social and Political Agendas in Genetic Studies of Homosexuality, 1940–1994

Garland E. Allen

In Jonathan Tollins's 1993 play, *The Twilight of the Golds*, a pregnant woman and her husband face the decision of whether or not to abort a fetus that has been identified genetically as a "homosexual." The decision is complicated by the fact that the mother's own brother is gay, and he has vowed never to see her again if the couple decides on abortion. Although supposedly set in "the very near future," the play deals with a theme that has received considerable public exposure in the last several years. Growing claims that a wide variety of personality and behavioral traits are genetic in origin—a view known by its critics as *biological determinism*—have become increasingly prominent in both scientific and lay circles. Combined with publicity flowing from the Human Genome Project claiming that genetic "diseases" can be detected early in pregnancy, and that afflicted fetuses can either be aborted or else "cured" through drug, hormone, or gene therapy, the Golds's situation presents a major ethical dilemma. Even UCLA neurobiologist Roger Gorski, who believes strongly that male and female brains are hardwired for gender roles, has remarked that "[t]here is something reductive and scary about a situation in which you *might* be able to ask a mother whether she wants testosterone treatment to avoid having a homosexual son" (qtd. in Longino 1990, 169).

Research on the genetic basis of many human personality and behavioral traits has been the object of a blitz of popular media presentations in recent years. The nation's most widely circulating magazines and newspapers have let loose a barrage of articles and cover stories claiming that scientists now have good evidence that criminality, alcoholism, manic depression, schizophrenia, shyness, general personality, male/female gender-role differences, and infidelity are largely genetic in origin.[1]

In this highly determinist *milieu*, particular prominence has been given to claims that sexual orientation—meaning, mostly, homosexuality—is also genetically based. In 1991 a paper in *Science* by openly gay, Salk Institute neurobiologist Simon LeVay claimed to have found a noticeable difference between gay and straight men in the volume of an area of the brain (the medial preoptic region of the hypothalamus, which regulates general metabolism along with aspects of sexual behavior). That work was highly publicized in the popular media and was the subject of a book by LeVay, *The Sexual Brain*, published by MIT Press in 1993. Even more prominent, in some respects, was the attention given to a report in the July 16, 1993, issue of *Science* by Dean Hamer and his coworkers at the National Cancer Institute/National Institutes of Health (NIH). Soberly titled, "A Linkage Between DNA Markers on the X Chromosome and Male Sexual Orientation," Hamer's report claimed that homosexual behavior in 33 out of 40 pairs of brothers was linked to a specific DNA region on the X chromosome. Perhaps not coincidentally, the Hamer study appeared in *Science* the very week that Congress was to vote on the issue of gays in the military. In a television interview, Hamer admitted that he hoped the work would eventually lead to a more accepting attitude toward homosexuality. He also vowed to patent his genetic testing techniques to insure that they could not be used in a discriminatory way.

But how realistic is this goal? What kind of science is being invoked? If scientific concepts are themselves socially constructed, as more and more people both inside and outside the scientific community recognize, what is the evidence that these concepts can be counted on to radically alter prevailing social attitudes? Historically, what kind of track record do biological theories—particularly genetic—have in expanding human rights? Furthermore, is it even philosophically valid for acceptance or rejection of any particular human behavior, or for the status of a minority group, to ride on demonstrating its biological or genetic basis?

I cannot answer all of these questions in the space of one essay, but I would like to address four major points:

(1) Attempts to demonstrate a genetic basis for complex human behavioral or personality traits have had a long and sad scientific history, from the early nineteenth through the whole of the twentieth century. None of the claims has ever withstood close scrutiny.

(2) Despite differences in subject matter or historical period, theories of genetic determinism have shared a variety of methodological pitfalls that recur time and time again, despite clear and overt criticism. It is as if these theories have had no history.

(3) Despite their often flimsy basis, genetic determinist views have repeatedly been given full coverage in the popular media of their day. Hamer's work, for example, was headlined as evidence for a "Homosexuality Gene," and LeVay's claims were promulgated as evidence for "the gay brain." Scientists themselves often contribute to this sensationalism, which, for obvious reasons, the press has been quick to pick up. But even if the researchers are publicly cautious, media hype usually involves considerable oversimplification and hyperbole.

(4) Theories of genetic determinism have had a double-edged history: they have more often led to restricting human opportunity (that is, telling people what their limitations are) than to enhancing it; more often to reinforcing cultural prejudices than to overriding them.

My aim in looking at this issue stems from several sources. In part it grows out of my research on the history of genetics and eugenics in the early twentieth century, when virtually all of the same personality traits being touted today were also claimed to arise from genetic causes. History has shown where such ideas, based on science that was often naïve and simplistic even for its own day, have led. It is time we got beyond the foolishly conceived and ultimately meaningless *nature-nurture* argument and the mechanistic view of genetics that it reflects. In what is increasingly realized to be the "age of genetics," it is clearly important to gain a more sophisticated view of what genes do—how they function in human development. This means understanding the limitations as well as strengths of genetics as a field.

Another motivation is to put the history and philosophy of science to good use in dealing with pressing issues in our modern world. As Marx exhorted, "Philosophers have only interpreted the world; the point, however, is to change it" (1888, 245). Historians and philosophers of science are in a strong position to change the way we—all of us, academic and nonacademic alike—understand and interpret claims about the genetic bases of our behavior. More important, historians and philosophers of science can help elucidate the complex of economic and social forces that lie behind the periodic recurrence of these ideas in both the scientific and public arenas. At the present time, for example, we face a challenge to help clarify some of the issues that surround claims regarding the genetic basis of sexual orientation, especially when such claims are being invoked in legislative battles over the constitutionality of laws that would exclude gays, lesbians, and bisexuals from protection against discrimination—for instance, the bitter struggles over Amendment 2 in Colorado in 1992 to 1994, or similar measures in Oregon and Idaho in 1994 and 1995. Given the recent turn of political events after the November 1994 elections, and the greatly increased conservative majority in Congress and elsewhere, we are likely to have more, rather than less, of these issues to face. I think my own and others' experiences can help avoid the pitfalls that have come up again and again in attempts to derive solutions to social or political problems from biological findings. Moreover, because current theories go far beyond homosexuality to include a large number of other personality traits, the present mood of biological determinism will likely touch us all in very important political, social, and economic ways in the not-too-distant future.

Historical Background

The history of genetic studies of homosexuality in this century can be roughly divided into two periods: pre-1973 and post-1973. In 1973, largely in response to growing pressure from gay activists, along with a reform movement within psychiatry itself, homosexuality was removed from the *Diagnostic and Statistical Manual II* (DSM-II), the psychiatric profession's handbook of recognized pathological behaviors (Bayer 1987). An important social stimulus for this change seems to have been the Stonewall riots of 1969 in New York, in which the gay community fought back openly against police harassment and brutality.[2] Thus homosexuality has been unique, among all the personality or behavioral traits that have been the subject of genetic studies during this century, in having officially made a transition from disease to nondisease status. While this change in status has altered the aims of some of those who have continued to argue for a genetic basis for homosexuality, it has not significantly improved the quality of the research or the cultural context in which the work is carried out.

In the pre-1973 period, at least in the United States, explanations of homosexuality focused largely on psychiatric/psychological causes, linking the occurrence of homosexual behavior to one or another aspect of family dysfunction (for example, close-binding mother and/or distant father for male homosexuality [Bieber 1965]). For the most part, homosexuality was thought to be *caused* by social, not biological factors. At the same time, as we will see shortly, throughout the twentieth century biological explanations were never completely absent, and in some periods—for example, the 1930s and 1940s—they gained a certain prominence with regard to the finding of supposed hormonal imbalances among homosexuals. Since the hormonal story is being discussed by Stephanie Kenen in this anthology, I will review briefly the genetic studies that appeared, albeit infrequently, during the pre-1973 period.

Genetic Studies of Homosexuality, 1900–1940

Given the prominence of the eugenics movement in the United States in the first three decades of the twentieth century, and its strong hereditarian claims for a wide variety of social behaviors, we might have expected that homosexuality would have figured among its objects of study. In fact, such was not the case. Eugenics, inspired by Francis Galton in England, was a movement that sought to study that which

> is good in stock, hereditarily endowed with noble qualities. [Eugenics] takes cognizance of all influences that tend in however remote a degree to give to the more suitable races or strains of blood a better chance of prevailing speedily over the less suitable than they would have had. (Galton 1883, 24–25)

Although eugenicists did not ignore sexuality as a topic, they did not pay special attention to homosexuality as a specific phenotype. For example, Charles B. Davenport, dean of American eugenicists, in his elaborate catalog of human hereditary conditions, *The Trait Book* (1919), included a whole category labeled "Constitutional Psychopathic State" (category 317), under which homosexuality is indexed as number 31761, along with a variety of other sexual pathologies (nymphomania, promiscuity, fetishism, bestiality, masochism), but is not given any special prominence (1919, 48). Contemporaneous work in Germany, from the classic studies of Richard von Krafft-Ebing in the 1880s to those of Magnus Hirschfeld (1936) in the first three decades of the twentieth century, assumed some innate biological cause of homosexuality, particularly physiological (hormonal). That hormonal imbalances could be caused by genetic factors (point mutations or chromosomal aberrations) was recognized by some investigators, but there was little evidence for such mechanisms at the time. Except for the Nazi period in Germany, overtly biological explanations for homosexuality in Europe and the United States took a back seat to Freudian-based psychodynamic theory from the 1910s through the late 1960s. All the while, however, homosexuality was regarded as a pathology to be cured if possible by such techniques as intensive psychotherapy, electric shock, or operant conditioning. In some European countries and most U.S. states, homosexuality remained a criminal activity as well.

There were, however, some direct claims for a genetic basis of homosexuality. One such theory was put forward in the early 1940s by Thomas Lang on the basis of studies of sex ratios in families of known male homosexuals in Germany (1945, 51–52). Lang's claim reflected his theory that male homosexuals were sex intergrades, chromosomal females in outwardly male bodies. If this were true, he reasoned, then the sex ratios in families with gay males ought to be skewed toward a higher-than-normal male-to-female ratio. In 1,015 families that he surveyed, Lang found a ratio of 121 males to 100 females, well above the average of 100 to 105 for the population at large. The theory was tested by C.M.B. Pare (1956), a psychiatric consultant at London's St. Bartholomew's Hospital. Pare used cytogenetic analysis of 50 gay men, compared to 25 non-gay men and 25 women. In all cases he found no chromosomal abnormalities in the XY pair (Pare 1956; see also a subsequent review by Pare 1965, 73–74). Pritchard (1962) also confirmed Pare's findings. Thus, prewar attempts to uncover any genetic links to homosexuality were both sparse and nonconclusive.

Enter Twin Studies: Franz Kallmann and the Eugenic Connection

Although most American eugenicists did not concern themselves directly with homosexuality, an émigré Austrian psychiatrist with a long history of interest in the eugenic treatment of mental illness clearly did. Franz Kallmann was born in Vienna, and worked much of the early part of his career (until 1938) in Berlin under his mentor, racial hygienist and psychiatrist Ernst Rüdin. In 1904 Rüdin described homosexuals as a "harm to the race," and recommended that they never reproduce, lest they transmit their pathological disposition (see Herrn 1995, 39). He subsequently gained notoriety as a member of the Nazi Party, most importantly for his work on the Task Force of Heredity Experts (headed by Heinrich Himmler), which drew up the 1933 German Sterilization Law (Kallmann 1938a, 1938b, 1953; Lewontin et al. 1984, 207). Like his teacher, Kallmann was a convinced hereditarian who claimed a genetic predisposition for many social traits, particularly schizophrenia and homosexuality, which he studied in Germany and later in New York (Breggin 1991, 103). While his work on homosexuality came after the war, Kallmann's studies on schizophrenia, carried out in the early to mid-1930s, reveal the degree to which his research was motivated by strong eugenical concerns.

As a thoroughgoing Mendelian, Kallmann (1938a) concluded in his book on schizophrenia that the condition must be due to a single recessive gene, a claim that subsequently was subjected to a devastating critique by Pastore (1949), Lewontin et al. (1984), and Breggin (1991). All three critics found evidence of pervasive hereditarian bias and sloppy research methods (see also Futuyma, n.d., 15). For Kallmann, writing in 1938, schizophrenics were "a source of maladjusted crooks, asocial eccentrics, and the lowest type of criminal offenders. Even the faithful believer in liberty," he continued, "would be much happier without [them]" (Moulton & Komoro, 1939, 145; qtd. in Lewontin et al. 1984, 208). Because he thought the gene for schizophrenia was recessive, Kallmann noted in 1936 that sterilizing all hospitalized patients would barely reduce the frequency of the gene in the population 1–3% (Lewontin et al. 1984, 208). To effect any real solution, he argued, it would be necessary to sterilize *all* family members, including distant relatives, who showed any "eccentricity." According to Müller-Hill (1988, 28–29) and Lewontin et al. (1984, 209), this would have amounted to sterilizing 18% of the entire German population, a practice that Kallmann actually proposed (Lewontin et al. 1984, 208). At the International Congress for Population Science in 1935, Fritz Lenz, one of the Reich's most enthusiastic eugenicists, spoke publicly against Kallmann's proposal as both impractical and unwarranted (Lewontin et al. 1984, 208). It is thus particularly ironic that Kallmann, more Nazi than the Nazis, was eventually forced to flee Germany in 1936 because of his half-Jewish ancestry. He subsequently took up lucrative positions as Chief of Psychiatric Research at the New York Psychiatric Institute and Professor of Psychiatry at the College of Physicians and Surgeons at Columbia University. That he did not renounce his former eugenic ties is indicated by the fact that he served as a defense witness at the Denazification Tribunal for his former mentor, Rüdin.[3] Despite these past connections, however, Kallmann was elected President of the American Society of Human Genetics in 1951.

After reaching the United States, Kallmann initiated his studies on the genetics of male homosexuality. How or why this switch in interests came about is not explained in his published work. In the 1940s and early 1950s he carried out the most extensive study of homosexuality in siblings that had been made up to that time. Kallmann's sample included 85 twin pairs: 40 pairs of monozygotic twins (that is, from one fertilized egg, and therefore genetically identical) and 45 pairs of dizygotic twins (that is, from fertilization of two separate eggs, and therefore no more genetically similar than non-twin siblings), all culled from psychiatric and correctional institutions in New York, as well as, he tells us, "through contacts with the clandestine homosexual world" (1952b, 139). This group became his "index subjects." As controls, Kallmann included 112 non-twin homosexuals of similar age to the index group, and 116 male employees from his own Psychiatric Institute in New York. All homosexuals in the sample were judged to be largely, if not exclusively, homosexual. As another aspect of the study, Kallmann also attempted to obtain data on the sexual orientation of the index cases' fathers, brothers, and half-brothers, as well as the ratio of male and female sibs in each family.

In his study, Kallmann reported some rather remarkable results. For the monozygotic (MZ) twin sample he found a concordance rate of 100% (that is, both members of the pair were homosexual). For dizygotic (DZ) twins the rate fell to a little over 60%, and for non-twin siblings it was 11.5% (1952b, 142–143). The data on sex ratios among siblings showed that the male-female figure for the index families was 125:100, and for the non-twin homosexuals' families, 126:100, a figure similar to Lang's unusually high ratios obtained in 1940. Kallmann also found that the majority of his twin pairs reported that they had developed their homosexuality independent of their sibling, and that specific preferential sexual behaviors exhibited by the two members of a twin pair were surprisingly similar. The range of behaviors *between* twin pairs, however, was much greater.

From these data Kallmann concluded that homosexuality was determined largely by genetic elements. That concordance rate declines as genetic similarity declines seemed to Kallmann to be an affirmation of the genetic hypothesis. How else, he argued, could you explain the 100% concordance rate among genetically identical pairs, compared to only 60% concordance rate for DZ pairs and 11% for non-twin siblings? To provide a possible biological mechanism for how genes might determine sexual orientation, Kallmann concluded (in a passage of considerable obscurity) that

> it seems advisable to view overt homosexual behavior in the adult male as an *alternative minus variant* [?] in the integrative process of psychosexual maturation rather than as a pathognomonically [diagnostically] determinative expression of a codifiable entity of behavioral immaturity. Apparently, the interactions between the biological components of sexual maturation and the adjustive phenomena of personality development form such a central and inseparable interrelationship that fractional deviations in the psychosomatic integration of the sex function from its pregenital elements to genital maturity may dislocate the axis, around which the organization of the personality takes place. (1952b, 143–144)

If I understand this statement, Kallmann seems to be arguing that while there is clearly an underlying genetic basis for sexual orientation (our modern term), the ultimate behavior an individual expresses is very much affected, at different maturational stages both before and after puberty, by psychological experiences. He compares sexual development to handedness, in which an underlying biological tendency can be redirected through training. Kallmann then toyed with Lang's idea that (male) homosexuals may represent genetic *intersexes* whose development toward homo- or heterosexuality might be affected by both hormonal balance and/or psychological experiences during childhood and early adolescence. However, as Kallmann notes, there is no good evidence for this theory from either an endocrinological or a cytological point of view, so he left it only as a theoretical possibility.

Kallmann himself acknowledged that family and prevailing cultural attitudes may have had much to do with determining male homosexuality, but to the end of his career he continued to maintain that there was a significant genetic component. Bieber et al. (1962) severely criticized Kallmann's work by pointing out that his conclusions are truly contradictory. How, they asked, could Kallmann claim a strong genetic basis for homosexual orientation, and yet admit that "the sex impulse is easily dislocated by experiential factors" (Bieber et al. 1962, 306). Furthermore, Kallmann's study shares all the problems associated with studying behavior in samples from a hospital or prison population. Such samples can hardly be claimed to be representative of the population as a whole. It should be pointed out that the same problem plagued Bieber's own psychodynamic theory of the origin of homosexuality, which utilized patients who had sought psychiatric treatment. Such sampling bias (reflecting also the bias of the investigators) from the outset supports the disease concept of homosexuality.

The methodological problems with Kallmann's study are legion, but a few examples will emphasize that his findings provide no basis whatsoever for the sweeping conclusions that he drew. No doubt the most devastating criticism is that Kallmann nowhere gave any indication that the two members of his twin pairs (either MZ or DZ) were reared apart (Futuyma n.d., 15). Thus, there is no way in which the similarities can be claimed to be more the result of genetics than environment. Moreover, it is well known that MZ twins are often treated more alike by their parents, teachers, and other adults than regular siblings, including DZ twins, are, thus easily accounting for their unusually high concordance rate for traits. The similarity would be especially apparent if the twins were reared together. Kallmann also does not indicate at what stage in the research he determined, or even *how* he determined, the zygosity of the twin pairs. Apart from these problems, Kallmann appears not to have bothered to carry out his analysis "blind"—that is, without knowing zygosity when comparing the two members of his twin pairs. Under these circumstances, the apparently greater behavioral similarity between MZ compared to DZ twins may well have reflected Kallmann's *a priori* knowledge of the degree of genetic relatedness. And finally, despite his claim that sexual orientation is largely genetic, Kallmann found no evidence of high concordance rate for homosexuality in either the DZ co-twins or the fathers of his MZ index cases when he could locate them. Surveying these criticisms, Futuyma concludes that Kallmann's work provides no reliable evidence that differences in sexual orientation are in any way genetically influenced (n.d., 18).

What is significant about Kallmann's work is not that it either demonstrated or did not (it clearly did not) a genetic basis for homosexuality, but that Kallmann came to the problem from a largely medical and eugenical point of view. Although he did not call for sterilization of homosexuals in the United States, as he had done for schizophrenics in Germany, Kallmann clearly thought of both "mental states" as pathological conditions that needed "treatment." Thus, in arguing for continuation of genetic research on homosexuality, Kallmann claimed: "The urgency of such work is undeniable as long as this aberrant type of behavior continues to be an inexhaustible source of unhappiness, discontentment, and a distorted sense of human values" (1952b, 146). In 1959 in a chapter on "The Genetics of Mental Illness" for the *Amer-*

ican Handbook of Psychiatry (1959, 188), Kallmann included homosexuality as one of a group of similar pathologies that included criminality, manic depression, schizophrenia, mongolism (*sic*), cerebral palsy, and "convulsive disease." Later, he described homosexuality as a "disorder" of psychosexual maturation (1963, 17). As late as 1959, he called for "eugenic considerations" (using those very words) regarding homosexuality on the grounds that failure to recognize the genetic aspect of psychiatric problems ran the risk of increasing the frequency of mutant genes in the population (1959, 192). He stated, "General public health measures for the prevention of such hazards [increased frequency of mutations] will require . . . the foresight implicit in a concern with the health of future generations" (1959, 192). Combined with his exuberant support for sterilization in his native Germany, it is not difficult to imagine that ultimately Kallmann would have liked to sterilize most homosexuals if public sentiment would have allowed.

A few additional studies in the 1960s attempted to replicate Kallmann's findings, but the results were inconclusive. One, carried out on 12 twin pairs in 1968, showed a concordance rate of 40–60% for the MZ twins and 14% for the DZ twins (Heston & Shields 1968). Although significantly lower than Kallmann's figures, the authors nevertheless concluded that the concordance rates were significant enough to suggest a genetic basis, and thus deserved further study.

Finally, in the pre-1973 period, the work of Alfred C. Kinsey was singular in its nonjudgmental, nonbiological, and nonmedical approach to the study of homosexuality (see Kenen's essay in this volume). Although Kinsey's nontypological, descriptive approach did not spread to wide segments of the psychiatric community, it did influence a growing, though specialized, group of psychologically oriented sex researchers, especially in the United States (Bayer 1987, 385). Most of this group rejected genetic explanations for the origin of homosexuality.

The Post-1973 Period

The period following Stonewall was one of increasingly open activism by proponents of gay rights and more vigorous demands for social acceptance of gays as a whole. Stonewall was, in turn, a product of the liberating effect of the earlier civil rights, women's, and sexual liberation movements. It is important not to underestimate the significant impact that the whole tide of political activism of that period had on the development of a new gay consciousness. It was under these circumstances that gay activists began to pressure the psychiatric community to reevaluate its stance on homosexuality as a disease. Many gays and lesbians began to recognize that if they indeed had more psychological problems than anyone else (and it was not always clear that they did), it was the result of repressive societal attitudes, including those of the psychiatric community, on their own self-images and sense of equality. A gay activist friend of mine once told me that attending one good, militant demonstration was more psychologically liberating than a month's worth of sessions on the psychiatrist's couch.

Although removal of homosexuality from *DSM-II* did not automatically eliminate its status as a "disease," it did begin to alter the sociological context of research into its *causes*. For one thing, an increasing number of researchers who were themselves gay began to enter the field—of which LeVay and Richard Pillard are the most recent and prominent. While this shift undoubtedly brought with it a political agenda of its own, it nonetheless helped to move psychiatrists and psychologists away from the medical model of studying a behavior primarily to "cure" it. For another, if homosexuality was not viewed as a pathology, then we cannot sensibly ask about its *cause* or *origins* separate from the causes or origins of heterosexuality and sexual practices in general. Since very little was, and is, known about how virtually any human sexual responses originate, a component of the new view (actually stemming from Kinsey) has been a call for more research into human psychosexual development in all its varied forms.

Indeed, as a result of the more liberal, environmentally oriented mood of the mid-1970s and 1980s, genetic studies on the origin of homosexuality remained relatively sparse. The research that did exist was largely twin and sibship studies, making use of pedigree analysis and/or heritability estimates. One study in the mid-1970s, however, created some media stir. Riding high on the tide of controversy and excitement surrounding E. O. Wilson's *Sociobiology, the New Synthesis* (1975), James Weinrich (1976), a student of Wilson's, developed an evolutionary theory of homosexuality that assumed, but did not provide any direct data to support, a genetic basis. Weinrich argued that recessive "genes" for homosexuality persist in the human population because homosexuals help raise children of their siblings, and thus indirectly contribute a selective advantage to the propagation of familial genes. This notion, an aspect of the general theory of "kin selection," was an important component of the sociobiological research program, and became a cornerstone of the work of Richard Dawkins and Irving De Vore, among others. However, the work of neither Weinrich nor other sociobiologists has produced any data that bore directly on the genetic basis of homosexuality. Indeed, for the theory of kin selection to provide any explanation at all, the genetic basis for homosexual behavior was *assumed*, not demonstrated.

Several studies in the late 1980s and early 1990s had begun to revive the issue of genetics, and provided a curtain-raiser to the flurry of excitement surrounding the Hamer study that was published in August 1993. In 1986 Richard Pillard and James Weinrich (of Boston University and University of California, San Diego, respectively) published a study of homosexuality among brothers, showing that the brothers of gay men had a 22% chance of being gay, while the brothers of straight men had only a 4% chance of being gay (1986, 811). Pillard later teamed up with Northwestern University psychologist Michael Bailey to produce a larger, more thorough study, using 56 pairs of MZ twins, 54 pairs of DZ twins, and 57 pairs of adoptive brothers (Bailey & Pillard 1991). Subjects were recruited through advertisements in gay newspapers, and, wherever possible, data were collected on sexual orientation of all male siblings in the families. Pillard and Bailey found the expected conclusions. In the MZ twins, 52% turned out to be concordant, in the DZ twins, only 22% (the same percentage found by Pillard and Weinrich), and in adoptive brothers, only 11%. This correlation rate between genetic relatedness and concordance parallels, though, is not as strong as Kallmann's findings. Bailey and Pillard (1991, 1094) concluded that the high concordance rate for MZ twins strongly supported a genetic hypothesis. Subsequently, Bailey and Pillard, with Michael Neale and Yvonne Agyei (1993), carried out a similar study on female twins (MZ and DZ) with more ambiguous, though somewhat positive, results: that is, a concordance rate that declined as the degree of genetic relatedness declined.

By his own admission, it was Bailey and Pillard's work that inspired Dean Hamer at the NIH in the early 1990s to undertake his genetic marker study (Hamer & Copeland 1994, 28). While the Bailey and Pillard studies received scant attention in the news media, in the summer and fall of 1993, Hamer's study became the focus of a media circus that included articles in all major newspapers and slick magazines and on numerous talk shows. The blitz of media publicity is what makes the issue all the more interesting and, at the same time, politically troublesome. In particular, it is the meaning of the *media attention* that is important to understand, because in that dynamic may lie a clue to the political role all theories of biological determinism are playing today, and what effect they may ultimately have in the larger social arena. The media attention has forced us to ask once again: Are the newer data so much better, or the conclusions so much more clear-cut than the pre– and immediate post–World War II studies? I turn in the next section to a detailed examination of Hamer's study.

The Hamer Study

In contrast to the previous investigators (Kallmann, Pillard and Bailey, and others), Hamer and his colleagues set out to find a *direct* genetic marker that could be linked to homosexuality in males. Admitting that homosexuality was not easy to define, Hamer decided to use only subjects who considered themselves primarily homosexual, with a self-rated score of 5 or 6 on the Kinsey scale (where 0 is exclusively heterosexual and 6 is exclusively homosexual). Hamer assembled two different sets of subjects in his study: (1) 76 index subjects (individuals only, not sibling pairs) recruited from three sources: the outpatient HIV clinic at the NIH, the Whitman-Walker Clinic (an AIDS clinic in Washington, D.C.), and local gay organizations. For 26 of the subjects one or more family members also participated, providing information about sexual orientation, for a total of 122 subjects. This group was used for pedigree analysis and confirmed the fact that more maternal relatives of a gay male were themselves gay than for paternal relatives. This finding supported an earlier hypothesis that homosexuality might be transmitted genetically on the X chromosome. (2) 40 pairs of gay brothers, along with their parents and other relatives where possible, were recruited through advertisements in local and national gay publications (total number of homosexual subjects—gay sibs and relatives—was 114). This group was used for the sib-pair pedigree analysis and genetic marker study.

The NIH group then searched the data repositories from the Human Genome Project for polymorphic DNA markers on the X chromosome. Twenty-two such markers were identified whose map locations were known. Hamer and his colleagues then compared their twin sets for all 22 of the marker sites by PCR (polymerase chain reaction, a method that greatly amplifies the amount of DNA from specific regions of a chromosome). These "marker segments" of DNA from the same locus, or site, on the chromosome can be compared, thus demonstrating similarities or differences in overall molecular structure among different individuals—a kind of fine-structure analysis of individual variability. The amplified DNA from the 22 sites was then separated out by gel electrophoresis and compared for their degrees of similarity/difference. For most of the sites, concordance for the total sample of twin pairs was low (that is, there were far more differences than similarities in the DNA patterns) but for one site, called Xq28, at the tip of the X chromosome's long arm, the concordance was extremely high: 33 of the 40 pairs (83%) had matching DNA variants. On average, 50% of the brother pairs should have the same X-linked allele from their mother by chance alone, so that 83% seemed well above the expected value. Using the low estimate of a 2% incidence of exclusive homosexuality for the population at large (based on an unpublished survey the researchers had themselves made of gay relatives of lesbians), Hamer and his colleagues calculated that this concordance rate could have occurred by chance in only one in a thousand cases. As a control, they had sampled 314 randomly selected pairs of brothers, most of whom were assumed to be heterosexual, and found the Xq28 markers to be randomly distributed, that is, concordant in both brothers in only about 50% of the cases.

To their credit, Hamer and his coworkers point out that their work does not even establish a genetic basis, much less an actual gene for homosexuality. They state clearly that their DNA analysis was only a linkage study, that is, it identified a neighborhood on the X chromosome within which a gene or genes might eventually be found; that neighborhood could include 200 genes as well as much redundant-repetitive and non-transcribed DNA. All the Hamer study claimed to do was provide a correlation of molecular *markers* (in the Xq28 region) with a given phenotype (homosexual behavior). Thus Hamer and his colleagues make it clear that they did not carry out a study of an actual gene (or genes) producing homosexuality. They also note that their results would need to be replicated in other samples, since similar linkage data for a number of other traits—for example, manic depression, schizophrenia, and alcoholism—have not stood up to the original claims when repeated in different sample sets, and have had to be withdrawn (Cooke 1990). Hamer also points out that seven pairs of brothers in their sample did not show the Xq28 sequence, yet were all gay. Using estimates of chance among the other 33 pairs suggests that as much as 36% of the sample *could* be nonconcordant in actuality, thus considerably weakening the possible connection between the marker and homosexual behavior.

Not daunted by these limitations, however, Hamer speculated—especially in his more popular *Scientific American* article with LeVay (1994) and in his book with Peter Copeland, *The Science of Desire* (1994)—how genes might actually determine homosexual behavior. He suggested that genes determining homosexuality might alter the amino acid sequence of a hormone receptor, or affect hormone synthesis and metabolism. In the past decade, such a mechanism has been suggested by genetic studies of the courtship and mating behavior of the fruitfly, *Drosophila* (Barinaga 1995, 791). Recent work has shown that, in a strain of flies in which certain brain cells in the males are "feminized" by a genetic insertion within the fly's DNA that switches on genes for female development, the flies court males and females indiscriminately. The feminized cells appear to have a chemical block in their ability to respond to pheromones (sexual attractants), thus allowing these males to court both male and female flies. Although Ralph Greenspan (1995) at New York University, in whose labs these "bisexual" flies have been developed, cautions that the organization of the insect brain is vastly different from that in higher animals, Hamer has drawn a possible connection between the *Drosophila* work and his own findings on the Xq28 marker (in Barinaga 1995, 792). In humans, Hamer points out, molecular geneticists have determined the sequence of the androgen receptor gene, which produces the protein that allows brain and other body cells to respond to the male sex hormone androgen. He reasoned that gay males might have, like Greenspan's *Drosophila*, a DNA variation that would make cells in certain regions of the brain insensitive to androgen, leading to an inability to respond to females, or, conversely, to the ability to respond sexually to other males. In collaboration with researchers at the Johns Hopkins, Hamer compared the molecular structure of the androgen receptor gene in 197 gay and 213 nongay men. However, the survey showed no significant differences in coding sequence between the two groups (Hamer & Copeland 1994, 156–58).

Methodological Flaws in Studies on the Inheritance of Social Behavior

There is good reason why studies on the inheritance of social behavior or personality traits have almost always ended up being retracted. They are based not only on what is often a lack of detailed knowledge of aspects of genetics, but also on a general philosophical misconception of genes, what they do, and how they function in the development of adult phenotypes. I will enumerate below some of those persistent problems that have plagued this area of research, past and present, as a way of indicating just how complex the problem is, and why we should not expect to ever find an answer to the question: What is/are the gene/genes for homosexuality?

1. Definition of Phenotype

Any repeatable genetic study must first have an agreed-upon definition of the phenotype to be studied.[4] Even the earliest Mendelians recognized that failure to make correct phenotypic identifications could easily lead to spurious results. If two observers cannot agree whether an individual has or does not have the trait in question, following that trait through family lines or breeding experiments is futile. Human behavioral traits, because they are the products of varying social contexts, will necessarily be fluid categories, varying in definition, social values, and even their very existence as a recognizable entity from one time or place to another. For example, what is an "alcoholic," a "schizophrenic," or a "homosexual"? By the elimination of homosexuality from the disease list in 1973 and, currently, by the debate on whether schizophrenia and manic depression are varying manifestations of a single condition or two separate conditions, the psychiatric community has demonstrated clearly that these categories are socially constructed. However, this point has scarcely made an impression on modern human behavioral geneticists. Behind much of this work appears to lie an essentialist or typological view of behaviors as fixed and objectively defined entities, ignoring the wide variability in any behavior both within and between human societies (Churchill 1971). Kinsey was among the first to try to introduce a more populational approach to sexual behavior when, for example, he introduced his 0 to 6 rating scale for heterosexuality-homosexuality. Homosexual, like heterosexual, behavior falls across a wide spectrum of responses, making it impossible to claim that something called "homosexuality" exists in the abstract.[5] The problem of grouping what may be a variety of behaviors under one name is what neurobiologist Steven Rose (1995) has called "artificial conglomeration."

In the Hamer study, the problem of phenotypic definition is further complicated by the use of the "self-rating" method. Kinsey's scheme, while somewhat arbitrary, at least called for rating by an independent observer using a standardized procedure. Imagine, for example, asking people to rate themselves as to whether they were schizophrenic, alcoholic, or criminal. Our social definition of sex in Western society is so geared to the binary mode of categorization—either male or female (see Fausto-Sterling in this volume)—that people come to see themselves as either exclusively homosexual or heterosexual, when in fact, everyone may be basically bisexual. In other words, all human beings may be fundamentally capable, both biologically and psychologically, of responding to members of either sex. The choice of categorizing oneself as *either* heterosexual or homosexual is thus socially contrived, artificial, and, from a biological and genetic point of view, meaningless. With a self-rating process as the means of identifying phenotypes, the artificiality of the definition is magnified manyfold.

In any behavior as complex and socially sensitive as homosexuality, cultural and geographic differences undoubtedly are important in diagnosing the phenotype, especially by a self-rating method. For example, Hamer's sample included 92% Caucasian non-Hispanic, 4% African-Americans, 3% Hispanic, and 1% Asian subjects (out of a total of 122 study participants). While the small number of non-Caucasian subjects may not have significantly influenced the results, the fact that cultural differences were not factored in further suggests the degree to which the authors tend to view sexual orientation as a single, abstract, phenotypic behavior, the same wherever it is found.

A further problem that Hamer did not take into account is that of developmental change, the fact that human behaviors, including sexuality, can undergo significant change in the course of a lifetime. A twenty-year-old and a fifty-year-old are likely to view their sexuality, including the nature of their sexual attraction, quite differently. The fact that such changes are often related to, or even directly influenced by, changing social mores underscores the fluidity and variability of the human sexual response. This fluidity means, among other things, that the age at which someone's sexuality is studied is critical to both interpreting and classifying the behavior. The Hamer study does not take age into account, except to point out that all subjects were over eighteen, and that the mean age was thirty-six plus or minus nine years. No information is given about the range of ages involved, or whether individuals have always considered themselves gay.

If anything is truly genetic about human sexuality and gender identification, it appears to be the wide range of variation of which it is capable. Expression of these variations appears to depend very much on present as well as past social, psychological, and other circumstances in which individuals find themselves. We might compare the problem of defining the phenotype of human sexuality to that of categorizing the phenotype of color in the common (Old World) chameleon. As is well-known, the chameleon's color is not fixed, but changes according to the background against which the animal is placed. The chameleon's phenotype cannot be described as green or brown or tan *per se*, but rather as the ability to alter color within a rather broad spectrum; the phenotype of any individual chameleon, then, must be described as encompassing a whole range of possible colors within a known (and broad) range of backgrounds. In both a developmental, as well as a social-cultural sense, human sexual orientation appears to show a similar broad range of expressions, both between individuals, and in the same individual under different social-environmental conditions. Genetic determinist studies seldom seem to take this fluidity into account.

2. *Selection of Subjects*

Human behavior genetics has been plagued by problems of selecting representative samples of the population for genetic studies. As we have seen, in the pre-1973 period, the study of homosexual behavior was based almost universally on samples taken from institutionalized populations (prisons, homes for delinquents, hospitals) or from psychiatrists' private practice; in other words, samples came almost exclusively from a population under institutional or medical care. In the more open, post-1973 period, subjects have been obtained from clinics and by advertising in gay or other publications. It is obvious that a sample obtained from institutions is biased; it is not so obvious that populations obtained through open advertisements may also be biased. For example, twins obtained by advertising may represent a particularly outgoing or flamboyant personality type whose behavior, or perception of their own behavior, may be quite atypical of the population as a whole. Such was apparently the case with the (in)famous Minnesota Twin Study, which turned up preposterous coincidences in the life histories of MZ twins reared apart. It now appears that many of the twin pairs exaggerated their similarities in order to remain in the study, or to capture researcher and media attention and appear on TV talk shows (Horgan 1993, 125). As we have seen, Hamer's study involved volunteers obtained through advertising in the gay press and at an HIV clinic. If any genetic correlation emerges from such a sample, it may well be for "openness" or "honesty" (being "out"), rather than for homosexuality *per se*. While Hamer admits that the Xq28 marker may be valid only for self-acknowledged, exclusively gay men, this restriction of the conditions to which the linkage applies does not do much for the original claim of finding a genetic basis for homosexuality in general.

3. *Use of Controls or Comparison Groups*

A lack of sufficient controls has plagued the study of inheritance of human social traits from the old eugenic days to the present. Many of the earlier studies of homosexuality, especially pre-1973, had no controls at all and focused only on homosexual samples; they were thus not corrected for age, socioeconomic status, race, or ethnic background. Even Hamer's more sophisticated study lacks sufficient control groups. For example, Hamer did not sample the occurrence of the Xq28 markers in the other, non-gay, brothers of his forty sibling pairs. Lacking this information makes the concordance rate between gay sibs difficult to assess. Its omission in the original study was justified on the grounds that, since homosexuality is, according to Hamer, "probably polygenic," by surveying non-gay family members, "too many exceptions [would be] included" (LeVay & Hamer 1994, 48). In other words, if many of the non-gay brothers of the gay pairs also shared the Xq28 markers, the correlation to homosexuality would be meaningless. By excluding those offspring in each generation that fail to show a trait, anything can be made to appear genetic. It is precisely the comparison—between those offspring in any generation that show a trait compared to those that do not show it—that has traditionally allowed geneticists to make any claims about the inheritance of phenotypes.

Hamer also biased the conclusion that Xq28 is a significant marker for homosexuality by choosing the conservative estimate of 2% for the frequency of homosexuality in the general population. This low rate makes the concordance within the sample seem all the more significant. However, Evan Balaban, of the Neurosciences Institute in La Jolla, California, has calculated that, at the slightly higher (and to many observers more realistic) estimate of 4% for the incidence of homosexuality in the general population, the distribution within the gay sample group becomes statistically insignificant (Balaban, pers. comm.).

Yet another problem, also related to Hamer's lack of controls, is the lack of information on homozygosity of the Xq28 marker in the mothers of the twin pairs. Since females have two X chromosomes, if each X contains the same Xq28 marker, *all* the sons will receive the marker, thus making a concordance rate meaningless. The ideal sample would contain brother pairs, all of whose mothers were heterozygous for the marker. Unfortunately, such information was not available in Hamer's study. Of the 40 sib pairs, only two mothers were known to be heterozygous, 12 were known to be homozygous, and no information was available on the other 23. The best Hamer and his group could do on this score was to gather information on heterozygosity levels for these markers in a random sample of women. Among this group, frequency of heterozygosity ranged from 0.3 to 0.8, a rather broad and thus not very useful comparison figure.

4. The Phenotype or the Genotype as Moving Target

It has been a hallmark of theories of biological determinism for more than a century that, as the sample base was broadened and new cases uncovered that displayed neither the biological marker nor the customary phenotype, one or both (marker or phenotype) was redefined—usually broadened—to include the new cases. For example, after years of collecting ambiguous family studies of alcoholism, the National Institute for Alcoholism and Alcohol Abuse (NIAAA) concluded recently that the failure to find a clear genetic basis for alcoholism resulted from too narrow a definition of the phenotype. As reported in *Science* magazine, the NIAAA claimed that the underlying behavior is not really alcoholism but *compulsivity,* which, in certain individuals, might express itself as alcohol abuse (Holden 1991). In a similar vein, failing to find any association between the Xq28 marker and a hormone-receptor gene on the X chromosome, LeVay and Hamer (1994, 49) suggest that homosexuality genes might determine not sex-object choice itself but more general personality features, so that, for example, "people who are genetically self-reliant might be more likely to acknowledge and act on same-sex feelings than are people who are dependent on the approval of others."

A similar "moving target" approach is often applied to the marker itself. LeVay and Hamer (1994, 49) explain the lack of concordance in seven of the twin pairs by claiming that "perhaps these men inherited different genes" from those associated with Xq28, or that different genes in different families predispose an individual to homosexual behavior. If one association will not produce the desired correlation, another is substituted for it. Thus, instead of recognizing that perhaps the search for a "gene or genes" for homosexuality might be a flawed enterprise in the first place, Hamer and colleagues simply redefine the nature of the marker or the phenotype in order to preserve the association. Philosophically speaking, if the genotypic or phenotypic definition—the "target"—continues to be redefined or expanded, it is impossible to come up with a negative result or to falsify any genetic hypothesis. Such a process eludes all critical judgment.

Now, to be fair, there is good historical precedence in genetics for being able to redefine both phenotype and genotype to account for new data. For example, between 1905 and 1925, genetic markers (that is, genotypes) were redefined for such seemingly non-Mendelian phenomena as epistasis (where two or more genes interact to produce a nonadditive effect, such as a totally new color) or quantitative inheritance (where two or more genes interact additively to produce increasing or decreasing expression of a trait). There is nothing wrong with this process as long as the "target" eventually stops moving, as it eventually did with conditions like epistasis and quantitative inheritance. However, in studies of human behavior genetics over the past half century or more, the targets have never stopped changing. Perhaps studies on the genetics of homosexuality will prove to be an exception, but current research does not seem to point in any more hopeful a direction.

The Nature of Genetic Explanation: Asking the Right Questions

The long and unproductive history of the so-called nature-nurture debate should alert historians and philosophers of science to the fact that some underlying problems are persistently at work.[6] Those problems lie, as far as I can see, in the historical way in which we have constructed our concept of genes and their modes of action. This chief difficulty stems from the mechanistic, materialist approach to genetics that has characterized much of classical genetics, especially that deriving from the Morgan School and its affiliates after 1915 (Allen 1985a, 1985b). By separating the functional, developmental aspects of heredity from the process of genetic transmission, the Morgan School and its more mechanistic (or "classical") school of genetics gave rise to one of the most erroneous myths in modern biology: that, independent of the environment, a gene or genes contains information for the production of an adult trait. That myth is characterized by the phrase "The gene for . . ." (insert eye color, height, intelligence, or homosexuality). The problem is more than merely the simplistic notion embodied in the idea of single genes determining single traits. Even disabused of a one-gene-one-trait conception, the phrase "The gene/genes for . . ." still conveys the serious misconception that genes, once transmitted to the next generation, develop into full-blown adult phenotypes, irrespective of environmental input. The view of genes as fixed blueprints has been perpetuated by most textbooks and other popular presentations of genetics for the past seventy-five years or more (Nelkin & Lindee 1995). Yet any experienced geneticist will tell you that, of course, it is not strictly true that genes directly determine traits independent of environment. The phrase "the gene for" is just a "shorthand," they say. Yet it is a shorthand that may ultimately conceal more than it reveals. This "shorthand" has contributed significantly to the confusion surrounding human behavior genetics in the past five or more decades.

At heart, the issue is this: What is clear is that genes contain information for the amino acid sequence of proteins.[7] However, how that information is initially read out and ultimately transformed into an adult phenotypic trait is a multistage process, the complete sequence of which remains unknown for almost any trait, even simple ones such as hair color or height. The process is clearly not a simple unfolding of a preconceived design. Even the early stages of DNA transcription can be influenced by environmental input.[8] For example, in the case of the "heat-shock syndrome" in plants, how and when initiation of transcription of specific DNA segments takes place, or which specific non-sense segments of mRNA are excised after transcription, is very much influenced by temperature. Thus, when plant seedlings are exposed to high temperatures, different DNA segments are transcribed, and thus different proteins are produced from when the seedlings are exposed to lower temperatures. More importantly, the processes by which the primary products of genes, the proteins, interact within the cell, and by which cells interact with each other during embryonic development, are all subject to environmental impact at every level of organization. Geneticists and developmental biologists know relatively little about how any of these higher levels of organization come about during embryogenesis, or how they are related to the full development of phenotypic traits. This lack of knowledge—partly lack of experience and techniques in studying these higher levels of organization, and partly a result of the naïve, reductionist philosophy that still pervades much of the genetic thinking of our day—is the legacy of the so-called mechanistic view of life that came to dominate the "new biology" in the early decades of the twentieth century (Allen 1978, 1985b). By separating the problem of embryonic development from that of genetic transmission, geneticists in the 1920s and 1930s may have been highly successful in establishing a unified "school" of Mendelian theory and in attracting funds for their research; but they have inevitably, and unwittingly, produced a view of the genetic process that now requires much undoing.

The highly mechanistic view that there is an invariable relationship between a gene and a specific phenotypic trait has maintained a life of its own outside the genetics community. It is simple and resonates well with the more pervasive, mechanistic, materialist view that has dominated much of Western society since the seventeenth century. The mechanistic view encompasses the notions that the whole is no more than the sum of its parts, and that interactive processes can best be understood by resolving them into their component parts, each of which can be studied independently. In genetics, this crude form of mechanism gives rise to a form of reductionism: a rigid, inflexible view of gene function that plays into the hands of naïve determinists, and leads to a simplistic view about the ontogeny of behavior.

A more productive way to understand all genetic processes is represented by the diagram shown in Figure 1. This schematic view emphasizes the constant interactions, feedback loops, and successively higher levels of organization that are involved in representing the processes of ontogeny in successive generations of organisms. Most modern geneticists, especially molecular geneticists, pay lip service to interactive processes, but in their research *practice* they usually focus on very specific, isolated elements in the processes of transmission, transcription, or translation.[9] What has become evident, however, is the way in which informational feedback loops affect successive stages in gene expression, thus ultimately indicating that the environment always has a role to play in formation of the phenotype. In a developing embryo, the environment within each cell is constantly changing,

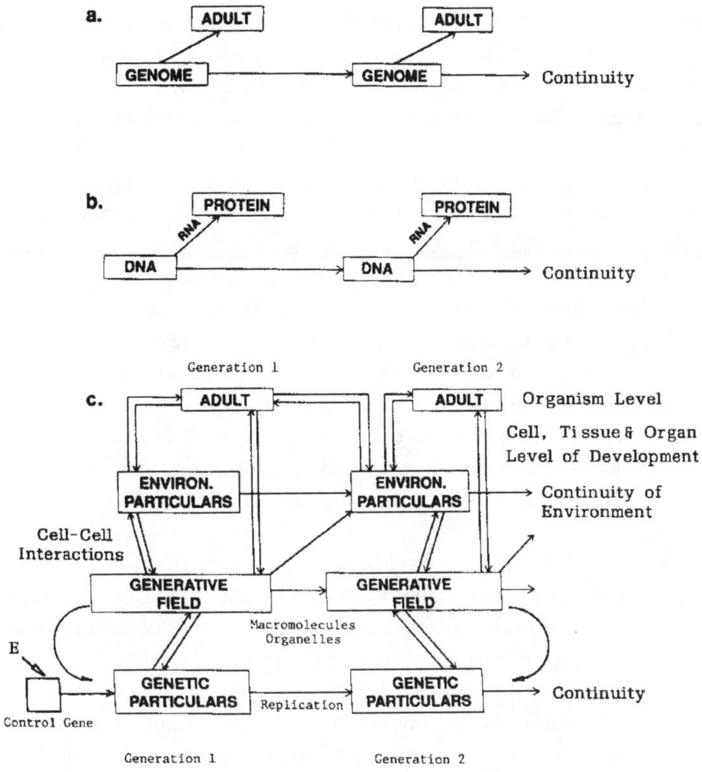

Figure 1. Various ways of visualizing how genes influence the development of adult characteristics (the genotype-phenotype interaction). All three representations see the genome as replicating itself and preserving continuity from one generation to the next (the bottom horizontal line in each diagram). However, the three models differ significantly in the complexity they impart to the genotype-phenotype interaction.

(a) The classical Mendelian theory of the gene sees genes developing into adult traits with no developmental input. In this model genes are seen as having relatively little plasticity.

(b) The view of molecular genetics after development of the Watson-Crick model of DNA in 1953. Here the gene is seen as giving rise to its direct product, a protein (represented by the "central dogma" sequence: DNA RNA PROTEIN), which, in a manner often unknown, yields an adult phenotype. This model suggests some avenues of genetic flexibility, since proteins interact with one another, but still preserves the basic one-to-one relationship between gene and adult trait.

(c) A modern developmental model that incorporates genetic, cell biological, and embryological perspectives, and thus sees the path from genotype to phenotype as highly complex and subject at many points toinput from many sources, including both the internal and external environment. This model suggests there is no straight-line or one-to-one correspondence between a gene and an adult trait.

Schemes (a) and (b) are reasonably accurate for simple traits such as color (but even then, many flower or animal colors are the product of multiple genes) or simple protein (enzyme) reflecting changes produced by sequential gene expression within that cell, as well as changes occurring in the physiological (embryonic) environment in which that cell exists. Gene expression in most cases is far more plastic than the classical view of the gene suggests. We are just now beginning to understand how this plasticity is generated.

An interactive model of gene expression is a first step in going beyond the old, unresolvable, and misguided nature-nurture controversy. All phenotypic traits, including the most complex human behaviors, are at some level a product of the interaction between genes and the cellular, organismic, and ecological environment with which the organism resides. However, the controversy cannot be resolved simply by making such a statement, for it is a truism that is ultimately meaningless. The important question is: To what extent and in what ways do genetic elements and particular environments interact to produce particular phenotypes? Phrased this way, the question sets a meaningful research agenda, as difficult as it may be to conceive of exactly how to carry it out with respect to behavioral aspects of human subjects. At least, however, the question makes biological sense, unlike the question: What is the gene for . . . ?

By suggesting that human behaviors and interactive processes in ontogeny are complex, I do not want to suggest that research on such topics is *a priori* hopeless. To tease apart interactions between genetic and environmental factors in ontogeny poses exciting prospects for developmental biology in the twenty-first century. But it also requires new ways of viewing the problem and new research methods that focus on the interaction of components in biological systems. We have, after all, had over three hundred years of research in natural science based on the mechanistic, reductionistic approach. It is perhaps time to devote some effort to developing other approaches that speak to complex, interacting systems. The illusion that we can understand the development of something as complex as sexual orientation by trying to locate "the gene for" amounts to no more than the fool's gold of modern genetic research, a field in which, I might add, there is plenty of true gold to be mined.

I want to make it completely clear that, in emphasizing the complexity of genetic processes, and by being highly critical of past and present research on behavioral genetics, I am not aiming to be a "gene-basher" or a "genetic Luddite," as Vernon Rosario phrased it in the introduction to this volume. I have spent much of the past thirty years studying the history of genetics, in part because the field as a whole, classical as well as molecular, represents one of the most exciting achievements of twentieth-century biology. I have no innate animosity to genetic explanations in humans or

---

deficiencies, but do not begin to illuminate the development of complex physical traits or behaviors. Because the latter are so highly subject to environmental input, any attempt to disentangle genetic from environmental components is extremely complex, especially for humans where the rigorous experimental methods that would be required are highly unethical. (Modified from Woodward 1994, 55.)

any other species. At the same time, however, it is a disservice to the achievements of the field to demand of it more than it can legitimately produce. Such demands only lead to unworkable models, however politically or philosophically useful they may appear (to some). Indeed, it is in their oversimplified but politically promulgated form that mechanical models of human behavior genetics become not just erroneous, but socially *dangerous*. It is to the political role that simplistic genetic models can play that I want to turn in the final segment of this essay.

The Politics of Human Behavior Genetics

One of the most important questions to arise from considering the manifold difficulties in doing human behavioral genetics, is: Why do we want to know, or appear to want to know, so badly? What are the characteristics of the social and political context in which genetic determinism has become such a burning issue?

Hamer's work serves as a classic example that speaks to these very questions. Hamer himself sees his work as having important social and political implications for the gay and lesbian community as a whole. In the conclusion to their *Scientific American* article, LeVay and Hamer state: "We believe scientific research can help dispel some of the myths about homosexuality that in the past have clouded the image of lesbians and gay men" (1994, 49).

Many gays and lesbians have welcomed the genetic, or at least biological, explanation of homosexuality as one way of bringing about greater understanding and acceptance—both within the gay community and from the larger society. The implications of the genetic research are that, at one level, if homosexuality can be shown to be inborn, and therefore beyond the individual's control, then perhaps it will be viewed as more natural and thus less stigmatized. Gays, lesbians, and their parents can feel less "guilty" that homosexuality was *caused* by a dysfunctional or disturbed family. "It's not my fault," is supposed to be a liberating conception. However, the genetic view can also work in just the opposite direction. In 1920s and 1930s Germany, homosexuality was regarded as a genetically determined trait (Weindling 1989, 104ff.), yet such research only played into the hands of the social pathologists. German eugenics of this time was adopted by the medical community, which treated many behavioral/social traits as pathologies (Proctor 1988). Thus, regarding social behaviors as genetically based allows them to be treated by "medical means"—that is, to be controlled or "managed." In today's context, claiming that homosexuality is genetic places it in the company of unabashedly pathological behaviors. If "guilt by association" has any power or force in the public arena, geneticizing homosexuality will not be likely to increase its acceptance.

More chilling is the prospect that by claiming a genetic basis for any human behavior we may actually undermine the social acceptance of homosexuality that has been achieved over the past twenty-five years. The mood of modern medicine, particularly psychiatry, to "treat" social behaviors by drug or hormone therapy, or even someday by genetic engineering, provides little hope that a biologically based theory of homosexuality will necessarily bring with it greater liberation. Michael T. McGuire of UCLA, a strong proponent of biological—especially genetic—explanations for human social behavior, has already argued that dominant or submissive behavior in monkeys can be manipulated by serotonin injections (in McDonald 1994, A11). And Frederick Goodwin, head of NIMH and enthusiastic advocate of the government project known as the Violence Initiative, suggested last year that so-called violent and criminal behavior in inner-city youths could be controlled by massive screening of elementary-school children for potentially violent individuals, followed by administration of mood-controlling drugs such as Prozac (Allen 1995). Biologizing homosexuality offers the same double-edged sword. The Nazis medicalized many human behaviors, only to declare individuals exhibiting those behaviors biologically incurable and thus "lives not worth living."

Already, Hamer's research has found its way into a court of law. In the fall of 1993 a test case of the constitutionality of Colorado's Amendment 2 (which prevented any city or county in the state from enacting laws that would protect homosexuals from discrimination), the gay and lesbian legal team opposing the bill decided, after much debate, to call in Dean Hamer as an expert witness. In response, the Colorado Citizens' Council (representatives of the religious right) called on one of the critics of Hamer's research, Evan Balaban, as their witness. To his credit, Balaban, who did not wish to provide fuel for anti-gay campaigns, refused to testify. In so doing, he articulated what I think is a crucial philosophical and social point: civil rights or any form of social justice should never hinge on biology. Biology may inform us about how to deal medically with particular human characteristics, but the decision to treat or not treat, or whether treatment is even necessary, is a social not a biological decision. The greater acceptance accorded gays and lesbians in the past twenty-five years has been achieved by social not biological means: by gay people increasing their visibility, by demanding their civil rights, and by political action. It is in the streets, not the laboratory, that the struggle for social justice is ultimately waged. In the era of AIDS especially, biological theories of sexual orientation are not likely to be much of an ally in that struggle. Worse, they can become an instrument of the very oppression they were meant to combat.

As to why there has been such a resurgence of research and intense publicity concerning the genetic basis for so much of our social behavior, I would point to several strong economic and political determinants. The renewed interest in human behavior genetics can be viewed as part of a larger attempt on the part of sectors of the financial world—particularly the medical and insurance industries, and their allies in government—to accomplish both economic and political/social goals:

(1) *Economic Goals.* By pathologizing many so-called antisocial behaviors, these behaviors can be treated more cost-effectively with drugs as opposed to individualized therapy—by less labor-intensive and thus less expensive means. Behavior modifying drugs do not cure, they simply *control.* In the same vein, current legal and

ethical problems arising from the Human Genome Project suggest that if diseases—of any sort, physiological or behavioral—can be viewed as genetic, they might qualify as "preexisting conditions," and thus their treatment excluded from coverage by insurance companies. In an era of skyrocketing health-care costs and the consolidation of mammoth health-care empires, a strictly biological approach to psychological/psychiatric conditions provides one way to reduce costs while maximizing profit.

(2) *Social/Political Goals.* In our present economic environment, human stress manifests itself in many ways: increased substance abuse, violence, crime, depression, and a variety of mental and personality problems. To locate those problems in the innate biology of individuals is to remove the blame from the economic and social system in which we live and to deflect responsibility for such problems away from society's privileged and powerful elite. Historically, theories of biological determinism have always functioned to such ends, and it is clear that they can continue to do so unless we blow the whistle on them in both the scientific as well as the political arena.

But why, then, do theories of biological determinism appear to be so popular with the general public, especially, in this case, within the gay and lesbian community? This is a complex question, but it can be approached in several ways. First, it is important to recognize that the lure of biological determinist theories has always been their relative simplicity. "Man's Genes Made Him Kill" read a headline recently in *The Wall Street Journal* (November 15, 1994, Sect. B1). Genes are abstract entities that can be blamed for all manner of complex problems—they are the "Other" that is somehow detached from ourselves, our beings, and thus are easy targets. They were the "devils" or "demons" of feudal theology that lurked within us and caused us to behave in "deviant" ways. Now, instead of receiving exorcism by a medieval priesthood, they are "treated" by the modern counterpart, the scientific "expert." This view is sometimes referred to as the "technological fix," for it puts the solution to social problems, no matter how complex, in the hands of technical "experts." The rest of us can go about our business and not ask the more penetrating questions of why such behaviors exist, whether they are truly pathological or not, and how we should respond both morally and ethically.

On the research front, significant funds, both private and public, are being made available for genetic determinist work, and researchers have been flocking to use it. Three years ago the NIAAA announced that $25 million has been appropriated to study the genetics of personality disorders leading to alcohol abuse. The NIMH and Center for Disease Control are currently collaborating on a $400 million Violence Initiative, a significant part of which is devoted to studying the genetic and hormonal basis of antisocial behavior. For over half a century the Pioneer Fund, a right-wing foundation originally organized in 1937 by eugenicists Madison Grant and Harry Laughlin in the United States, has funded research on the genetics of human social behaviors, including the work of Arthur Jensen and William Shockley in the 1960s and 1970s, and of J. Philippe Rushton in the 1980s and 1990s. Along with the Heritage Foundation, the Pioneer Fund has also funded the work of Thomas Bouchard of the Minnesota Twin Studies project (Mehler 1989, 1994). The funds *are* being made available, and in a period of shrinking research grants, for some investigators "any port in a storm" will do. The individual scientists who pursue such work, gratified that their work is being funded and has some possible social relevance, are only partly responsible for the widespread promulgation of biological determinist theories. The scientific and academic community bears some responsibility to critique and evaluate these views openly, and to make it clear where the data is circumstantial or faulty. Historians of science have a particularly rich opportunity to point out the past consequences of widespread belief in such theories, especially when those beliefs have become translated into social policy. But all of us, as human beings, have a responsibility to work for a more equitable and just society, one in which the true roots of human behavior can be better understood, and one in which there is no need for blaming victims and seeking simplistic answers to economic, social, and moral problems. It behooves us all to examine these issues carefully and critically, if our true aim is to understand and accept the different forms of sexuality and the different lifestyles they generate within our society.

Notes

1 For examples, see the cover stories of: *U.S. News and World Report*, Apr. 13, 1987, and Nov. 30, 1987; *Time*, Nov. 30, 1987; Jan. 17, 1994, and Aug. 15, 1994; *New Republic*, July 9 and 16, 1990, and Oct. 31, 1994; *Newsweek*, May 28, 1990, and Oct. 24, 1994; *Harvard Magazine*, May–April, 1992; *Atlantic*, March 1993, and September 1994; the *Chronicle of Higher Education*, September 1994; *Discover*, November 1994. See also the *Science* June 17, 1994 issue devoted to behavioral genetics. Most recently, Richard Herrnstein and Charles Murray's *The Bell Curve* (1994) has received widespread publicity.

2 On June 27, 1969, at the Stonewall Inn on Christopher St. in New York's Greenwich Village, angry gays attacked a police vice squad when it attempted to raid the bar shortly after midnight. Street fighting lasted for several hours and skirmishes continued for days, but the "Stonewall Riot" came to symbolize for decades the new assertiveness and activism that was beginning to sweep through the gay community.

3 As a result of the Denazification trial, Rüdin was classified by the Tribunal as a Nazi "Fellow-Traveler," a category less severe than "War Criminal" (Müller-Hill 1988, 176, 122n.).

4 "Phenotype" designates the individual's *observable* characteristics, which are presumed to be a product of genetic determinants ("genotype") and environmental influences.

5 Cf. Darwin's populational view in which variation, not fixed essential qualities, became the point of definition of a species.

6 The nature-nurture debate involves a long-standing controversy over whether heredity (nature) or environment (nurture) is the more important in determining the outcome of any particular trait in organisms, especially humans. In many respects it is a meaningless debate, similar to debating whether the area of a rectangle is determined more by its height or its width. As usually discussed, however, the issue revolves around *how much* either heredity or environment contributes to the overall form of a trait. This is, of course, the aspect that is most

difficult to determine with respect to human behavioral traits, where it is not usually possible to do the necessary controlled experiments to separate one component from the other.

7 The sequence of nucleotide bases in a segment of DNA codes for the sequence of amino acids making up a specific protein. Changes in nucleotide sequence can alter amino acid sequence, thus changing the specific properties of the protein, and thereby the role it plays in the development or maintenance of physiological properties of cells.

8 "Transcription" refers to the process of copying the nucleotide sequence from DNA to an intermediate nucleic acid, messenger RNA (mRNA). "Translation" refers to the process of converting the nucleotide sequence of mRNA into the specific amino acid sequence of a protein.

9 "Transmission" refers to the processes involved in passing on DNA from parent to offspring.

References

Allen, Garland E. 1978. *Thomas Hunt Morgan: The Man and His Science*. Princeton: Princeton University Press.

———. 1985a. Heredity under an embryological paradigm: The case of genetics and embryology. *Biological Bulletin* 168:107–121.

———. 1985b. Thomas Hunt Morgan: Materialism and experimentalism in the development of modern genetics. *Trends in Genetics* 1:151–154; 186–190.

———. 1995. Modern biological determinism: The Violence Initiative, the Human Genome Project and the New Eugenics. Forthcoming in *Yearbook of the Social Sciences*, ed. Everett Mendelsohn.

Bailey, J. Michael, and Richard C. Pillard. 1991. A genetic study of male sexual orientation. *Archives of General Psychiatry* 48:1089–1096.

Bailey, J. Michael, Richard C. Pillard, Michael C. Neal, and Yvonne Agyei. 1993. Heritable factors influence sexual orientation in women. *Archives of General Psychiatry* 50:217–223.

Barinaga, Marcia. 1995. Bisexual fruit flies point to brain courtship centers. *Science* 267:791–792.

Barnouw, Victor, and John A. Stern. 1963. Some suggestions concerning social and cultural determinants of human sexual behavior. In *Determinants of Human Sexual Behavior*, ed. George Winokur, 206–209. Springfield, IL: Charles C. Thomas.

Bayer, Ronald A. 1987. Politics, science, and the problem of psychiatric nomenclature: A case study of the American Psychiatric Association referendum on homosexuality. In *Scientific Controversies. Case Studies in the Resolution and Closure of Disputes in Science and Technology*, ed. H. Tristram Engelhardt and Arthur L. Caplan, 381–400. New York: Cambridge University Press.

Beach, Frank A., ed. 1976. *Human Sexuality in Four Perspectives*. Baltimore: Johns Hopkins University Press.

Bell, Alan P., and Martin S. Weinberg. 1978. *Homosexualities: A Study of Diversity Among Men and Women*. New York: Simon & Schuster.

Bieber, Irving, Harvey J. Dain, Paul R. Dince, Marvin G. Drellich, Henry G. Grand, Ralph H. Gundlach, Malvina W. Kremer, Alfred H. Rifkin, Cornelia B. Wilbur, and Toby B. Bieber. 1962. *Homosexuality, A Psychoanalytic Study*. New York: Basic Books.

Bieber, Irving. 1965. Clinical aspects of male homosexuality. In *Sexual Inversion: The Multiple Roots of Homosexuality*, ed. Judd Marmor, 248–267. New York: Basic Books.

Billings, Paul R., Jonathan Beckwith, and Joseph S. Alper. 1992. The genetic analysis of human behavior: A new era? *Social Science and Medicine* 35:227–238

Bleuler, M., and H.R. Wiedemann. 1956. Chromosomengeschlecht und Psychosexualität. *Archiv für Psychiatrie und Nervenkrankheiten* 195:14–19.

Breggin, Peter R. 1991. *Toxic Psychiatry*. New York: St. Martin's Press.

Brooks, Kelly. 1994. Homosexuality and genetics: Does "X" mark the spot? Unpublished course paper, Washington University, St. Louis.

Byne, William. 1994. The biological evidence challenged. *Scientific American* 270:50–55.

Byne, William, and Bruce Parsons. 1993. Human sexual orientation: The biological theories reappraised. *Archives of General Psychiatry* 50:228–239.

Churchill, Wainright. [1967] 1971. *Homosexual Behavior Among Males. A Cross-cultural and Cross-species Investigation*. 2nd ed. New York: Spectrum Books.

Cohen, D.J., E. Dibble, J.M. Grause, and W. Pollin. 1975. Reliably separating identical from fraternal twins. *Archives of General Psychiatry* 32:1371–1375.

Cooke, Robert. 1990. Now you see 'em, now you don't. *Newsday* (October 23): 6–7.

Dank, Barry M. 1971. Six homosexual siblings. *Archives of Sexual Behavior* 1:193–204.

Davenport, Charles B. 1919. *The Trait Book*. Cold Spring Harbor, NY: Carnegie Institution of Washington.

Ferveur, Jean-François, Klemens F. Stortkuhl, Reinhard F. Stocker, and Ralph J. Greenspan. 1995. Genetic feminization of brain structures and changed sexual orientation in male *Drosophila*. *Science* 267:902–905.

Futuyma, Douglas J. n.d. Sexual orientation and human evolution: A review of biological theories of homosexuality. Typescript, pers. com.

Galton, Francis. 1883. *Inquiries into Human Faculty and its Development*. London: Macmillan.

Gifford, Fred. 1990. Genetic traits. *Biology and Philosophy* 5:327–347.

Greenspan, Ralph. 1995. Understanding the genetic construction of behavior. *Scientific American* 272:72–78.

Hamer, Dean, Stella Hu, Victoria L. Manguson, Nan Hu, and Angela M.L. Pattatucci. 1993. A linkage between DNA markers on the X chromosome and male sexual orientation. *Science* 261:321–327.

Hamer, Dean, and Peter Copeland. 1994. *The Science of Desire: The Search for the Gay Gene and the Biology of Behavior*. New York: Simon & Schuster.

Harmsen, Hans, and Franz Lohse, eds. [1936] 1969. *Bevolkerungsfragen; Bericht des Internationalen Kongresses für Bevolkerungswissenschaft, Berlin, 26 August–1 September, 1935*. Munich: Lehmann. Reprint of original edition, Nedeln/Liechtenstein: Kraus Reprint.

Herrn, Rainer. 1995. On the history of biological theories of homosexuality. In *Sex, Cells, and Same-Sex Desire: The Biology of Sexual Preference*, ed. John DeCecco, and David Allen, 31–56. Binghamton, NY: Harrington Park.

Heston, L.L., and J. Shields. 1968. Homosexuality in twins: A family study and registry study. *Archives of General Psychiatry* 18:149–160.

Hirschfeld, Magnus. [1936] 1954. The homosexual as an intersex. Reprinted in *The Homosexuals: As Seen by Themselves and Thirty Authorities*, ed. Aaron M. Krich, 119–134. New York: Citadel Press.

Hirschhorn, K., and H.L. Cooper. 1961. Chromosomal aberrations in human disease. *American Journal of Medicine* 31:442–470.

Holden, Constance. 1991. Probing the complex genetics of alcoholism. *Science* 251: 163–164.

Horgan, John. 1993. Eugenics revisited. *Scientific American* 268:122–131.

Kallmann, Franz J. 1938a. *The Genetics of Schizophrenia. A Study of Heredity and Reproduction in the Families of 1,087 Schizophrenics*. New York: J.J. Augustin.

———. 1938b. Heredity, reproduction and eugenic procedure in the field of schizophrenia. *Eugenical News* 23:105–113.

———. 1952a. Comparative twin study on the genetic aspects of male homosexuality. *Journal of Nervous and Mental Disease* 115:283–298.

———. 1952b. Twin and sibship study of overt male homosexuality. *American Journal of Human Genetics* 4:136–146.

———. 1953. *Heredity in Health and Mental Disorder*. New York: W.W. Norton.

———. 1959. The genetics of mental illness. In *American Handbook of Psychiatry*, ed. S. Arieti, 175–196. New York: Basic Books.

———. 1963. Genetic aspects of sex determination and sexual maturation potentials in man. In *Determinants of Human Sexual Behavior*, ed. George Winokur, 5–18. Springfield, IL: Charles C. Thomas.

Kleemeier, Robert W., and Mildred Kantor. 1963. Methodological considerations in the study of human sexual behavior. In *Determinants of Human Sexual Behavior*, ed. George Winokur, 201–209. Springfield, IL: Charles C. Thomas.

Krafft-Ebing, Richard von. [1886] 1924. *Psychopathia Sexualis*. Brooklyn, NY: Physicians and Surgeons Book Co.

Lang, Thomas. 1940. Studies on the genetic determination of homosexuality. *Journal of Nervous and Mental Disease* 92:55–64.

Lang, Thomas. 1945. Zur Frage nach der genetischen Struktur von Homosexullen und deren Eltern. *Archiv Julius Klaus Stiftung* 20: 51.

LeVay, Simon. 1993. *The Sexual Brain*. Cambridge: MIT Press.

LeVay, Simon, and Dean H. Hamer. 1994. Evidence for a biological influence in male homosexuality. *Scientific American* 270:44–49.

Lewontin, R.C., Steven Rose, and Leon J. Kamin. 1984. *Not in Our Genes*. New York: Pantheon Books.

Longino, Helen. 1990. *Science as Social Knowledge. Values and Objectivity in Scientific Inquiry*. Princeton, NJ: Princeton University Press.

McDonald, Kim A. 1994. Biology and behavior. Social scientists and evolutionary biologists discuss and debate new findings. *The Chronicle of Higher Education* (September 14): A10–20.

Marmor, Judd. 1965. Introduction. In *Sexual Inversion: The Multiple Roots of Homosexuality*, ed. J. Marmor, 1–24. New York: Basic Books.

Marx, Karl. [1888] 1959. Theses on Feuerbach. In *Marx and Engels. Basic Writings on Politics and Philosophy*, ed. Lewis S. Feuer, 243–245. Garden City, NY: Anchor Books.

Mehler, Barry. 1989. Foundations for fascism: The new eugenics movement in the United States. *Patterns of Prejudice* 23:18–25.

———. 1994. In genes we trust. When science bows to racism. *Reform Judiasm* 23:10–14, 77–79.

Money, John. 1963. Factors in the genesis of homosexuality. In *Determinants of Human Sexual Behavior*, ed. George Winokur, 19–43. Springfield, IL: Charles C. Thomas.

Moulton, Forest Ray, and P. O. Komoro, eds. 1939. *Mental Health*. Publication No. 9.Washington, DC: American Association for the Advancement of Science.

Müller-Hill, Benno. 1988. *Murderous Science*. New York: Oxford University Press.

Nelkin, Dorothy, and Susan Lindee. 1995. *The DNA Mystique. The Gene as a Cultural Icon*. New York: W. H. Freeman.

Pare, C.M.B. 1956. Homosexuality and chromosomal sex. *Journal of Psychosomatic Research* 1:247–251.

———. 1965. Etiology of homosexuality: Genetic and chromosomal aspects. In *Sexual Inversion: The Multiple Roots of Homosexuality*, ed. J. Marmor, 70–80. New York: Basic Books.

Pastore. N. 1949. The genetics of schizophrenia. *Psychiatric Bulletin* 46: 285–302.

Perkins, Muriel W. 1973. Homosexuality in female monozygotic twins. *Behavior Genetics* 3:387–388.

Pillard, Richard C., and James D. Weinrich. 1986. Evidence of familial nature of male homosexuality. *Archives of General Psychiatry* 43:808–812.

Pritchard, Michael. 1962. Homosexuality and genetic sex. *Journal of Mental Science* 108:616–623.

Proctor, Robert. 1988. *Racial Hygiene: Medicine Under the Nazis*. Cambridge: Harvard University Press.

Rose, Steven. 1995. The rise of neurogenetic determinism. *Nature* 373 (February 2): 380–384.

Rosenthal, David. 1970. Homosexuality. In *Genetics of Psychopathology*, ed. D. Rosenthal, 250–255. New York: McGraw-Hill.

Rosenzweig, Saul. 1973. Human sexual autonomy as an evolutionary attainment, anticipating proceptive sex choice and idiosyncratic bisexuality. In *Contemporary Sexual Behavior: Critical Issues in the 1970's*, ed. Joseph Zubin and John Money, 189–230. Baltimore: Johns Hopkins University Press.

Ruse, Michael. 1988. *Homosexuality: A Philosophical Inquiry*. Oxford: Basil Blackwell.

———. 1994. Knowledge in human genetics: Some epistemological questions. In *Genes and Human Self-Knowledge*, ed. Robert Weir, Susan Lawrence, and Evan Fales, 34–45. Iowa City: University of Iowa Press.

Schlegel, W.S. 1962. Die konstitutionsbiologischen Grundlage der Homosexualität. *Zeitschrift für menschlische Konstitutionslehre* 36:341–364.

Sines, Jacob O., and David J. Pittman. 1963. Male homosexuality: The relevance of cross-species studies of sexual behavior. In *Determinants of Human Sexual Behavior*, ed. George Winokur, 189–192. Springfield, IL: Charles C. Thomas.

Suppe, Frederick. 1979. The Bell/Weinberg study and future priorities for research on homosexuality. Typescript, presented January 5 at AAAS Meeting, Houston.

Taylor, Charlotte C. 1972. Identical twins: Concordance for homosexuality? *American Journal of Psychiatry* 129:486–487

Van Wyck, P.H., and C.S. Geist. 1984. Psychosocial development of heterosexual, bisexual and homosexual behavior. *Archives of Sexual Behavior* 13:505–544

Weindling, Paul. 1989. *Health, Race and German Politics Between National Unification and Nazism, 1870–1945*. New York: Cambridge University Press.

Weinrich, James D. 1976. Human reproductive strategy. Ph.D. dissertation, Harvard University, Cambridge. *Dissertation Abstracts International* 37(10): 5339-B. University Microfilms No. 77–8348.

———. 1987. *Sexual Landscapes*. New York: Scribners.

Wilson, E.O. 1975. *Sociobiology, The New Synthesis*. Cambridge: Harvard University Press.

Woodward, Val. 1994. Can we draw conclusions about human societal behavior from population genetics? In *Challenging Racism and Sexism. Alternatives to Genetic Explanations*, ed. Ethel Tobash and Betty Rosoff, 35–65. New York: Feminist Press at The City University of New York.

The Seductive Power of Science in the Making of Deviant Subjectivity

Jennifer Terry

As part of an attempt to situate the AIDS epidemic historically and culturally, much of my work is devoted to making sense of the discursive association between homosexuality and pathology over the past one hundred years or so. I am concerned with what the confluence of these two terms—homosexuality and pathology—means for the construction of queer subjectivities, particularly in the United States now, at the end of a century and of a millennium.[1] My method is to examine critically medical and scientific projects designed to gain epistemological and social control over homosexuality. I do not presume that one can do this effectively by focusing on scientific practices and discourses alone. Instead, my method is to read scientific practices as both embedded in and expressive of culturally and historically specific conditions. In short, I presume science to be situated always among competing meanings and explanations, and never to be in a domain free from political, economic, and cultural processes. For many readers, I am sure, understanding science *as* culture and *in* culture is a first premise, or a given of any intelligent analysis of scientific knowledge. Likewise, the notion that science is both embedded in and constitutive of dynamics of social power is by now beyond question, even (or especially) from the perspectives of many scientists themselves. But demonstrating these points seems important now, at a time when the magical signs of rationality, objectivity, and scientific authority continue to shape the terms by which we imagine ourselves, our bodies, and the environments we occupy.

I would like to offer some ideas for assessing the contemporary relationship of lesbians and gay men to scientific knowledge by saying a little bit about the paradoxical history of this relationship. By now, we have voluminous evidence to show that science and medicine have played a big part in the making of homophobia. And yet, paradoxically, science has on occasion had a seductive power over gay men and lesbians, especially when it purports to offer us truth, authenticity, the security of identity, and even liberation. Why and how has homosexuality become the object of scientific scrutiny? What cultural anxieties generate scientific studies of homosexuality? And why would lesbians and gay men agree to be studied by scientists? I want to pose these questions through a brief historical survey of what I think represent the main kinds of scientific research on homosexuality undertaken in the U.S. during this century. Hopefully, this survey will shed some light on the cultural salience of recent biological research on sexual orientation, to which I will turn during the second half of the chapter.

The Paradox of Seduction and Repulsion

Over the past several years I have encountered a particularly difficult and troubling problem in my research on the history of the formation of lesbian and gay subjectivities. This problem in many ways precipitated my specific interest in analyzing how science thinks about homosexuality: in trying to map what produces or constructs "queer" subjectivities in the twentieth century, I have been constantly reminded that one cannot simply disentangle the discursive conflation of homosexuality and pathology. This led me to investigate specific instances where lesbians and gay men were brought under the medical and scientific gaze (Terry 1990, 1992, 1995). I am immensely curious about how the processes of clinical and scientific scrutiny operate in relation to the production of queer subjectivities. And, frankly, I am most intrigued in cases where lesbians and gay men actually volunteered to be studied by experts and to be examined physically in ways that we might find utterly repulsive today.

In order to take up the question of why lesbians and gay men volunteer to be studied by doctors and scientists and why some are inclined to embrace science, we need first to note how this question is itself located in a particular historical moment. Many of us now are deeply skeptical about the grandiose promises of science, but for most of this century in the United States, science has held the status of being the sacred avenue to truth as well as a source of national strength. Throughout this discussion I deliberately use the term science broadly to refer to a wide range of disciplines, from the natural, to the physical, to the social sciences, including medicine—disciplines that share certain philosophical and methodological assumptions and approaches based on the idea that science is the privileged mode for discovering Truth. What these disciplines have in common is that they generally believe (1) in the importance of testing hypotheses through careful techniques of data gathering, experimentation, and observation; (2) that truth is empirically measurable and can be reproduced in an experimental setting; (3) that the scientist can maintain impartiality and neutrality by following certain procedures; and (4) that what scientists find in their laboratories, through their questionnaires, or through their clinical observations has some utility to humankind.

Reputable practitioners of science are seen to be objective, impartial, neutral, and, indeed, virtuous on account of helping us know more about the world. Moreover, science has been heralded in the United States, especially in the earlier part of this century, as a primary method for solving social problems such as crime, poverty, and disease. However, now, in the late twentieth century, after revelations about Nazi medicine, after the invention of the nuclear bomb and germ warfare, and after the ecological horrors wrought by technological development, many of us have developed a skeptical view of the doctrine of rationality and its practitioners.

Ironically, coexisting alongside this general cultural skepticism about science and doubt about its ability to "discover" the truth is a persistent faith in science, if not in particular scientists. In and of itself, scientific knowledge continues to be seen as virtuous. On top of this, research projects on a grand scale—such as the Human Genome Project, the Strategic Defense Initiative ("Star Wars"), the Strategic Computing Initiative, and cancer research—are justified in terms of their essential importance to the vitality and security of human beings. So at the end of the twentieth century, the utopian and dystopian images of science exist concurrently in a curious way.

It is worth noting that skepticism toward scientists and doctors among some groups of people—namely women, people of color, poor people—is the result of a long history of abuse and neglect (Jones 1981; Ehrenreich & English 1978). But where are lesbians and gay men situated in relation to this contradictory state of horror and hope about science? We have particularly complicated histories, which must be brought to bear on this question. Lesbians and gay men can thank scientists and doctors for naming them as pathological, beginning in the latter half of the nineteenth century (Westphal 1869; Krafft-Ebing 1886). And for much of this century we have been regarded as anomalies to be explained, if not patients to be treated. As a result, many are deeply ambivalent about the theories and applications of science to questions about sexuality.

We, as deviant subjects, have had to account for ourselves as anomalies. We are compelled to ask certain *questions of the self*, beyond the generic question of: Who am I? In addition, we ask: How did I come to be this way? How and why am I different? Is there something wrong with me? Is there something in my background that would explain my homosexuality? Is there something different about my body? Am I a danger to myself or others? Deviant subjectivity is forged in the relay of these questions, where a number of intended and unintended effects are produced (Terry 1994). What follows is a brief sketch of several different kinds of studies in which homosexual subjects have been motivated to ask particular questions of the self—that is, to account for themselves—through the authority of science.

A Brief Survey of Scientific Studies of Homosexuality

Scientific inquiry into homosexuality is particularly interesting to analyze because, as I hope to show, each episode or mode of scientific research aimed at studying queers has been shaped by and, in turn, influences the social relations and the cultural context from which it emerged. I propose that we look at various kinds of inquiry as they encode and enact particular cultural anxieties. How have these anxieties shaped the terms of deviant subjectivity? Through individual case histories of patients, nineteenth-century neurologists described homosexuality as a manifestation of innate degeneracy and nervousness, likening it to the morally and physically dissipating practice of masturbation (Westphal 1869; Krafft-Ebing 1886; Charcot & Magnan 1882). At the heart of much of this early scientific discourse and subsequent studies of homosexuality was a fascination and obsession with the body—its structure, motions, and behaviors—as a territory of perversions. Through techniques of clinical surveillance and diagnosis, homosexual bodies were objects to be measured, zones to be mapped, and texts to be read by both scientists and the subjects who inhabited those bodies. Machines and morals functioned instrumentally and phantasmatically to "find" the sources and traces of perversions. It was both on the surfaces of perverse bodies and in their dark interiors that homosexual desire was presumed to originate and proliferate as a dyshygienic threat to the whole and wholesome organic body of the *human* (read: white, heterosexual, property-owning gentleman). For the homosexual subjects themselves, the body was both constrained by this scientific moral quest and always excessive to any such quest. Historically, deviant subjectivity is profoundly bound up with contests about the roles, functions, possibilities, and violations performed by queer bodies.

Homosexuals were one of a number of late nineteenth-century *internal others* explored for stigmata of degeneracy within the West—alongside criminals, prostitutes, the feebleminded—whose bodies were believed to carry the germs of ruin. In this way, the clinical study of perverts was linked with a larger scientific interest in classifying human cultural diversity in biological terms. In nineteenth-century Europe and America, the belief that moral character and psychical features were fundamentally tied to biology came to the fore with a vengeance at a moment of heated debate about who would enjoy the privileges of legal and economic enfranchisement in a newly reconfigured public sphere. In the United States, anxieties about the abolition of slavery in 1865 and the rise of feminist agitation for the vote fueled scientific research aimed at demonstrating that social inequality was merely a matter of biology and nature. It was around this moment when the sodomite emerged as a threat to public hygiene, and the mannish woman was characterized as a threat to the private realm of the family—nothing short of a woman on strike against marriage and motherhood. Science and medicine were installed as keepers of the public trust, and a fascination with all things modern made the idea of eugenic engineering of a population's genetic stock compelling across the political spectrum.

Interestingly, the early clinical study of perverts and inverts engendered the resistant tradition of Magnus Hirschfeld, whose Institute for the Study of Sexual Science used the idea as well as the textual conventions of the case history to document that those with "contrary sexual feeling" were benign natural anomalies, afflicted not by biological defects but by the social hostility that surrounded them (Hirschfeld 1914, 1935; Nunberg & Federn 1962). In this early instance of what we might call (at the risk of being "presentist") gay-positive science, Hirschfeld and those who voluntarily offered up their stories and bodies to scrutiny believed that scientific knowledge would bring social tolerance, legal protection, and even personal liberation. The "secrets of the self" that Foucault (1978, 1980) described as central to the modern psychoanalytic confession were conveyed by homosexual subjects in the hopes of gaining a greater sense of self-knowledge. Science was viewed as a powerful means for gaining visibility and eradicating prejudice (see Oosterhuis and Steakley in this volume).

Following the nineteenth-century clinical case history model, knowledge about homosexuality in the first half of the twentieth century was gleaned from an array of behavioral surveys undertaken by biologists, sociologists, and anthropologists, often working in conjunction with psychiatric physicians. This behavioral research used statistical methods to quantify the incidence and nature of homosexuality as part of a larger interest in studying and constituting norms within the general population. This kind of research did not wholly supplant the clinical case model; homosexuality continued to be seen both as a medical malady afflicting certain individuals, and as a danger that was potentially spreading throughout the population. Thus, while medical doctors focused on individual cases as the primary unit of analysis for exemplifying particular perversions, behavioral surveys of sexual practices were the product of scientists seeking to determine norms at the collective level of society. Their studies were tied to other normalization efforts linked to military recruitment in World Wars I and II, to public health campaigns related to venereal disease and eugenics, and to marital adjustment surveys aimed at policing the institutions of marriage and family.[2] A scientific zeal to measure everything from intelligence to vocational abilities to rates of sexual pleasure characterized the behavioral surveys and subsequent social engineering of the first half of this century. Anxieties engendered by economic depressions, waves of immigration into the United States by Southern and Eastern Europeans, and internal migration of African-Americans to northern cities fueled the scientific rationale to solve social problems through techniques of quantification.

One study of homosexuality from this period combined the clinical case history method with scientific methods in a very interesting fashion. It was conducted in the late 1930s in New York City, under the auspices of the Committee for the Study of Sex Variants, a group made up of twenty biological and social scientists, and doctors from various specialty areas (Henry 1941). The subjects of the study included forty lesbians and forty homosexual men, who volunteered to be interviewed and to be examined physically in great detail by all kinds of different doctors, including surgeons and gynecologists.

One of the most interesting facets of the study, for my purposes, is that it was largely made possible by the volunteer work of a lesbian named Miss Jan Gay, who was a freelance journalist and novelist in the Greenwich Village lesbian scene of the 1920s and 1930s. During the 1920s, Gay traveled to Europe, looking for information about homosexuality. In addition to the many libraries she consulted, Jan Gay visited Magnus Hirschfeld's institute, and gathered information about how to conduct a survey about sexuality, including what kinds of questions to ask. She put her new knowledge to work, interviewing some three hundred lesbians in Paris, London, Berlin, and New York. This sample survey, which was based on a questionnaire she adapted from Hirschfeld, formed the methodological basis for the study conducted by the Sex Variants Committee during the 1930s. The interview questionnaire asked the subjects about their family background and ancestors, childhood experiences, adult experiences, sexual desires, and opinions about society's attitude toward homosexuality. In addition, the protocol for research included various physical examinations designed to determine any anatomical features which distinguished homosexuals from the "general population."

How could the subjects have said yes to science in this way? It is impossible to determine with certainty what specifically motivated each of the eighty subjects to be interviewed and examined by doctors. But I do know that they were not coerced, at least not in any simple way. They received no money, nor did they get any special favors in return for their participation. This put them in a different position from involuntary subjects of other scientific studies—for example, mental patients, prisoners, parolees, potential army recruits, soldiers, and reform school inmates—who were forced, more or less, to comply with the demands of probing experts.

What reward was offered the sex-variant subjects, if not money or special favors and privileges? Why did they talk to psychiatrists and allow doctors to probe and measure them? There are several possible explanations. Clearly, Jan Gay was crucial in getting the eighty subjects for this study because she was part of a homosexual subculture in New York at the time. Many of these subjects were acquaintances and friends of Gay, and, as a favor to her, agreed to take part in the study. Beyond that simple fact, the psychiatrist who authored the volume compiling the case histories assured readers that most of the subjects agreed to participate in the study because they believed it would advance the cause of social tolerance toward lesbians and gay men. Indeed, this motivation was more than mere conscientious duty; no doubt the occasion of the study inspired many of its subjects to avow homosexuality as a desirable alternative to heterosexuality. And they were able to intervene in the terms of homosexual representation at one of its most powerful points of generation—medico-scientific discourse.

But these explanations alone fail to capture the complexity of how medico-scientific discourse came to be an avenue of self-enunciation for these people, who, in many ways, had physicians and scientists to thank for their social stigmatization. Perhaps in addition to relying upon science to defend them, the subjects volunteered to be studied because they believed that they might also learn something valuable about themselves in the process. And they might have also believed that being studied by scientists was a way of becoming visible and thus tolerated within the larger society.

Around the same time this research was being done, Alfred Kinsey and his team of researchers (1948, 1953) were busy attempting to survey sexual behavior in the general population. As Stephanie Kenen points out in this volume, Kinsey argued that previous studies of homosexuality were deeply flawed, because they presumed the homosexual to be a psychically and somatically distinct type of person. Instead, Kinsey's research opened up a space for thinking about homosexual practice as widespread and "natural," and powerfully disrupted a scientific tradition of looking for signs of homosexuality in certain bodies—although only momentarily.

Immediately following the publication of Kinsey's research, a number of very vicious books were written mainly for mass audiences by psychiatrists and psychoanalysts who vehemently opposed Kinsey's claim that homosexuality was natural and widespread in the population. They used case histories of homosexual mental patients to argue that lesbianism and male homosexuality were indeed morbid pathological conditions (Bergler 1958, 1959; Bergler & Kroger 1954). Symptoms included immaturity, deception, and even treason, making the homosexual just as dangerous to the nation's security as the treacherous communists. Deeply homophobic psychiatrists such as Edmund Bergler were more than willing to concede that homosexuality was not a biologically based condition but a diseased lifestyle that should be subject to psychotherapy. In his book, *Homosexuality: Disease or Way of Life* (1956), Bergler argued that homosexuals were a small, psychotic group of people, and that it was only because homosexuality had been glamorized that these maladjusted and self-indulgent people gravitated toward it. Bergler, along with Frank Caprio (1955) and Irving Bieber (1965), produced what we might call the xenophobic Cold War texts attacking homosexuality as a morbid psychological condition that threatened the security of the family and the nation. A host of treatments and so-called aversion therapies were devised to treat the treacherous malady.[3] Even while they argued that the body and biology had nothing to do with homosexuality, these experts attempted to single out the homosexual as a pathological type of person, and thus to allay social anxieties unleashed by Kinsey's findings of widespread homosexual practice. But it was against this hostile and speculative psychoanalysis that Alfred Kinsey was able to appear as a careful, unbiased, and methodologically sound scientist among those in the early homophile organizations.

In their eyes, Kinsey stood out as the hero and, of course, the ultimate truth-teller, based on the belief that "statistics don't lie," and that the documented frequency of homosexual behavior in the population meant that it was both natural and normal. In the emergent homophile discourse of the late 1940s and early 1950s, one can hear the appeal of social scientific techniques of statistical analysis which rendered a broader and—in the minds of many—a more accurate picture of homosexuality. This was accompanied by explicit opposition to patient-based psychoanalytic or medical studies. Homophile activists in the Mattachine Society and the Daughters of Bilitis (DOB) argued that, for one thing, the famous psychiatric studies of Bergler and others drew their conclusions about homosexuality from mental patients or people who were, in some other way, maladjusted to society. Homophile activists argued that scientists should study homosexuals who were not patients, and who were "adjusted" in every other way. Of course, this carried with it a valorization of assimilationism and a dependency upon science to articulate political claims for mainstream tolerance of homosexuality.

The homophile embrace of social science promoted two main points. First, it sought to argue that homosexuals were not, by definition, sick. In fact, it stressed that homosexuals were average people, just like everyone else. Obviously this emphasis banked on social conformity and resulted in the homogenization of differences among homosexuals into a model of the perfect, "adjusted" homosexual. Second, the homophile interest in scientifically generated statistical surveys was related to arguing that homosexuals represented a minority, but a substantial one, worthy of some recognition for its social and cultural contributions. Scientific surveys became a strategy for visibility. In fact, the Daughters of Bilitis stated one of its foundational principles to be the gathering and dissemination of authoritative and reliable information about lesbians. For this they sought the expertise of sympathetic psychiatrists and social scientists.

Gradually, by about 1963, it is possible to trace the emergence of a split between various chapters of the Mattachine Society and DOB over the question of how important it was to have scientific studies conducted about homosexuality. It is interesting to note that no one was particularly in favor of biological or medical research on homosexuality at this moment. This consensus fits with that of the general public at a time when the horrors of Nazi medicine were making headline news, and the whole idea of biological explanations for social inequality was coming in for harsh criticism. Frank Kameny (1965), a gay man and founder of the Mattachine Society of Washington, fought against the homosexual purges from the U.S. government during the 1950s. He argued in the pages of the DOB publication, *The Ladder*, that spending so much time on scientific and psychological research was a waste of energy for homosexuals. Kameny, a scientist himself, argued that most existing scientific studies lacked rigor and relied on an unsupported assertion that homosexuals were sick or defective. To counter this assertion, he insisted on a militant position that refused the notion that lesbians and gay men were sick, and argued that it was time to fight for homosexual rights and for homosexuals to speak for themselves rather than taking the meek position of hoping that doctors and scientists would find them normal enough. The only scientific studies Kameny condoned were those that helped lesbians and homosexual men to understand their own worlds and lives better, not those that were meant to persuade the general public or other experts that homosexuals should be tolerated. Florence Conrad, chair of the DOB research committee, countered Kameny's editorial, arguing that lesbians and homosexual men needed to have their experiences translated by scientists, so that other scientists and the lay public would listen with interest and be persuaded that being gay was okay. For Conrad, militant action would only allow them to ignore and marginalize homosexuals. Instead, she recommended a careful course of cooperation. Conrad had a great deal of faith particularly in the virtues and possibilities of social scientific investigations (Conrad 1965).

Then, in 1972, Del Martin and Phyllis Lyon published *Lesbian/Woman*, which they describe as a *subjective* account of lesbianism. In their introduction, they explicitly set out to recuperate the experiences of lesbians from the distortions of most medical and scientific accounts. Martin and Lyon claimed to have produced neither a true confession nor a scientific book, but one that was written from subjective experience. They affirmed the book as partisan, not only rejecting the idea of objectivity and scientific neutrality, but also making the argument that lesbians must speak in their own terms, not through those set out in the experts' frameworks. But one of the things that is most interesting to me about *Lesbian/Woman*, a foundational text of lesbian-feminism, is how much it, in many respects, resembles previous social scientific surveys and early psychiatric case histories produced as a result of voluntary lesbian participation in studies. One can identify a similarity in the discursive structure of the subjects' self-descriptions reported in *Lesbian/Woman* and those of the early psychiatric interviews that were part of the Sex Variants study of the 1930s. Again we find the articulation of questions of the self—What am I? How did I come to be this way? How and why am I different? Is there something wrong with me? Hence lesbian-feminist discourse took on some of the same questions raised earlier by medical and scientific discourses that conflated homosexuality with pathology. This time, however, these questions provided the means for explicitly generating a counterdiscourse that replaced scientific authority with new, authentic evidence called "personal experience" in order to claim that homosexuality was healthy. Any pathology surrounding it was caused by social prejudice and homophobic and sexist hostility.

Whither the Homosexual Body?

What was happening to the scientific search for homosexuality in the body during this time? Earlier studies from the 1930s, aimed at determining distinct somatic features of homosexuals, for the most part failed to produce any such evidence. Most of them focused on the overall structure of bodies, measuring skeletal features, pelvic angles, and aspects such as muscle density and hair distribution. They hypothesized that homosexuals would show physical characteristics of the opposite sex, but none could provide conclusive evidence of this. Furthermore, endocrinological studies from the first part of this century relied on crude methods and were entirely unsuccessful in their attempts to link homosexuality with specific hormonal activity. But these failures by no means put to rest the hope of finding innate biological markers of homosexuality. Beginning in the 1960s, a growing number of hormonal experiments were conducted on both rodents and on nonhuman primates as part of a renewed attempt to determine the effects of hormones on sexual behavior, and especially to find a link between hormonal activity and homosexuality (Dörner 1968, 1976). Scientists conducting these hormonal experiments conjectured that homosexuality was a congenital condition, originating in the earliest stages of development, and arresting the natural maturation process of the male so that it behaved more like the *species type*: that is, more like a female. By contrast, female offspring, showered by storms of androgens in the womb, would falsely mature beyond their primary status to develop masculine characteristics.[4] Some psychiatrists took a keen interest in this type of research as a way of accounting for sissy-boys and tomboys.[5] Many acknowledged that hormonal activity could be influenced by the environment and by family relations. But, to a great degree, they biologized the process of psychosexual development to emphasize that sexual orientation is deeply embedded in the body from an early age—perhaps a result of a genetic predisposition to hormonal anomalies, or the outcome of maternal stress that subverted the processes by which male and female embryos normally develop (Dörner et al. 1975, 1983).

Interestingly, during the late 1960s and 1970s, even while it was busily taking place in scientific laboratories, this kind of research was roundly criticized by other biologists for lacking scientific rigor, as well as by social scientists for its pretensions to explain complex human relations in biologically reductive, trans-species terms. Meanwhile, during this period, feminists, Marxists, and liberals decried attempts to explain social differences and inequalities in terms of biology. Hormonal research involving human subjects was seen by many as downright ghoulish, reminiscent of Nazi medicine, and fundamentally retrograde because it defined homosexuality as an abnormal condition or defect. To a great degree, among liberals and radicals, scientific projects to discover the biological basis of homosexuality were regarded with no less disdain than medical efforts to treat homosexuality as a mental disorder. Feminists and gay liberationists were among the most vocal critics of biological determinism.

Now, in the 1990s, I am interested in asking how and why, more than twenty years later, scientific research purporting to find a biological basis for sexual orientation in the body is being welcomed among some gay men and lesbians as a means for understanding ourselves better and for defending ourselves against growing homophobic hostility. As I have argued, scientific interest in finding homosexuality in the body never really went away; but why is new research on the biology of homosexuality being embraced by certain gay organizations and individuals? What has made this shift in thinking possible?

Where Are We Today?

I would like to take a moment to juxtapose two bold quotes, one from 1973, the other from 1993, to illustrate a point about the significant shift in thinking concerning the place of biology in constructing lesbian and gay subjectivities and political identities. In 1973, Anne Koedt articulated a common tenet among radical lesbian-feminists at that time:

> Basic to the position of radical feminism is the concept that biology is not destiny, and that male and female roles are learned—indeed that they are male political constructs that ensure power and superior status for men. (Koedt 1973, 248).

Twenty years later, in March of 1993, gay journalist, Chandler Burr, in a cover-page article in *The Atlantic Monthly*, asserted a very different position, and one that seems to be oblivious to either leftist or feminist critiques of biological determinism:

> Homosexuality's invitation to biology has been standing for years. Homosexuals have long maintained that sexual orientation, far from being a personal choice or lifestyle (as it is often called), is something neither chosen nor changeable; heterosexuals who have made their peace with homosexuals have often done so by accepting that premise. The very term "sexual orientation," which in the 1980s replaced

> "sexual preference," asserts the deeply rooted nature of sexual desire and love. It implies biology. (Burr 1993, 48)

Maybe Chandler Burr is correct in reporting the interests of *some* gay men in establishing biological explanations for homosexuality and beseeching scientists to study us more. But Burr's assertion stages a false consensus on the matter among lesbians and gay men. Some gay men's narratives of "having always felt this way" are very powerful indeed at the subjective level. And they can also perform the rhetorical function (albeit fundamentally defensive) of telling homophobes to "fuck off." But I think it is important to note that many women, in particular, feel a great deal of ambivalence about grounding identity and personal narratives in biological difference since biological explanations have historically been deployed to keep women in a subordinate position to men. Likewise, there is considerable resistance among many lesbians and gays of color to the idea that homosexuality is biologically based, again because biological explanations have been largely in the service of marginalizing certain groups defined as naturally inferior to white men (Hammonds 1993).

Perhaps it would be useful to take a look at the larger cultural and historical context out of which this new biological evidence of homosexuality is emerging in order to make sense of this shift from radical feminism in 1973 to gay rights politics in the 1990s. It strikes me that there are several key cultural and political developments that make the 1990s a very different place to be from the 1970s. To begin, let us consider some of the changes in the relation of scientific knowledge to society generally, and then try to analyze how these changes position lesbians, gay men, and queers today with respect to being studied by scientists.

We are living now in the age of the magical sign of the gene. There is a great deal of hope riding on this "holy grail" of the late twentieth century. Scientists promise that if we can figure out the exact function and location of specific genes within the human body, the human population could be rid of diseases and defects (Gilbert 1992; Hood 1992; Caskey 1992). And even more compelling, knowledge of genetics is marketed as an avenue for self-knowledge—knowledge of our proficiencies, our possibilities, our limits, our histories, and our futures (Haraway 1992). We are told by scientists working on the Human Genome Project that genes can explain to us who we are at the most fundamental level of DNA. Lobbyists for the Human Genome Project (with its present annual budget exceeding $135 million) market this new "Manhattan Project" on the one hand as a means to both unify humans as a population sharing many genetic traits, and on the other, as a means of making distinctions between types of people. No doubt, this latter option offers great appeal among insurance companies and employers who would like to be able to deny coverage to those who have "genetic predispositions" to disease. Likewise, people such as Frederick Goodwin, head of the National Institutes of Mental Health, are interested in locating the genetic and neurochemical bases for violence, and propose the screening of inner-city children who seem to be "incorrigible" to see if their bodies house the evil seed (Goodwin 1992). Genetic explanations for social inequalities are extremely attractive at a time when the welfare state is in decline, and the brutality of poverty diminishes the life expectancy of an entire generation of children of color living in our cities.[6]

The promises of genetics are grandiose. Not only will the world be rid of disease, but knowledge of genetics will help us to maximize biological resources at a moment of fear over global agricultural scarcity (Kloppenburg 1988; Smith 1991). For Americans, genetic research promises to do even more than fortify our human and natural resources: it promises to save our economy in the face of fierce global competition. Biotechnology is to the 1990s what nuclear weapons development was to the 1960s—the putative guarantor of America's economic and political influence over the destiny of the planet. Never mind that metanational corporations dealing in biotechnology and genetic research will be selling our genes back to us once they isolate and patent key fragments (Hubbard & Wald 1993; Lewontin 1994).

I mention the magical sign of the gene and its political economy because over the past several years two scientific teams have reported a "genetic" basis for homosexuality.[7] In 1991, psychologist Michael Bailey and psychiatrist Richard Pillard reported in their study of gay men with identical twins, that 52 percent of the co-twins were also gay or bisexual. Twenty-two percent of fraternal co-twin brothers were both gay or bisexual. An even smaller number of about 11 percent of those gay men who were raised as brothers through adoption and thus were not related genetically both identified as gay or bisexual. Even with these meager findings, the headlines in the popular press cried out: "Scientists Find That Homosexuality Is Genetic." Although Bailey and Pillard's research has been criticized on numerous grounds, including that the twins they studied were not reared apart, perhaps the most troubling issue raised by their study was that they gave no explanation as to how they were using or measuring the term *sexual orientation*. The categories of homosexual, heterosexual, and bisexual were taken at face value as the subjects defined themselves, as if we (or they) all agree on the meanings of these terms. Furthermore, the study was not based upon random sampling techniques, but recruited its subjects through gay newspapers, thus effectively weeding out men who may engage in homosexuality from time to time but do not read gay magazines or would be loathe to answer such an advertisement. Critics of this method of self-selection suggest that instead of finding a correlation to sexual orientation *per se* (that is, the sexual desire of a man for other men), Bailey and Pillard's twin studies could just as well indicate that there is a genetic underpinning to coming out of the closet. In other words, their research may indicate only the presence of a gene for self-assertiveness or bravery (Byne & Parsons 1993). Because the research required the cooperation of the gay subjects' brothers, it also weeded out those men who were not out of the closet to their families, or who came from homophobic families with brothers who would never agree to be part of such a study. Using the same problematic methods, the later study of female identical twins produced virtually the same statistical findings (Bailey, Pillard et al. 1993). But even with these problems of method and conjecture, both studies were touted as evidence for a genetic basis for homosexuality, because the concordance rate for sexual orientation was higher in identical twins, or those who shared the same genetic material, than it was in dizygotic twins or adopted siblings. Each pair of identical twins was reared together, yet no method was used for determining the influence of social environment and familial relations on sexual orientation. In other words, the researchers did not consider how parents and relatives might treat identical twins differently (that is, as more alike) from dizygotic or unrelated adopted siblings who were reared together, nor what effect this might have on sexual orientation. A good half of the identical twins did *not* show concordance for sexual orientation.

It is interesting to note that neither of the principal researchers involved in the so-called gay twins studies was a geneticist or a molecular biologist, in spite of the media representations of them. As with other demographic heredity studies (for instance, family pedigree studies from the nineteenth century and early work on the genetic marker for Huntington's chorea), the twin study researchers took neither tissue nor blood samples of subjects to analyze their DNA or genetic material. Even as psychiatrist Richard Pillard was featured in *Newsweek* (Figure 1) holding the magical icon of his study, the molecular model, the actual properties of the participants' DNA did not even enter into the discussion (Gorman 1991). Self-reported homosexuality was taken as a clear-cut phenotypic trait (like Huntington's chorea) from which to infer the presence of genetic material that had been passed down from previous generations. It was on the basis of subjects' self-identification that the researchers determined that homosexuality was genetic, but in no more than fifty percent of the cases. Nevertheless, the magical sign of the gene was invoked to make sense of this research and to represent the researcher as an engaged scientist. Indeed, in the media blitz surrounding this research, Pillard's posed photograph mimics the traditional iconography of great men of science, from Copernicus to Watson and Crick, holding their mythical objects of study, in spite of the fact that his study was only "genetic" in the

'A genetic component in sexual orientation says, "This is not a fault, and it's not your fault".'
Dr. Richard Pillard, coauthor of a study on male twins

Figure 1. Dr. Richard Pillard. From *Newsweek* (24 Feb. 1992). Courtesy of Richard Howard.

crudest sense of the word. Perhaps it would have been more fitting for him to be holding a copy of a gay newspaper from which his subjects were recruited.

What else has gone on in science and culture in the last twenty years to make this new research on sexual orientation possible? In 1973, when Anne Koedt made her impassioned statement denouncing biology as destiny, no one had ever heard of AIDS. Since then, the AIDS epidemic has profoundly and devastatingly transformed the nature of lesbian and gay life in the United States. Our relations with one another, our understandings of ourselves, our sense of sexual possibilities, and our ideas about political mobilization have undergone massive transformations in the face of the deadly HIV, and the social neglect and homophobic contempt that have accompanied it. Our bodies are bound up in medical discourse and practices once again, but this time under new, urgent, and deadly conditions. And these new conditions produce new ways of imagining the body in relation to subjectivity. It is not surprising that the privileged domain of the body, where our innermost secrets and sexual passions are thought to reside, is being imagined as a source of meanings in the face of this social atrocity. These days, even as they are theoretically and materially disintegrating, we imagine our bodies as a point of origin for exploring contemporary and very pressing questions of the self. Neuroscientist Simon LeVay's own story of what compelled him to undertake research on sexual orientation is a tale of grieving, of trying to make sense of himself as a gay man in the face of deep depression about the loss of his lover to AIDS. By his own account, LeVay's shift in focus from work on the neuroanatomy of vision to the neuroanatomy of sex and sexual orientation was a crucial part of his recovery process (LeVay 1993; Dolce 1993).

And there is a more palpable, material relationship between the epidemic and much of this new research. Indeed, AIDS provided LeVay (1991) with the very brain tissue he used to conduct his research on the hypothalamus. It was men who died of AIDS who constituted the majority of his subject population, and it was their autopsied brain tissue he used to produce his distinction between the categories of homosexual and heterosexual upon which his findings are based. What was the basis LeVay used for determining which tissue belonged to homosexual and which to heterosexual men? In contrast to Bailey and Pillard's study, which relied on the self-reports of subjects on their sexual orientation, in LeVay's study, a single line in the subject's medical charts, stating his mode of HIV transmission, became the grounds for classifying a man as either gay or not. Those whose charts indicated the mode of transmission was "male-to-male" sexual contact were defined as gay, and those with other modes of transmission (intravenous drug use, blood transfusions, and so on) were, by default, presumed to be heterosexual. Of course, these other cases might just as well have been men who occasionally engaged in homosexual sex but who reported a different mode of transmission, for whatever reasons. In other words, the journey of the human immunodeficiency virus was relied upon to account for the complexity of these men's sexual subjectivities in a masterful instance of scientific reductivism. Were it not for the early deaths of gay men through HIV infection, and the availability of information on modes of transmission in medical charts, LeVay's study could not have been conducted. And although LeVay's "objective" method for determining sexual orientation contrasts with Bailey and Pillard's "subjective" method (that is, voluntary self-reporting), neither approach takes into account the complexity of how sexual orientation is variously defined and experienced in the course of an individual's lifetime and across historical periods and cultural contexts (Kinsey 1941; Terry 1995, 1996). My main point here is that AIDS provided the actual bodies for the hypothalamus study, and it provided a way to classify those bodies. It also provided the impetus for Simon LeVay to recover from his depression through the healing power of neuroscientific research, during what George Bush (the president who brought us Dan Quayle) officially proclaimed the "Decade of the Brain."

Simon LeVay on the cover of *The Advocate* (1 June 1993). Courtesy of Liberation Publications, Inc.

AIDS also made possible the now-famous genetic study reported in July of 1993 by Hamer et al. Researchers at the National Cancer Institute (NCI) reported the discovery of DNA markers linking male homosexuality with a region on the X chromosome, the chromosome boys get from their mothers (prompting the facetious T-shirt I saw at the gay beach in Provincetown: "Love you, Mom. Thanks for the genes"). Unlike the twins studies, this one actually did involve blood samples, but again, it relied mainly on the self-reporting of gay volunteers who recounted a greater number of lesbians and gay men on their mothers' side of the family than on their fathers' (Ebers, qtd. in Crewdson 1995). Although it was no doubt colored by the fact that in general, in American culture, many of us know much more about our mother's family than our father's, this self-reporting led researchers to look for the marker of homosexuality on that gift from mom, the X chromosome. This study, like the others before it, was not based on random sampling, so there is no way of knowing how often this marker exists among men who practice homosexuality often or seldom, but who would never identify as gay. Furthermore, Hamer's team did not check the heterosexual brothers of the gay subjects to see if they, too, carry the corresponding markers. Hamer's neglect in not conducting such an obvious control experiment has led to harsh criticisms from scientists who have tried and failed to reproduce Hamer's findings (see Crewdson 1995 and Allen and Pillard in this volume). Similarly, for a variety of reasons, few of the subjects' mothers were checked for markers on their DNA; some mothers were dead, others had been lost track of, or were unaware that their sons were gay. If Hamer were to have found the marker in a significant number of heterosexual brothers or mothers, his findings of a genetic influence for homosexuality would have been seriously weakened.[8]

But the relationship of this study to the AIDS epidemic is worthy of note: the money used to fund this research had been earmarked for NCI research on Kaposi's sarcoma (KS) and lymphoma. To support his research, Hamer appealed to the National Cancer Institute, proposing a study of whether homosexuals had a genetic susceptibility to KS. According to NIH director Harold Varmus, it was only in the course of Hamer's study on KS and homosexuality that the linkage between sexual orientation and DNA markers on the X chromosome was discovered. By funding this study, the NCI entertained the possibility that there was a genetic relationship between KS and male homosexuality—rather than conditions suffered more often by HIV-infected men of any sexual orientation than women. In this move, the NCI researchers reiterated—perhaps inadvertently—the idea that AIDS is a gay disease that affects particular types of people who are genetically predisposed to it. As historian of medicine Evelynn Hammonds (1993) has noted, researchers at the NCI and the Human Genome Project have money to study genetic predispositions; now they are looking for problems to solve. KS and homosexuality are just two of those "problems." Hamer, in his statements to the gay and popular press, stresses that he is merely curious about the possible genetic correlates to homosexuality, not because it is pathological, but because it is a benign trait, like eye color or handedness. Yet in his proposals for funding, male homosexuality and disease are clearly associated with one another. The innocence of scientific curiosity thus works discursively in an uneasy relationship to the otherwise quite obvious funding politics of scientific research on the controversial topics of homosexuality and AIDS.[9]

There is yet another way that AIDS figures into this new cultural and scientific context, and it has to do with the nature of the current homophobic backlash against gays and lesbians. Right-wing Christian fundamentalists have declared that homosexuality is to the 1990s what abortion was to the 1980s: the enemy in a battle of moral cleansing to determine the future of the world. Not long ago I attended a lecture at the Ohio State University sponsored by the Fellowship of Christian Students, entitled "Gay Agony: Can Homosexuals Be Healed?" The guest speaker, fresh from an appearance on Pat Robertson's 700 Club, began his lecture by saying that the compulsive disorder of homosexuality has brought AIDS into the world. But, he urged, it is not too late to change, to recover from this compulsion, to turn to others for fellowship and guidance, and to overcome this deeply rooted sexual addiction. Throughout the entire lecture, homosexuality and AIDS were virtually synonymous.[10] This illustrates a crucial point: AIDS provides a rationale for both this kind of homophobia and a gay rights opposition to it.[11] Indeed, the good Christian proclaimed that, contrary to what the liberal-dominated media says, there is no sound "glandular" or genetic evidence of the immutability of homosexuality. Beseechingly, he repeated, "You can change, you can change." It is in the face of this hostile homophobia, dressed up as Christian compassion, that LeVay's and the NCI research are being proposed as tools of political opposition. But the limitations of the gay-rights-through-biology defense are striking: Biology makes us act this way. We can't be cured. We can't seduce your children. Talk about surplus powerlessness (Minkowitz 1993; Halley 1994).

In addition to a decade of governmental neglect of and indifference to AIDS, we are now faced with a growing grass-roots backlash against lesbians and gay men of significant proportions. Public displays of homophobia bring rewards these days: from Pat Buchanan's self-satisfied homophobia at the 1992 Republican Convention, to the officially sanctioned brutality toward gay men and lesbians in the military, to the staggering rise of homophobic bashings in city streets, to the suspension of child custody for lesbian mothers around the country, to the local campaigns against lesbian and gay rights. It is quite clear that lesbians and gay men are surrounded by growing numbers of enemies. And it is in these times of defensiveness and of feeling beleaguered that our bodies, presented to us through the authority of science, appear to be refuges for staking a desperate claim for tolerance. As if the knowledge of a gene for homosexuality would stop the basher's club from crashing down on our heads. . .

An idiosyncratic reading of civil rights law provides the backdrop to why hope is invested in the biological proof of homosexuality. Now we have gay scientists and some gay leaders arguing that homosexuality is an immutable characteristic, which they liken to race or skin color. Thus the reasoning follows that homosexuals, like African-Americans, ought to be protected from discrimination. In the first place, this way of thinking ignores the scientific consensus that clear-cut or mutually exclusive racial differences do not exist at the genetic or biological level; race, it is agreed, is primarily a social or demographic concept that, at best, describes reproductive pools with arbitrary and varying boundaries (Marshall 1968; Barkan 1992). But in a larger political sense, the use of race as an analogy to sexual orientation relies on a strange and limited reading of the history of the civil rights movement as well as of the current status of racial minorities. The civil rights movement, after all, focused its antiracism efforts on grass-roots actions, public marches, demonstrations, and the courts. The main goal was equality and respect for all people, regardless of race, religion, or creed; arguments valorizing the biological immutability of race were by no means central. The civil rights movement was most effective in the streets through valorizing cultural diversity, not by African-Americans beseeching those in authority to see them as biologically different. In the 1960s, biological arguments about race had long been seen as the handmaidens of racism, just as those about gender were identified as a central part of the architecture of sexism.

The argument for homosexual immutability betrays a misreading of the scientific research itself. Nothing in any of these studies can fully support the idea that homosexuality is biologically immutable; each study leaves open the possibility that homosexuality is the result of a combination of biological and environmental factors, and several suggest that homosexuality may be tied to a predisposition in temperament that could manifest in a number of ways (LeVay 1993; LeVay & Hamer 1994). All agree that biological, social, and psychological factors interact to produce and change the signs of homosexuality. Furthermore, these studies cannot comment effectively on the frequency of homosexuality in the general population. Nor do they offer much in the way of understanding women's complex relationship to questions of sexuality in general, let alone sexual orientation, growing up in a culture where almost every sexual act is put off-limits as potentially damaging to one's feminine reputation. It is small wonder that many lesbians' stories about their own homosexual desire are not lodged in a prenatal moment or even in early childhood, when boys first experience the privilege of exclusive prerogative over sexual expression. More often, lesbians describe their homosexuality as originating in a process of feminist politicization, or in the context of an adult situation where they began to recognize desire for other women.

The new affinity and hope invested in the biology of homosexuality might be seen as the swan song of economically comfortable white men (quietly lip-synched by straight, politically liberal essentialists) who are the only ones who know the lyrics to each verse, and who, but for their homosexual desire, have many reasons to regard science and social order with great affection. Maybe biology is a more comforting way to narrate their desires than to make sense of them in terms of cultural and historical contradictions, conflicts, and contingencies.

I want to close by coming back to the question of the relationship between scientific knowledge and sexual subjectivity. I have tried to suggest that, throughout this century, the nature of this relationship has been as political as it has been personal. That is, different queer people have thought about scientific knowledge in different ways, some more likely to be swept up by its promises and reassurances than others. Their personal stakes have varied. And in each of the episodes I have described here, including the present, scientific inquiry about homosexuality is politically situated in relation to cultural anxieties. One way to shore up anxieties has been to insist that there be a definitive line drawn between "normal" heterosexuals and "diseased" (or, at best, merely anomalous) homosexuals. This is the dynamic in relation to which deviant subjectivity has been largely—but not thoroughly—fashioned. Thus we can read the recent scientific studies produced by politically engaged, gay scientists such as LeVay and Pillard as expressions of a kind of separatism that finds power through claiming biological uniqueness (Pillard 1992; Dolce 1993). The idea of biology being destiny is less chilling, and perhaps even liberating, to these gay scientists. Indeed, as Evelyn Fox Keller (1992) has noted in reference to molecular biologists, scientists—gay, straight, or otherwise—have an intimate relationship to a newly imagined "nature" in the laboratory in this final decade of the late twentieth century. Particularly in the genetics laboratory, where genes are engineered and bodies can be elementally reconfigured, scientists may feel that "nature" really is more liberating than "nurture," if only because the former is more manipulable than ever before and the latter is imagined as hostile, hopeless, and homophobic. This sense of animated and manipulated nature no doubt acquires some of its appeal from its historical location in relation to the decline of the welfare state. Such a decline, experienced in the midst of antisocial cynicism characteristic of Newt Gingrich's Contract with America, serves to underscore a sense that the "nurture" side of arguments about causality and amelioration is either passé or moot and a get-tough punitive model is preferable.

At the same time that Keller's ideas about a newly created nature in the laboratory may appeal to gay scientists and the public, both Dean Hamer and Simon LeVay, in their respective books and public presentations, seem to argue against the prospect of engineering homosexuality out of the genome (LeVay 1993; Hamer & Copeland 1994). They appear to be more attracted to the foundational narrative of genetics which would cast homosexuality as an eternal, transhistorical, transspecies trait, rather than a novel or even undesirable perversion to be weeded out. But regardless of LeVay's and Hamer's attempts to control the implications of their research, there is a growing popular trend toward regarding biological evidence for things like homosexuality as a possible means for targeting "carriers" and removing them from the gene pool (Hubbard & Wald 1993).

Among those gay men who are economically and socially powerful in the world, conceding that nature makes them gay is apparently less damaging than it might seem to working-class, gay teenagers. A social worker who works with suicidal gay teens recently remarked that the biology-is-destiny line can be deadly. Thinking they are "afflicted" with homosexual desire as a kind of disease or biological defect, rather than it being a desire they somehow affirmatively choose, is, for many gay teenagers, one more reason to commit suicide rather than live in a world so hostile to their desires (Acqueno 1993).

In *The Epistemology of the Closet*, Eve Sedgwick invites us to "denaturalize the present" and to call into question any idea that "homosexuality as we know it today" is singular, knowable, or unified. Instead, she is interested in the "performative space of contradiction" in what could be our present understandings of homosexuality; she wants to bring out the multiplicity of narratives of "homosexuality as we know it today" (Sedgwick 1990). What would it mean if "homosexuality as we know it today" became reduced in the popular imagination to a strip of DNA, or to a region of the brain, or to a hormonal condition? What would we lose in the defensive move to believe science to be our rational savior and to base our politics in biology? What does science do *for* us? What does it do *to* us? And where can we turn for new questions of the self and new ways of *performing*—as opposed to biologically manifesting—deviance?

Notes

Earlier versions of this paper were presented at Rutgers University, the American Historical Association conference, UC San Diego, American University, Miami University, the History of Science Society Meeting. Thanks to the following people for their insights and suggestions: Margaret Cerullo, Katherine Diaz, Marla Erlien, Evelynn M. Hammonds, Ira

Livingston, Donna Penn, Vernon A. Rosario, Andrea Slane, Jacqueline Urla, and Carole S. Vance.

1 The term "queer," a word used in popular discourse throughout the twentieth century to refer to homosexuality and homosexuals in pejorative terms, has recently been appropriated by self-proclaimed "queers" for the purposes of articulating a new kind of confrontational political rhetoric that embraces eccentricity and perversity while rejecting the normality and predictability of straight (that is, heterosexual) conventions and prejudices. I use the term here with some ambivalence precisely because it collapses important differences between the experiences of men and women vis-à-vis the hierarchically structured sex/gender system operating in the United States. But I find the term queer useful in my discussion here because it signals the elastic character of most of the scientific and medical inquiries into homosexuality, which encompass an increasingly vast number of individuals whose sexual practices came to be classified as essentially abnormal. For further analyses of the debates surrounding the term see: de Lauretis 1991, Bérubé and Escoffier 1991, Duggan 1992, Warner 1993, Penn 1995, Abelove 1995.

2 See Davis 1929; Dickinson and Beam 1934; Kinsey et al. 1948, 1953; Landis et al. 1940; Henry 1934; Henry and Galbraith 1934; Strecker 1946; Strecker and Appel 1945; Terman 1938.

3 See Caprio 1955; London and Caprio 1950; Bieber 1965.

4 See Ellis and Ames 1987; Meyer-Bahlburg 1979, 1984; Money 1987.

5 See Friedman et al. 1977; Friedman and Stern 1980; Green 1987; Stoller 1978.

6 See Murray and Herrnstein 1994; Fraser 1995; Jacoby and Glauberman 1995; Lewontin et al. 1993.

7 These were not the first twin studies on homosexuality; see Kallmann (1952, 1953), and Allen's discussion of twin studies in this volume.

8 Other problems surround Hamer's 1993 research. In the summer of 1995, the Office of Research Integrity (ORI) at the National Institutes of Health, the parent institution of the National Cancer Institute, investigated a claim by one of Hamer's collaborators, who alleged that Hamer selectively reported his data in ways that enhanced the study's conclusions. Because ORI investigations are conducted behind closed doors, it is not known exactly what data are alleged to have been omitted, nor how the inclusion of that data might have affected the results. The controversy surrounding Hamer's research moved into the halls of Congress, where debate over the relevance of research on the genetics of sexual orientation to cancer research was aired. Throughout this controversy, the fact that Hamer is an openly gay scientist has been invoked to allege that he "cooked" the data to produce results that homosexuality was genetically based as a strategy for claiming that gays should have a right to protection against discrimination on similar grounds to preventing racial discrimination—that is, that sexual orientation, like race, is a matter of biology, not choice (Crewdson 1995).

9 The NIH and NCI have been under some attack for funding studies like Hamer's, whose findings appear to bear no relationship to cancer research. When questioned by Senator Bob Smith (R-N.H.) as to why the NIH and NCI seemed to be funding research that had little or nothing to do with cancer, NIH director Harold Varmus stated that Hamer's research was indeed intended to uncover any possible links between male homosexuality and KS. A companion study on lesbians proposed by Hamer and his collaborator, Angela Pattatucci, similarly sought funding to investigate a genetic link between lesbianism and breast cancer. As a condition for funding in both of these cases, researchers had to hypothesize a link between homosexuality and disease. Furthermore, proponents of the studies defend

them from attacks by the taxpaying public on the grounds that they contribute to medical knowledge. Thus, the discursive web that historically tied homosexuality together with disease is tightened once again, this time in the context of high-tech genetics research and taxpayer revolt.

10 Lesbians were never mentioned explicitly in the lecture, but are clearly implied in the Christian Fundamentalist conflation of homosexuality with disease, moral degeneracy, and death.

11 The issue of whether or not sexual orientation is a biologically determined characteristic has played a significant role in a number of recent political and legal battles over antigay discrimination. In the state court challenge to Colorado's Amendment 2 (which would remove protections against discrimination on the basis of sexual orientation from all state and municipal jurisdictions in Colorado), Dean Hamer gave testimony that homosexuality was genetically influenced. The Colorado judge who overturned the amendment as unconstitutional concluded that "the preponderance of credible evidence suggests that there is a biologic or genetic 'component' of sexual orientation." Similar arguments have been made in the debates over whether to allow gays and lesbians to serve openly in the military (Crewdson 1995; Kevles 1995).

References

Abelove, Henry. 1995. The queering of lesbian/gay history. *Radical History Review* 62:44–57.

Acqueno, Frank. 1993. Remarks at Out/Write Conference on Lesbian and Gay Writing and Publishing, Boston, MA.

Bailey, J. Michael, and Richard C. Pillard. 1991. A genetic study of male sexual orientation. *Archives of General Psychiatry* 48:1089–1096.

Bailey, J. Michael, Richard C. Pillard, Michael C. Neale, and Yvonne Agyei. 1993. Heritable factors influence sexual orientation in women. *Archives of General Psychiatry* 50:217–223.

Barkan, Elazar. 1992. *The Retreat of Scientific Racism: Changing Concepts of Race in Britain and the United States Between the World Wars*. Cambridge: Cambridge University Press.

Bergler, Edmund. 1956. *Homosexuality: Disease or Way of Life*. New York: Hill & Wang.

———. 1958. *Counterfeit Sex: Homosexuality, Impotence, Frigidity*. New York: Grune & Stratton.

———. 1959. *One Thousand Homosexuals: Conspiracy of Silence, or Curing and Deglamorizing Homosexuals?* Paterson, NJ: Pageant Books.

Bergler, Edmund, and W. Kroger. 1954. *Kinsey's Myth of Female Sexuality: The Medical Facts*. New York: Grune & Stratton.

Bérubé, Allan, and Jeffrey Escoffier. 1991. Queer/Nation. *OUT/LOOK* 11 (Winter): 12.

Bieber, Irving. 1965. Clinical aspects of male homosexuality. In *Sexual Inversion: The Multiple Roots of Homosexuality*, ed. Judd Marmor. New York: Basic Books.

Burr, Chandler. 1993. Homosexuality and biology. *The Atlantic Monthly* 271(March): 47–65.

Byne, William, and Bruce Parsons. 1993. Human sexual orientation: The biological theories reappraised. *Archives of General Psychiatry* 50:228–239.

Caprio, Frank S. 1955. *Female Homosexuality*. London: Peter Owen.

Caskey, C. Thomas. 1992. DNA-based medicine: Prevention and therapy. In *The Code of Codes: Scientific and Social Issues in the Human Genome Project*, ed. Daniel J. Kevles and Leroy Hood. Cambridge: Harvard University Press.

Charcot, Jean-Martin, and Valentin Magnan. 1882. Inversions du sens genital et autres perversions sexuelles. *Archives de neurologie* 3: 53–60; 296–322.

Conrad, Florence. 1965. Research is here to stay. *The Ladder* (July/August): 15–21.

Crewdson, John. 1995. Author [Dean Hamer] defends findings against allegations. *Chicago Tribune* (June 25).

Davis, Katherine Bement. 1929. *Factors in the Sex Lives of Twenty-Two Hundred Women*. New York: Harper and Row.

de Lauretis, Teresa. 1991. Queer theory: Lesbian and gay sexualities, an introduction. *differences* 3(2):iv–v.

Dickinson, Robert Latou, and Lura Beam. 1934. *The Single Woman: A Medical Study in Sex Education*. Baltimore: Williams & Wilkins.

Dolce, Joe. 1993. And how big is yours? (Interview with Simon LeVay). *The Advocate* 630 (June 1):38–44.

Dörner, Günter. 1968. Hormonal induction and prevention of female homosexuality. *Journal of Endocrinology* 42:163–4.

———. 1976. *Hormones and Brain Differentiation*. Amsterdam: Elsevier.

Dörner, Günter, et al. 1975. A neuroendocrine predisposition for homosexuality in men. *Archives of Sexual Behavior* 4:1–8.

———. 1983. Stressful events in prenatal life of bi- and homosexual men. *Experiments in Clinical Endocrinology* 81:83–87.

Downey, Jennifer, et al. 1987. Sex hormones in lesbian and heterosexual women. *Hormones and Behavior* 21:347–357.

Duggan, Lisa. 1992. Making it perfectly queer. *Socialist Review* 22 (January–March): 11–31.

Ehrenreich, Barbara, and Deirdre English. 1978. *For Her Own Good: 150 Years of Experts' Advice to Women*. Garden City, NY: Anchor Press.

Ellis, Lee, and M. Ashley Ames. 1987. Neurohormonal functioning and sexual orientation: A theory of homosexuality-heterosexuality. *Psychological Bulletin* 101(2):233–258.

Foucault, Michel. 1978. *The History of Sexuality: An Introduction*. Trans. Robert Hurley. New York: Vintage Books.

———. 1980. The confession of the flesh. In *Power/Knowledge: Selected Interviews and Other Writings by Michel Foucault, 1972–1977*, ed. Colin Gordon, 194–228. New York: Pantheon Books.

Fraser, Steven. 1995. *The Bell Curve Wars: Race, Intelligence, and the Future of America*. New York: Basic Books.

Friedman, Richard C., et al. 1977. Hormones and sexual orientation in men. *American Journal of Psychiatry* 134:571–572.

Friedman, Richard C., and Leonore O. Stern. 1980. Juvenile aggressivity and sissiness in homosexual and heterosexual males. *Journal of the American Academy of Psychoanalysis* 8:427–440.

Gilbert, Walter. 1992. A vision of the grail. In *The Code of Codes*, ed. D. Kevles and L. Hood. Cambridge: Harvard University Press.

Goodwin, Frederick. 1992. Conduct disorder as a precursor to adult violence and substance abuse: Can the progression be halted? Address presented to the American Psychiatric Association Annual Convention, May, Washington, D.C.

Gorman, Christine. 1991. Are gay men born that way? *Newsweek* 138(10):48.

Green, Richard. 1987. *The "Sissy Boy Syndrome" and the Development of Homosexuality*. New Haven: Yale University Press.

Halley, Janet E. 1994. Sexual orientation and the politics of biology: A critique of the argument from immutability. *Stanford Law Review* 46:503–568.

Hamer, Dean, Stella Hu, Victoria Magnuson, Nan Hu, and Angela Pattatucci. 1993. A linkage between DNA markers on the X chromosome and male sexual orientation. *Science* 261:321–327.

Hamer, Dean, and Peter Copeland. 1994. *The Science of Desire: The Search for the Gay Gene and the Biology of Behavior*. New York: Simon & Schuster.

Hammonds, Evelynn M. 1993. Remarks at Out/Write Conference on Lesbian and Gay Writing and Publishing, Boston, MA.

Haraway, Donna. 1992. The promise of monsters: A regenerative politics for inappropriate/d others. In *Cultural Studies*, ed. Lawrence Grossberg, Cary Nelson, and Paula Treichler, 295–337. New York: Routledge.

Henry, George W. 1934. Psychogenic and constitutional factors in homosexuality; their relation to personality disorders. *Psychiatric Quarterly* 8:243–264.

———. 1941. *Sex Variants: A Study in Homosexual Patterns*. 2 vols. New York: Paul Hoeber & Sons.

Henry, George W., and Hugh Galbraith. 1934. Constitutional factors in homosexuality. *American Journal of Psychiatry* 13:1249.

Henry, George W., and Alfred Gross. 1941. The homosexual delinquent. *Mental Hygiene* 25:420–442.

Hirschfeld, Magnus. 1914. *Die Homosexualität des Mannes und des Weibes*. Berlin: Louis Marcus.

———. [1935] 1975. *Sex in Human Relationships*. Trans. John Rodker. New York: AMS Press.

Hood, Leroy. 1992. Biology and medicine in the twenty-first century. In *The Code of Codes*, ed. D. Kevles and L. Hood. Cambridge: Harvard University Press.

Hubbard, Ruth, and Elijah Wald. 1993. *Exploding the Gene Myth: How genetic information is produced and manipulated by scientists, physicians, employers, insurance companies, educators, and law enforcers*. Boston: Beacon Press.

Jacoby, Russell, and Naomi Glauberman. 1995. *The Bell Curve Debate: History, Documents, Opinions*. New York: Times Books.

Jones, James H. [1981] 1993. *Bad Blood: The Tuskegee Syphilis Experiment*. New York: The Free Press.

Kallmann, Franz J. 1952. Comparative twin study on the genetic aspects of male homosexuality. *Journal of Nervous and Mental Disease* 115:283–298.

———. 1953. *Heredity in Health and Mental Disorder: Principles of Psychiatric Genetics in the Light of Comparative Twin Studies*. New York: Norton.

Kameny, Frank E. 1965. Does research into homosexuality matter? *The Ladder* (May): 14–20.

Keller, Evelyn Fox. 1992. Nature, nurture, and the human genome project. In *The Code of Codes*, ed. D. Kevles and L. Hood. Cambridge: Harvard University Press.

Kevles, Daniel J. 1995. The X factor: The battle over the ramification of a gay gene. *New Yorker* (April 3): 85–90.

Kinsey, Alfred. 1941. Criteria for a hormonal explanation of the homosexual. *The Journal of Clinical Endocrinology* 1:424–428.

Kinsey, Alfred, et al. 1948. *Sexual Behavior in the Human Male*. Philadelphia: W.B. Saunders Co.

———. 1953. *Sexual Behavior in the Human Female*. Philadelphia: W.B. Saunders Co.

Kloppenburg, Jack Jr. 1988. *Seeds and Sovereignty: The Use and Control of Genetic Resources*. Durham, NC: Duke University Press.

Koedt, Anne. 1973. Lesbianism and feminism. In *Radical feminism*, ed. Anne Koedt, Ellen Levine, and Anita Rapone. New York: Quadrangle Books.

Krafft-Ebing, Richard von. 1886. *Psychopathia sexualis. Eine klinisch-forensische Studie.* Stuttgart: Enke.

Landis, Carney, et al. 1940. *Sex and Development: A study of the growth and development of the emotional and sexual aspects of personality together with physiological, anatomical, and medical information on a group of 153 normal women and 142 female psychiatric patients.* New York: Paul B. Hoeber.

LeVay, Simon. 1991. Evidence for anatomical differences in the brains of homosexual men. *Science* 253:1034–1037.

———. 1993. *The Sexual Brain*. Cambridge: MIT Press.

LeVay, Simon, and Dean H. Hamer. 1994. Evidence for a biological influence in male homosexuality. *Scientific American* 270(May): 44–49.

Lewontin, R.C. 1994. The dream of the human genome. In *Cultures on the Brink: Ideologies of Technology*, ed. Gretchen Bender and Timothy Druckrey. Seattle: Bay Press.

Lewontin, R.C., Steven Rose, and Leon J. Kamin. 1993. I.Q.: The rank ordering of the world. In *The "Racial" Economy of Science*, ed. Sandra Harding. Bloomington: Indiana University Press.

London, Louis S., and Frank S. Caprio. 1950. *Sexual Deviations: A Psychodynamic Approach.* Washington, DC: Linacre Press.

Marshall, Gloria. 1968. Racial classifications: Popular and scientific. In *Science and the Concept of Race*, ed. Margaret Mead et al. New York: Columbia University Press.

Martin, Del, and Phyllis Lyon. 1972. *Lesbian/Woman.* San Francisco: Glide Publications.

Meyer-Bahlburg, Heino F.L. 1979. Sex hormones and female homosexuality: a critical examination. *Archives of Sexual Behavior* 8(2): 101–119.

———. 1984. Psychoendocrine research on sexual orientation: Current status and future options. In *Progress in Brain Research*, ed. G.J. DeVries et al. Amsterdam: Elsevier Science Publishers.

Minkowitz, Donna. 1993. Trial by science: In the fight over Amendment 2, biology is back and gay allies are claiming it. *Village Voice* (November 30): 27–30.

Money, John. 1987. Sin, sickness, or status?: Homosexual gender identity and psychoendocrinology. *American Psychologist* 24(4):384–399.

Murray, Charles, and Richard Herrnstein. 1994. *The Bell Curve: Intelligence and Class Structure in American Life*. New York: Free Press.

Nunberg, Herman, and Ernst Federn, eds. 1962. *Minutes of the Vienna Psychoanalytic Society, Volume 1, 1906–1908.* Trans. M. Nunberg. New York: International Universities Press.

Penn, Donna. 1995. Queer: Theorizing politics and history. *Radical History Review* 62:24–42.

Pillard, Richard. 1992. Just what do gay twins reveal? *The Guide* (Boston) 12 (February): 24–28.

Sedgwick, Eve Kosofsky. 1990. *Epistemology of the Closet*. Berkeley: University of California Press.

Smith, Alistair. 1991. Biodiversity and food security. *Science as Culture* 2 (Pt. 4, No. 3):591–601.

Stoller, Robert C. 1978. Boyhood gender aberrations: Treatment issues. *Journal of the American Psychoanalytic Association* 26:541–58.

Strecker, Edward. 1946. *Their Mother's Sons: The Psychiatrist Examines an American Problem.* New York and Philadelphia: J.B. Lippincot.

Strecker, Edward, and Kenneth Appel. 1945. *Psychiatry in Modern Warfare*. New York: Macmillan.

Terman, Lewis M. 1938. *Psychological Factors in Marital Happiness.* New York: McGraw-Hill.

Terry, Jennifer. 1990. Lesbians under the medical gaze: Scientists search for remarkable differences. *Journal of Sex Research* 27(3):317–340.

———. 1992. Siting homosexuality: A history of surveillance and the production of deviant subjects (1935–1950). Ph.D. diss., University of California, Santa Cruz.

———. 1994. Theorizing deviant historiography. In *Feminists Revision History,* ed. Ann-Louise Shapiro. New Brunswick: Rutgers University Press.

———. 1995. Anxious slippages between "us" and "them": A brief history of the scientific search for homosexual bodies. In *Deviant Bodies: Critical Perspectives on Difference in Science and Popular Culture,* ed. Jennifer Terry and Jacqueline Urla, 129–169. Bloomington: Indiana University Press.

———. 1996. "Unnatural acts in nature": A look at the scientific fascination with queer animals.

Warner, Michael, ed. 1993 *Fear of a Queer Planet: Queer Politics and Social Theory.* Minneapolis: University of Minnesota Press.

Westphal, Karl. 1869. Die konträre Sexualempfindung: Symptom eines neuropathologischen (psychopathischen) Zustandes. *Archiv für Psychiatrie und Nervenkrankheiten* 2:73–108.

Notes on Contributors

Garland E. Allen is Professor of Biology at Washington University, St. Louis. He has published on the history of genetics, evolution, and theories of biological determinism, particularly genetic determinism and eugenics. He is the coauthor (with Jeffrey Baker and Scott Gilbert) of *The Study of Biology* (5th ed.), and is currently revising *Life Science in the Twentieth Century* for Cambridge University Press.

Erin G. Carlston is an instructor in the Program in Cultures, Ideas and Values at Stanford University, where she received her Ph.D. in Modern Thought and Literature. She does research on Western European and U.S. literature, politics, and culture of the 1930s, and is the author of *Thinking Fascism: Sapphic Modernism and Fascist Modernity* (forthcoming from Stanford University Press).

Julian Carter is a doctoral candidate in the History Department and a Chancellor's Fellow of the University of California at Irvine. She is writing a dissertation on "The Evolution of the Lesbian Object: Race Degeneration and Abnormal Sexuality, 1900–1940."

Alice D. Dreger is Assistant Professor in Science and Technology Studies at the Lyman Briggs School of Michigan State University. She received her Ph.D. in the History and Philosophy of Science from Indiana University in 1995, and is author of a forthcoming book on the medical history of hermaphroditism in France and Britain, 1868–1915. She is currently studying the history of the Western biomedical treatment of "Siamese" twins.

Anne Fausto-Sterling is Professor of Molecular Biology, Cell Biology, and Biochemistry in the Division of Medical Science at Brown University. She is the author of *Myths of Gender: Biological Theories About Women and Men* (2d ed., 1992).

Margaret Gibson is an independent scholar in the history of medicine. She graduated from the Department of the History of Science at Harvard University and is currently doing research on the medical theorizing of lesbian bodies in the nineteenth- and twentieth-century United States.

Stephanie H. Kenen is a doctoral candidate in the Program in the History of Science and Technology, Department of History, at the University of California, Berkeley, where she is completing a dissertation on scientific categories of sexual difference, 1920–1955.

Hubert Kennedy, a former professor of mathematics, is an independent researcher on gay political history and a manuscript editor for the *Journal of Homosexuality*. He has written on John Henry Mackay, and is the author of *Ulrichs: The Life and Works of Karl Heinrich Ulrichs, Pioneer of the Modern Gay Movement* (1988).

Harry Oosterhuis is Assistant Professor of History at the State University of Limburg in Maastricht, The Netherlands. He studied history at the University of Groningen, and has a Ph.D. in Sociology from the University of Amsterdam. He was a lecturer in gay and lesbian studies at the Catholic University of Nijmegen. His recent publications include: *Homoseksualiteit in Katholiek Nederland. Een sociale geschiedenis 1900–1970* (1992) and *Homosexuality and Male Bonding in Pre-Nazi Germany* (1991). He is coeditor (with Gert Hekma and James Steakley) of *Gay Men and the Sexual History of the Political Left* (1995).

Richard C. Pillard is Professor of Psychiatry at Boston University School of Medicine. He was the first publicly identified gay psychiatrist in the United States and cofounder of the Homophile Community Health Center in Boston. He has done research on the psychopharmacology of psychoactive drugs and the frequency of homosexuality in siblings.

Vernon A. Rosario is currently an Andrew W. Mellon Fellow at the University of Pennsylvania. He received his Ph.D. in the History of Science from Harvard University and his M.D. from the Harvard Medical School—Massachusetts Institute of Technology Division of Health Sciences and Technology. He is coeditor (with Paula Bennett) of *Solitary Pleasures: The Historical, Literary, and Artistic Discourses of Autoeroticism* (1995), and author of *Sexual Psychopaths: Doctors, Patients, and Novelists Narrating the Erotic Imagination* (forthcoming from Oxford University Press).

James D. Steakley is Professor of German at the University of Wisconsin-Madison. He is the author of *The Homosexual Emancipation Movement in Germany* (1975), and has also published on sodomy in eighteenth-century Prussia, homosexuals in the Third Reich, and gays in the former East Germany. He has lectured widely on gay history, and has taught as a guest professor at the universities of Berlin and Hannover.

Jennifer Terry is Assistant Professor of Comparative Studies at Ohio State University, and author of articles on women and medical surveillance, queer theory, and the history of sexual science in the United States. She is coeditor, with Jacqueline Urla, of *Deviant Bodies: Critical Perspectives on Difference in Science and Popular Culture* (1995) and is presently completing *Mapping an American Obsession: Science, Homosexuality, and Defining Norms of Citizenship*.

Index